Empirical Econometric Modelling

PcGive™ 11: Volume I

Jurgen A. Doornik
David F. Hendry

Published by Timberlake Consultants Ltd
www.timberlake.co.uk
www.timberlake-consultancy.com
www.oxmetrics.net

Empirical Econometric Modelling

PcGive™ 11: Volume I

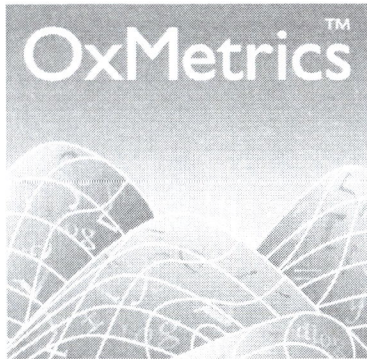
OxMetrics™

Empirical Econometric Modelling - PcGive 11: Volume I
Copyright @ 2006 Jurgen A. Doornik and David F. Hendry

British Library Cataloguing-in-Publication Data
A catalogue record of this book is available from the British Library

Library of Congress Cataloguing-in-Publication Data
A catalogue record of this book is available from the Library of Congress
Jurgen A. Doornik and David F. Hendry
p. cm. – (Empirical Econometric Modelling – PcGive 11 Vol I)

ISBN 0-9542603-4-1

Published by
Timberlake Consultants Ltd
Unit B3, Broomsleigh Business Park
London SE26 5BN, UK
http://www.timberlake.co.uk

842 Greenwich Lane,
Union, NJ 07083-7905, U.S.A.
http://www.timberlake-consultancy.com

In memory of Denis Sargan

Contents

Figures

Tables

Preface

PcGive for Windows is the latest in a long line of descendants of the original GIVE program. Over its life, many scholars, researchers and students have contributed to its present form. We are grateful to them all for their help and encouragement.

The current version, 11, has been designed to work with OxMetrics 4 and offers more convenient access to the many econometric procedures in the program. Version 11 contains all the improvements that were made available as minor upgrades to version 10. PcGive remains almost entirely written in Ox. This complete rewrite for Ox was achieved with version 10.

The original mainframe ancestor was written in Fortran, PC versions in a mixture of Fortran with some C and Assembly. Version 7 was a complete rewrite in C (with the graphics in Assembly). Version 9 was a mixture of C and C++, while versions 10 and later are written in Ox, with a small amount of code still in C.

Sections of code in PC-GIVE 6 were contributed by Neil Ericsson, Giuseppe Mazzarino, Adrian Neale, Denis Sargan, Frank Srba and Juri Sylvestrowicz, and their important contributions are gratefully acknowledged. Despite the algorithms having been rewritten in C, their form and structure borrows from the original source. In particular, Adrian Neale's code for graphics from PC-NAIVE was incorporated in PC-GIVE 6.0 and much of that was carried forward to PcGive 7 and 8. The interface of PcGive 7 and 8 was based on D-FLAT, developed by Al Stevens for *Dr. Dobb's Journal*. Version 9 relied on the Microsoft Foundation Class for its interface, for version 10 the interface is provided by OxPack. We are grateful to Bernard Silverman for permission to include his code for density estimation.

Many people made the development of the program possible by giving their comments and testing out β-versions of version 10 and earlier versions. With the risk of forgetting some, we wish to thank Willem Adema, Peter Boswijk, Gunnar Bårdsen, Mike Clements, Neil Ericsson, Hans-Martin Krolzig, Bent Nielsen, Marius Ooms, Jaime Marquez, and Neil Shephard for their help. We are also grateful to the Oxford Institute of Economics and Statistics, especially to Gillian Coates, Candy Watts, and Alison Berry for help with earlier versions. We also wish to thank Maureen Baker and Nuffield College.

The documentation for GIVE has evolved dramatically over the years. We are indebted to Mary Morgan and Frank Srba for their help in preparing the first (mainframe) version of a manual for GIVE. Our thanks also to Manuel Arellano, Giorgio Bodo, Peter Boswijk, Julia Campos, Mike Clements, Neil Ericsson, Carlo Favero, Chris Gilbert, Andrew Harvey, Vivien Hendry, Søren Johansen, Siem Jan Koopman, Adrian Neale, Marius Ooms, Robert Parks, Jean-François Richard, Neil Shephard, Timo Teräsvirta and Giovanni Urga for their many helpful comments on the documentation for PC-GIVE 6 and later versions.

MikTeX in combination with Scientific Word and OxEdit eased the development of the documentation in LaTeX, further facilitated by the more self-contained nature of recent PcGive versions and the in-built help system.

Over the years, many users and generations of students have written with helpful suggestions for improving and extending PcGive, and while the current version will undoubtedly not yet satisfy all of their wishes, we remain grateful for their comments and hope that they will continue to write with good ideas (and *report any bugs!*).

DFH owes a considerable debt to Evelyn and Vivien during the time he has spent on this project: their support and encouragement were essential, even though they could benefit but indirectly from the end product. In a similar fashion, JAD is delighted to thank Kate for her support and encouragement.

We wish you enjoyable and productive use of

PcGive for Windows

Part I

PcGive Prologue

Chapter 1

Introduction to PcGive

1.1 The PcGive system

PcGive is an interactive menu-driven program for econometric modelling. Version 11 for Windows, to which this documentation refers, runs on under Windows XP/2000. PcGive originated from the AUTOREG Library (see Hendry and Srba, 1980, Hendry, 1986c, 1993, Doornik and Hendry, 1992, and Doornik and Hendry, 1994), and is part of the OxMetrics family.

The PcGive system comprises the following econometric techniques:

- **Econometric Modelling (PcGive)**
    - **Cross-section Regression**
    - **Single-equation Dynamic Modelling**
    - **Nonlinear Modelling**
    - Multiple-equation Dynamic Modelling
      VAR and cointegration, simultaneous equations analysis
      Multivariate modelling is described in Volume II (Doornik and Hendry, 2006a).

- Limited Dependent Models (LogitJD)
    - Logit and Probit
    - Multinomial Logit
    - Count data (Poisson and Negative Binomial)

- Volatility Models (Garch)
    - GARCH
    - GARCH in mean, GARCH with Student-t, EGARCH
    - Estimation with Nelson&Cao restrictions

- Panel Data Models (DPD)
    - Static panel data models,
    - within groups, between groups
    - Dynamic panel data:Arellano-Bond GMM estimators

3

- Time Series Models (Arfima)
    - ARFIMA(p,d,q) models
    - Exact maximum likelihood, modified-profile
    - likelihood or non-linear least squares
- X12Arima for OxMetrics (not yet available)
    - regARIMA modelling
    - Automatic model selection
    - Census X-11 seasonal adjustment
- **Descriptive Statistics**
    - **Means, standard deviations and correlations**
    - **Normality tests and descriptive statistics**
    - **Correlogram (ACF) and Portmanteau statistic**
    - **Unit-root tests**
    - **Principal component analysis**

The documentation of PcGive is contained in several volumes. The current book, Volume I, describes single equation modelling, as marked in bold above. PcGive uses OxMetrics for data input and graphical and text output. OxMetrics is described in a separate book (Doornik and Hendry, 2006b). Even though PcGive is largely written in Ox (Doornik, 2006), it does not require Ox to function.

1.2 Single equation modelling

This book describes the single equation modelling features of PcGive. This part of PcGive is designed for modelling economic data when the precise formulation of the relationship is not known *a priori*. The present version is for individual equations with jointly determined, weakly or strongly exogenous, predetermined, and lagged endogenous variables. A wide range of individual equation estimation methods is available. Particular features of the program are its ease of use, edit facilities, flexible data handling, extensive set of preprogrammed diagnostic tests, and its focus on recursive methods, supported by powerful graphics. System estimation methods are incorporated in PcGive, but described in a separate volume.

The documentation aims to provide an operational approach to econometric modelling using the most sophisticated yet easy-to-use software available. Thus, this book is especially extensive to fully explain the econometric methods, the modelling approach, and the techniques used, as well as bridge the gap between econometric theory and empirical practice. It transcends the old ideas of 'textbooks' and 'computer manuals' by linking the learning of econometric methods and concepts to the outcomes achieved when they are applied by the user at the computer. Because the program is so easy to learn and use, the main focus is on its econometrics and application to data analysis. Detailed tutorials in Chapters 2–8 teach econometric modelling by walking the user through the program in organized steps. This is supported by clear explanations of econometrics in Chapters 9–14. The material spans the level from introductory to frontier research, with an emphatic orientation to practical modelling. The exact definitions of all statistics calculated by PcGive are described in Chapters 15–17. The context-sensitive help system supports this approach by offering help on both the program and the econometrics.

This chapter discusses the special features of PcGive, describes how to use the documentation, provides background information on data storage, interactive operation, help, results storage, and filenames, then outlines the basics of using the program (often just point-and-click with a mouse).

1.3 The special features of PcGive

(1) *Ease of use*

- PcGive is **user friendly**, being a **fully interactive and menu-driven** approach to econometric modelling: pull-down menus offer available options, and dialog boxes provide access to the available functions.

- PcGive has a **high level of error protection**, making it suitable for students acquiring experience in econometrics on computers, for live teaching in the classroom, or fraught late-night research.

- PcGive provides an extensive context-sensitive **help system** explaining both the program usage and the econometrics.

- **High quality screen presentations** in edit windows allow documentation of results as analysis proceeds, with easy review of previous results and cutting and pasting within or between windows.

- Both text and graphics can be controlled by a **mouse**, allowing powerful and flexible editing, rapid menu and dialog access, and easy documentation of graphs.

- **Estimation options** can be set to automatically activate or inhibit model evaluation procedures, set the format for results presentation and control the detail and sophistication of the output.

(2) *Advanced graphics*

- OxMetrics provides easy adjustment of graph types, layout and colours.

- As many as **36 graphs** can be shown simultaneously, with easy user control or automatic selection.

- **Graphs can be documented and edited** via direct screen access with reading from the graph.

- **Time series and cross-plots** are supported with flexible adjustment and scaling options, including several bivariate linear regression lines with joint presentation of reverse regressions, or non-parametric fits, as well as spectra, correlograms, histograms and data densities.

- **Descriptive results, recursive statistics, diagnostic tests, likelihood projections and forecasts** can be graphed in many combinations.

(3) *Flexible data handling in OxMetrics*

- The **data handling system provides convenient storage** of large data sets with easy loading to PcGive either as a unit, or for subsamples or subsets of variables.

- **Excel and Lotus spreadsheet files** can be loaded directly, or using 'cut and paste' facilities.

- **Large data sets** can be analyzed, with with as many variables and observations as memory allows.

- Database variables can be transformed by a **calculator**, or by entering **mathematical formulae** in an editor with easy storage for reuse; the database is easily viewed, incorrect observations are simple to revise, and variables can be documented on-line.

- **Appending** across data sets is simple, and the data used for estimation can be any subset of the data in the database.

- **Several data sets** can be open simultaneously, with easy switching between the database.

(4) *Efficient modelling sequence*

- The underlying **Ox algorithms** are **fast, efficient, accurate** and carefully **tested**; all **data are stored in double precision**.

- PcGive is designed specifically for **modelling time-series** data, and creates lags, and analyzes dynamic responses and long-run relations with ease; it is simple to change sample, or forecast, periods or estimation methods: models are retained for further analysis, and general-to-specific sequential simplifications are monitored for reduction tests.

- The **structured modelling approach** is fully discussed in this book, and guides the ordering of menus and dialogs, but application of the program is completely at the user's control.

- The **estimators** supported include least squares, instrumental variables, error autocorrelation, non-linear least squares, and non-linear maximum likelihood: powerful numerical optimization algorithms are embedded in the program with easy user control and most methods can be calculated recursively over the available sample.

- PcGive offers **powerful preprogrammed testing facilities** for a wide range of hypotheses of interest to econometricians and economists undertaking substantive empirical research, including tests for unit roots, dynamic specification, cointegration, linear restrictions and common factors.

- PcGive is also **applicable to cross-section data** and most of its facilities and tests are available for such analyses.

- **Large models** can be formulated, with no restrictions on size, apart from those imposed by available memory.

- A **Batch language** allows automatic estimation and evaluation of models, and can be used to prepare a PcGive session for teaching.

(5) *Thorough evaluation*

- **Equation mis-specification tests are automatically provided**, including residual autocorrelation, autoregressive conditional heteroscedasticity (ARCH), heteroscedasticity, functional form, parameter constancy, and normality (with residual density functions), as well as a complete set of encompassing tests.

- The **recursive estimators provide easy graphing** of coefficients and residuals with their confidence intervals, or 't'-values: parameter constancy statistics scaled by selected nominal significance levels are also calculated.

- All estimators provide **graphs** of fitted/actual values, residuals, and forecasts against outcomes with 1-step error bars.

(6) *Output*

- **Graphs can be saved** in several file formats including for later recall, further editing, and printing, or for importing into many popular word processors, as well as directly by 'cut and paste'

- **Results window** information can be saved as an ASCII (human readable) document for input to most word processors, or directly input by 'cut and paste'.

- Model residuals and recursive output can be **stored in the database** for additional graphs or evaluation.

We now consider some of these special features in greater detail.

Advanced graphics

- Users have full control over **screen and graph colours**. The colour, type (solid, dotted, dashed etc.) and thickness of each line in a graph can be set; graphs can be drawn inside boxes, and with or without grids; axis values can be automatic or user defined; areas highlighted as desired; and so on.
- Up to **36 different graphs** can be shown simultaneously on-screen, which is especially valuable for graphical evaluation of equations and recursive methods. Combinations of graphs displaying different attributes of data can be shown simultaneously — examples are reported below.
- Once on-screen, text can be entered for **graph documentation**, or a mouse used to highlight interesting features during live presentations. Graphs can be both rapidly saved and instantly recalled. Coordinates can be read from each graph, however many are displayed at once.
- Much of PcGive's output is provided in **graphical form** which is why it is written as an interactive (and not a batch) program. Dozens of time series can be graphed together using a wide range of adjustment and prescaling options. Two variables can be cross-plotted as points or joined by lines (to show historical evolution), with least-squares lines for subsamples, selected recursively (so growing in size) or sequentially (a fixed % of the whole sample), showing projections of points from the lines; alternatively, both bivariate regression lines and/or a non-parametric regression can be drawn. Or they can be plotted by the values of a third variable. Spectral densities, correlograms, histograms and interpolated data densities and distributions also can be graphed in groups of up to 36.
- The option to see **multiple graphs** allows for more efficient evaluation of large amounts of information. Blocks of graphs can simultaneously incorporate descriptive results (fitted and actual values, scaled residuals and forecasts etc.) and diagnostic test information; or show many single-parameter likelihood grids.

Efficient modelling sequence

- **Dynamic econometrics** involves creating and naming lagged variables, controlling the available sample and forecast period etc., and assigning the appropriate status to all variables, so such operations are either automatic or very easy. The basic PcGive operator is a lag polynomial. Long-run solutions, unit-root tests, cointegration tests, the significance of lagged variables (or groups of lags), the choice between deterministic or stochastic dynamics, roots of lag polynomials, tests for common factors etc. are all calculated. If the recommended general-to-specific approach to model construction is adopted, the sequence of reductions is monitored and F-tests, information criteria etc. are reported.
- This **extensive program book** seeks to bridge the gap between econometric theory and empirical modelling: the tutorials walk the user through every step from

inputting data to the final selected econometric model of the variables under analysis. The econometrics chapters explain the theory and methods with reference to the program with detailed explanations of all the estimators and tests. The statistical output chapters carefully define all the estimators and tests used by PcGive.

- The **ordering of the menus and dialogs** is determined by the theory: first establish a data coherent, constant parameter model, investigate cointegration, reduce the model to a stationary, near orthogonal and simplified representation and finally check for parsimonious encompassing of the system: see Hendry and Ericsson (1991) and Hendry (1993, 1995a) for further details. Nevertheless, the application and sequence of the program's facilities remain completely under the user's control.

- **Estimation methods** currently supported include ordinary and recursive least squares, two-stage least squares, instrumental variables and recursive instrumental variables, r^{th}-order autoregressive least squares, non-linear least squares and recursive non-linear least squares and maximum likelihood. models are easily revised, transformed and simplified; up to 15 models are remembered for easy recall and progress evaluation.

- **Powerful testing facilities** for a wide range of specification hypotheses of interest to econometricians and economists undertaking substantive empirical research are preprogrammed for automatic calculation. Available tests include dynamic specification, lag length, cointegration, and tests of reduction or parsimonious encompassing. Wald tests of linear restrictions are easily conducted.

Thorough evaluation

- **Evaluation tests** can either be automatically calculated, calculated in a block as a summary test option, or implemented singly or in sets merely by selecting the relevant dialog option. A comprehensive and powerful range of mis-specification tests is offered to sustain the methodological recommendations about model evaluation. Equation mis-specification tests include residual autocorrelation, ARCH, heteroscedasticity, functional form mis-specification and normality. Constancy tests can be computed automatically or via recursive procedures. A range of encompassing tests can be undertaken (just by a single keystroke or click!) once two rival models have been estimated.

- **Graphical diagnostic information** includes plots of residual correlograms, residual density functions and histograms, and QQ plots.

- Much of the power of PcGive resides in its extensive use of **recursive estimators**. These provide voluminous output (coefficients, standard errors, t-values, residual sums of squares, 1-step residuals and their standard errors, constancy tests etc. at every sample size), but recursive statistics can be graphed for easy presentation (up to 36 graphs simultaneously). The size of models is only restricted by the available memory, as long as fewer than 100 variables are involved.

- All estimators provide **graphs** of residuals, fitted and actual values and their cross-plots, as well as 1-step forecasts or forecast errors with 95% confidence intervals shown by error bars.
- Full graphics facilities can be applied to any or all of these graphs (e.g., adding regression lines etc.)

Considerable experience has demonstrated the practicality and value of using Pc-Give as an operational complement to learning econometrics and conducting empirical studies. It is also easy and helpful to run PcGive live in classroom teaching as an adjunct to theoretical derivations. On the research side, the incisive recursive estimators and the wide range of preprogrammed tests make PcGive the most powerful interactive econometric modelling program available; Chapter 14 discusses its application to a range of important practical econometrics problems. These roles are enhanced by the flexible and informative graphics options provided.

1.4 Documentation conventions

The convention for instructions that you should type is that they are shown in Typewriter font. Capitals and lower case are only distinguished as the names of variables in the program and the mathematical formulae you type. Once OxMetrics has started, then from the keyboard, the Alt key accesses line menus (at the top of the screen); from a mouse, click on the item to be selected using the left button. Common commands have a shortcut on the toolbar, the purpose of which can be ascertained by placing the mouse on the relevant icon. Icons that can currently operate are highlighted. Commands on menus, toolbar buttons, and dialog items (buttons, checkboxes etc.) are shown in Sans Serif font.

Equations are numbered as (chapter.number); for example, (8.1) refers to equation 8.1, which is the first equation in Chapter 8. References to sections have the form §chapter.section, for example, §8.1 is Section 8.1 in Chapter 8. Tables and Figures are shown as Figure chapter.number (e.g.) Figure 5.2 for the second figure in Chapter 5. Multiple graphs are numbered from left to right and top to bottom, so (b) is the top-right graph of four, and (c) the bottom left.

1.5 Using PcGive documentation

The documentation comes in five main parts: Part I comprises this introductory chapter, and instructions on starting the program. Part II then has six extensive tutorials on all aspects of econometric modelling, emphasising the data analytic facilities over simply program usage. Part III has six chapters discussing the econometrics of PcGive from introductory to advanced levels. Part IV offers a detailed description of the statistical and econometric output of PcGive. Finally, Part V contains appendices. The documentation ends with references and a subject index. As discussed above, the aim is to provide a practical textbook of econometric modelling, linking the econometrics of PcGive to empirical modelling through tutorials which implement applied modelling exercises. In more detail:

(1) A separate book explains and documents the companion program **OxMetrics** which records the output and provides data loading and graphing facilities.

(2) The **Prologue** discusses the main feature provided by PcGive, sketches how to use the program and illustrates some of its output. In particular, Chapter 2 provides a quick start for the PcGive system.

(3) The **Tutorials** in Chapters 2 to 8 are specifically designed for joint learning of econometric analysis and use of the programs. They describe using the editor, data input, graphics control, dynamic model formulation, estimation and evaluation; dynamic analysis; econometric modelling; and advanced features. By implementing empirical research exercises, they allow rapid mastery of PcGive and an understanding of how the associated econometric theory operates in practice.

(4) The **Econometric overview** in Chapter 9 briefly reviews the background econometrics of PcGive.

(5) Chapters 10–14 explain the **Econometrics** at all levels from elementary, through intermediate to advanced, including Chapter 12 covering statistical theory, as well as a chapter on important practical problems.

(6) The **Statistical Output** in Chapters 15 to 17 explain in detail the econometric and statistical calculations of PcGive.

(7) Chapter A1 gives information about PcGive **languages**. The on-line help system documents the menu structure and dialogs. Most dialogs are easy to understand, but the on-line help can be accessed at any time if required.

The appropriate sequence is to first install PcGive on your system. Next, read the remainder of this introduction, then follow the step-by-step guidance given in the **tutorials** to get familiar with the operation of PcGive. Part III explains the required econometrics, starting at an elementary level and building up to advanced tools.

To use the documentation, either check the index for the subject, topic, menu or dialog that seems relevant; or look up the part relevant to your current activity (for example, econometrics, tutorials or description) in the **Contents**, and scan for the most likely keyword. The references point to relevant publications which analyze the methodology and methods embodied in PcGive.

1.6 Citation

To facilitate replication and validation of empirical findings, PcGive should be cited in all reports and publications involving its application. The appropriate form is to cite

PcGive in the list of references.

1.7 World Wide Web

Consult `www.oxmetrics.com` or `www.pcgive.com` pointers to additional information relevant to the current and future versions of PcGive. Upgrades are made available for downloading if required, and a demonstration version is also made available.

1.8 Some data sets

The data used in Hendry (1995a) is provided in the files `ukm1.in7/ukm1.bn7`. The DHSY data (see Davidson, Hendry, Srba and Yeo, 1978) is supplied in the files `dhsy.in7/dhsy.bn7`. An algebra file, `dhsy.alg`, contains code to create variables used in the paper. A batch file, `dhsy.fl`, loads the data, executes algebra code, and estimates the two final equations reported in the paper.

For the data sets used in Hendry and Morgan (1995), consult: `www.nuff.ox.ac.uk/users/hendry`.

Part II

PcGive Tutorials

Chapter 2

Tutorial on Cross-section Regression

2.1 Starting the modelling procedure

The purpose of this tutorial is to explain the use of PcGive for estimating linear regression equations. The background to regression and least squares estimation methods is explained in Chapters 10 and 11. If you are unfamiliar with regression, proceed with this chapter till you feel lost, then read Chapter 10 and return here later. Our starting point is cross-section regression, because that has fewer options than dynamic regression, making it easier to use.

Start OxMetrics, and load the `data.in7` and `data.bn7` files in OxMetrics as explained in the OxMetrics book. If you have used this data set in a previous session, you can right-click on the Data folder in the workspace, and look under Open Recent Data File in the context menu. We assume that you've made yourself somewhat familiar with OxMetrics first, for example by reading the getting started chapters in the OxMetrics book.

You can start modelling with PcGive from OxMetrics in three ways:

- By clicking on the Model entry under Modules in the workspace on the left-hand side.
- Via Model on the Model menu.
- Using the Model toolbar button:

Once started, the databases loaded in OxMetrics are accessible from PcGive.

The modelling dialog gives access to all the modelling features of the OxMetrics modules, including PcGive:

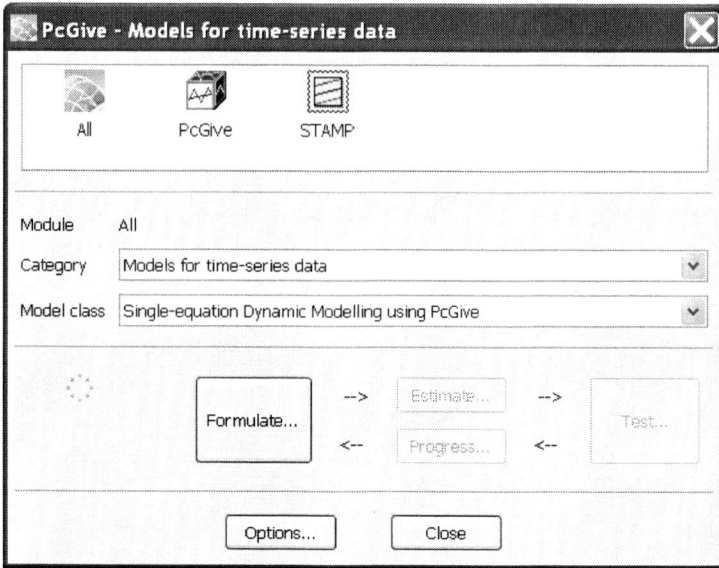

The first step is to select a model category, and for the category a model type. The images at the top allow you to see the choices for all available modules, or to restrict it to a specific module such as PcGive. In your case, it is likely that Module is set to all (if not, click on the OxMetrics item for All, or on PcGive).

Before we can estimate our first model, we have two choices to make:

(1) Change the **Category** to Models for cross-section data:

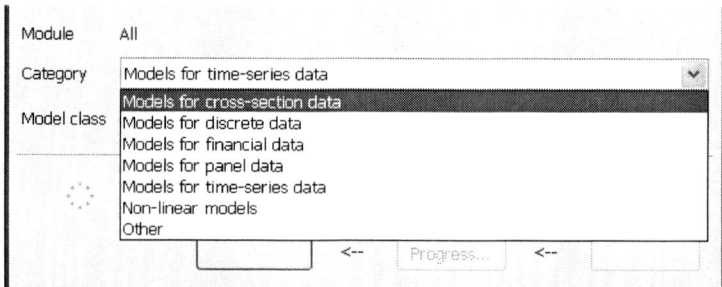

(2) select a **model class**, in this case there is only one, but other modelling modules may add more:

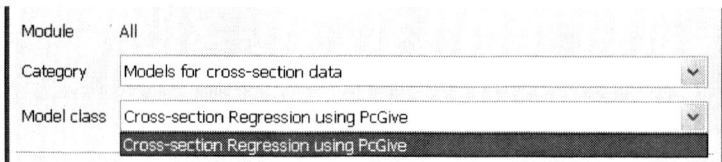

To facilitate the modelling process, PcGive has several model classes, from cross-section regression to multiple-equation dynamic modelling. They are categorized according to the type of data to which they usually apply. Two separate classes are for non-linear modelling and descriptive statistics. These are not particularly associated with a data type, and fall in separate categories.

2.2 Formulating a regression

Selecting the cross-section regression using PcGive class, and pressing the Formulate button takes you to the Model Formulation dialog:

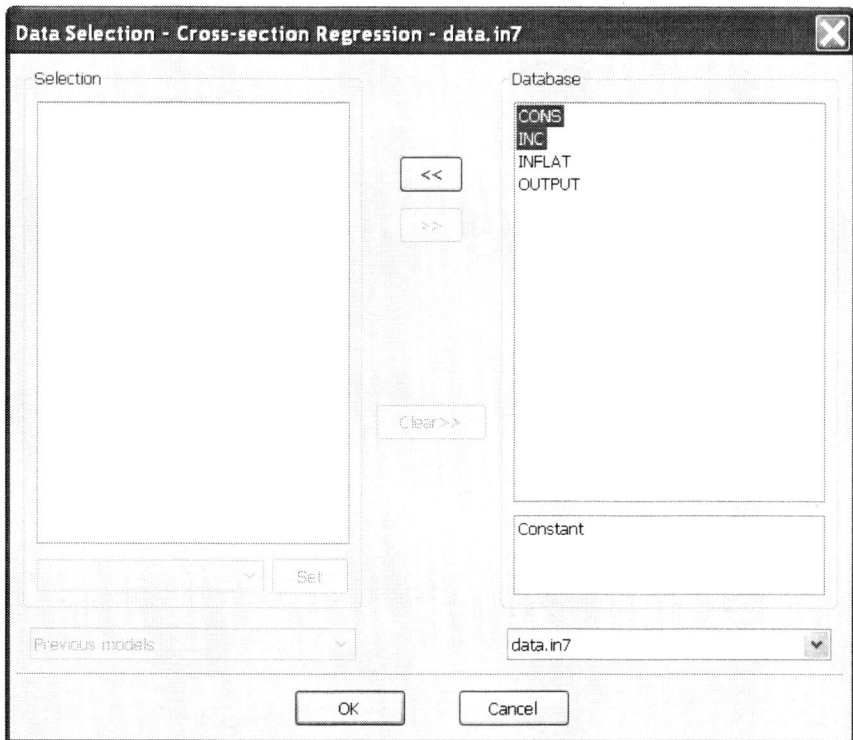

This is a dialog which you will use often, so, at the risk of boring you, we consider it in detail. At the bottom are the two familiar OK and Cancel buttons, while the remainder is grouped in three columns. On the right are the variables that can be added to the model and the databases that are open in OxMetrics. In the middle are buttons for moving between the database and the selection (i.e. the model). For dynamic models, the lag length is also there. On the left is current selection, options to change status, and the possibility to recall previous models.

The following actions can be taken in this dialog:

- Mark a variable by clicking on it with the mouse. To select several variables, use the Ctrl key with the mouse, to select a range, use Shift plus the mouse.
- Press >> to add selected variables to the model.
- Double click to add a database variable to the model.
- Remove a model variable by pressing >> or double clicking.
- Empty the entire model formulation by pressing Clear>>.
- The box immediately below the database contains the so-called 'special' variables. These are made available even when not present in the database, and are added to the selection in the same way as database variables.
- Below that, still on the database side, is the option to change databases, if more than one are open in OxMetrics. But the model only works on one database.
- On the left-hand side, below the selection (the model formulation), is a drop-down box to change the status of selected variables. It becomes active when a selection variable is selected. For the cross-section regression there are three types:

  Y the endogenous (dependent) variable, by default the first,
  Z regressor, the default for all other variables,
  A an additional instrument (for instrumental variables estimation, considered in Ch. 5),
  S an optional variable to select observations by.

  To change status, select one or moore variables, then a status type, and click on Set.
  It is also possible to change status by right-clicking on a variable.
- Finally, the last drop-down box below the selection allows the recall of a previously formulated model (none as yet). indexPcGive dialogs!Formulate!Previous models

Select CONS and INC, and add the marked variables to the model, as shown in the capture below:

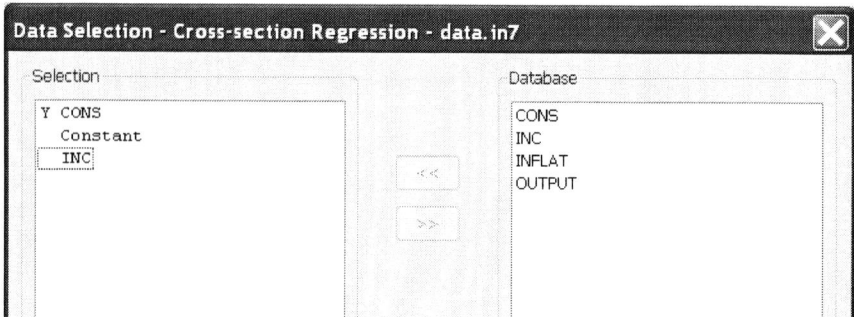

The marked variable that is highest in the database becomes the dependent variable, because it is the first to enter the model. A two-step procedure might be required to make a lower variable into the dependent variable: first mark and add the dependent variable, then add the remaining variables.

Note that a Constant is automatically added, but can be deleted if the scale of the variables lets a regression through the origin have meaning. CONS is marked with a Y to show that it is an endogenous (here, the dependent) variable. The other variables do not have a status letter, and default to regressor (Z).

2.3 Cross-section regression estimation

Pressing the OK button in the Model Formulation dialog immediately jumps to the Estimation dialog.

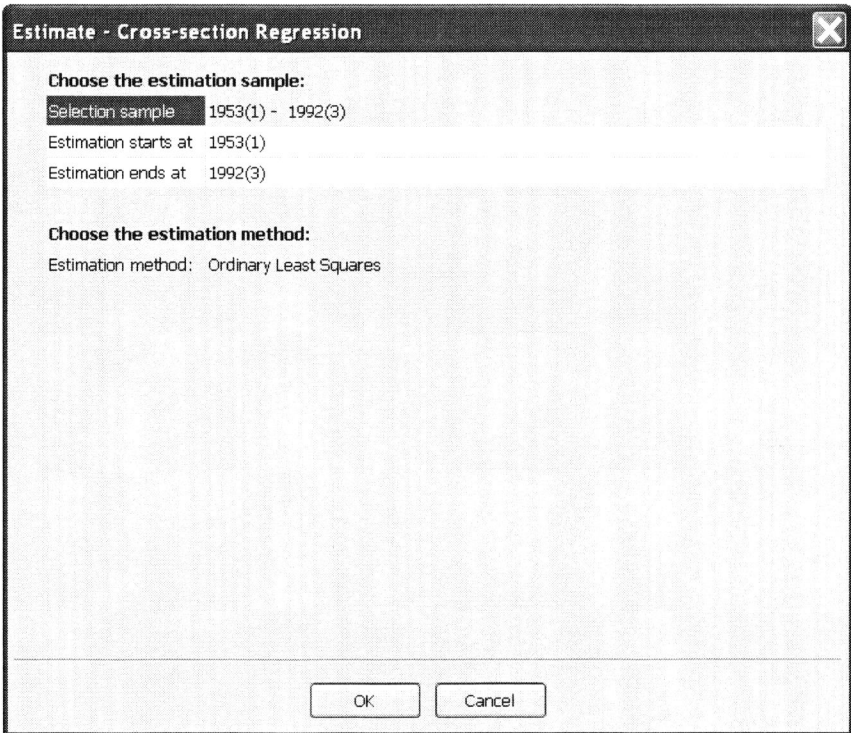

Other ways of activating the Estimation dialog from OxMetrics are the short-cut key Alt+l, in which the l stands for least squares; however, the toolbar button (the second: the blocks put together) will be the most convenient way of activating the dialog.

This style of dialog is used througout PcGive. It presents a list of options: check boxes, edit fields, radio buttons etc. To change a value, click on the item with the mouse. A check box and radio button changes immediately, for an edit field the value can be changed in the edit box. From the keyboard use the arrow up and down buttons to move between items, and the space bar to change the value. Pressing the return key has the same effect as clicking the OK button, unless the caret is in an edit field.

Under cross-section regression, the only available option is estimation by **ordinary least squares** (OLS) (unless the model has more than one endogenous variable — additional estimation methods are discussed in Chapter 5).

The dialog allows selection of the sample period: by default the full sample is used after deleting observations which have missing values (as we shall discuss later, the sample can also be selected by a variable).

Press the OK button (or Enter) to estimate the model.

The equation we fitted is:

$$\text{CONS}_i = a + b\text{INC}_i + u_i$$

where a and b are selected to minimize the sum of squares of the $\{u_i\}$. The resulting estimated values for a and b are written $\hat{a}$ and $\hat{b}$.

2.3.1 Simple regression output

The regression results are written to the Results window. As you may already know, this window does not reside in PcGive, but in OxMetrics. After estimation, focus switches automatically to the Results window in OxMetrics. The output is:

```
EQ( 1) Modelling CONS by OLS-CS (using data.in7)
        The estimation sample is: 1953(1) - 1992(3)

                      Coefficient  Std.Error  t-value  t-prob Part.R^2
Constant                 -181.270      30.03    -6.04   0.000   0.1884
INC                       1.18563    0.03367     35.2   0.000   0.8876

sigma                      4.5537  RSS              3255.58444
R^2                      0.887596  F(1,157) =      1240 [0.000]**
log-likelihood           -465.639  DW                    0.365
no. of observations           159  no. of parameters         2
mean(CONS)                 875.94  var(CONS)           182.159
```

These results cannot be regarded as substantive but their meaning can be described. To do so, we remain in OxMetrics, and turn to a scatter plot of CONS and INC. Access the Graphics dialog and graph a scatter plot of CONS against INC. Then double click on the graph to add a regression line with projections: the outcome is shown in Fig. 2.1.

The slope of the line is the tangent of the angle at b: a tangent is calculated by the ratio of the length opposite over the length adjacent. Using the point facility (Alt+p) to read off the values at the two extremes of the line as drawn, we find the approximate slope:

$$\hat{b} = \frac{(896.864 - 853.136)}{(909.367 - 872.379)} = \frac{43.728}{36.988} = 1.182.$$

This value closely matches the coefficient just reported.

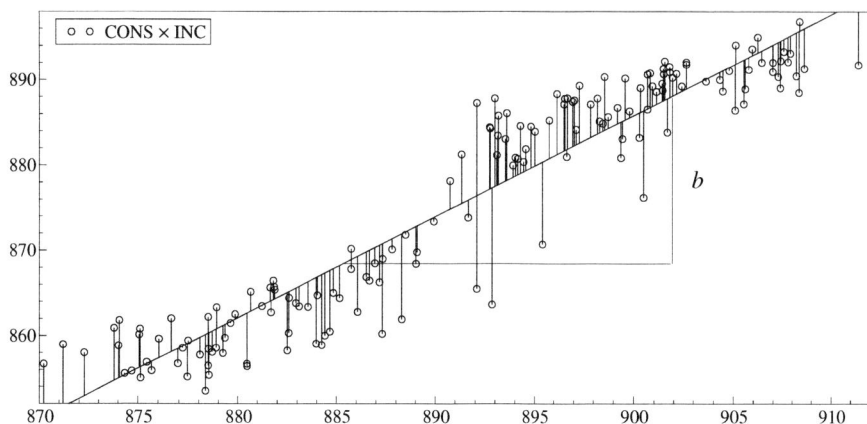

Figure 2.1 Cross-plot of CONS against INC.

The intercept is the value of CONS when INC equals zero, or more usefully, using an overbar $^-$ to denote the mean value, a is given by:

$$\hat{a} = \overline{\text{CONS}} - \hat{b} \times \overline{\text{INC}}.$$

To calculate the mean values, set focus to the `data.in7` database in OxMetrics, and select Summary statistics from the View menu. The results from the descriptive statistics are (we deleted the minimum and maximum):

```
Database:  Data.in7
Sample:    1953 (1) to 1992 (3) (159 observations)
Variables: 4
Variable        leading sample   #obs  #miss     mean   std.dev
CONS          1953( 1)-1992( 3)   159      0   875.94    13.497
INC           1953( 1)-1992( 3)   159      0   891.69    10.725
INFLAT        1953( 1)-1992( 3)   159      0   1.7997    1.2862
OUTPUT        1953( 1)-1992( 3)   159      0   1191.1    10.974
```

Substituting the means of the variables into our formula, we obtain:

$$\hat{a} = 875.94 - 1.182 \times 891.69 = -178.$$

Thus, the regression coefficients simply show the values of the slope and intercept needed to draw the line in Figure 2.1. Their interpretation is that a unit increase in INC is associated with a 1.18 unit increase in CONS. If the data purport to be consumption expenditure and income, we should be suspicious of such a finding taken at face value. However, there is nothing mysterious about regression: it is simply a procedure for fitting straight lines to data. Once we have estimated the regression coefficients $\hat{a}$ and $\hat{b}$, we can compute the fitted values:

$$\widehat{\text{CONS}}_i = \hat{a} + \hat{b} \, \text{INC}_i,$$

and the residuals

$$\hat{u}_i = \text{CONS}_i - \widehat{\text{CONS}}_i.$$

The fitted values correspond to the straight line in Fig. 2.1, and the residuals to the vertical distance between the observed CONS values and the line (as drawn in the graph).

Next, the standard errors (SEs) of the coefficients reflect the best estimate of the variability likely to occur in repeated random sampling from the same population: the coefficient $\pm 2\text{SE}$ provides a 95% confidence interval. When that interval does not include zero, the coefficient is often called 'significant' (at the 5% level). The number 2 derives from the assumption that $\hat{\beta}$ has a student-t distribution with $n - k = 159 - 2 = 157$ degrees of freedom. This, in turn, we know to be quite close to a standard normal distribution, and: $P(|Z| > 2) \approx 95\%$ where $Z \sim N(0, 1)$.

The t-value of $\hat{b}$ is the ratio of the estimated coefficient to its standard error:

$$t_b = \frac{\hat{b}}{\text{SE}\left(\hat{b}\right)} = \frac{1.18563}{0.03367} = 35.2.$$

This can be used to test the hypothesis that b is zero (expressed as $H_0 : b = 0$). Under the current assumptions we reject the hypothesis if $t_b > 2$ or $t_b < -2$ (again, using a 95% confidence interval, in other words, a 5% significance level), so values with $|t| > 2$ are significant. Here, the non-random residuals manifest in Figure 2.1 make the interpretation of the SEs suspect (in fact, they are downwards biased here, and hence the reported 't'-values are artificially inflated – despite that, they are so large that even the 'correct' SEs would yield t-values greater than 2 in absolute value).

The last statistic in the regression array is the partial r^2. This is the squared correlation between the relevant explanatory variable and the dependent variable (often called regressor and regressand respectively), holding all other variables fixed. For the regression of CONS on INC, there are no other variables (after all, the Constant is not called that for nothing!), so the partial r^2 equals the simple correlation squared (shown above in the descriptive statistics output). As can be seen, that is also the value of the coefficient of multiple correlation squared, R^2, which measures the correlation between the actual values CONS_i and the fitted values $\widehat{\text{CONS}}_i$, and is reported immediately below the regression output. When there are several regressors, r^2 and R^2 differ.

Moving along the R^2 row of output, the F-test is a test of $R^2 = 0$. For a bivariate regression, that corresponds precisely to a test of $b = 0$ and can be checked using the fact that $t^2(k) = F(1, k)$. Here, $(35.21)^2 = 1239.74$ which is close for a hand calculation. The next item [0.000] is the probability that $F = 0$, and the ** denotes that the outcome is significant at the 1% level or less.

The value of $\hat{\sigma}$ is the standard deviation of the residuals, usually called the equation standard error:

$$\hat{\sigma} = \sqrt{\frac{1}{n-k} \sum_{t=1}^{n} \hat{u}_i^2},$$

for n observations and k estimated parameters (regressors). Since the errors are assumed to be drawn independently from the same distribution with mean zero and constant variance σ, an approximate 95% confidence interval for any one error is $0 \pm 2\hat{\sigma}$. That represents the likely interval from the fitted regression line of the observations. When $\hat{\sigma} = 4.55$, the 95% interval is a huge 18.2% of CONS – the government would not thank you for a model that poor, as it knows that consumers' expenditure rarely changes by more than 5% from one year to the next even without your model. We learn that not all regressions are useful. RSS is the acronym from residual sum of squares, namely $\sum_{t=1}^{n} \hat{u}_i^2$, which can be useful for hand calculations of tests between different equations for the same variable.

The statistic listed after the log-likelihood is the DW (Durbin–Watson) test statistic. That checks whether the residuals are indeed successively related (called serial correlation): tables of significance values are presented in many textbooks, but the assumptions needed to justify the application of the test in economics are rarely satisfied. It is reported more as a historical relic than as a fundamental test. Here, it is invalid but nevertheless suggests non-random residuals (values outside $[1, 3]$ are usually significant: its mean is 2 and its extreme lower and upper values are zero and 4 respectively).

Finally, the last line gives the mean and variance of the dependent variable. The variance corresponds to the squared standard deviation:

$$\overline{\mathrm{CONS}} = \frac{1}{n} \sum_{i=1}^{n} \mathrm{CONS}_i, \qquad \hat{\sigma}^2 = \frac{1}{n} \sum_{i=1}^{n} \left(\mathrm{CONS}_i - \overline{\mathrm{CONS}}\right)^2.$$

2.4 Regression graphics

Of course, there are other ways to represent the findings, and one of the more useful is a time-series graph of the fitted values, namely $\widehat{\mathrm{CONS}}_i$, with the outcomes, a cross-plot of the same two variables, and the scaled residuals:

$$\hat{u}_i = \frac{\left(\mathrm{CONS}_i - \widehat{\mathrm{CONS}}_i\right)}{\hat{\sigma}}.$$

Select the Test menu in OxMetrics; again there are three ways Alt+t, sf Model/sf Test or the Test toolbar button. Check Graphic analysis:

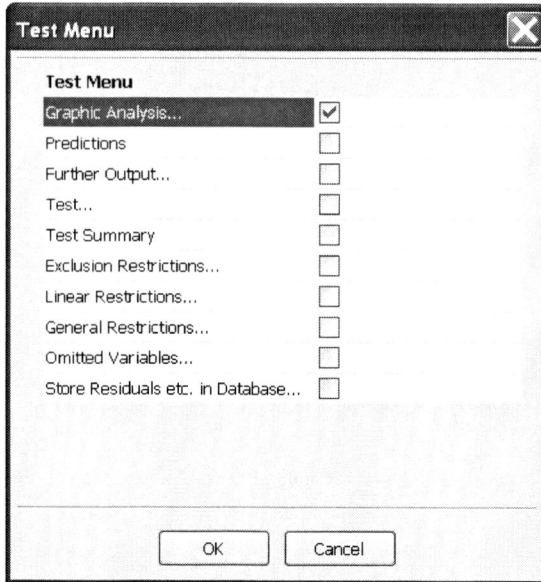

Press sf OK. The Graphic analysis dialog lets you plot and/or cross-plot the actual and fitted values, the residuals scaled by $\hat{\sigma}$, the forecasts if any were assigned, and a variety of graphical diagnostics to which we return below. Mark Actual and fitted values, Cross plot of actual and fitted, and Residuals (scaled) as shown here:

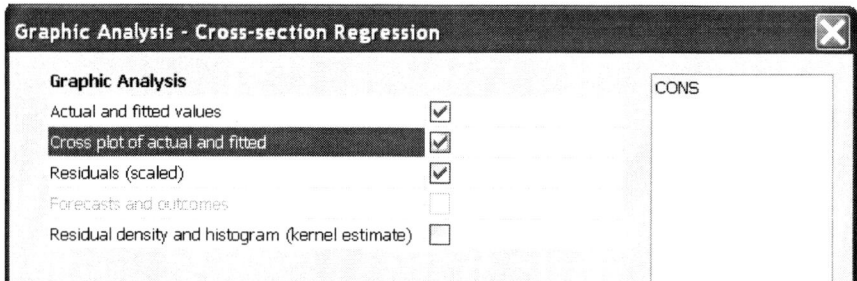

Accepting produces Figure 2.2 in OxMetrics. Any graphs can be saved, edited or printed.

The first plot shows the 'track' of the outcome by the fitted model as time series. The overall tracking is fair, but is not very precise. This is perhaps easier to see here from the cross-plot, where two groups of scatters can be seen on either side of 875: the outcome would be a straight line for a perfect fit. Finally, the scaled residuals do not look very random: when the value is high in one period, you can see that it is more likely to be high again in the next period, and similarly low (that is, large negative) values are followed by other low values.

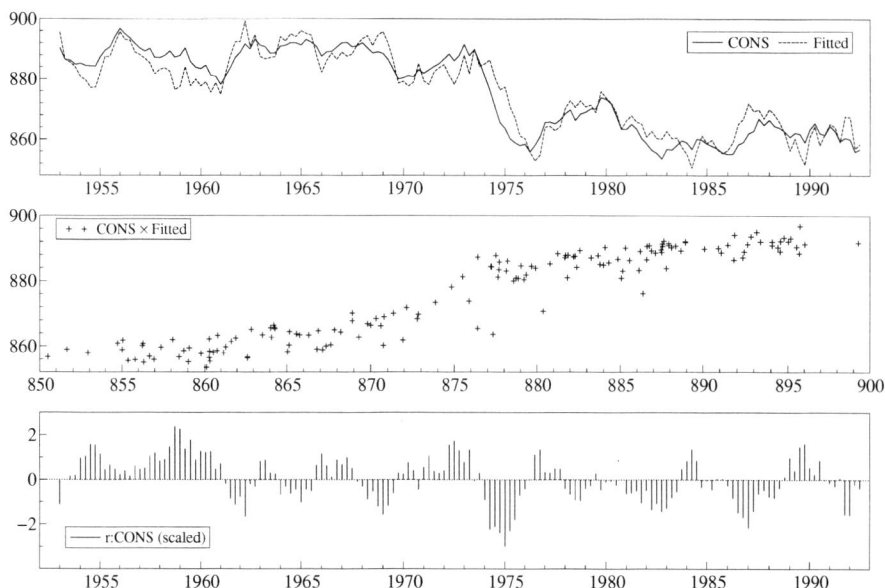

Figure 2.2 Goodness-of-fit graphs for bivariate model of CONS.

2.5 Testing restrictions and omitted variables

We will only compute two tests in this part of the tutorial: the first is for a subset of the regressors being zero. With only one actual variable, there is not much scope, but we can check that the test yields the same outcome as the (squared) t-test already reported. Select the Test menu, Exclusion restrictions, and mark INC. Now accept to produce:

```
Test for excluding: INC
Subset F(1,157) =   1239.8 [0.0000]**
```

This is identical to the F-test value above.

The same test can be made through Test/Linear Restrictions. In this case restrictions are entered in the form

$$\mathbf{R}\boldsymbol{\beta} = \mathbf{r},$$

where $\boldsymbol{\beta}$ is the $k \times 1$ coefficient vector, $\mathbf{R}$ the $s \times k$ restrictions matrix when s restrictions are imposed, and $\mathbf{r}$ the desired value of the summation, an $s \times 1$ vector. For a single restriction in our simple model:

$$\begin{pmatrix} R_{11} & R_{12} \end{pmatrix} \begin{pmatrix} a \\ b \end{pmatrix} = r_1.$$

Specifically, to test that b is zero:

$$\begin{pmatrix} 0 & 1 \end{pmatrix} \begin{pmatrix} a \\ b \end{pmatrix} = 0.$$

Access Test/Linear Restrictions and enter 0 1 0 in the edit field. The format is **R** followed by **r**, so the leading 0 1 are the elements of **R**, and the final zero is **r**:

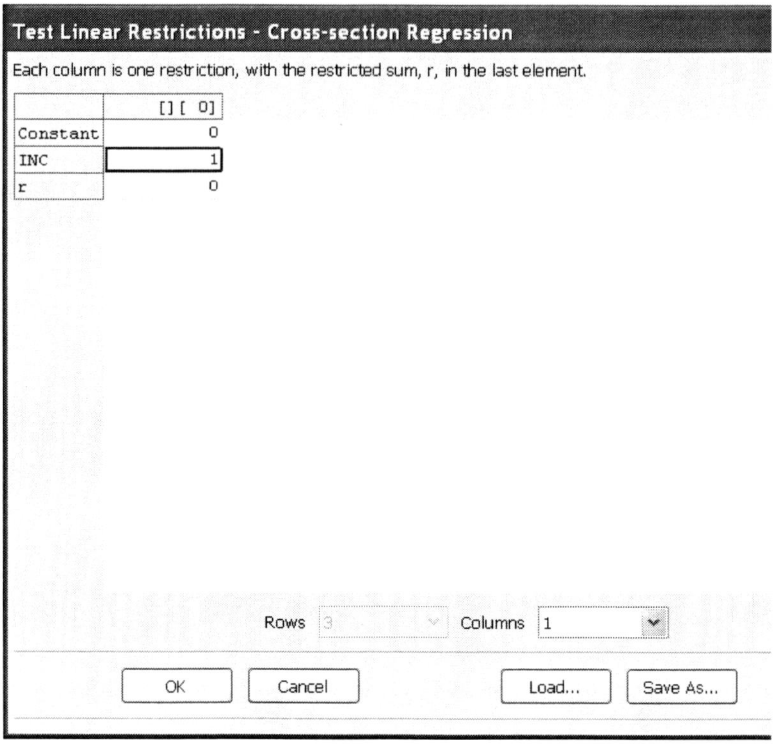

Test Linear Restrictions - Cross-section Regression

Each column is one restriction, with the restricted sum, r, in the last element.

	[] [0]
Constant	0
INC	1
r	0

Rows 3   Columns 1

OK   Cancel   Load...   Save As...

Further examples are given in the next chapter. Press OK to see:

```
Test for linear restrictions (Rb=r):
R matrix
     Constant              INC
      0.00000          1.0000
r vector
      0.00000
LinRes F(1,157) =    1239.8 [0.0000]**
```

As a second test, we consider adding a variable to the existing model. Select Test/Omitted variables and mark INFLAT as in:

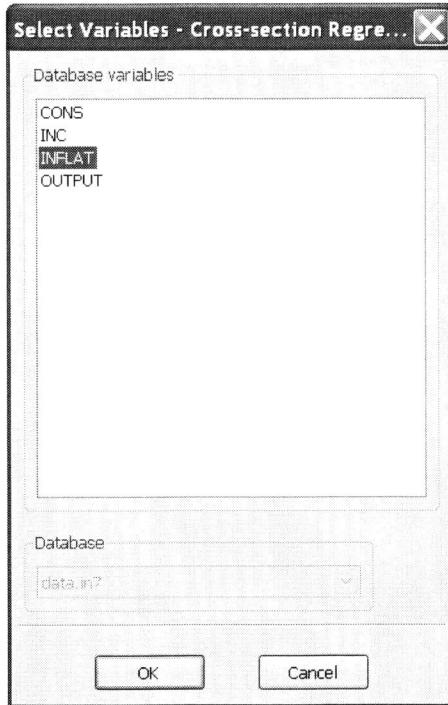

This dialog offers a choice of lag length, provided that the lagged variables match the estimation sample (so no lags can be added here). Accept to obtain:

```
Omitted variables test: F(1,156) = 149.072 [0.0000] **
Added variables:
[0] = INFLAT
```

This result strongly suggests that INFLAT has an important impact on the relation between CONS and INC, as the hypothesis that the effect is zero would essentially never produce such a large test outcome by chance.

2.6 Multiple regression

That last result suggests using a multiple explanatory variable model, with both INC and INFLAT as regressors. From a methodological viewpoint, expanding a model in response to test rejections is not a good way to do research: we could have found 10 different flaws with the first regression, and where we finally ended up would depend critically on the order in which we 'fixed' them. However, in a tutorial on the use of the program, we can claim some poetic licence and proceed to the more interesting stage of a multiple regression by adding INFLAT to the set of regressors. Select Model, Formulate using the toolbar button, or the 'hot-key' Alt+y (remember y_i is usually the symbol for the dependent variable in econometrics since Koopmans, 1950).

Double click on INFLAT to add it to the model. Click on OK – then OK (or the Enter key) again at the Estimation dialog) to obtain:

```
EQ( 2) Modelling CONS by OLS-CS (using data.in7)
        The estimation sample is: 1953(1) - 1992(3)
```

	Coefficient	Std.Error	t-value	t-prob	Part.R^2
Constant	-147.390	21.72	-6.79	0.000	0.2279
INC	1.15263	0.02431	47.4	0.000	0.9351
INFLAT	-2.47468	0.2027	-12.2	0.000	0.4886

sigma	3.26673	RSS	1664.75821
R^2	0.942522	F(2,156) =	1279 [0.000]**
log-likelihood	-412.319	DW	0.605
no. of observations	159	no. of parameters	3
mean(CONS)	875.94	var(CONS)	182.159

The added variable is apparently highly significant (but *DW* remains too low to allow any trust in the standard errors reported).

The square of the t-test on INFLAT is precisely the Omitted variable F-test. Otherwise, the INC coefficient is not greatly altered, and still exceeds unity, but $\hat{\sigma}$ is somewhat smaller, allowing a 95% confidence around the line of about 13% of CONS, which remains too large for the model to be useful.

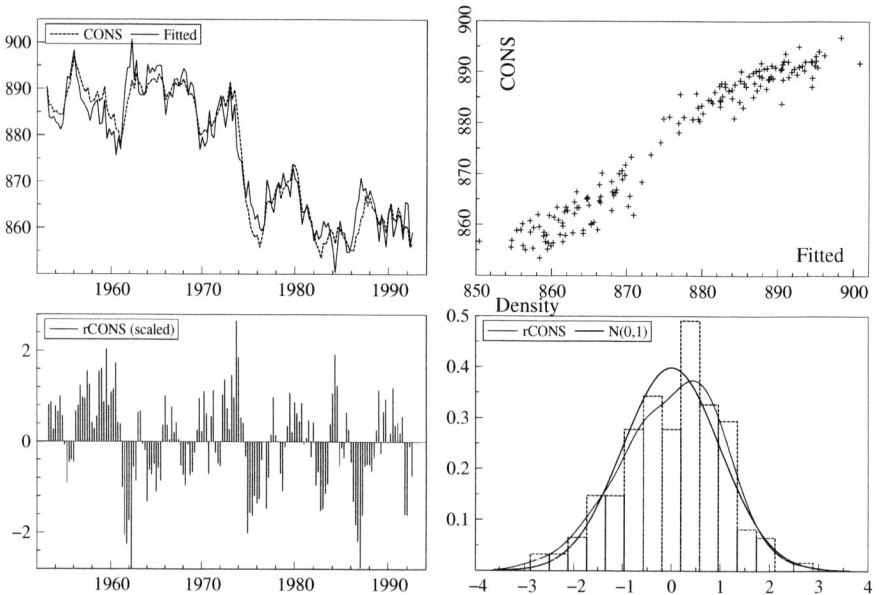

Figure 2.3   Goodness-of-fit graphs for extended model of CONS.

The partial r^2 for INC has risen relative to the simpler regression despite adding

INFLAT: in fact INC only has a correlation of -0.11 with INFLAT. Nevertheless, some of the explanation of CONS is being spread across the two regressor variables although more is being explained in total. Replot the graphical output, this time marking the options for Actual and fitted values, Cross plot of actual and fitted, Residuals (scaled), and finally, Residual density and Histogram. The graphs now appear as in Figure 2.3.

The improvement in the fit over Figure 2.1 should be clear. The new plot is the histogram with an interpolation of the underlying density. This lets us see the extent to which the residuals are symmetric around zero, or have outliers etc.; more generally, it suggests the form of the density. It is drawn together with the normal density (standardized, because the standardized residuals were used in the histogram and density).

2.7 Formal tests

Econometricians have constructed formal tests of such hypotheses as serial correlation or normality, and these are easily implemented in PcGive. For example, to test normality of the errors, select the Test... command from the Test menu and the Test dialog appears. Mark Normality as shown below, and accept.

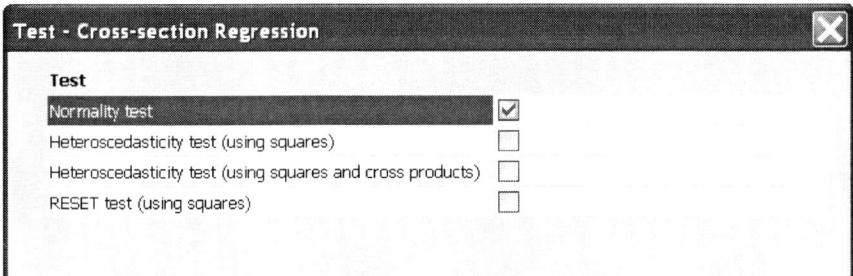

The output comprises the first four moments of the residuals and a χ^2 test for these being from a normal distribution:

```
Normality test for Residuals
Observations                159
Mean                    0.00000
Std.Devn.                3.2358
Skewness               -0.32415
Excess Kurtosis       -0.083166
Minimum                 -9.0491
Maximum                  8.6025
Asymptotic test:  Chi^2(2) =   2.8303 [0.2429]
Normality test:   Chi^2(2) =   3.2519 [0.1967]
```

Note that the mean of the residuals is zero by construction when an intercept is included, and the standard deviation is the equation standard error (but uses the wrong degrees of freedom, as it divides by n, rather than $n - k$). The skewness statistic measures the deviation from symmetry, and the excess kurtosis measures how 'fat' the tails of the distribution are: fat tails mean that outliers or extreme values are more common than in a normal distribution. Finally, the largest and smallest values are reported. Here, the normality χ^2 test does not reject: the probability of such a value or larger is 0.1967.

2.8 Storing residuals in the database

Occasionally it can be useful to store the residuals in the OxMetrics database for further analysis. Select Test/Store in Database and mark Residuals:

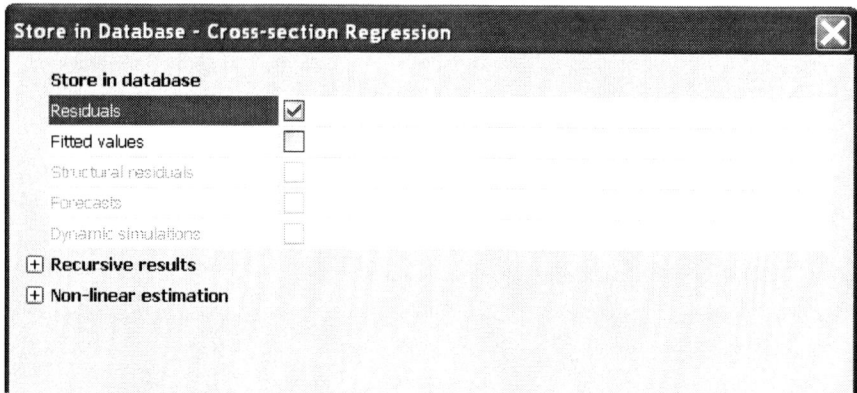

Accept, and confirm the new variable name in OxMetrics. Now the variable is stored in the data.in7 database. This is held in memory by OxMetrics, and not committed to disk until you save it from inside OxMetrics (to keep this tutorial dataset clean, you may prefer not to save the modified version).

Bring the database in focus (remaining in OxMetrics), and select View/Summary statistics to confirm that the mean of the residuals variable is zero (well, not exactly: numerical computations on a computer are usually accurate but never exact), and the standard deviation (dividing by n) 3.2358.

This concludes the first tutorial on regression estimation. We now move on to descriptive statistics, and then to formulating and estimating dynamic models. The mechanics of the program remain the same, although the level of technique needed is higher. Chapter 11 describes the analysis of linear dynamic models, with the objective of learning the econometrics. Chapter 4 shows how to do it in PcGive.

Chapter 3

Tutorial on Description Statistics and Unit Roots

The previous tutorial introduced the econometrics of PcGive for a simple bivariate regression, and explained the mechanics of operating PcGive. We have mastered the skills to start the program, access menus and operate dialogs, load, save and transform data, use graphics, including saving and printing and estimate simple regression models. And remember, there is always help available if you get stuck: just press F1. Now we're ready to move to more substantial activities. Usually, a data analysis starts by exploring the data and transforming it to more interpretable forms. These activities are the subject of this chapter. The OxMetrics book describes the 'Calculator' and 'Algebra.'

If you're not inside PcGive at the moment, restart and load the tutorial data set data.in7/data.bn7 into OxMetrics. Inside PcGive ensure that the Package menu is set to Descriptive Statistics.

Use the OxMetrics calculator to create DCONS as the first difference of CONS (in the calculator, mark CONS in the database list box, then press the Diff button and accept lag length one to get the expression diff(CONS,1) in the calculator display, finally press the = button to accept DCONS). Fig. 3.1 shows how different CONS and DCONS appear when graphed.

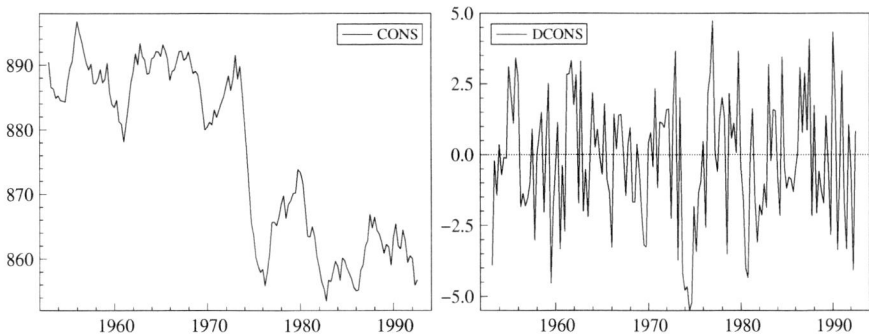

Figure 3.1   Time-series plot of CONS and DCONS.

31

3.1 Descriptive data analysis

Select Package/Descriptive Statistics, and then Model/Formulate. This dialog is similar to that discussed in the previous section. Select CONS and DCONS:

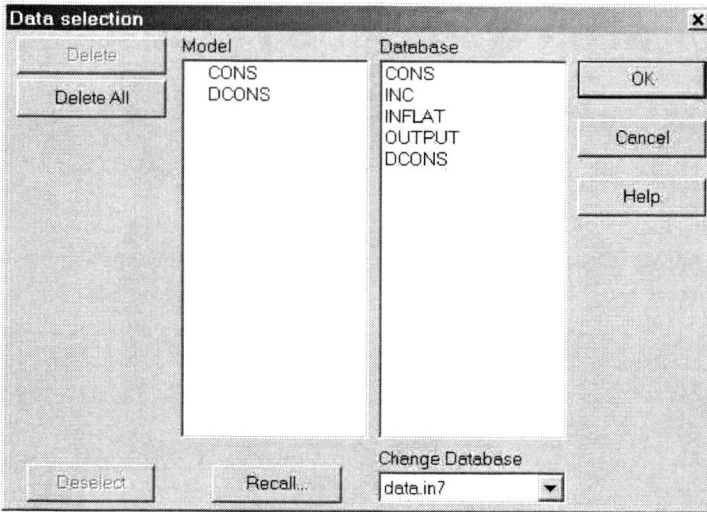

In the next dialog, select means, standard deviations and correlations as shown here (the unit-root tests are described in §3.3):

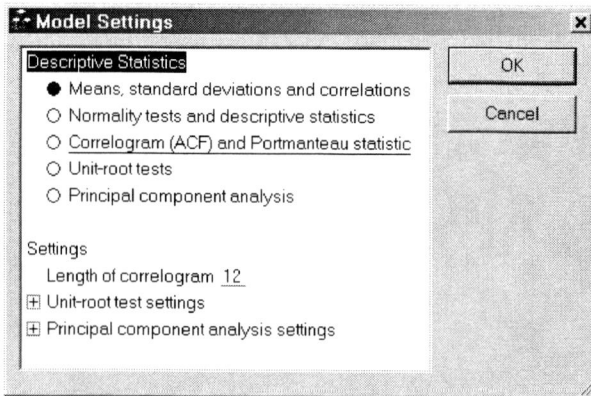

Press OK, and OK again in the next dialog to accept the maximum sample size. First listed in the output are the means and standard deviations, followed by the correlation matrix:

```
Means, standard deviations and correlations (using data.in7)
The sample is 1953 (2) - 1992 (3)
Means
          CONS         DCONS
        875.85      -0.21341
Standard deviations (using T-1)
          CONS         DCONS
        13.533        2.2101
Correlation matrix:
                   CONS         DCONS
CONS             1.0000      0.098638
DCONS          0.098638        1.0000
```

The sample standard deviation of a variable x is defined here as

$$\bar{x} = \frac{1}{T}\sum_{t=1}^{T} x_t, \quad s = \sqrt{\frac{1}{T-1}\sum_{t=1}^{T}(x_t - \bar{x})^2}.$$

The sample correlation between two variables x and y is:

$$r_{xy} = \frac{\sum_{t=1}^{T}(x_t - \bar{x})(y_t - \bar{y})}{\sqrt{\sum_{t=1}^{T}(x_t - \bar{x})^2 \sum_{t=1}^{T}(y_t - \bar{y})^2}}. \tag{3.1}$$

CONS is hardly correlated with its difference, matching its high correlation with its own one-lagged value (as we shall see later).

Now repeat, selecting Normality tests and descriptive statistics. The normality test output consists of the first four moments, extrema and a test statistic. The output is the same as §2.7, but applied to CONS and DCONS instead of the model residuals:

```
Normality tests and descriptive statistics (using data.in7)
The sample is 1953 (2) - 1992 (3)

Normality test for CONS
Observations              158
Mean                   875.85
Std.Devn.              13.490
Skewness             -0.17195
Excess Kurtosis       -1.6251
Minimum                853.50
Maximum                896.83
Asymptotic test:  Chi^2(2) =   18.165 [0.0001]**
Normality test:   Chi^2(2) =   52.808 [0.0000]**

Normality test for DCONS
Observations              158
Mean                 -0.21341
Std.Devn.              2.2031
Skewness             -0.11208
```

```
Excess Kurtosis        -0.55302
Minimum                -5.4897
Maximum                 4.7393
Asymptotic test:  Chi^2(2) =   2.3442 [0.3097]
Normality test:   Chi^2(2) =   2.2958 [0.3173]
```

For a standard normal distribution (denoted by $N(0, 1)$) the numbers would be:

$$\begin{array}{llll} \text{mean} & 0 & \text{skewness} & 0 \\ \text{standard deviation} & 1 & \text{excess kurtosis} & 0 \end{array}$$

Note the difference between the standard deviation of CONS under the normality test and under correlations. This can be explained by:

$$\hat{\sigma} = \sqrt{\frac{1}{T} \sum_{t=1}^{T} (x_t - \bar{x})^2} \quad \text{versus} \quad s = \sqrt{\frac{1}{T-1} \sum_{t=1}^{T} (x_t - \bar{x})^2}.$$

The normality test reports the former:

$$13.490 \times \sqrt{\frac{158}{157}} = 13.533.$$

The normality test statistic is a function of the skewness and excess kurtosis. The value of the test for CONS is 52.81. The probability of getting a number at least as large if CONS would really have a normal distribution is given between the square brackets. It is zero (not exactly, but so close to zero that we need not bother how close). The two stars indicate that the test is significant at the 1% level, in other words it tells us that 0% (the p-value) < 1%. It is extremely unlikely that CONS was generated by a normal distribution. DCONS is another picture, as we can see in Fig. 3.2: its shape is not significantly different from an $N(-0.21, (2.2)^2)$ distribution.

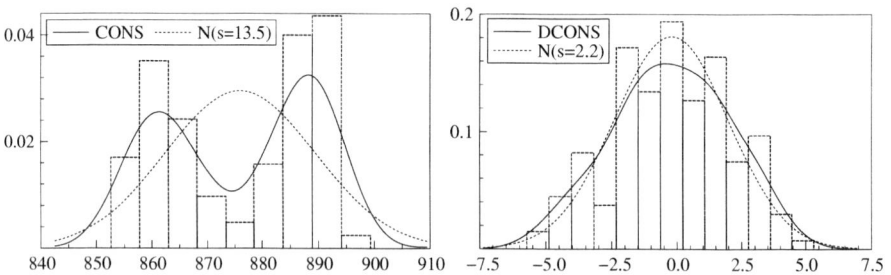

Figure 3.2   Histogram and estimated density plot of CONS and DCONS.

3.2 Autoregressive distributed lag

Figure 3.3 shows the sample autocorrelation function (ACF) of CONS and DCONS. CONS is highly correlated with its own lags, but not much autocorrelation is present

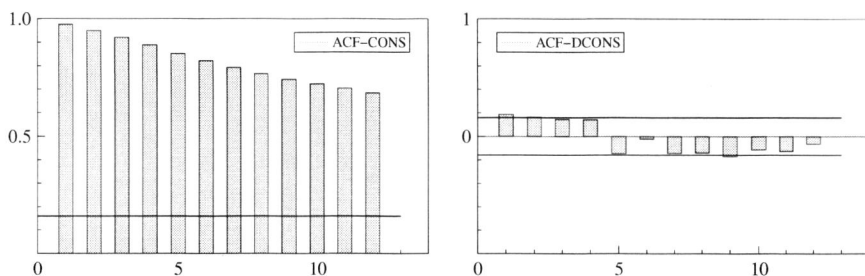

Figure 3.3 Sample autocorrelation function of CONS and DCONS.

in DCONS, the distribution of which resembled an independent normal distribution in Fig. 3.2b. Both graphs in Fig. 3.3 indicate approximate significance under the assumption that the data constitutes an independent sample from the normal distribution as absolute values in excess of:

$$\frac{2}{T^{1/2}} = \frac{2}{\sqrt{159}} \approx 0.16$$

for the first graph (the second has $T = 158$, because one observation is lost when taking the first difference).

From this, we could entertain the hypothesis that CONS is appropriately described by a first-order autoregressive process, denoted by AR(1). In mathematical form:

$$y_t = \alpha + \beta y_{t-1} + \epsilon_t, \quad t = 1, \ldots, T. \tag{3.2}$$

The coefficient α is the intercept. If β were zero, y_t would be perturbed by a random disturbance around a constant. When $\beta = 1$, then Δy_t is random. Assumptions about the error term are that it has mean 0 and variance which is constant over time:

$$\mathsf{E}\left[\epsilon_t\right] = 0, \ \mathsf{V}\left[\epsilon_t\right] = \mathsf{E}\left[\epsilon_t - \mathsf{E}\left[\epsilon_t\right]\right]^2 = \mathsf{E}\left[\epsilon_t^2\right] = \sigma^2.$$

Autoregressions are a subset of autoregressive-distributed lag (ADL) models, and are easily estimated in PcGive using the techniques of the previous chapter. The only difference is that we need to estimate a *dynamic* model. Therefore, select the Model/Single-equation Dynamic Modelling menu to formulate a regression of CONS on a Constant and CONS_1 (the first lag of CONS). The dialog is only slightly different from before: a default lag length will be set (the initial default is one; choosing Query, would result in a little pop-up box, asking the lag length for each variable). After selecting one lag:

```
Data selection                                                    x
  Delete        Model              Database
                Y  CONS             CONS
  New Model        Constant         INC               OK
                   CONS_1           INFLAT
 Status                             OUTPUT          Cancel
  Clear                             DCONS
                                                     Help
  Y: endogenous
  Z: variable                                      Special
  A: instrument                                    Constant
                                                   Trend
                                                   Seasonal
                                                   CSeasonal

                                                  Lag length
                                 Change Database   C Query
  Deselect All      Recall...     data.in7    ▼    ⊙ 1    ▲▼
```

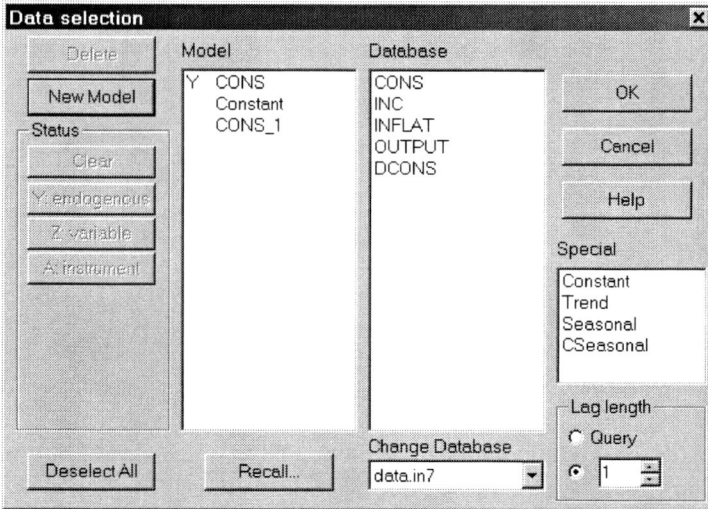

In the next screen, select ordinary least squares (the default), and then accept the
default full sample period.

The estimation results from the AR(1) model are:

```
EQ( 3) Modelling CONS by OLS (using data.in7)
        The estimation sample is: 1953 (2) to 1992 (3)

                   Coefficient  Std.Error  t-value  t-prob Part.R^2
CONS_1                0.989378    0.01308     75.6   0.000   0.9734
Constant              9.09221       11.46    0.793   0.429   0.0040

sigma                 2.21251  RSS                  763.648214
R^2                   0.97344  F(1,156) =     5717 [0.000]**
log-likelihood       -348.658  DW                          1.6
no. of observations       158  no. of parameters             2
mean(CONS)            875.848  var(CONS)              181.971
```

The output from simple regression was already discussed in §2.3.1. The col-
umn marked coefficients gives $\hat{\beta}$ and $\hat{\alpha}$. Next to that are their estimated standard errors, from which we could derive a rough 95% confidence interval, for $\hat{\beta}$:
$(0.9894 \pm 2 \times 0.01308)$. The number 2 derives from the assumption that $\hat{\beta}$ has a
student-t distribution with $T - k = 158 - 2 = 156$ degrees of freedom. This, in turn,
we know to be quite close to a standard normal distribution. Soon we shall see that this
assumption might not be valid; if so, the confidence interval will change. Alternatively,
we could use the t-value of $\hat{\beta}$:

$$t_\beta = \frac{\hat{\beta}}{\text{SE}\left(\hat{\beta}\right)} = \frac{0.9894}{0.01308} = 75.6$$

to test the hypothesis that β is zero (expressed as $H_0 : \beta = 0$). Under the current assumptions we reject the hypothesis if $t_\beta > 2$ or $t_\beta < -2$ (again, using a 95% confidence interval, in other words, a 5% significance level). The observed value of 75.6 is very much larger than 2, making it highly unlikely that β is zero.

3.3 Unit-root tests

It is more interesting to test whether β equals one, $H_0 : \beta - 1 = 0$. The t-value is computed as

$$\frac{0.9894 - 1}{0.01308} = -0.8.$$

It is convenient to rewrite (3.2) by subtracting y_{t-1} from both sides:

$$y_t - y_{t-1} = \alpha + \beta y_{t-1} - y_{t-1} + \epsilon_t,$$

or:

$$\Delta y_t = \alpha + (\beta - 1) y_{t-1} + \epsilon_t. \tag{3.3}$$

With DCONS in the database, we can check whether (3.3) is identical to (3.2). Reformulate the model of the previous section as a regression of DCONS on a Constant and CONS_1. The result should be:

```
EQ( 4) Modelling DCONS by OLS (using data.in7)
        The estimation sample is: 1953 (2) to 1992 (3)
```

	Coefficient	Std.Error	t-value	t-prob	Part.R^2
Constant	9.09221	11.46	0.793	0.429	0.0040
CONS_1	-0.0106221	0.01308	-0.812	0.418	0.0042

sigma	2.21251	RSS	763.648214
R^2	0.00420671	F(1,156) =	0.659 [0.418]
log-likelihood	-348.658	DW	1.6
no. of observations	158	no. of parameters	2
mean(DCONS)	-0.213409	var(DCONS)	4.85363

Comparing RSS shows that the outcomes are identical. What has changed dramatically are R^2 and the F-statistic, corresponding to switching between y_t and Δy_t as dependent variables.

The hypothesis $H_0 : \beta = 1$ is called the **unit-root hypothesis** (which implies that y_t is non-stationary). It is of special interest, because under the null hypothesis, it is incorrect to use the student-t distribution. Moreover, many economic variables appear to have a unit root. If CONS has one unit root, we say that CONS is **integrated of order 1**, denoted I(1); this corresponds to saying that DCONS is I(0). The correct distribution to use for the t-value is the 'Dickey-Fuller' distribution. Unfortunately, the precise distributional form depends on the presence or absence of a Constant or Trend term. (If the distribution of a test depends on other ('nuisance') parameters, it is called 'not similar'.)

To obtain correct critical values, use Package/Descriptive Statistics to re-estimate (3.3). Select CONS, in the formulation dialog, press OK and check Unit-root tests in the next dialog. Keep the default of just using a constant term, but switch off the Report summary table only option, and set the lag length for differences to zero:

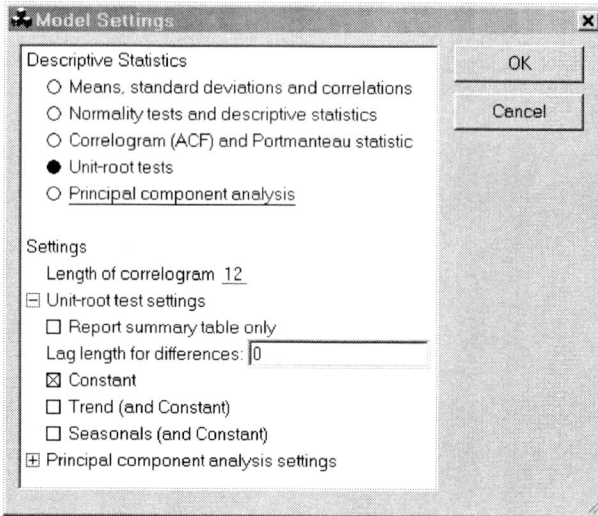

Press OK to accept. (Note that, if necessary, the sample is automatically adjusted for the required differences and lags.) The current estimation uses the full sample:

```
Unit-root tests (using data.in7)
The sample is 1953 (2) - 1992 (3)

Augmented Dickey-Fuller test for CONS; regression of DCONS on:

              Coefficient    Std.Error      t-value
CONS_1          -0.010622     0.013085     -0.81180
Constant         9.0922      11.464         0.79309

sigma = 2.21251  DW = 1.598  DW-CONS = 0.02639  ADF-CONS = -0.8118
Critical values used in ADF test: 5%=-2.88, 1%=-3.473
RSS = 763.6482142 for 2 variables and 158 observations
```

DW is the Durbin-Watson statistic of the OLS regression residuals, whereas DW-CONS is the Durbin-Watson of CONS (see Chapter 15). ADF-CONS is the t-statistic we computed earlier. The 5% critical value for the Dickey-Fuller test is reported as -2.88. The negative number is given, because the interesting alternative hypothesis is that $\hat{\beta} < 1$; $\hat{\beta} > 1$ corresponds to an exploding process, which we tend not to see in economic variables. The critical values are based on response surfaces in MacKinnon (1991); 5% significance is marked by *, 1% by **. Here we can *not* reject the hypothesis that $\beta - 1 = 0$: CONS appears to have a unit root (is I(1)). As with all statistical tests, some caution is required. It can be seen in the time-series graph of CONS in

Fig. 3.1a that it has a break around 1975, and it has been found that a break can cause I(0) variables to appear I(1) in DF tests.

The augmented Dickey-Fuller(ADF) test derives from the DF test by adding lagged differences, for example, for the ADF(1) test:

$$\Delta y_t = \alpha + (\beta - 1) y_{t-1} + \gamma \Delta y_{t-1} + \epsilon_t,$$

or more general for the ADF(s):

$$\Delta y_t = \alpha + (\beta - 1) y_{t-1} + \sum_{i=1}^{s} \gamma_i \Delta y_{t-i} + \epsilon_t.$$

ADF(0) corresponds to the DF test. The purpose of these additional lags is to 'whiten' the residuals.

Tip   The null hypothesis is that of a unit root. A significant test statistic would reject that hypothesis and suggest stationarity.

To facilitate the computation of ADF tests, and the decision about the lag length, Pc-Give can be instructed to print a summary table of ADF tests. Select Model/Descriptive Statistics, mark INFLAT and CONS, and select Unit-root tests. The default is the summary table starting from lag 4. The output consists of the sequence of ADF(4)...ADF(0) tests:

```
Unit-root tests (using data.in7)
The sample is 1954 (2) - 1992 (3)
```

```
CONS: ADF tests (T=154, Constant; 5%=-2.88 1%=-3.47)
D-lag    t-adf    beta Y_1   sigma   t-DY_lag  t-prob     AIC  F-prob
  4      -1.466   0.98058    2.157    1.268    0.2068    1.576
  3      -1.308   0.98278    2.161    1.450    0.1492    1.573  0.2068
  2      -1.135   0.98512    2.169    1.712    0.0889    1.574  0.1594
  1      -0.9463  0.98759    2.183    2.491    0.0138    1.581  0.0874
  0      -0.6500  0.99139    2.220                       1.608  0.0135
```

```
INFLAT: ADF tests (T=154, Constant; 5%=-2.88 1%=-3.47)
D-lag    t-adf    beta Y_1   sigma   t-DY_lag  t-prob     AIC  F-prob
  4      -5.095** 0.85178    0.3534   0.5232   0.6016   -2.042
  3      -5.340** 0.85784    0.3526   1.078    0.2829   -2.053  0.6016
  2      -5.354** 0.86932    0.3527   1.090    0.2774   -2.058  0.4910
  1      -5.363** 0.87997    0.3530  11.40     0.0000   -2.063  0.4577
  0      -2.398   0.92835    0.4799                     -1.456  0.0000
```

The first column is the number of lagged differences, so the first line gives the results for the ADF(4) test. The second column is the t-value, which is the ADF test statistic, the third column is the coefficient on y_{t-1} (the coefficient used in t-adf), the next column gives the equation standard error. The next two columns, t-DY_lag and t-prob, give the t-value of the highest lag (of γ_s, $s = 4, 3, 2, 1$), followed by the p-value of that lag. The suggested strategy is to select the highest s with a significant last γ_s (the distribution of $\hat{\gamma}_s$ is the conventional student-t distribution). So for both INFLAT and CONS we use an ADF(1) test. The only place where it makes a difference is in using ADF(1) or ADF(0) for INFLAT. Using the lag criterion we conclude that INFLAT is stationary, so if we did not check for the importance of lagged values of INFLAT, we might mistakenly think that it is non-stationary. Note that all tests used the same sample period, which explains why the table lists ADF-CONS(0)= -0.65, while we previously found -0.81. We deleted the column labelled AIC; the last column, labelled F-prob, is the p-value of the F-tests on all lags dropped up to that point.

We have avoided the issue of including a constant, or a constant and trend. The implications are as follows:

	$\beta = 1$	$\beta < 1$
$\Delta y_t = (\beta - 1) y_{t-1} + \epsilon_t$	zero growth	mean zero
$\Delta y_t = \alpha + (\beta - 1) y_{t-1} + \epsilon_t$	trend in y_t	non-zero mean
$\Delta y_t = \alpha + (\beta - 1) y_{t-1} + \mu t + \epsilon_t$	quadratic trend in y_t	trend in y_t

Few variables have quadratic trends, but it is often advisable to include t in case the variable is stationary around a linear trend. Equally, include an intercept unless it is clear that the variable has a zero mean. Technically, including a polynomial in time of order n (for example, having α and μt corresponds to $n = 1$) makes the test similar despite the presence of the nuisance parameters of a polynomial of order $n - 1$.

Some variables could be thought to be I(2). Then you could start with checking whether the second differences are stationary. If so, move on to test stationarity of the first differences.

That concludes the data description. The PcGive unit-root test and issues of cointegration are discussed in §11.6.

Chapter 4

Tutorial on Dynamic Modelling

Dynamic modelling normally consists of a cycle of three steps: formulation or re-formulation, estimation and evaluation. The modelling process takes place within the Model and the Test menus described in the previous tutorials, but we reproduce several dialogs here for convenience. This tutorial will guide you through a simple model sequence based on the artificial data set. Hopefully you will agree at the end that PcGive combines sophistication with great simplicity.

Before we start, a brief digression on lags is called for. PcGive names lagged variables by appending an underscore and then the lag length. So CONS_1 is CONS one period lagged. PcGive uses this naming scheme to keep track of the lag length. Suppose the database holds both a CONS and a CONS_1 variable. Then, when formulating a model involving the first lag of CONS, PcGive will use CONS, to create that lag. So the database CONS_1 variable is never used. When CONS_1 is the only CONS variable in the database, PcGive will start using it.

4.1 Model formulation

Load `data.in7` in OxMetrics, if you are starting this tutorial afresh. Then click on the Model icon (or use Model on the Model menu or `Alt+y`). Change the Category to Models for time series data and the Model class to Single-equation dynamic modelling using PcGive:

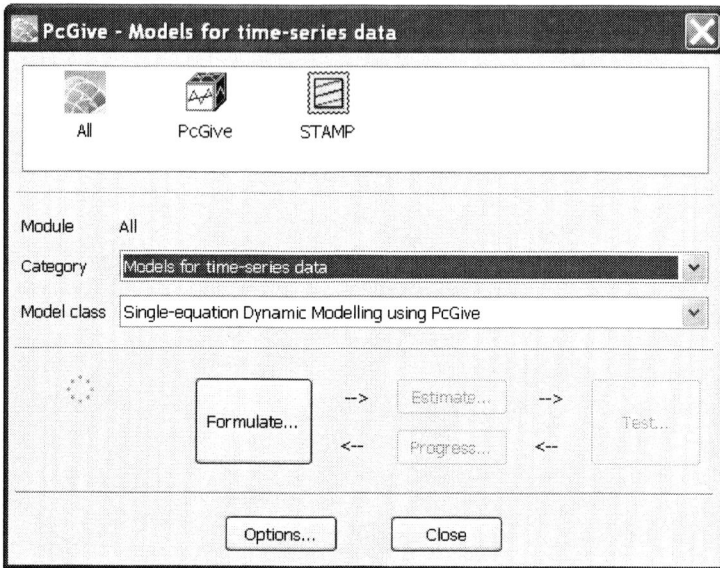

Click on Formulate to initiate the Formulate a Model dialog, discussed extensively in Chapter 2. The first model to formulate is CONS on a Constant, CONS lagged, INC, INC lagged and INFLAT, as shown overleaf. There are various ways of formulating such a model, including:

- Assuming that the lag selection is set from lag0 to 1, Double click on CONS, INC, INFLAT respectively. Then select INFLAT_1 in the Model list box, and delete (using the `Delete` key, double clicking, or pressing the >> button).
- After adding CONS and INC with lags 0 and 1, set the lag length to lag 0 to 0, and add INFLAT.
- Using the mouse, select the CONS, INC, INFLAT variables. Note that a single click only selects one variable. To select a range, hold the `Ctrl` key down, and click on the three variables. Finally, you could click on CONS, then hold the `Shift` key down and click on INFLAT. With the three variables selected, press <<. Then delete INFLAT_1.

There are three ways to use the lag settings:
- None to add without lags;
- Lag to add obly the specified lag;
- Lag 0 to to set a lag range.

Note that a Constant is automatically added, but can be deleted if the scale of the variables lets a regression through the origin have meaning. Neither the Constant nor the Trend will be offered for lagging (lagging these would create redundant variables). Seasonals are not used here, but you could add them and delete them if you wish. In that case, you'll see that PcGive automatically adds the correct number of seasonals (three here as the data are quarterly: see Chapter 10). It takes the constant term into account; without the constant, four seasonals would have been added. Seasonal is always unity in the first period (first quarter in this case). So Seasonal_1 is one in the second quarter. Delete the seasonals from the model.

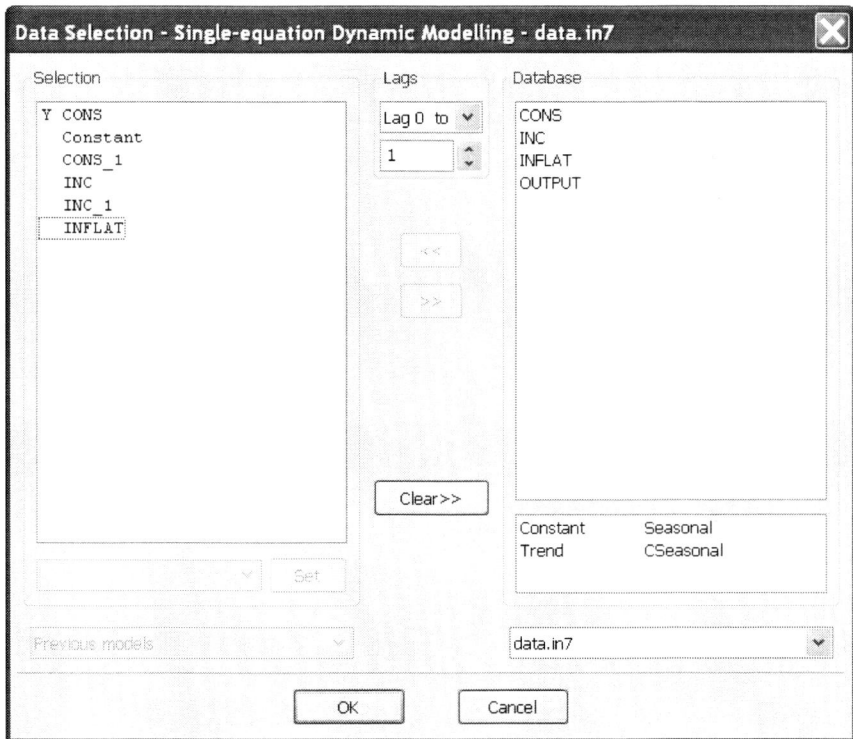

4.2 Model estimation

Estimation methods are discussed in Chapter 11; Chapter 16 reviews the statistical output reported following estimation. Here we only need OLS; examples of the other estimation methods are given in the next chapter. Pressing OK after model formulation brings up the model settings dialog. Select the default of OLS:

Model Settings - Single-equation Dynamic Modelling   ☒

Choose a model type:

Ordinary least squares	◉
Instrumental variables	○
Autoregressive least squares	○
from lag	1
to lag	1

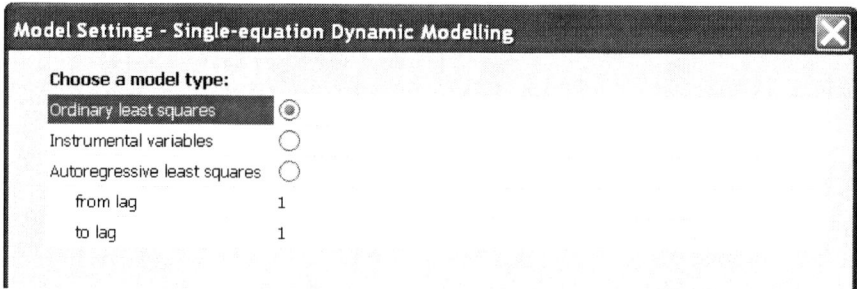

The next step is the the Estimation dialog where the sample period can be set. The short-cut key for model estimation is Alt+l, in which the l stands for least squares. However, pressing OK in the Model Settings dialog takes us directly to the Estimation dialog.

The dialog also allows you to retain some data for static forecasting. The sample period can be adjusted, but the one shown is always admissible and will either be the maximum available or the one used in the previous model. *Please verify that the sample size on your screen corresponds to the one shown here*, the full sample: 1953 (2) − 1992 (3). Retain *eight* observations for parameter constancy using the Less forecasts text entry field (the default is none, and the maximum is determined by the sample size):

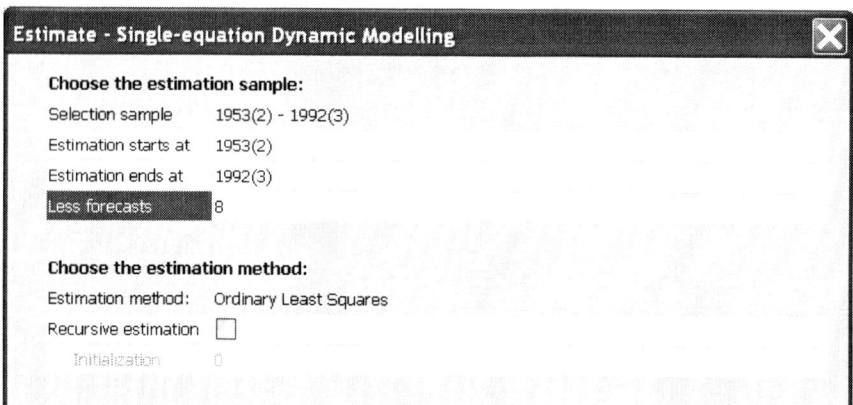

Estimate - Single-equation Dynamic Modelling   ☒

Choose the estimation sample:

Selection sample	1953(2) - 1992(3)
Estimation starts at	1953(2)
Estimation ends at	1992(3)
Less forecasts	8

Choose the estimation method:

Estimation method:	Ordinary Least Squares
Recursive estimation	☐
Initialization	0

Tip   It is easy to refit models to subsamples and hence conduct tests of constancy based on the residual sums of squares. The recursive estimation option allows testing over the entire set of subsamples.

4.3 Model output

4.3.1 Equation estimates

The estimated equation has the form:

$$y_t = x_t'\beta + \epsilon_t, \quad t = 1, \ldots, T,$$

where x_t contains a '1' for the intercept, y_{t-1} for the lagged dependent variable, as well as the other regressors. Assumptions about the error term are that it has mean 0 and variance which is constant over time:

$$\mathsf{E}\left[\epsilon_t\right] = 0, \ \mathsf{V}\left[\epsilon_t\right] = \mathsf{E}\left[\epsilon_t - \mathsf{E}\left[\epsilon_t\right]\right]^2 = \mathsf{E}\left[\epsilon_t^2\right] = \sigma^2.$$

We can write the estimated autoregressive-distributed lag (ADL) model in more detail as:

$$\text{CONS}_t = a_1\text{CONS}_{t-1} + c + b_0\text{INC}_t + b_1\text{INC}_{t-1} + \gamma\text{INFLAT}_t + \epsilon_t. \tag{4.1}$$

The equation estimation results are written to the OxMetrics Results window where further editing is easy. We assume that you have the default options setting, which generates the minimum number of statistics. Section 4.8 discusses the options. The reported results include coefficient estimates; standard errors; t-values; the squared partial correlation of every regressor with the dependent variable; the squared multiple correlation coefficient (denoted R^2); an F-test on R^2 equalling zero; the equation standard error (σ); the residual Durbin–Watson statistic (DW); the Residual Sum of Squares (RSS); these were all introduced in §2.3.1.

```
EQ( 1) Modelling CONS by OLS (using data.in7)
        The estimation sample is: 1953(2) - 1990(3)

                  Coefficient  Std.Error  t-value  t-prob Part.R^2
CONS_1               0.809091    0.02548     31.8   0.000   0.8743
Constant            -18.5178      8.726     -2.12   0.036   0.0301
INC                  0.506687    0.02882     17.6   0.000   0.6807
INC_1               -0.296493    0.03560    -8.33   0.000   0.3236
INFLAT              -0.992567    0.08618    -11.5   0.000   0.4777

sigma                 1.07598  RSS                 167.872396
R^2                   0.993693  F(4,145) =     5712 [0.000]**
log-likelihood     -221.283    DW                        1.96
no. of observations     150   no. of parameters          5
mean(CONS)          876.685   var(CONS)           177.453

1-step (ex post) forecast analysis 1990(4) - 1992(3)
Parameter constancy forecast tests:
Forecast  Chi^2(8) =    9.3241 [0.3157]
Chow      F(8,145) =    1.1500 [0.3337]
```

The sample period was automatically adjusted for the lags created on CONS and INC. The figure in [·] after the F (·) value is the probability of obtaining that value from a central F-distribution with the degrees of freedom shown. Should it be desired, the output can also be printed in LaTeX or equation format, as shown in §4.8.

4.3.2 Analysis of 1-step forecast statistics

The forecast tests are a Chow test and a forecast Chi^2 (8) which is an index of numerical parameter constancy. For H forecasts, values $> 2H$ imply poor *ex ante* accuracy. The χ^2 value always exceeds that of H times the Chow test. Later, we will graph the outcomes, forecasts and the error bars for ± 2 standard errors of the 1-step forecasts. The forecast tests are reported with the regression output. To see the full results, select Test/Further Output, and select Static (1-step) forecasts:

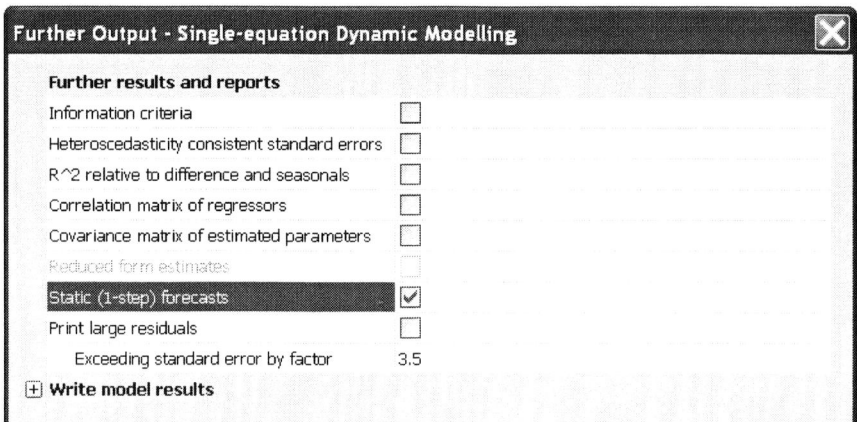

```
1-step forecasts for CONS (SE with parameter uncertainty)
   Horizon     Forecast       SE      Actual        Error    t-value
   1990-4       862.235     1.097    861.484    -0.751532    -0.685
   1991-1       862.136     1.090    864.444     2.30801      2.117
   1991-2       863.237     1.085    862.750    -0.487490    -0.449
   1991-3       860.146     1.091    859.413    -0.732399    -0.671
   1991-4       862.243     1.106    860.480    -1.76260     -1.594
   1992-1       860.796     1.092    860.002    -0.793439    -0.727
   1992-2       856.477     1.113    855.908    -0.568310    -0.511
   1992-3       856.995     1.089    856.731    -0.264312    -0.243
   mean(Error) =    -0.38151    RMSE =      1.1616
   SD(Error)   =     1.0972     MAPE =      0.11126
```

The RMSE and MAPE are discussed in §4.10.

4.4 Graphical evaluation

The next major step is to evaluate the estimated model. Select the Graphic Analysis dialog from the Test menu (or press the toolbar button), and mark the first six items:

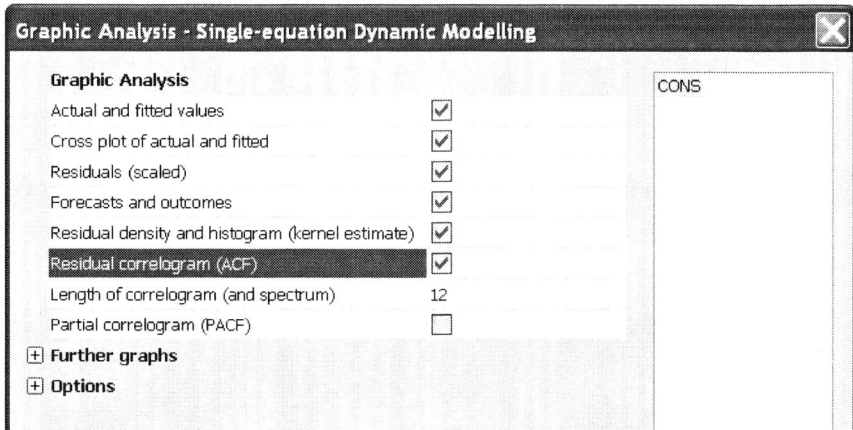

The dialog lets you plot or cross-plot the actual and fitted values for the whole sample, the residuals scaled by σ, so that values outside the range $[-2, +2]$ suggest outlier problems, the forecasts, and some graphical diagnostic information about the residuals (their spectrum, correlogram, histogram, density and cumulative distribution). The forecast period start is marked by a vertical line (see Figure 4.1). Notice the good fit: the earlier high R^2, and good Chow test are consistent with this. As before, any graphs can be saved for later recall, editing and printing.

Accept the dialog, and the graphs appear in the PcGive Graphics window in Ox-Metrics, as in Figure 4.1. There are two new graphs. The first is the correlogram, which extends the idea behind the DW test to plot the correlations between successive lagged residuals (that is, the correlation of $\hat{\epsilon}_t$ with $\hat{\epsilon}_{t-1}$, then with $\hat{\epsilon}_{t-2}$, $\hat{\epsilon}_{t-3}$ and so on up to $\hat{\epsilon}_{t-12}$). A random (independent) residual would have most such correlations close to zero: visually, the dependence between successive residuals is small. The second plots the forecasts which we printed earlier, with the error bands changed to error fans.

Tip If you wish to use a non-default sample size, adjust the area in OxMetrics.

4.5 Dynamic analysis

Next, activate Dynamic Analysis from the Test menu. Select Static long-run solution, Lag structure analysis, and both Graph normalized weights and Graph cumulative normalized weights, as shown:

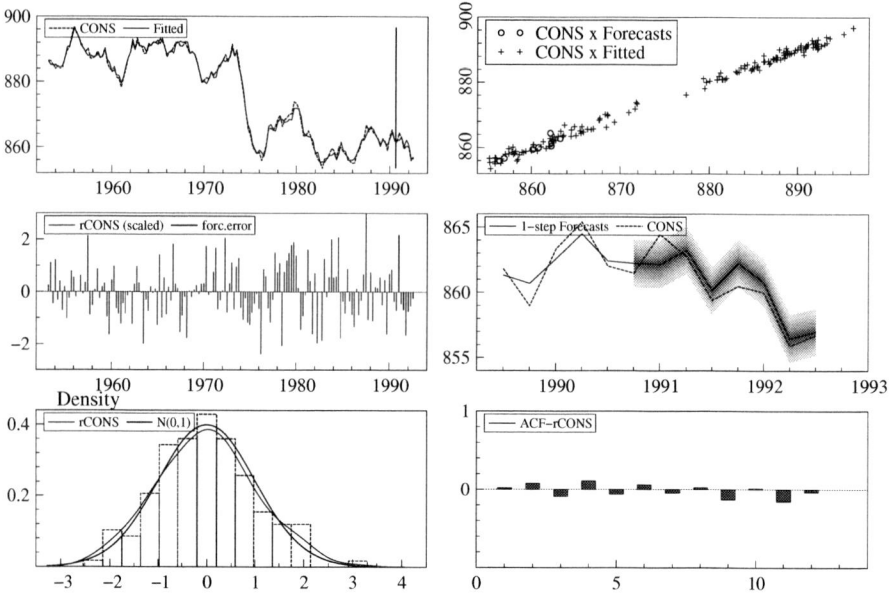

Figure 4.1 Graphical evaluation of CONS model.

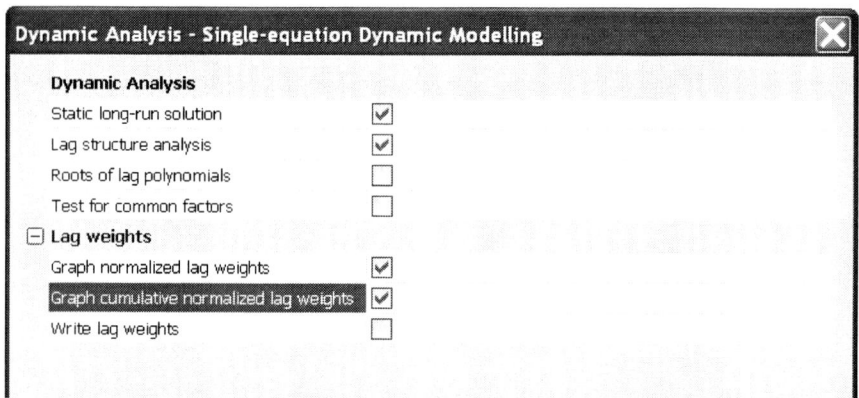

The dynamic analysis commences with the long-run solution. Chapter 11 provides an explanation. The solved long-run model (or static solution) is calculated, together with the relevant standard errors as follows. Write the dynamic equation as

$$a(L) y_t = b(L) x_t + \epsilon_t,$$

where L is the lag operator so that $Lx_t = x_{t-1}$ and $b(L) = \sum_{i=0}^{n} b_i L^i$ is a scalar polynomial in L of order n, the longest lag length. Similarly, $a(L) = \sum_{i=0}^{n} a_i L^i$, with $a_0 = -1$. With $a(1) = \sum_{i=0}^{n} a_i$ (that is, $a(L)$ evaluated at $L = 1$), then if $a(1) \neq 0$

the long run is:

$$y = \frac{b\,(1)}{a\,(1)}x = Kx.$$

Under stationarity (or cointegration inducing a stationary linear relation), standard errors for derived coefficients like K can be calculated from those of $a\,(\cdot)$ and $b\,(\cdot)$. Here the long-run coefficients are well determined, and the null that they are all zero (excluding the constant term) is rejected.

```
Solved static long run equation for CONS
                Coefficient  Std.Error  t-value  t-prob
Constant           -96.9979      40.68    -2.38   0.018
INC                 1.10102    0.04534     24.3   0.000
INFLAT             -5.19917     0.5558    -9.35   0.000
Long-run sigma = 5.63611

ECM = CONS + 96.9979 - 1.10102*INC + 5.19917*INFLAT;
WALD test: Chi^2(2) = 824.782 [0.0000] **
```

Next, the lag polynomials are analyzed, listing the individual coefficients a_0, a_1, etc. (normalized so that $a_0 = -1$), followed by their sum $a(1)$, $b(1)$, etc. and their standard errors (remember that the standard error of the sum is not simply the sum of the standard errors!):

```
Analysis of lag structure, coefficients:
            Lag 0    Lag 1     Sum  SE(Sum)
CONS           -1    0.809  -0.191   0.0255
Constant    -18.5        0   -18.5     8.73
INC         0.507   -0.296    0.21   0.0313
INFLAT     -0.993        0  -0.993   0.0862
```

This is followed by the F-tests of the joint significance of each variable's lag polynomial:

```
Tests on the significance of each variable
Variable    F-test          Value [ Prob]    Unit-root t-test
CONS        F(1,145) =    1008.5 [0.0000]**       -7.4931**
Constant    F(1,145) =     4.503 [0.0355]*
INC         F(2,145) =    155.67 [0.0000]**         6.7226
INFLAT      F(1,145) =    132.64 [0.0000]**        -11.517

Tests on the significance of each lag
Lag 1       F(2,145) =    617.11 [0.0000]**
```

The hypothesis that $a(1) = 0$ can be rejected, with a PcGive unit-root test value of -7.49 (or $-0.191/0.0255$ from the previous output). The two stars mark significance, suggesting cointegration between the variables in the model in levels (see Banerjee, Dolado, Galbraith and Hendry, 1993, or Johansen, 1995). Finally, tests on the significance of each lag length are provided (here we deleted three columns with zeros):

The unit-root t-test (also called the PcGive unit-root test) does not in fact have a t-distribution, but the marked significance (* for 5%, ** for 1%, dependent variable only) is based on the correct critical values, see Banerjee, Dolado and Mestre (1998).

Since we also chose Lag weights, there are four new graphs in the PcGive Graphics window, as in Figure 4.2.

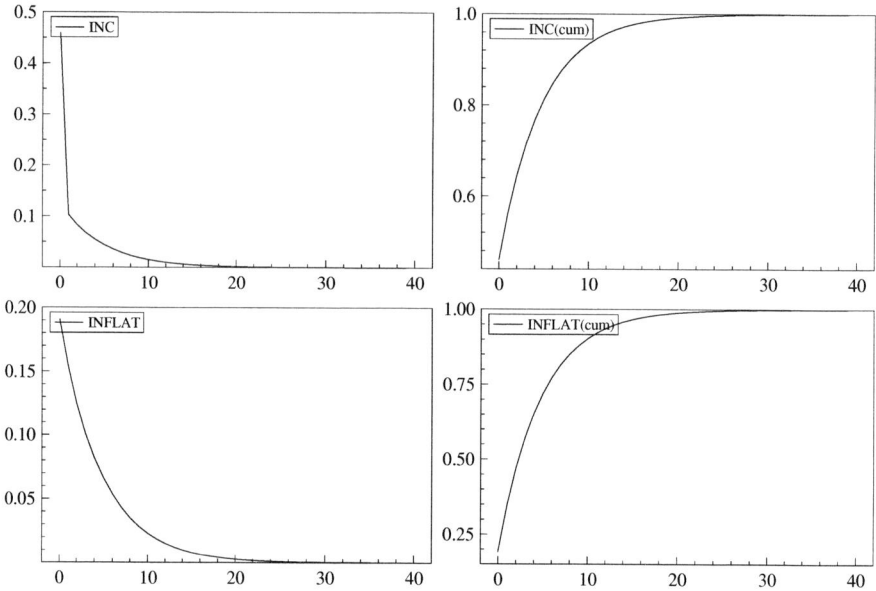

Figure 4.2   Lag weights from CONS model.

4.6 Mis-specification tests

Test/Test Summary conducts a summary testing sequence on the residuals for a range of null hypotheses of interest, including: autocorrelation, autoregressive conditional heteroscedasticity (ARCH), the normality of the distribution of the residuals, heteroscedasticity, and functional form mis-specification. The output is:

```
AR 1-5 test:      F(5,140)  =  0.90705 [0.4784]
ARCH 1-4 test:    F(4,137)  =  0.55687 [0.6943]
Normality test:   Chi^2(2)  =  0.67529 [0.7134]
hetero test:      F(8,136)  =  1.0169  [0.4263]
hetero-X test:    F(14,130)=  0.93848 [0.5199]
RESET test:       F(1,144)  =  1.8185  [0.1796]
```

Note how easy these tests are to calculate; and to see how informative they are about the match of model and evidence, try computing them when any regressor is dropped (why does dropping INC not lead to rejection?).

Tests can also be undertaken individually, or in different groups from that embodied in the test summary. From the Test menu, select Test, which brings up the Test dialog:

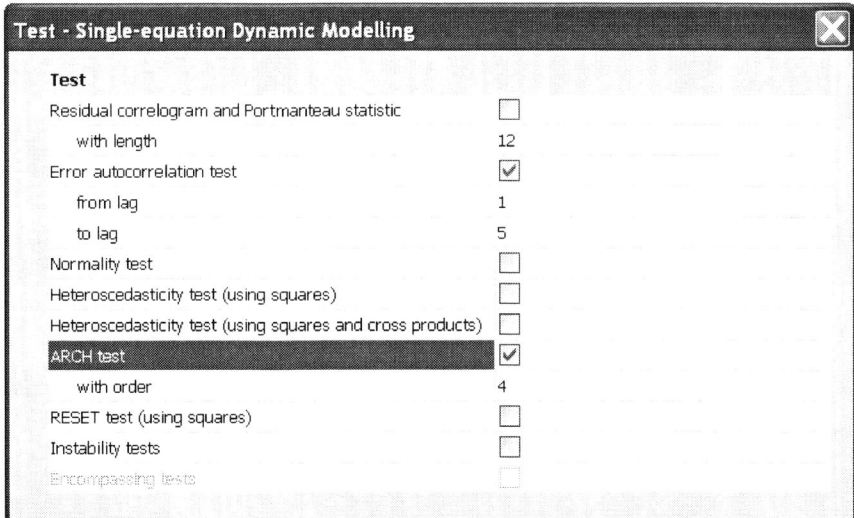

Test - Single-equation Dynamic Modelling	
Test	
Residual correlogram and Portmanteau statistic	☐
with length	12
Error autocorrelation test	☑
from lag	1
to lag	5
Normality test	☐
Heteroscedasticity test (using squares)	☐
Heteroscedasticity test (using squares and cross products)	☐
ARCH test	☑
with order	4
RESET test (using squares)	☐
Instability tests	☐
Encompassing tests	☐

Any or all available tests can be selected.

Tip The default values for the lag length of the AR and ARCH tests are based on the data frequency and the sample size. Different lag lengths can be selected in the Test dialog.

The output is rather more extensive than with batch tests. For example, the error auto-correlation test (or AR test) and ARCH test produce:

```
Error autocorrelation coefficients in auxiliary regression:
  Lag Coefficient   Std.Error
   1     0.054381      0.0909
   2     0.071683     0.08987
   3    -0.088316     0.08768
   4      0.12258     0.08856
   5    -0.051648      0.0885
RSS = 162.605   sigma = 1.16146

Testing for error autocorrelation from lags 1 to 5
 Chi^2(5) = 4.7067 [0.4527]   and F-form F(5,140) = 0.90705 [0.4784]

ARCH coefficients:
  Lag Coefficient   Std.Error
   1    -0.065174     0.08551
   2    -0.077844      0.0854
   3     0.063463     0.08545
   4     0.034848     0.08569
RSS = 345.559   \sigma = 1.58818

Testing for error ARCH from lags 1 to 4
```

```
ARCH 1-4 test:    F(4,137) =   0.55687 [0.6943]
```

Similarly, the normality test leads to the low-order moments being reported. The density of the scaled residuals was shown in Figure 4.1 and revealed slight skewness and somewhat fatter tails than the standard normal distribution. These mis-specification test outcomes are satisfactory, consistent with the equation being a congruent model, so we now consider some specification tests.

Note that you can use Test/Store to store residuals and fitted values from the regression in the OxMetrics database.

4.7 Specification tests

4.7.1 Exclusion, linear and general restrictions

First, we test whether a subset of the coefficients is zero. Choose Exclusion Restrictions from the Test menu to test whether one or more coefficients are zero. At the dialog mark INC and INC_1 and accept:

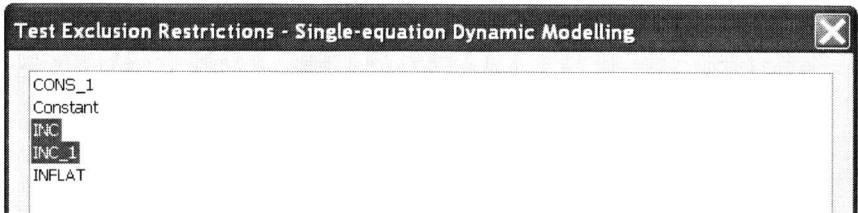

Before looking at the subset test result, we shall also do a linear restrictions test on homogeneity of CONS with respect to INC. This time, select Linear Restrictions. To complete, edit the restrictions as follows:

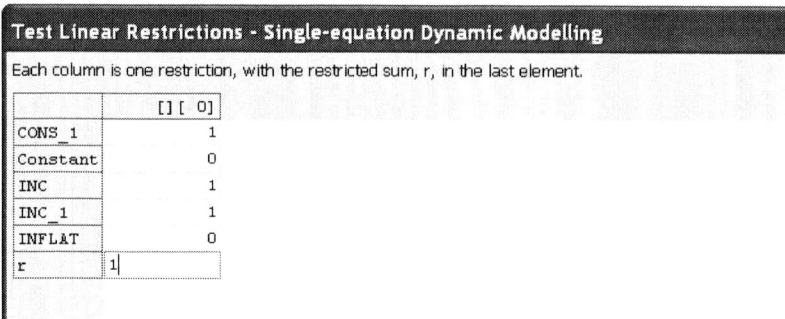

This formulates one restriction. The last element is the r vector, specifying what the restriction should add up to. In terms of (4.1) the restrictions are:

$$(1\ 0\ 1\ 1\ 0) \begin{pmatrix} a_1 \\ c \\ b_0 \\ b_1 \\ \gamma \end{pmatrix} = a_1 + b_0 + b_1 = 1.$$

One further way of implementing this test is in the form of general restrictions. These are expressed as $\mathbf{f}(\boldsymbol{\theta}) = \mathbf{0}$. Complete the dialog as follows, and accept:

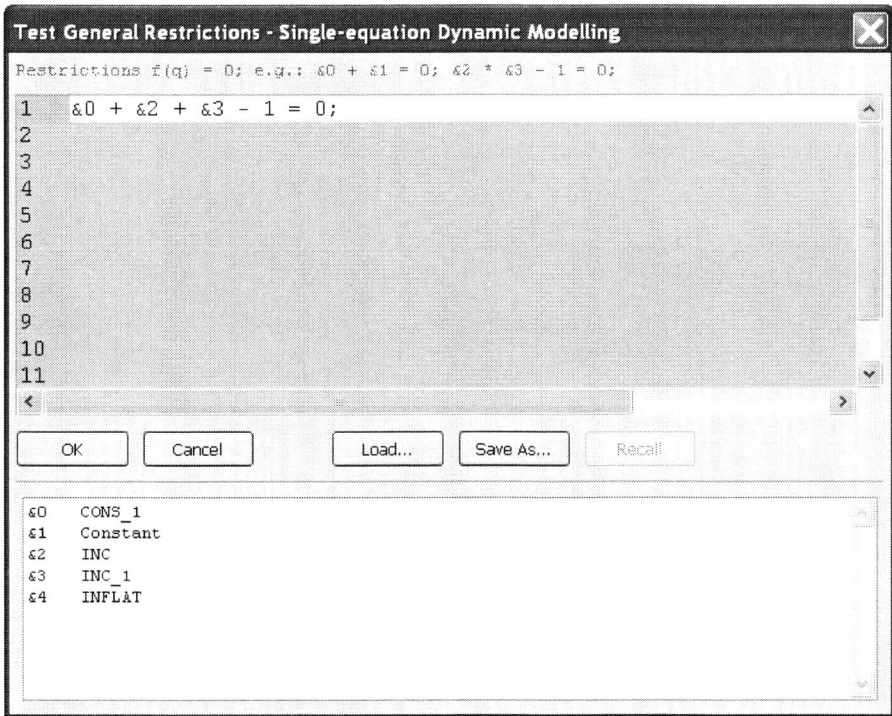

The results of the three tests are:

```
Test for excluding:
[0] = INC
[1] = INC_1
Subset F(2,145) =    155.67 [0.0000]**

Test for linear restrictions (Rb=r):
R matrix
          CONS_1       Constant        INC         INC_1        INFLAT
          1.0000       0.00000         1.0000      1.0000       0.00000
```

```
r vector
        1.0000
LinRes F(1,145) =    4.0348 [0.0464]*

Test for general restrictions:
&0 + &2 + &3 - 1 = 0;
GenRes Chi^2(1) =    4.0348 [0.0446]*
```

The output of the homogeneity test shows slight evidence of rejection of long-run homogeneity if conventional critical values are used. The previous exclusion test reveals strong rejection of the null.

Finally, we conduct an omitted variables test for INFLAT_1. At the dialog, mark INFLAT, and set the lag length to one:

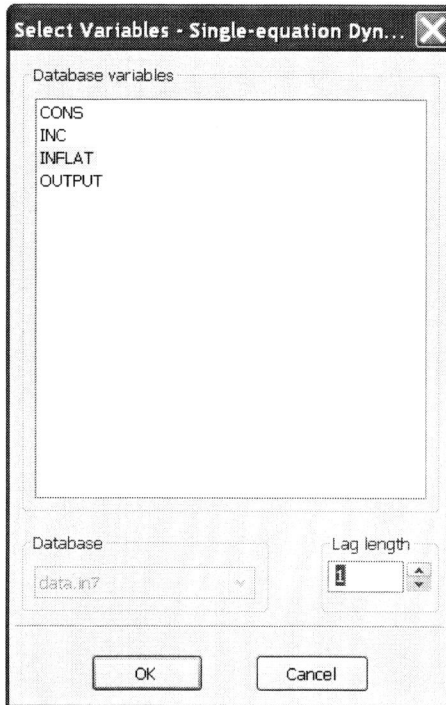

```
Omitted variables test: F(1,144) = 1.44885 [0.2307]
Added variables: INFLAT_1
```

The additional lag is indeed irrelevant.

4.7.2 Test for common factors

Testing for for common factors (COMFAC; also see Chapter 11) is part of Dynamic analysis. It is also a specification test, motivating its inclusion here. When the dynamic equation is:

$$a\left(L\right)y_t = b\left(L\right)x_t + c\left(L\right)z_t + \epsilon_t,$$

COMFAC involves testing whether $a(L) = a(1 - \rho L)$ when $b(L) = b(1 - \rho L)$ and $c(L) = c(1 - \rho L)$ so that $(1 - \rho L)$ is the factor of the lag polynomials in common. COMFAC is discussed by Hendry and Mizon (1978).

To select COMFAC tests, the minimum lag length must be unity for all non-redundant variables (variables that are redundant when lagged can occur without lags: PcGive notices the Constant and Trend if such terms occur). First, we must revise the model to have one lag on INFLAT: select the Model Formulation dialog, mark INFLAT in the database, and add it to the model using a lag length of one. PcGive notices that current INFLAT is already in the model and doesn't add it a second time. Estimate over the previously selected sample (the full sample, with 8 forecasts). Now select Dynamic analysis, and mark Test for common factors. Since the lag polynomials are first-order, only the Wald test of one common-factor restriction is presented following the roots of the lag polynomials. Here the restriction is rejected so the dynamics do not have an autoregressive error representation, matching the very different roots of the lag polynomials. The output is:

```
COMFAC Wald test table, COMFAC F(2,144) = 51.3999 [0.0000] **
Order   Cumulative tests              Incremental tests
  1     Chi^2(2) =  102.8 [0.0000]**   Chi^2(2) =  102.8 [0.0000]**
```

The remainder of this chapter uses the model without lagged INFLAT, so re-estimate the previous model (still with 8 static forecasts).

4.8 Options

The Options entry on the OxMetrics Model dialog allow you to control the settings for iterative maximization (which we have not used yet), and select additional output options. Clicking on Additional output in the Options dialog expands the item. Marking any of these items will result in the output automatically appearing after estimation. All Options settings are saved between runs of PcGive. Note however, that all items are also available on demand from the Test menu.

Options - Single-equation Dynamic Modelling

Convergence

Strong convergence tolerance   .0001

Weak convergence tolerance   .005

Default

Reset default   ☐

Additional output to be printed after estimation

Correlation matrix of regressors   ☐

Heteroscedasticity consistent standard errors   ☐

    HACSE (default is HCSE if selected)   ☐

Information criteria   ☐

Instability tests (single equation only)   ☐

R^2 relative to difference and seasonals (single equation only)   ☐

Covariance matrix of estimated parameters   ☐

Test Summary   ☐

Static long-run solution   ☐

Equation format   ☐

Cointegration test   ☐

⊞ Further options

OK   Cancel

Further Output - Single-equation Dynamic Modelling

Further results and reports

Information criteria   ☐

Heteroscedasticity consistent standard errors   ☐

R^2 relative to difference and seasonals   ☐

Correlation matrix of regressors   ☐

Covariance matrix of estimated parameters   ☐

Reduced form estimates   ☐

Static (1-step) forecasts   ☐

Print large residuals   ☐

    Exceeding standard error by factor   3.5

⊟ Write model results

Equation format   ☑

LaTeX format   ☐

Non-linear model format   ☐

Significant digits for parameters: 4

Significant digits for std.errors: 3

4.9 Further Output

Other output formats may prove more convenient for direct inclusion in final reports. To make PcGive write the output in equation format, for example, activate the Further Output, (on the Test menu) and mark as shown on the previous page.

Reporting only the equation format, this produces:

```
CONS = 0.8091*CONS_1 - 18.52 + 0.5067*INC - 0.2965*INC_1 - 0.9926*INFLAT
(SE)   (0.0255)       (8.73) (0.0288)      (0.0356)        (0.0862)
```

4.10 Forecasting

To end this chapter, we briefly compare dynamic and static forecasts for this model. When we started, 8 observations were kept for static (1-step) forecasts, and these were listed in §4.3.2 and graphed in Fig. 4.1d.

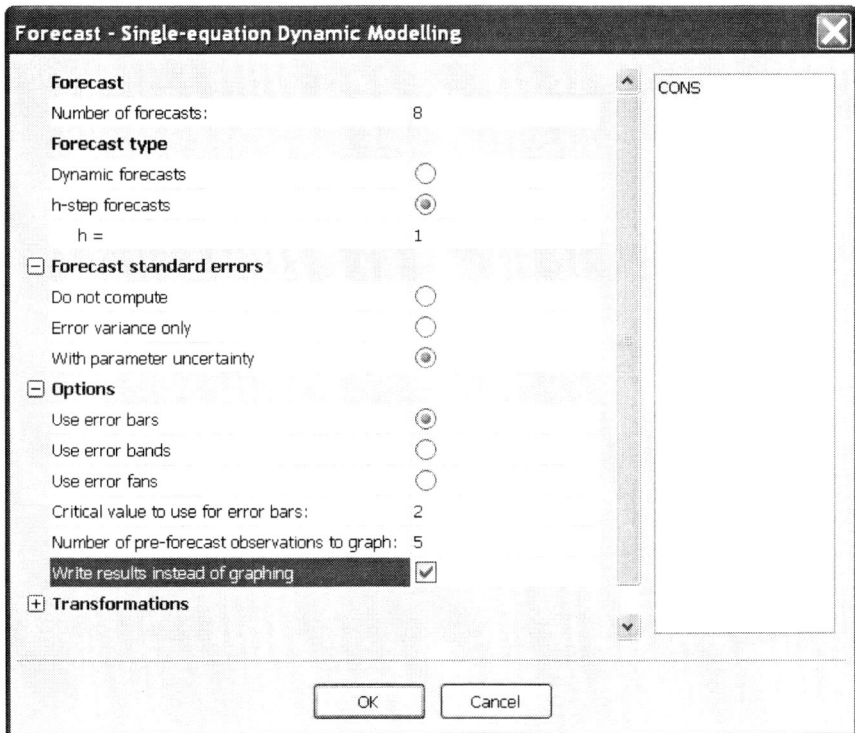

To replicate the results of §4.3.2, activate Test/Forecast (or click on the forecast icon on the toolbar). In the subsequent dialog, select the h-step forecasts radio button (keeping $h = 1$), expand Forecast standard errors, and select With parameter uncertainty. Finally, expand options, and select Write results instead of graphing, as shown in the capture above. The output in the OxMetrics results window matches that listed in §4.3.2; for the summary measures:

```
mean(Error) =      -0.38151    RMSE =      1.1616
SD(Error)   =       1.0972     MAPE =      0.11129
```

The numbers are as before, but two additional statistics are reported. The first is the Root Mean Square Error:

$$\text{RMSE} = \left[\frac{1}{H} \sum_{t=1}^{H} (y_t - f_t)^2 \right]^{1/2},$$

where the forecast horizon is H (8 here), y_t the actual values, and f_t the forecasts. The second statistic is the Mean Absolute Percentage Error:

$$\text{MAPE} = \frac{100}{H} \sum_{t=1}^{H} \left| \frac{y_t - f_t}{y_t} \right|.$$

Both are measures of forecast accuracy, see, e.g. Makridakis, Wheelwright and Hyndman (1998, Ch. 2). Note that the MAPE can be infinity if any $y_t = 0$, and is different when the model is reformulated in differences. For more information see Clements and Hendry (1998).

The default for forecast standard errors in the dialog is based on equation standard error only, reported as sigma in the estimation output. In that case, the listed SE would be 1.076 for all 1-step forecasts: generally the two forms of standard error are relatively close and converge asymptotically (because the parameter uncertainty vanishes).

The one-step forecasts are also called *ex-post* forecasts: they require actual data of all explanatory variables. To obtain the one-step forecast of CONS for 1990Q4, we need to know the INC and INFLAT values for 1990Q4, and CONS from the previous period. The next static forecast is again based on observed values for INC, INFLAT and previous CONS. For pure forecasting purposes, we need to make *dynamic forecasts*, usually requiring forecasts of all explanatory variables as well. One solution is to switch to multiple-equation dynamic modelling, and to make INC and INFLAT endogenous in a system such that all the variables are jointly forecast. That is beyond our current scope, but we can do something comparable by at least using forecasted values of CONS when available. In a simple autoregressive model $y_t = \beta y_{t-1} + \epsilon_t$, writing $\hat{y}_t$ for forecasted values, and assuming that $T + 1$ is the first forecast period:

Forecast horizon	Static Forecast	Dynamic Forecast
$T + 1$	$\hat{y}_{T+1} = \hat{\beta} y_T$	$\hat{y}_{T+1} = \hat{\beta} y_T$
$T + 2$	$\hat{y}_{T+2} = \hat{\beta} y_{T+1}$	$\hat{y}_{T+2} = \hat{\beta} \hat{y}_{T+1}$
$T + 3$	$\hat{y}_{T+3} = \hat{\beta} y_{T+2}$	$\hat{y}_{T+3} = \hat{\beta} \hat{y}_{T+3}$

The first forecast is the same, but thereafter the forecasts differ.

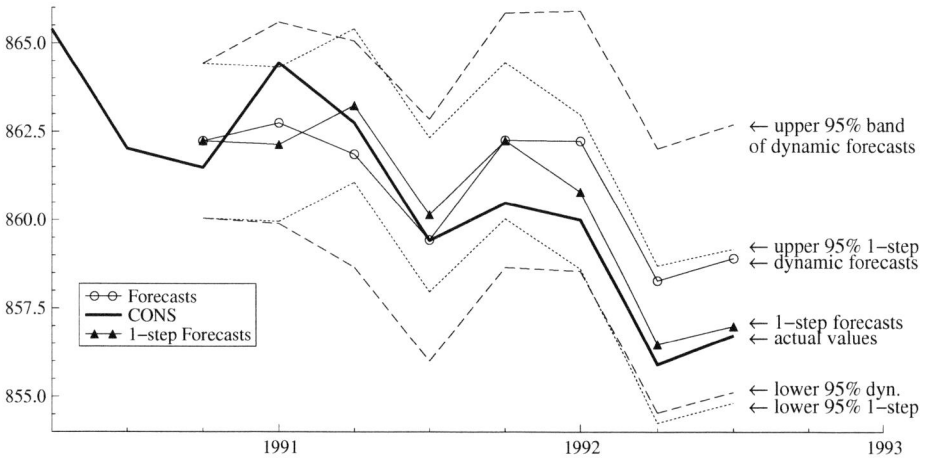

Figure 4.3 Static and dynamic forecasts from CONS model.

In the next Chapter we try some of the other estimators, which either produce different output or need different input instructions.

Chapter 5

Tutorial on Estimation Methods

Three main groups of single equation dynamic modelling estimation methods will be explained. The first is recursive estimation where we describe recursive least squares in detail. Next, we examine instrumental variables estimation, then turn to estimating models with autoregressive errors. That provides a convenient introduction to non-linear optimization and the tutorial concludes by considering non-linear least squares methods, which is a separate model class. Maximum likelihood estimation, which is also is part of the non-linear modelling class, is considered in Chapter 8.

5.1 Recursive estimation

Formulate a model consisting of CONS on Constant, CONS_1, INC and INC_1, as explained in the previous chapter. Keep ordinary least squares in the Model Settings dialog. Move to the model estimation dialog, set the maximum possible estimation sample, and keep 8 observations for forecasting. Now tick the Recursive estimation box. Chapter 12 explains the algebra of recursive estimation; the logic is simply to fit the model to an initial sample of $M - 1$ points and then fit the equation to samples of M, $M + 1$, ... up to T observations. The main output will be graphs of coefficients, $\hat{\sigma}$ etc. over the sample. This is a powerful way to study parameter constancy (especially in its absence!).

The number of observations for initialization (the $M - 1$ above) is set to 15 (to be changed from the default of 10). Press the OK button to estimate. In a trice, all $T - M$ estimates and associated statistics are computed. The final (full sample) estimates are shown in the Results window.

The one new statistic reported to the Results window is for the mean of the innovations being zero. Here we have:

```
1-step (ex post) forecast analysis 1990(4) - 1992(3)
Parameter constancy forecast tests:
Forecast  Chi^2(8) =    7.505 [0.4833]
Chow      F(8,146) =  0.90149 [0.5171]
CUSUM     t(7)     =   -1.317 [0.2292]   (zero forecast innovation mean)
```

so that this test does not detect any non-constancy. Interestingly, neither do the instability statistics (based on Hansen, 1992): select Test/Test and mark Instability tests for
the reported outcomes (significance would be marked by one or two stars):

```
Instability tests:
variance              0.36720
joint                  1.0166
Individual instability tests:
CONS_1                0.21030
Constant              0.20566
INC                   0.21021
INC_1                 0.21033
```

The main new option on the Test menu is the Recursive Graphics dialog. Activate
this:

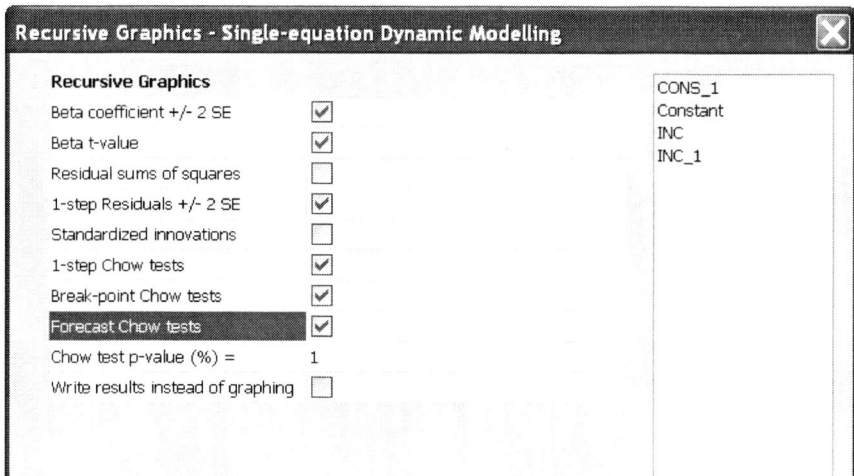

The right column has all the variables to be plotted in beta coefficients and beta t-
values. Select the statistics which they are to be plotted: beta coefficients, beta t-values,
1-step residuals, and all three Chow tests. First, the graph of the coefficient of CONS_1
over the sample in Figure 5.1 shows that after 1978, $\hat{\beta}_t$ lies outside of the previous
confidence interval which an investigator pre-1974 would have calculated as the basis
for forecasting. Other coefficients are also non-constant. Further, the 1-step residuals
show major outliers around 1974.

The 1-step residuals are $\tilde{u}_t = y_t - \mathbf{x}_t'\hat{\beta}_t$ and they are plotted with $\pm 2\hat{\sigma}_t$ shown on
either side of zero. Thus $\tilde{u}_t$ which are outside of the error bars are either outliers or
are associated with changes in $\hat{\sigma}$. Note the increase in $\hat{\sigma}_t$ around 1974 (the oil crisis
...). The 1-step Chow tests amply reflects this. A further summary graph is the break-
point Chow test graph. Each point is the value of the Chow F-test for that date against
the final period, here 1990(3), scaled by its 1% critical value (which becomes the line
at unity), so the forecast horizon N is decreasing from left to right (hence the name
Ndn tests). Figure 5.1 illustrates. Note that the critical value can be set for any desired

probability level.

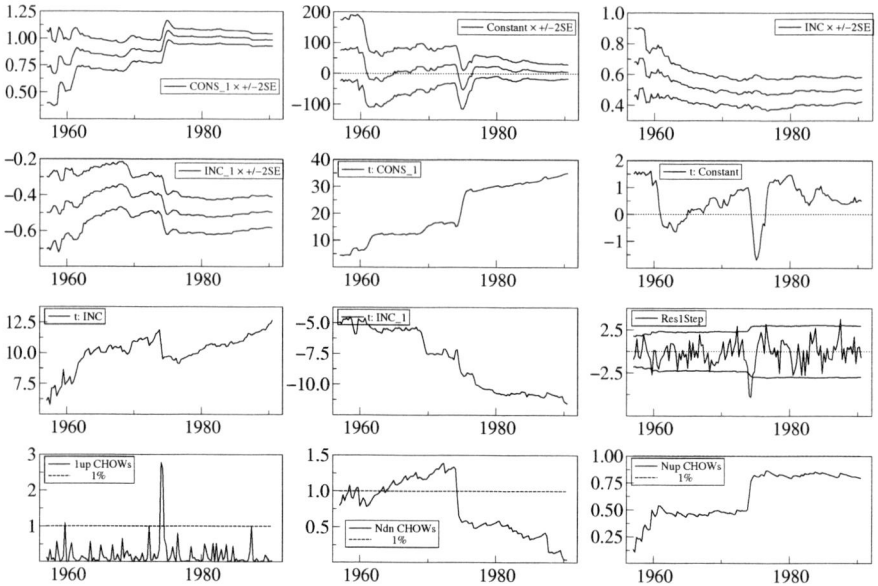

Figure 5.1   Recursive least squares graphical constancy statistics.

Peruse other options as you wish: see how the standardized innovations often high-light the outliers, or how the residual sums of squares confirm that a break occurred in 1974. Any of these graphs can be edited and printed, or saved for later recall and printing.

Next, select the Graphic analysis dialog and look at the full sample residuals:

$$\hat{u}_t = y_t - \mathbf{x}_t' \hat{\boldsymbol{\beta}}_T$$

where $\hat{\boldsymbol{\beta}}_T$ is the usual full-sample OLS estimate. The full-sample estimates somewhat smooth the outliers evident in the recursive figures, so now the largest is not much more than 3.5 standard errors (partly because $\hat{\sigma}$ increased by about 50% over the sample).

That completes RLS. Note that RLS can be used to check the constancy of pre-tests such as (Augmented) Dickey-Fuller tests for the order of integration of a time series, and the recursive graphs may help to discriminate between genuine unit roots and autoregressive coefficients driven towards unity by a failure to model a regime shift.

5.2 Instrumental variables

In many situations it may not be legitimate to treat all regressors as valid conditioning variables, hence instrumental variables (IV) (which for extraneous reasons are known to be valid) must be used. Reselect Model/Formulate as a first step towards the IV option. To compute instrumental variables, PcGive needs to know the status (dependent – or normalized – variable, endogenous, and exogenous or lagged) that you wish to assign to each variable. Given the present model, with a predefined dependent variable (CONS), known lags (CONS_1, INC_1) and a known status for the Constant (exogenous, as it is deterministic), only INC needs a status. Thus, make INC endogenous: right click on it and select Y: endogenous as shown:

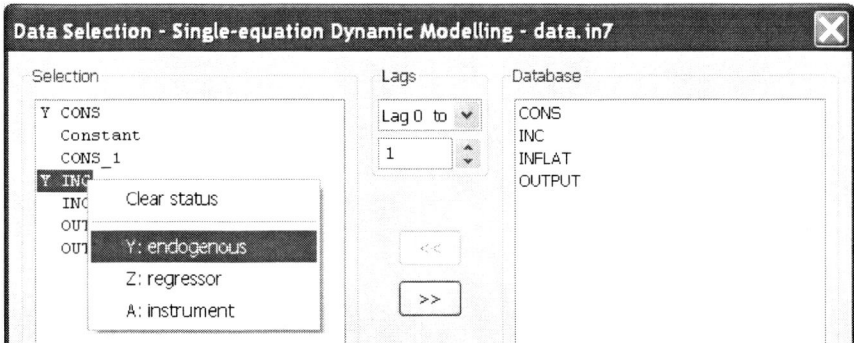

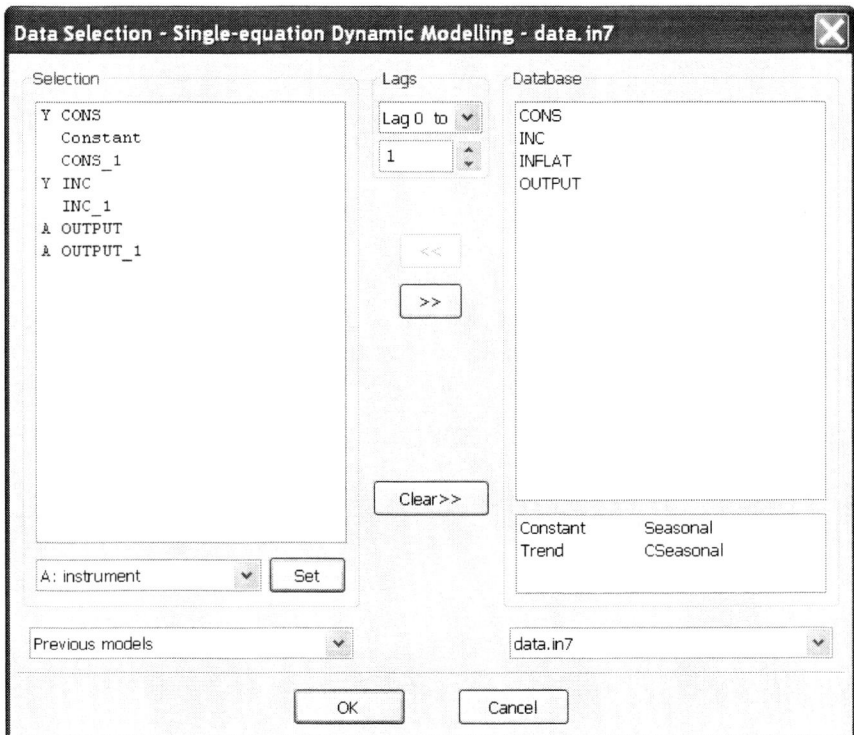

Next, the instruments must be selected. The lag polynomial choices for additional instruments must be sufficient to identify the equation: add OUTPUT with one lag to the model. Highlight both in the model, and select A: instrument in the drop-down box below the model, and press the Set button to mark these as Additional instruments. The model is now as shown above.

OK to accept and bring up the Model Settings dialog, if it is not already the default, switch to Instrumental variables, and press OK again. The available estimation method is two-stage least squares (TSLS). Keep 8 observations for static forecasting.

5.2.1 Structural estimates

The structural estimates from the IV estimation appear in OxMetrics:

```
EQ( 3) Modelling CONS by IVE (using data.in7)
        The estimation sample is: 1953(2) - 1990(3)

                     Coefficient  Std.Error  t-value  t-prob
INC              Y      0.373349     0.1025      3.64   0.000
CONS_1                  1.01559     0.03633     28.0    0.000
INC_1                  -0.407460    0.07771     -5.24   0.000
Constant               16.6558      14.38        1.16   0.249

sigma                   1.53761  RSS                345.179245
Reduced form sigma      2.0505
no. of observations        150  no. of parameters           4
no. endogenous variables     2  no. of instruments          5
mean(CONS)             876.685  var(CONS)             177.453
Additional instruments:
[0] = OUTPUT
[1] = OUTPUT_1

Specification test: Chi^2(1) =    14.883 [0.0001]**
Testing beta = 0:   Chi^2(3) =    10986. [0.0000]**

1-step (ex post) forecast analysis 1990(4) - 1992(3)
Forecast test:    Chi^2(8) =   6.5087 [0.5904]
```

The specification χ^2-test is for the validity of the instruments – and strongly rejects. Did you anticipate that? If so, which variables are the culprits? The $\chi^2(3)$ testing $\beta = 0$ is the analogue of the OLS F-test of R^2 equal to zero (so testing whether all the coefficients except the constant term are zero). Note how the coefficient of CONS_1 is larger than unity. All of these counter indicators suggest serious mis-specification.

Next we test the model for other problems, similar to the approach and methods used for least squares. The test summary produces:

```
AR 1-5 test:      F(5,141) =   7.2440 [0.0000]**
ARCH 1-4 test:    F(4,138) =   7.3218 [0.0000]**
Normality test:   Chi^2(2) =   5.0900 [0.0785]
```

```
hetero test:      F(6,139) =    1.1346 [0.3455]
hetero-X test:    F(9,136) =    1.1152 [0.3562]
```

Note the significant residual autocorrelation, invalidating most of the inferences you may have been tempted to make *en route*. The use of instrumental variables may correct a simultaneity or measurement error problem, but the basic model specification must be sound before their use.

5.2.2 Reduced forms

The reduced form estimates are the regressions of each endogenous variable on the instruments alone, so there are two equations (for CONS and INC). Select Test/Further Output and mark Reduced form estimates. Press OK to see:

```
Reduced form estimates
RRF coefficients
                        CONS            INC
CONS_1                1.0171       0.023619
INC_1              -0.079785        0.72756
Constant             6.2285        -58.808
OUTPUT              0.20994         0.26855
OUTPUT_1           -0.16812       -0.032723

RRF coefficient standard errors
                        CONS            INC
CONS_1             0.046472       0.064342
INC_1              0.050468       0.069875
Constant             25.118         34.777
OUTPUT             0.053144       0.073581
OUTPUT_1           0.054809       0.075885

RRF equation standard errors
          CONS            INC
       2.0505         2.8390

correlation of RRF residuals
                  CONS           INC
CONS            1.0000
INC            0.73243        1.0000
```

If these reduced form equations fit badly (in terms of their $\hat{\sigma}s$), the IV estimates will be poorly determined later. Note that these equations are unrestricted; once the structural model (here CONS on CONS_1, INC, INC_1 and a Constant) is estimated, the reduced form equation for INC can be used to eliminate it from the structural equation to produce a restricted reduced form for CONS. Thus, a comparison of the unrestricted and restricted reduced forms allows a test for the validity of the instruments (see Sargan, 1964). This was shown with the structural estimates above: could you expect a good or bad outcome on such a test from what you have seen here?

Dynamic forecasting is not available for IVE. Instead, build a simultaneous equations model using the multiple equation class, which allows dynamic forecasting from such a model.

5.3 Autoregressive least squares (RALS)

In this section we require the first difference of CONS. If you do not have this in the database yet, switch to OxMetrics, and use the Calculator to create DCONS (or use Algebra: `DCONS = diff(CONS,1);`).

The following assumes that ΔCONS is the dependent variable and that the regressors are only Constant, CONS_1, INC and INC_1: if you do not wish to create DCONS, simply add unity to the coefficient of CONS_1 below; if any INFLAT variables remain, delete these.

To access RALS (r^{th} order autoregressive least squares), check the Autoregressive least squares option in the model settings dialog:

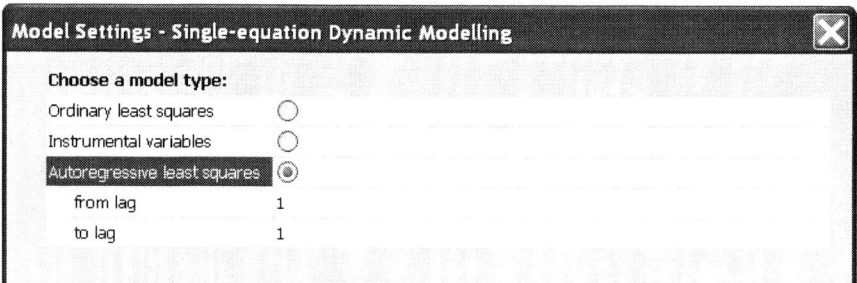

Model Settings - Single-equation Dynamic Modelling		
Choose a model type:		
Ordinary least squares	○	
Instrumental variables	○	
Autoregressive least squares	◉	
from lag	1	
to lag	1	

You can also change the start and end lag order, but here we only estimate first order, which is the default. There is only one estimation option, Non-linear Estimation:

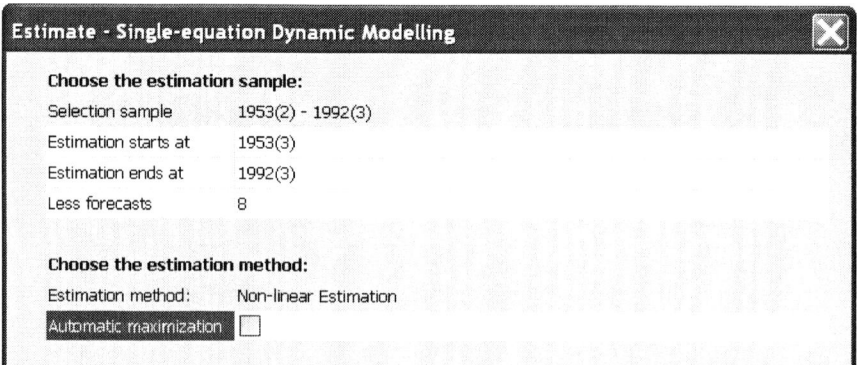

Estimate - Single-equation Dynamic Modelling	
Choose the estimation sample:	
Selection sample	1953(2) - 1992(3)
Estimation starts at	1953(3)
Estimation ends at	1992(3)
Less forecasts	8
Choose the estimation method:	
Estimation method:	Non-linear Estimation
Automatic maximization	☐

As usual, PcGive offers the sample period for your approval in the next dialog. Set it to 1953(3) - 1992(3), which is the maximum available sample, and use 8 forecasts. RALS requires lagged information for estimation. Here there is one observation additional required: 1953(2); however, if you do not change the sample, PcGive will do it automatically.

There is also a choice whether to do automatic estimation or not. Automatic maximization, will estimate the model directly, and is usually adequate. Non-automatic maximization offers a dialog to control the iterative estimation process or for a grid search. Uncheck automatic maximization to see:

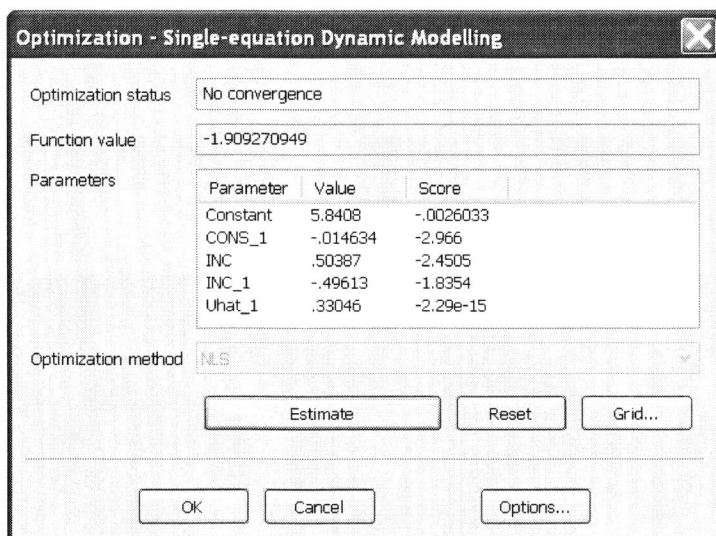

Optimization - Single-equation Dynamic Modelling

Optimization status	No convergence

Function value	-1.909270949

Parameters

Parameter	Value	Score
Constant	5.8408	-.0026033
CONS_1	-.014634	-2.966
INC	.50387	-2.4505
INC_1	-.49613	-1.8354
Uhat_1	.33046	-2.29e-15

Optimization method NLS

[Estimate]   [Reset]   [Grid...]

[OK]   [Cancel]   [Options...]

The initial values for RALS are provided by OLS. The parameters are the coefficients from OLS estimation, followed by an nth-order autoregressive error process (initialized by an LM-test, the order being set at the frequency+1, or the maximum lag length, whichever is smaller) and the function is minus the residual sum of squares divided by the sample size T.

5.3.1 Optimization

The available options are:

(1) Choose the orders (s, r) of the error process:

$$u_t = \sum_{j=s}^{r} \alpha_j u_{t-j} + \epsilon_t$$

This must be done in the model settings dialog.

(2) Coefficient values can be set to any particular desired value by double clicking on the coefficient in the list box.

(3) Reset the initial values to those at dialog entry.

(4) Estimate, to optimize the objective function starting from the listed coefficient values.

(5) Press Options to control the maximization process:

- Change the maximum number of iterations (that is, steps in which the function value reduces); if this number is reached, the optimization process will abort, despite not finding the minimum yet.
- Specify how often (if at all) iteration output is printed; and .
- Set the convergence criterion.

(6) Conduct a Grid search over the model parameters, most importantly for the α_i (labelled Uhat_1,...Uhat_p in the dialog).

Begin with a grid, to view the graph of the function against the first-order autoregressive parameter. The dialog allows you to select the region for the grid search, as well as the resolution of the search. Press Grid, and select Uhat_1 in the parameter box. The grid center is automatically set to the current value of the parameter, $0.33045\ldots$ here. Change the grid center to 0, and set the step size to 0.1:

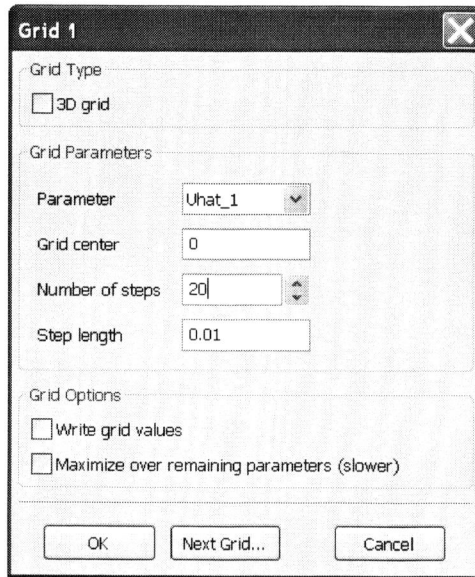

Set the Grid Options to Max: maximize over remaining parameters. With this option, we can read the actual maximum from the graph (and it is fast enough to use). Press Next Grid for a second grid, again for Uhat_1, but now centred on 0.9, in steps of 0.01. Press OK to compute and graph the grids.

The results are in Figure 5.2. There is a local maximum around 0.4, but the line goes up again after 0.8. The second graph inspects the rightmost section of the grid: centred at 0.9. Use the point facility when the graph is on the screen (View/Point): a maximum of about -1.86 seems to be around 0.97. We can also do a more accurate grid around 0.4 and read the maximum off the screen. Centre the grid around 0.4 and select a step length of 0.01. Here we find a minimum of -1.87 around 0.43 to 0.44. The optimum appears to be at 0.97, but the two minima have similar function values.

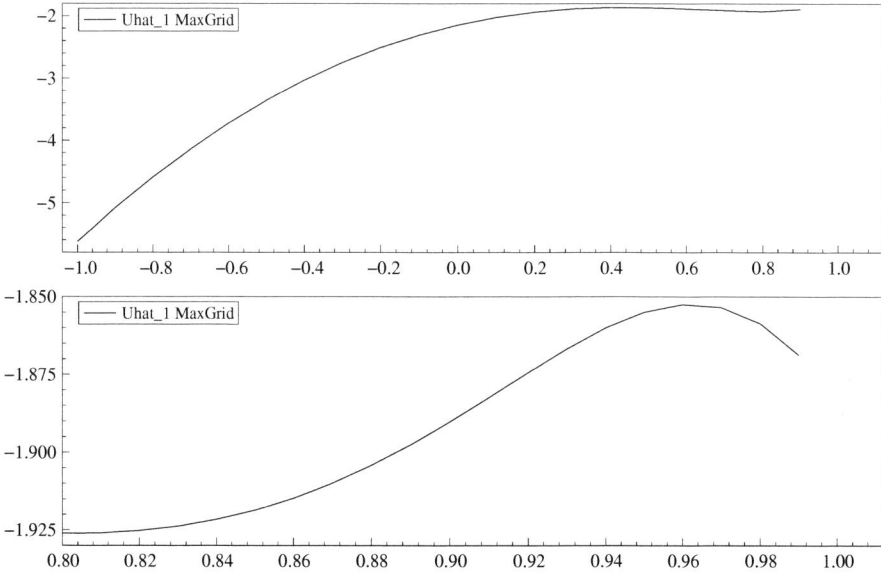

Figure 5.2 Autoregressive least squares grids.

On completion of the grid, the RALS estimation dialog reappears. Now select Alt+e for estimation. Note that iterations can be interrupted (for example, if too slow or diverging), but here convergence is achieved very rapidly. After convergence, the OK button lights up. Press OK to write the RALS output to the Results window.

```
EQ( 1) Modelling DCONS by RALS (using data.in7)
        The estimation sample is: 1953(3) - 1990(3)
                   Coefficient  Std.Error  t-value  t-prob Part.R^2
Constant              -11.2824      18.52   -0.609   0.543   0.0026
CONS_1              -0.101503    0.05330    -1.90   0.059   0.0246
INC                  0.505354    0.03716     13.6   0.000   0.5623
INC_1              -0.393064    0.05540    -7.09   0.000   0.2590
Uhat_1              0.436339    0.09860     4.43   0.000   0.1197

sigma                 1.39231  RSS              279.147933
no. of observations       149  no. of parameters          5
mean(DCONS)         -0.164562  var(DCONS)            4.78466

NLS using analytical derivatives (eps1=0.0001; eps2=0.005):
Strong convergence
Roots of error polynomial:
          real         imag     modulus
       0.43634      0.00000     0.43634
```

```
1-step (ex post) forecast analysis 1990(4) - 1992(3)
Forecast test:    Chi^2(8) =  0.97324 [0.9984]
Chow test:        F(8,143) =  0.95324 [0.4751]
```

Return to the RALS estimation dialog through Model/Estimate. Double click on Uhat_1 in the parameters list box and type in the desired new value (0.97 here, which we read off Figure 5.2). In this way the iteration can be recommenced from any point to check for multiple maxima – note what happens here:

```
EQ( 3) Modelling DCONS by RALS (using data.in7)
       The estimation sample is: 1953(3) - 1990(3)
                  Coefficient  Std.Error  t-value  t-prob  Part.R^2
Constant              209.681      60.39     3.47   0.001    0.0773
CONS_1              -0.645411    0.08478    -7.61   0.000    0.2869
INC                 0.505128    0.03635     13.9   0.000    0.5728
INC_1              -0.107236    0.05425    -1.98   0.050    0.0264
Uhat_1              0.962562    0.02605     36.9   0.000    0.9046

sigma                 1.38908  RSS               277.855447
no. of observations       149  no. of parameters          5
```

Thus, the existence of the two optima is real and the latter delivers the smaller RSS (the largest $-RSS/T$). The function value in the grid is $-RSS/T$, which with $-277.855/149 = -1.865$ corresponds to what we read off the graph. Note that the grid we plotted is the 'concentrated' grid: for each value of α_1 (the coeffficient on Uhat_1) the rest of the model is completely re-estimated. This allows us to read the maximum off the screen.

Now exit RALS estimation, re-enter the Model settings dialog, and set the end lag to two, estimate from 1953(4). This allows a second order RALS model. Again, convergence is rapid and both $\{\hat{\alpha}_i\}$ are significant. In fact, if one of the roots of the error polynomial $\left(1 - \hat{\alpha}_1 L - \hat{\alpha}_2 L^2\right)$ is close to unity, this would suggest a specification problem. As before, forecasts and fitted graphics can be perused as in Figure 5.3.

5.3.2 RALS model evaluation

Alt+t,t brings up the usual Test dialog; select some or all options and observe the output (only valid selections will be calculated, others are simply ignored). The residual correlogram shows that the residuals are close to white noise once the second-order error process is removed, although they are not in fact an innovation process (see Chapter 13). The summary results for the second-order model are:

```
ARCH 1-4 test:   F(4,134) =    1.6573 [0.1636]
Normality test:  Chi^2(2) =    1.4527 [0.4837]
hetero test:     F(6,137) =   0.28748 [0.9421]
hetero-X test:   F(9,134) =   0.86621 [0.5572]
```

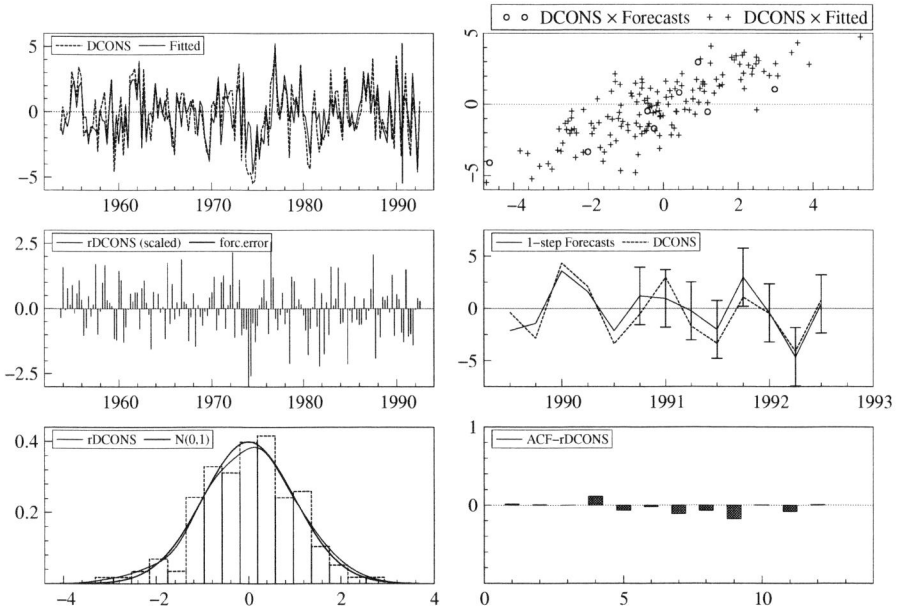

Figure 5.3   Autoregressive least squares graphical statistics.

The estimated coefficients are (using the Equation format option from Test/Further results):

```
DCONS =    -4.532 - 0.1544*CONS_1 + 0.5154*INC - 0.3586*INC_1 +
(SE)       (24.9)  (0.0817)         (0.0365)      (0.0687)
           0.3743*Uhat_1 + 0.2786*Uhat_2
           (0.116)         (0.0913)
```

5.4 Non-linear least squares

We now turn to non-linear least squares (NLS) estimation. This method is shown separately on the Category list since it applies to any type of data. It also requires a different method of equation formulation.

PcGive expects us to define a variable called 'actual' and a variable called 'fitted', expressed in Algebra code. The program can then go ahead to minimize the sum of squares (more precisely, PcGive maximizes $-RSS/T$, see Chapter 16):

$$\min \sum_{t=1}^{T} \hat{\epsilon}_t^2,$$

with $\hat{\epsilon}_t^2$ defined as:

$$\hat{\epsilon}_t = actual - \widehat{fitted},$$

and $\widetilde{fitted}$ is fitted evaluated at the current parameter values. Parameters are written as &0, &1, ..., although the numbering does not have to be consecutive. Starting values must always be provided with the code.

We have already considered one method requiring non-linear optimization, namely RALS. The principles behind NLS are similar except that the flexibility needed in formulation to cover a wide class of possible models makes the initial specification more complex. We are cheating here initially and have simply set up a linear-least squares equation.

To facilitate the model formulation, first do OLS of CONS on a Constant, CONS_1, INC and INC_1 over 1953 (2) to 1992 (3) less 8 forecasts. Then use the Non-linear model format option from Test/Further results) to write the following Algebra code to OxMetrics:

```
actual=CONS;
fitted=&0*CONS[-1] + &1 + &2*INC + &3*INC[-1];
// starting values:
&0=0.9854; &1=5.841; &2=0.5039; &3=-0.4961;
```

Then bring up the Non-linear model formulation dialog by selecting the Non-linear modelling Model Class menu and pressing the Formulate button. Copy and paste the Agebra code of the linear model from OxMetrics to the dialog. This formulates the model we just estimated in algebraic code, complete with starting values.

```
Nonlinear Model - Non-linear Modelling - data.in7                      [X]

Example:
actual = CONS;
fitted = &0 + CONS[-1] + &1*INC + (&1 - 1.0)*INC[-1];
&0=2; &1=1;

1    actual=CONS;                                                        ^
2    fitted=&0*CONS[-1] + &1 + &2*INC + &3*INC[-1];
3    // starting values:
4    &0=0.9854; &1=5.841; &2=0.5039; &3=-0.4961;
```

Accepting the model as shown in the capture below leads to the Non-linear model estimation dialog.

This is similar to the estimation dialog for RALS, with again a choice between direct estimation or the maximization control dialog. Sample periods and forecasts can still be set here, but now we can also activate recursive estimation. We will just use the full sample with 8 forecasts and Non-linear estimation (dialog):

Estimate - Non-linear Modelling

Choose the estimation sample:

Selection sample	1953(2) - 1992(3)
Estimation starts at	1953(2)
Estimation ends at	1992(3)
Less forecasts	0

Choose the estimation method:

Estimation method:	Non-linear Estimation
Automatic maximization	☑
Recursive estimation	☑
Initialization	10

The control dialog is again similar to that seen above for RALS. The starting values are shown, together with the gradients at those values. Here starting values are not so important, since OLS has a quadratic sum of squares function (we have good ones anyway from the earlier OLS estimation). Press estimate to commence the optimization. Press the OK button after convergence. The output produced is:

```
EQ( 2) Modelling actual by NLS (using data.in7)
        The estimation sample is: 1953 (2) to 1990 (3)

                   Coefficient  Std.Error  t-value  t-prob Part.R^2
&0                    0.985366    0.02809     35.1   0.000   0.8940
&1                     5.84075      11.68    0.500   0.618   0.0017
&2                    0.503870    0.03974     12.7   0.000   0.5240
&3                   -0.496128    0.04287    -11.6   0.000   0.4784

sigma                  1.48378  RSS                321.435502
R^2                   0.987924  F(3,146) =      3981 [0.000]**
log-likelihood        -270.003  DW                       1.34
no. of observations        150  no. of parameters          4
mean(actual)           876.685  var(actual)           177.453

Standard errors based on information matrix
BFGS/warm-up using numerical derivatives (eps1=0.0001; eps2=0.005):
Strong convergence

1-step (ex post) forecast analysis 1990 (4) to 1992 (3)
Parameter constancy forecast tests:
Forecast  Chi^2(8) =   7.5050 [0.4833]
Chow      F(8,146) =  0.90149 [0.5171]
```

Now we return to undertake a more interesting non-linear estimation, namely mimicking RALS. Reselect non-linear estimation, which will show the model we had before. This time, restrict the coefficients of the dynamic relation to satisfy the autoregressive error (that is, COMFAC) restriction for a static regression of CONS on INC:

$$\text{CONS}_t = \alpha\text{CONS}_{t-1} + \mu + \beta\text{INC}_t - \alpha\beta\text{INC}_{t-1} + \epsilon_t,$$

referring to the previous Algebra code, this imposes $\&3 = -\&0 * \&2$:

```
actual=CONS;
fitted=&0*CONS[-1] + &1 + &2*INC - &0 * &2 * INC[-1];
// starting values:
&0=0.9854; &1=5.841; &2=0.5039;
```

Delete the starting value for $\&3$, and accept this formulation; then in the estimation dialog, check recursive estimation and set the initialization number to 50. OK to move to the Non-linear estimation dialog. Press Estimate to estimate, and OK to start recursive estimation.

This is a rather time-consuming computation, which can be interrupted by clickin on the moving icon in the model dialog, to the left of the Formulate button. If you abort, no estimation results will be available.

```
EQ( 4) Modelling actual by NLS (using data.in7)
        The estimation sample is: 1953 (2) to 1990 (3)
```

	Coefficient	Std.Error	t-value	t-prob	Part.R^2
&0	0.985760	0.01426	69.1	0.000	0.9701
&1	6.00308	6.077	0.988	0.325	0.0066
&2	0.503653	0.03733	13.5	0.000	0.5533

sigma	1.47873	RSS	321.436087
R^2	0.987865	F(2,147) =	5983 [0.000]**
log-likelihood	-270.003	DW	1.34
no. of observations	150	no. of parameters	3
mean(actual)	876.685	var(actual)	177.453

Occasionally, recursive estimation may suffer from a problem in that the RSS value drops from one period to the next. This could happen when there are multiple optima in the likelihood.

The Recursive graphics dialog is somewhat different from that for RLS:

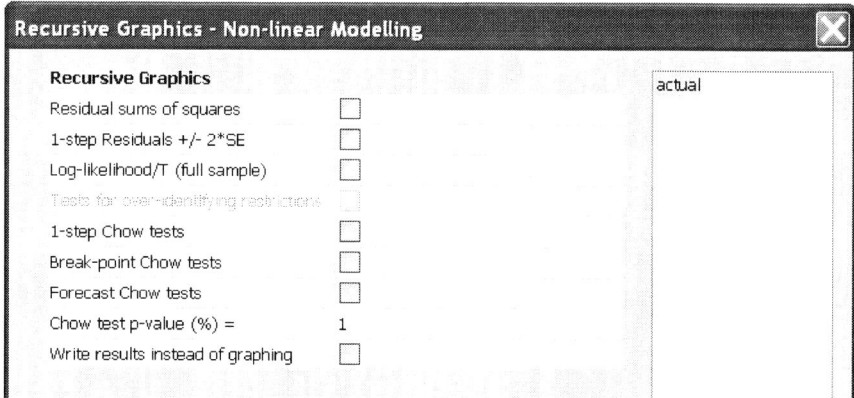

Parameter non-constancy is obvious from the two Chow-test sequences in Fig. 5.4.

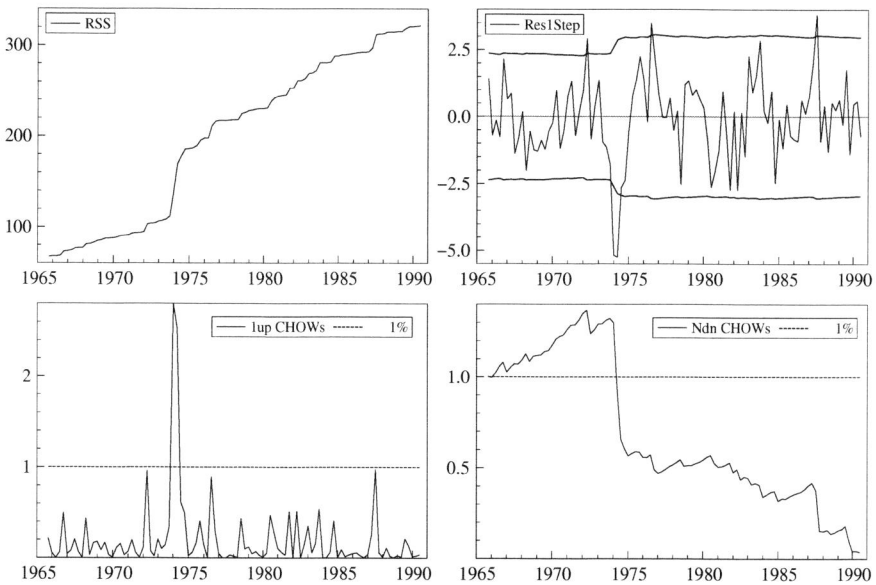

Figure 5.4 Recursive non-linear least squares constancy statistics.

We could also have taken our initial values for the parameters from RALS on the static model

$$\begin{aligned} \text{CONS}_t &= \mu^* + \beta\text{INC}_t + u_t, \\ u_t &= \alpha u_{t-1} + \epsilon_t. \end{aligned}$$

Pre-multiplying the first equation with $1 - \alpha$ gives:

$$\text{CONS}_t = \alpha\text{CONS}_{t-1} + (1 - \alpha)\mu^* + \beta\text{INC}_t - \alpha\beta\text{INC}_t + \epsilon_t.$$

The RALS output is:

```
EQ( 1) Modelling CONS by RALS (using data.in7)
        The estimation sample is: 1953 (2) to 1990 (3)

                    Coefficient  Std.Error  t-value  t-prob Part.R^2
Constant                421.558      33.88     12.4   0.000   0.5147
INC                    0.503653    0.03733     13.5   0.000   0.5550
Uhat_1                 0.985760    0.01426     69.1   0.000   0.9703

sigma                   1.47873  RSS               321.436087
no. of observations         150  no. of parameters          3
mean(CONS)              876.685  var(CONS)            177.453
```

but note the difference in the intercept: in RALS this is μ^* so is much larger than the value for $\mu = (1 - \alpha)\mu^*$ in the NLS formulation we have adopted. Which form is used can substantially affect convergence when α is close to unity. Indeed, if you want to create a very badly behaved problem, alter the definition of the intercept to $\mu/(1 - \alpha)$ and plot the grid over a wide range! Great care is needed in formulating the function to be minimized. Note also the huge time advantage of specifically programmed methods (e.g. RALS) over doing the equivalent in a generic NLS algorithm. Finally, the alternative specification of the constant term $((1 - \alpha)\mu^*)$ will lead to different recursive behaviour: the constant in the former vanishes when α becomes one. If this happens in the RNLS estimation, this parameter will not be able to get away from 1.

This concludes our tutorial on estimation methods. There are many others to be explored, and the disk provides several .ALG files for formulating some of the more common non-linear models. Further examples are given in Chapter 8.

Chapter 6

Tutorial on Batch Usage

In this book, the emphasis is very much on interactive use of PcGive. Sometimes, command driven operation can be useful, e.g. as a method of documenting research, or for preparation of a teaching session. For this purpose PcGive supports a batch language. As with many other facilities, batch mode operates in cooperation with OxMetrics. It is in OxMetrics that the batch commands are issued. OxMetrics then decides whether it can handle the command (e.g. data loading and saving, algebra, database selection). If not, the command is passed on to the active module (use the module command to switch between e.g. PcGive and STAMP when both are open).

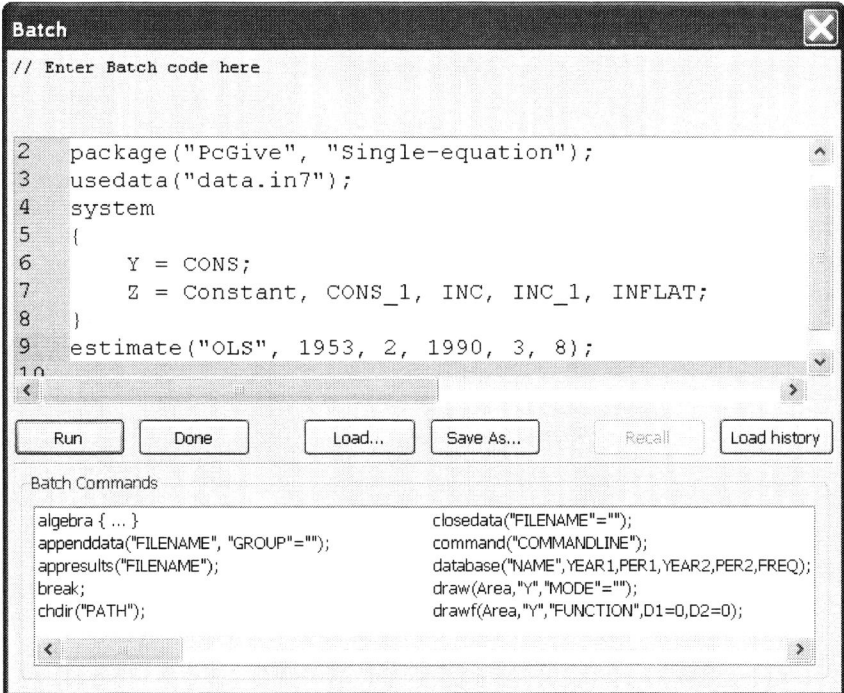

To see an example, estimate the familiar model of CONS on a Constant, CONS_1, INC, INC_1, and INFLAT, using the maximum sample with 8 forecasts. Then switch to OxMetrics, and Tools/Batch Editor or use the toolbar button to activate the batch editor: The edit dialog appears, with the current model already formulated in the PcGive batch language, as shown above.

Add some algebra code to create DCONS and DINC, replace CONS and INC in the model by the first differences, and add the testsummary command, as shown in the code below:

```
package("PcGive", "Single-equation");
usedata("data.in7");
algebra
{
    DCONS = diff(CONS, 1);
    DINC = diff(INC, 1);
}
system
{
    Y = DCONS;
    Z = Constant, CONS_1, DINC, INC_1, INFLAT;
}
estimate("OLS", 1953, 2, 1992, 3, 8);
testsummary;
```

Press Run to execute the batch file. Once saved to disk, a batch file can also be run directly using File/Open, or even by double clicking on the batch file in the Explorer or File Manager. Batch files have the .fl extension, which originally stood for Fiml Language.

As a last example, use Test/Further Output to write the non-linear model code. Then activate Model/Non-linear modelling to re-estimate the model using NLS. Finally, activate the Batch editor in OxMetrics. Again, an outline batch file has already been written by OxMetrics:

```
package("PcGive", "non-linear");
usedata("data.in7");
nonlinear
{
    actual=DCONS;
    fitted=&0 + &1*CONS[-1] + &2*DINC + &3*INC[-1] + &4*INFLAT;
    // starting values:
    &0=-18.52; &1=-0.1909; &2=0.5067; &3=0.2102; &4=-0.9926;
}
estimate("NLS", 1953, 2, 1992, 3, 8);
```

Chapter A1 documents the PcGive batch commands for single equation modelling, and gives a further example.

Chapter 7

Tutorial on Model Reduction

7.1 The problems of simple-to-general modelling

While the models used above were mainly selected as illustrations of the use of PcGive, they actually highlighted four important issues:

(1) Powerful tests can reveal model inadequacies: it is not sensible to skip testing in the hope that the model is valid.

(2) A reject outcome on any test invalidates all earlier inferences, rendering useless the time spent up to then – empirical research becomes highly inefficient if done that way.

(3) Once a problem is revealed by a test, how do you proceed? It is a dangerous *non sequitur* to adopt the alternative hypothesis of the test which rejected: did you nearly do this with residual autocorrelation, by assuming it was error autoregression and looking for Cochrane–Orcutt [that is, RALS here]?

(4) What can be done if two or more statistics reject? Which has caused what? Do both or only one need to be corrected? Or should third factors be sought?

As discussed in Chapters 11 and 13, the whole paradigm of postulating a simple model and seeking to generalize it in the light of test rejections or anomalies is suspect, and in fact makes sub-optimal use of PcGive's structure and functioning. Let us now switch to its mode of general-to-specific modelling.

7.2 Formulating general models

We wish to start this chapter with a clean modelling sheet. So exit PcGive and re-enter if you want your model numbering to coincide with the output presented in this chapter.

Turn to the formulation dialog to create a completely new, general specification. In substantive research, the starting point should be based on previous empirical research evidence (to test in due course that earlier findings are parsimoniously encompassed), economic (or other relevant subject matter) theory, the data frequency – and common sense. Here, we base the initial model on Davidson, Hendry, Srba and Yeo (1978) (denoted DHSY below) and begin by formulating an equation with CONS, INC, INFLAT and Constant as its basic variables (you could add in OUTPUT too if you like, but logic suggests it should be irrelevant given income).

Choose CONS, INC, and INFLAT with two lags each: please note that we are still only illustrating – in practice, five lags would be a better initial lag length for quarterly data, but in a tutorial, the mass of detail could swamp the principles if we reported all the numbers for a long lag length. Do not retain any forecasts for this run and select full sample OLS:

```
EQ( 1) Modelling CONS by OLS (using data.in7)
       The estimation sample is: 1953(3) - 1992(3)

                  Coefficient  Std.Error  t-value  t-prob Part.R^2
CONS_1               0.823338    0.08223     10.0   0.000   0.4038
CONS_2             -0.0315462    0.07151   -0.441   0.660   0.0013
Constant             -20.7434      9.070    -2.29   0.024   0.0341
INC                  0.500117    0.02922     17.1   0.000   0.6643
INC_1              -0.295872    0.05568    -5.31   0.000   0.1602
INC_2              0.0255575    0.04471    0.572   0.568   0.0022
INFLAT             -0.844115     0.2521    -3.35   0.001   0.0704
INFLAT_1          -0.0801516     0.4348   -0.184   0.854   0.0002
INFLAT_2           -0.137750     0.2633   -0.523   0.602   0.0018

sigma                 1.09027  RSS                   175.92662
R^2                  0.993857  F(8,148) =     2993 [0.000]**
log-likelihood       -231.708  DW                         2.02
no. of observations       157  no. of parameters             9
mean(CONS)             875.78  var(CONS)               182.397
```

Scan the output, noting the coefficient estimates *en route* (e.g. four t-values are small). Select the dynamic analysis to compute the static long-run solution:

```
Solved static long run equation for CONS
                  Coefficient  Std.Error  t-value  t-prob
Constant             -99.6282      38.05    -2.62   0.010
INC                   1.10372    0.04237     26.0   0.000
INFLAT               -5.10074     0.5484    -9.30   0.000
Long-run sigma = 5.23645

ECM = CONS + 99.6282 - 1.10372*INC + 5.10074*INFLAT;
WALD test: Chi^2(2) = 981.088 [0.0000] **
```

Note the coefficient values (for example, INC is close to unity, INFLAT to -5) and their small standard errors (so INC is apparently significantly different from unity).

7.3 Analyzing general models

The analysis of the lag structure is now more interesting: the unit-root t-tests show that the three basic variables matter as long-run levels (less so if very long lags were selected initially), which rejects a lack of cointegration. The F-tests on the (whole) lag polynomials show that each also matters dynamically. However, lag length 2 is irrelevant, whereas the first lag cannot be removed without a significant deterioration in fit.

```
Analysis of lag structure, coefficients:
             Lag 0    Lag 1    Lag 2      Sum   SE(Sum)
CONS            -1    0.823   -0.0315   -0.208    0.0322
Constant     -20.7        0        0    -20.7     9.07
INC            0.5   -0.296    0.0256    0.23     0.038
INFLAT      -0.844  -0.0802   -0.138    -1.06     0.132


Tests on the significance of each variable
Variable    F-test         Value [ Prob]     Unit-root t-test
CONS        F(2,148) =    306.93 [0.0000]**        -6.4716**
Constant    F(1,148) =     5.2302 [0.0236]*
INC         F(3,148) =    102.74 [0.0000]**         6.0458
INFLAT      F(3,148) =     32.254 [0.0000]**        -8.039


Tests on the significance of each lag
Lag 2       F(3,148) =    0.17158 [0.9155]
Lag 1       F(3,148) =     38.745 [0.0000]**


Tests on the significance of all lags up to 2
Lag 2 - 2   F(3,148) =    0.17158 [0.9155]
Lag 1 - 2   F(6,148) =     207.76 [0.0000]**
```

These four perspectives on the model highlight which reductions are consistent with the data, although they do not tell you in what order to simplify. That issue can be resolved in part by more experienced researchers (for one example see the discussion in Hendry, 1987). For the moment, we will follow a sequential simplification route, although generally it is better to transform to near orthogonality prior to simplification.

Can we trust the tests just viewed? The natural attack on that issue is to test all of the congruency requirements listed in the Help: so test using the test summary. Many of these tests will already have been conducted during earlier tutorials. The residual plot looks normal, and no test rejects, although either of the autocorrelation or RESET tests suggests a possible problem may be lurking in the background (the former option gives significant negative autocorrelation possibly owing to overfitting – keep an eye on how that evolves as simplification proceeds). COMFAC accepts that one common factor can be extracted (matching the insignificant 2nd order lag, which would imply that the common factor had a coefficient of zero) but strongly rejects extracting two. The omitted variables test reveals that OUTPUT is indeed irrelevant. And the linear restrictions test confirms that long-run homogeneity of CONS with respect to INC is rejected at the 5% level. Tentatively, therefore, we accept the general or statistical model as data-congruent, with no need for the second lag.

```
AR 1-5 test:       F(5,143)  =    2.1861 [0.0589]
ARCH 1-4 test:     F(4,140)  =    0.95118 [0.4365]
Normality test:    Chi^2(2)  =    1.6495 [0.4384]
hetero test:       F(16,131)=    0.69832 [0.7916]
hetero-X test:     F(44,103)=    0.74453 [0.8634]
RESET test:        F(1,147)  =    3.5374 [0.0620]
```

```
COMFAC Wald test table, COMFAC F(4,148) = 21.0177 [0.0000] **
Order   Cumulative tests              Incremental tests
  2     Chi^2(2) = 0.39429 [0.8211]    Chi^2(2) = 0.39429 [0.8211]
  1     Chi^2(4) =  84.071 [0.0000]**  Chi^2(2) =  83.676 [0.0000]**
```

```
Omitted variables test: F(2,146) = 0.252122 [0.7775]
Added variables:
[0] = OUTPUT
[1] = OUTPUT_1
```

```
Test for linear restrictions (Rb=r):
R matrix
    CONS_1    CONS_2    Constant      INC     INC_1     INC_2
    1.0000    1.0000    0.00000    1.0000    1.0000    1.0000
    INFLAT   INFLAT_1  INFLAT_2
    0.00000   0.00000   0.00000
r vector
         1.0000
LinRes F(1,148) = 4.71427 [0.0315] *
```

7.4 Sequential simplification

For comparability with later models, transform the dependent variable to DCONS = ΔCONS. Use the OxMetrics calculator to create DCONS, return to model formulation, delete CONS from the model, then add DCONS and mark it as endogenous. Now delete all the lags at 2 periods and repeat estimation, keeping the sample starting point to 1953(3) to match the initial model (this is the default behaviour of PcGive: sample periods are sticky). Note the coefficient estimates as you proceed:

```
EQ( 2) Modelling DCONS by OLS (using data.in7)
       The estimation sample is: 1953(3) - 1992(3)
```

	Coefficient	Std.Error	t-value	t-prob	Part.R^2
Constant	-19.9390	8.584	-2.32	0.022	0.0345
CONS_1	-0.202149	0.02725	-7.42	0.000	0.2670
INC	0.500235	0.02857	17.5	0.000	0.6700
INC_1	-0.277320	0.03808	-7.28	0.000	0.2599
INFLAT	-0.784047	0.1857	-4.22	0.000	0.1056
INFLAT_1	-0.262993	0.2057	-1.28	0.203	0.0107

```
sigma                 1.08126  RSS                     176.538482
R^2                  0.765599  F(5,151) =       98.64 [0.000]**
log-likelihood       -231.981  DW                            1.95
no. of observations       157  no. of parameters              6
mean(DCONS)         -0.189886  var(DCONS)               4.79712
```

The lag analysis and test options can be reused although the model has been modified by a valid deletion – later, the Progress dialog will be used to take care of testing the validity of reductions. Using test summaries, few keystrokes or mouse clicks are needed to completely re-estimate, regraph and retest the simplified model. Now the apparent residual autocorrelation has gone, suggesting that the earlier interpretation of overfitting was valid. RESET, too, is a little better. After testing whatever hypotheses are desired, select Progress on the OxMetrics Model dialog. A dialog appears, listing all the estimated models:

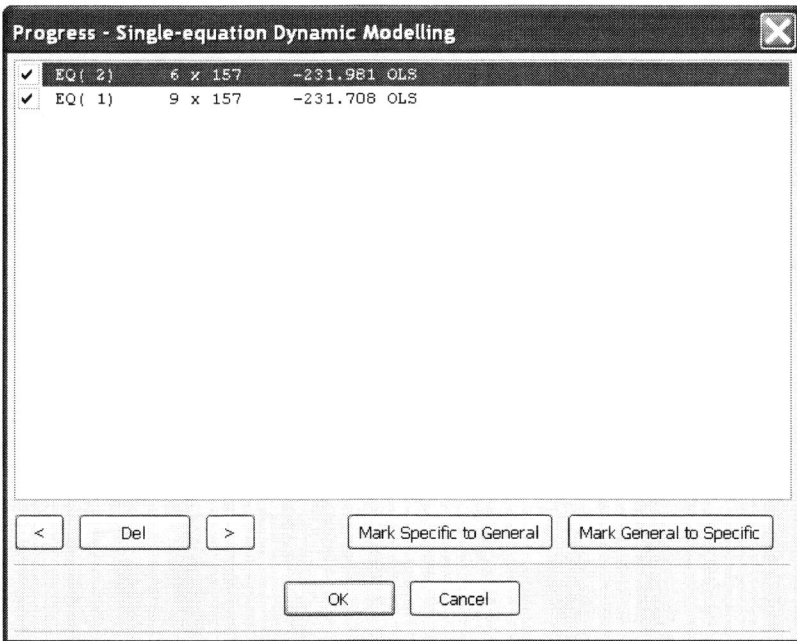

To offer a default sequence, PcGive decides that model A could be nested in model B if the following conditions hold:

- model A must have a lower log-likelihood (i.e. higher RSS),
- model A must have fewer parameters,
- model A and B must have the same sample period and database.

PcGive does not check if the same variables are involved, because transformations could hide this. As a consequence PcGive does not always get the correct nesting sequence, and it is the user's responsability to ensure nesting.

There are two options on the dialog:

- Mark Specific to General
  Marks more general models, finding a nesting sequence with strictly increasing log-likelihood.
- Mark General to Specific
  Marks all specific models that have a lower log-likelihood.

The default selection is found by first setting the most recent model as specific, and then setting the general model that was found as the general model. In this case, PcGive has marked both models,

Press OK to see the progress output:

```
Progress to date
Model        T    p        log-likelihood       SC        HQ       AIC
EQ( 1)      157   9   OLS      -231.70831     3.2415    3.1375    3.0663
EQ( 2)      157   6   OLS      -231.98086     3.1484<   3.0790<   3.0316<

Tests of model reduction
(please ensure models are nested for test validity)
EQ( 1) --> EQ( 2): F(3,148) =  0.17158 [0.9155]
```

T is the number of observations, and p the number of esstimated parameters. This is followed by the estimation procedure (OLS here) and the log-likelihood. Finally, three information criteria are listed: SC (Schwarz criterion), HQ (Hannan–Quinn) and AIC (Akaike information criterion). The F-test is the likelihood-ratio test for deleting all 2-lagged variables.

Next, we will transform the model to a more interpretable specification, similar to DHSY. Bring up the calculator to transform the variables to sustain a new model of the form:

$$\Delta \text{CONS}_t = \beta_0 + \beta_1 \Delta \text{INC}_t + \beta_2 (\text{INC} - \text{CONS})_{t-1} + \beta_3 \text{INFLAT}_t$$
$$+ \beta_4 \text{INC}_{t-1} + \beta_5 \text{INFLAT}_{t-1}.$$

Create (INC-CONS) by subtracting CONS from INC; call it SAVING, These new variables need to be added to the model: add DINC and SAVING with one lag. Then INC, current SAVING and CONS_1 (or INC_1) must be deleted. Note that it is exactly the same model as model 2 but with a different parametrization and hence a different extent of collinearity (see Chapter 14). Therefore, there is no need to re-estimate this model. But note in the previous output that INFLAT_1 is insignificant, so delete INFLAT_1 to retain only DCONS, Constant, DINC, SAVING_1, INFLAT and INC_1 (that is, 5 regressors). Estimate over the same sample period as previous models, to get model 3:

```
EQ( 3) Modelling DCONS by OLS (using data.in7)
        The estimation sample is: 1953(3) - 1992(3)

                  Coefficient  Std.Error  t-value  t-prob Part.R^2
Constant            -19.6232       8.598    -2.28   0.024   0.0331
```

```
DINC                0.507352    0.02808    18.1   0.000   0.6823
SAVING_1            0.188689    0.02519    7.49   0.000   0.2696
INC_1               0.0205447   0.009459   2.17   0.031   0.0301
INFLAT             -0.994858    0.08552   -11.6   0.000   0.4710

sigma               1.08352  RSS                178.449873
R^2                 0.763061 F(4,152) =     122.4 [0.000]**
log-likelihood   -232.826  DW                       1.95
no. of observations     157  no. of parameters        5
mean(DCONS)      -0.189886  var(DCONS)            4.79712
```

Test as before and return to check the reduction sequence (again acceptable). Note the greater interpretability of the regression parameters in this differences and levels form; also note that the effect of INC_1 is small, but matching the earlier static long run, is significantly different from zero when conventional critical values are used (but see, for example, Banerjee, Dolado, Galbraith and Hendry, 1993 for an analysis). In fact, the DGP for CONS does have a long-run coefficient of unity for INC, so we will next delete that variable (albeit anticipating a 'significant' reduction this time: in fact, INC is endogenous here, and given the number of tests we planned to use, a 1% level for each would be sensible so the deletion is not deleterious). Thus, delete INC_1, and go back through estimation and testing (note the greatly improved precision of the coefficients estimates in exchange for the cost of an increase in the residual standard error). Again select the nesting sequence in the Progress dialog.

All the diagnostic tests are acceptable from the test summary, and the Progress report is:

```
Progress to date
Model        T   p      log-likelihood        SC       HQ      AIC
EQ( 1)     157   9  OLS    -231.70831       3.2415   3.1375   3.0663
EQ( 2)     157   6  OLS    -231.98086       3.1484   3.0790   3.0316
EQ( 3)     157   5  OLS    -232.82621       3.1270   3.0692   3.0296
EQ( 4)     157   4  OLS    -235.22574       3.1253   3.0791   3.0475

Tests of model reduction
EQ( 1) --> EQ( 2): F(3,148) =  0.17158 [0.9155]
EQ( 1) --> EQ( 3): F(4,148) =  0.53068 [0.7134]
EQ( 1) --> EQ( 4): F(5,148) =  1.3565 [0.2441]

EQ( 2) --> EQ( 3): F(1,151) =  1.6349 [0.2030]
EQ( 2) --> EQ( 4): F(2,151) =  3.1863 [0.0441]*

EQ( 3) --> EQ( 4): F(1,152) =  4.7180 [0.0314]*
```

At the 5% level, Model 4 is 'significantly' worse than both models 2 and 3 but not than model 1; however, its SC is smaller ($\log T \approx 5.0$ here, so SC falls for all values of F less than about 5) and hence model selection depends in this sample on the choice of criterion and the level of significance. All further reductions by elimination will be significant, although other transformations plus reductions might prove successful: try using the ECM which imposes the long-run inflation coefficient as well.

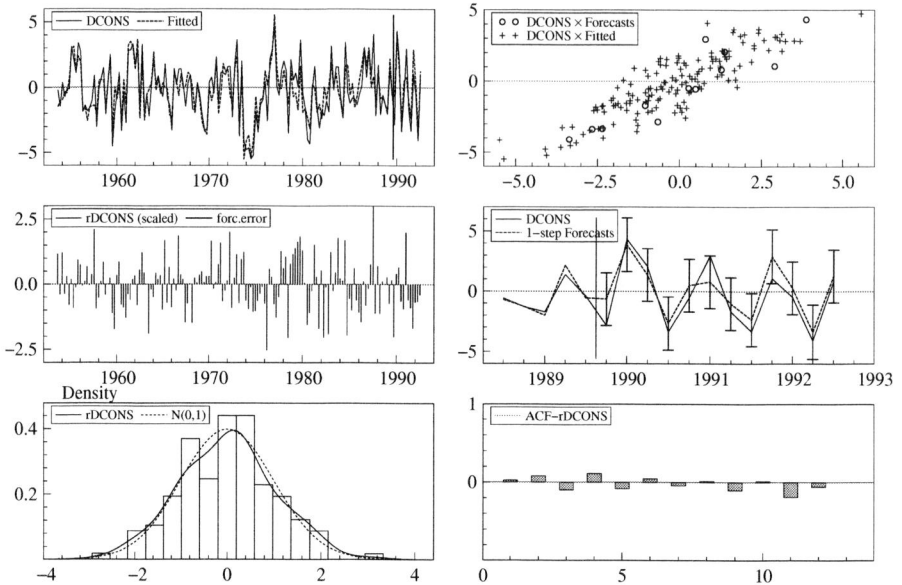

Figure 7.1   Graphical statistics for the final model with 12 forecasts.

Finally, the resulting model can be re-estimated by RLS to test recursively for parameter constancy (actually, the above model is not fully congruent, and the anomalous results are reflections of that, although the estimates are quite close to those used in the DGP, see Appendix A2). Figure 7.1 shows the graphical analysis of this final model, re-estimated with 12 forecasts.

Tip   Until a data set is saved, all changes within a run are transient; thus, changes will not be kept if you exit prior to saving your data. This is important if new transformations have been created and so automatically added to the database. OxMetrics will enquire as you exit if you wish to save the data. If you forget to save the transformed data, you will still have a record of the transformations in the results file. You could then paste the code of the transformations to the Algebra editor, save it and then load the algebra file to transform on each run. This economizes on disk space for data storage, and if you alter the base data, transformed variables are easily recreated.

7.5 Encompassing tests

The final necessary condition is to ensure that the empirical model which was obtained in the previous section is in the set of useful contenders, i.e. it is not dominated by any other model. More stringently, one might desire that no other model (M$_2$ say) explained features of the data which one's own model (M$_1$) could not. This idea will be formalized in §11.7.5 by *encompassing* (also see §13.5.6). We end this tutorial with a test for encompassing, which necessitates two non-nested models.

Start by regressing DCONS on CONS_1, INC, INC_1 and INFLAT_1, keeping the sample as before: 1953 (3) to 1992 (3). For the next model, delete INFLAT_1, adding INFLAT instead, and estimate. Then select Encompassing from the Test/Test dialog. The output comprises:

```
Encompassing test statistics: 1953(3) - 1992(3)

M1 is: DCONS on
   Constant    CONS_1      INC         INC_1       INFLAT_1
M2 is: DCONS on
   Constant    CONS_1      INC         INC_1       INFLAT

Instruments used:
   Constant    CONS_1      INC         INC_1       INFLAT_1
   INFLAT

sigma[M1] = 1.13957  sigma[M2] = 1.08352  sigma[Joint] = 1.08126

Test          Model 1 vs. Model 2           Model 2 vs. Model 1
Cox           N(0,1)   = -5.039 [0.0000]**  N(0,1)   = -1.382 [0.1670]
Ericsson IV   N(0,1)   =  4.407 [0.0000]**  N(0,1)   =  1.312 [0.1895]
Sargan        Chi^2(1) = 16.057 [0.0001]**  Chi^2(1) = 1.6281 [0.2020]
Joint Model   F(1,151) = 17.835 [0.0000]**  F(1,151) = 1.6349 [0.2030]
```

All the tests listed are automatically computed; none rejects model 2 and all reject model 1 (see Chapter 11 for details). How many hours would that have taken with another program? And we have many tools yet untried to dig deeper into the performance of econometric equations. Naturally you can extend, contract, transform or abandon your model, switch sample period or estimation methods, save the model's predictions, etc.

7.6 Model revision

If you have made it this far, you can manage on your own for a bit. We hope you enjoyed doing empirical econometrics using PcGive and found it easy, powerful and friendly to use. It is well worth reading through the econometrics Chapters 10–14. You will learn a great deal about the inadequacy of conventional methods when you see what you can investigate about claimed models. Or read the final tutorial chapter to delve further into non-linear models.

Chapter 8

Non-linear Models

8.1 Introduction

The emphasis of this book is mainly on interactive econometric modelling, primarily using OLS, IVE or RALS. However, the non-linear modelling option allows for a wide class of additional models to be estimated. In the remainder of this chapter we shall focus on advanced estimation, using the non-linear model option. Both time-series and cross-section examples will be considered. We assume you are familiar with preceding tutorials, especially with the material in Chapters 3 and 5. Note that all models in this chapter can also be estimated using the appropriate packages (discussed in Volume III). This would be more robust, and often gives additional flexibility. However, for teaching purposes, it is often useful to also implement the model using the non-linear modelling option.

8.2 Non-linear modelling

Several examples of non-linear least squares estimation were given in Chapter 5. In particular, we saw that a linear model can be set up as a non-linear model, but that direct estimation by OLS is much more efficient. Estimating RALS and NLS models confronted us with some of the potential problems of estimating non-linear models:

(1) choosing bad starting values;
(2) multiple optima;
(3) for recursive NLS: RSS which is not monotonically increasing with sample size;
(4) optima which are hard to locate, maybe resulting in failure to converge;
(5) choosing a 'difficult' parametrization (for example, maximizing a concentrated likelihood might be easier than the original likelihood).

We can add to that:

(1) programming errors, as we have to program the function ourselves (just try reversing the sign of the 'loglik' function);

(2) reaching a region of the parameter space where the function is not defined (such as taking the logarithm of a negative number);

(3) failure to compute numerical first derivatives (these are essential for finding an upward direction);

(4) upon convergence: failure to compute numerical second derivatives (these provide standard errors);

The following four precautions could make the difference between a diverging and converging estimation:

(1) **scale the parameters**, so that they fall between 0.1 and 1 (as a rule of thumb: scale the explanatory variables to be in the range 0.1–1);

(2) **find good starting values**, maybe solving a closely related problem which can be estimated by OLS;

(3) use a careful implementation, e.g. take the absolute value (or square) of parameters that must be positive (such as variances);

(4) in case of divergence, estimate first with fewer parameters.

All these problems have to be taken into account, making non-linear estimation an option for the advanced user. But it is a powerful feature, and a lot of fun to experiment with. Many examples are given below.

Sometimes we can show that the log-likelihood is concave, in which case there is only one maximum. This makes it easier to locate the maximum, and if we find one, we know that it's the only one. Some things can still go wrong, in the case where the starting values are too far away from the maximum, or when reaching an area where the function is numerically flat. Numerical issues must be considered throughout: e^{10000} does exist, but our computer cannot handle such a large number.

8.3 Maximizing a function

The second non-linear estimation method (following NLS) is called ML, which stands for maximum likelihood. This option maximizes a function of the parameters. This does not need to be a likelihood function. Consider, for example, minimizing the so-called Rosenbrock function (see Fletcher, 1987):

$$f(\alpha, \beta) = 100 * \left(\beta - \alpha^2\right)^2 + (1 - \alpha)^2.$$

No data are involved. It is easily seen that the minimum is at $(1, 1)$ with function value 0. The contours are rather banana-shaped. To estimate, create a database of just *two* observations in OxMetrics; in that database create a variable with two non-missing values. Then in PcGive select Model/Non-linear model and load the tutorial file TutRosen.alg:

```
actual=1; fitted=1;
loglik= -100 * (&2 - &1^2)^2 - (1 - &1)^2;
&1=0; &2=0;
```

The variables labelled 'actual' and 'fitted' are required by PcGive, but serve no other purpose here (they are used in the graphic analysis). The 'loglik' variable is summed over the sample size, and this sum is minimized. Non-linear modelling requires us to provide starting values, here we choose zero. Accept, select Non-linear estimation (dialog), accepting the default sample size of two observations. This leads to the Non-linear Estimation dialog; the top line says 'Press Estimate to start iterating', because the maximization has not started yet. Push the Estimate button, leading to convergence quickly (the message changes to 'Strong convergence').

Choosing OK gives the output:

```
EQ( 4) Modelling actual by ML (using Data3)
        The estimation sample is: 1 to 2

                   Coefficient  Std.Error  t-value  t-prob
&1                     0.999999     0.5000     2.00   0.000
&2                     0.999999      1.001    0.999   0.000
loglik = -9.172049474e-013 for 2 parameters and 2 observations

Standard errors based on numerical second derivatives
BFGS/warm-up using numerical derivatives (eps1=0.0001; eps2=0.005):
Strong convergence
```

The output also has a message 'Warning: invertgen: singular matrix', which you can safely ignore here.

8.4 Logit and probit estimation

A discrete choice model is one where the dependent variable is discrete, and denotes a category. In this section we use this type of model to do maximum likelihood estimation in PcGive. General references are Cramer (2001), McFadden (1984) and Amemiya (1981) among others. Examples of categorical dependent variables are:

$$y_i = 0 \quad \text{if household } i \text{ owns no car,}$$
$$y_i = 1 \quad \text{otherwise,}$$

or

$$y_i = 0 \quad \text{if individual } i \text{ travels to work by car,}$$
$$y_i = 1 \quad \text{if } i \text{ travels to work by bike,}$$
$$y_i = 2 \quad \text{otherwise.}$$

The first example is a binary choice problem (two categories), the second is multinomial. Here we restrict ourselves to the former: the dependent variable is a dummy. With a discrete dependent variable, interest lies in modelling the probabilities of observing a certain outcome. Write

$$p_i = P\{y_i = 1\}.$$

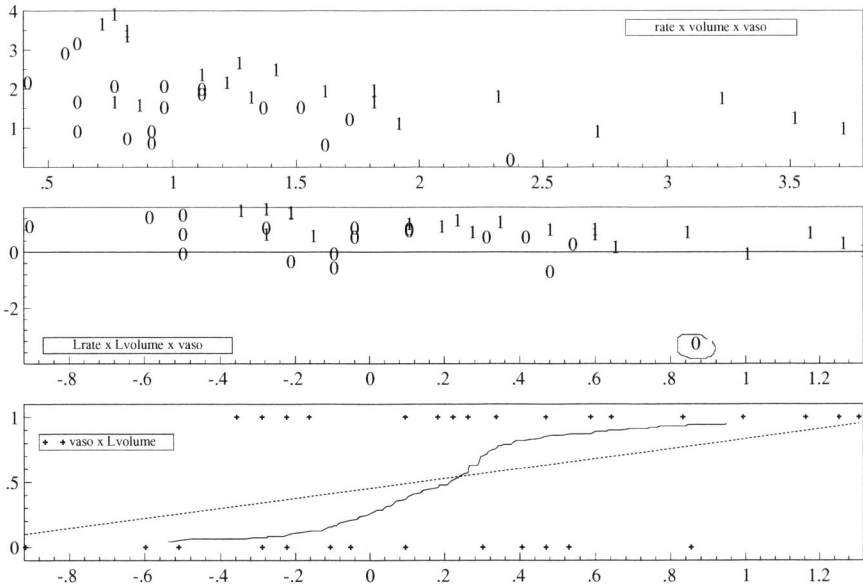

Figure 8.1   Finney's data.

To illustrate this method we use the data from Finney (1947), provided in the files FINNEY.IN7 and FINNEY.BN7. This data set holds 39 observations on the occurrence of vaso-constriction (the dummy variable, called 'vaso') in the skin of the fingers after taking a single deep breath. The dose is measured by the volume of air inspired ('volume') and the average rate of inspiration ('rate'). Load the data set into PcGive. A graphical inspection is provided by Figure 8.1. Figure 8.1(a) shows a cross-plot of volume and rate by vaso; a 1 indicates the occurrence of vaso-constriction. This graph suggests that response is determined by the product of rate and volume. The next graph uses log(rate) and log(volume). The point inside the circle appears to be an outlier. The data are taken from the table in Finney (1947), which has a typing error for observation 32. The correct value is (presumably) 0.3 instead of 0.03 (0.3 corresponds to the graph in the paper). The straight line in Fig. 8.1(c) shows what regressing vaso on log(volume) would lead to; the hand-drawn line shows a better approach, corresponding to a cumulative distribution function. Applying the straight line (that is, OLS) has several disadvantages here. First, it doesn't yield proper probabilities, as it is not restricted to lie between 0 and 1 (OLS is called the linear probability model: $p_i = \mathbf{x}_i'\beta$). Secondly, the disturbances cannot be normally distributed, as they only take on two values: $\epsilon_i = 1 - p_i$ or $\epsilon_i = 0 - p_i$.

Finally, they are also heteroscedastic: $\mathsf{E}[\epsilon_i] = (1 - p_i)p_i + (0 - p_i)(1 - p_i) = 0$, $\mathsf{E}[\epsilon_i^2] = (1 - p_i)^2 p_i + (0 - p_i)^2(1 - p_i) = (1 - p_i)p_i$.

A simple solution is to introduce an underlying continuous variable y_i^*, which is not observed. Observed is:

$$y_i = \begin{cases} 0 & \text{if } y_i^* < 0, \\ 1 & \text{if } y_i^* \geq 0. \end{cases} \tag{8.1}$$

Now we can introduce explanatory variables:

$$y_i^* = \mathbf{x}_i'\boldsymbol{\beta} - \epsilon_i.$$

and write

$$p_i = \mathsf{P}\{y_i = 1\} = \mathsf{P}\{\mathbf{x}_i'\boldsymbol{\beta} - \epsilon_i \geq 0\} = F_\epsilon\left(\mathbf{x}_i'\boldsymbol{\beta}\right).$$

Observations with $y_i = 1$ contribute p_i to the likelihood, observations with $y_i = 0$ contribute $1 - p_i$:

$$L\left(\boldsymbol{\beta} \mid \mathbf{X}\right) = \prod_{\{y_i=0\}} (1 - p_i) \prod_{\{y_i=1\}} p_i,$$

and the log-likelihood becomes:

$$\ell\left(\boldsymbol{\beta} \mid \mathbf{X}\right) = \sum_{i=1}^{N} \left[(1 - y_i) \log\left(1 - p_i\right) + y_i \log p_i\right].$$

The choice of F_ϵ determines the method. Using the logistic distribution:

$$F_\epsilon\left(z\right) = \frac{e^z}{1 + e^z}$$

leads to *logit*. Logit has a linear *log-odds ratio*:

$$\log\left(\frac{p_i}{1 - p_i}\right) = \mathbf{x}_i'\boldsymbol{\beta}.$$

The standard normal gives *probit*. As we can multiply y_i^* by any non-zero constant without changing the outcome, the scale of these distributions is fixed: the logistic has variance $\pi^2/3$, the standard normal has variance equal to 1. The corresponding Algebra code for our application is :

```
actual = vaso;
xbeta = &0 + &1 * Lrate + &2 * Lvolume;
fitted = 1 / (1 + exp(-xbeta));
loglik = actual * log(fitted) + (1 - actual) * log(1 - fitted);
// starting values:
&0 = -0.744;  &1 = 1.346;  &2 = 2.303;
```

and for probit:

```
actual = vaso;
xbeta = &0 + &1 * Lrate + &2 * Lvolume;
fitted = probn(xbeta);
loglik = actual * log(fitted) + (1-actual) * log(tailn(xbeta));
// starting values:
&0 = -0.465;  &1 = 0.842;  &2 = 1.439;
```

The starting values for both problems were obtained from an OLS regression of vaso on a constant, Lrate and Lvolume, and then transforming the parameters following Amemiya (1981) as:

	constant	rest
logit	$4\,(\alpha_{OLS} - 0.5)$	$4\beta_{OLS}$
probit	$2.5\,(\alpha_{OLS} - 0.5)$	$2.5\beta_{OLS}$

First estimate the binary logit model: load the Finney data set in OxMetrics, in PcGive type Alt+m,1 to activate Model/Non-linear modelling. Change database to finney.in7, then load TutLogit.alg, accept (if you get the message 'vaso not found in database' you forgot to change to the finney database) and accept again. In the Non-linear estimation dialog press Estimate to start estimating, and OK to accept the result after convergence. The results are:

```
EQ( 1) Modelling actual by ML (using Finney.in7)
        The estimation sample is: 1 to 39

                  Coefficient  Std.Error  t-value  t-prob
&0                   -2.87555      1.321    -2.18   0.036
&1                    4.56176      1.838     2.48   0.018
&2                    5.17939      1.865     2.78   0.009
loglik = -14.61368766 for 3 parameters and 39 observations

Standard errors based on numerical second derivatives
BFGS/warm-up using numerical derivatives (eps1=0.0001; eps2=0.005):
Strong convergence
```

A graphic analysis which will use the variables 'actual' and 'fitted' as we defined them is not so interesting here. Better is Figure 8.2. Select Test/Store in database, expand non-linear estimation, click on click on select, and select fitted in the drop-down list. In OxMetrics, rename fitted to plogit. Repeat the same procedur for loglik, renaming it to liklogit. Next, switch to OxMetrics and graph vaso, plogit and liklogit. This graph looks different from 8.2, which is sorted by 'liklogit'. This is achieved by sorting the whole database by the 'liklogit' variable using Algebra; enter:

```
index = trend();
_sortallby(liklogit);
```

in the Algebra editor and execute. The index variable allows us to undo the sorting operation. The 'plogit' variable is p_i, whereas 'liklogit' is the log-likelihood contribution

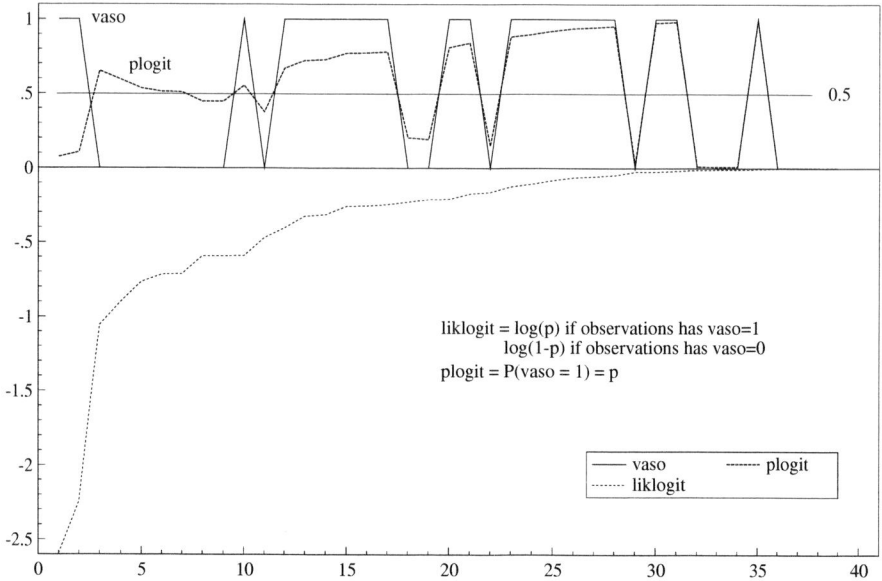

Figure 8.2   Log-likelihoods, probabilities and outcomes for the logit model.

of observation i: the log of the probability of being in the observed state. Ideally, we predict a probability of one, corresponding to a likelihood of 0. So as we move from left to right, the 'fit' improves. From the top part of the graph we see that if for $p_i > 0.5$ we would classify the outcome as a 1, then the misclassifications are on the left.

To see whether the typo in observation 32 matters much, move it to the end of the database through:

```
deselect = (index == 32);
_sortallby(deselect);
```

deselect will be 1 for observation 32 and 0 otherwise, and sorting all variables by deselect moves number 32 to the bottom. Do a logit model over the sample 1–38: there is hardly any difference at all.

The index variable corresponds to the original observation index, so to restore the original order in the database, execute:

```
_sortallby(index);
```

and turn to the probit estimation using TutProbit.alg:

```
EQ( 2) Modelling actual by ML (using Finney.in7)
        The estimation sample is: 1 to 39
                Coefficient  Std.Error  t-value  t-prob
&0              -1.50440     0.6375     -2.36    0.024
&1               2.51233     0.9365      2.68    0.011
&2               2.86200     0.9081      3.15    0.003
loglik = -14.64353075 for 3 parameters and 39 observations
```

Although the coefficients of logit and probit are quite different, this is mainly owing to the choice of scaling parameter. It is more useful to compare probabilities (or derivatives of probabilities with respect to explanatory variables). Sorting the database again, and combining logit and probit results, gives Figure 8.3. Here we see that the differences between the results are very small indeed: there is no reason to prefer one over the other (also see Chambers and Cox, 1967).

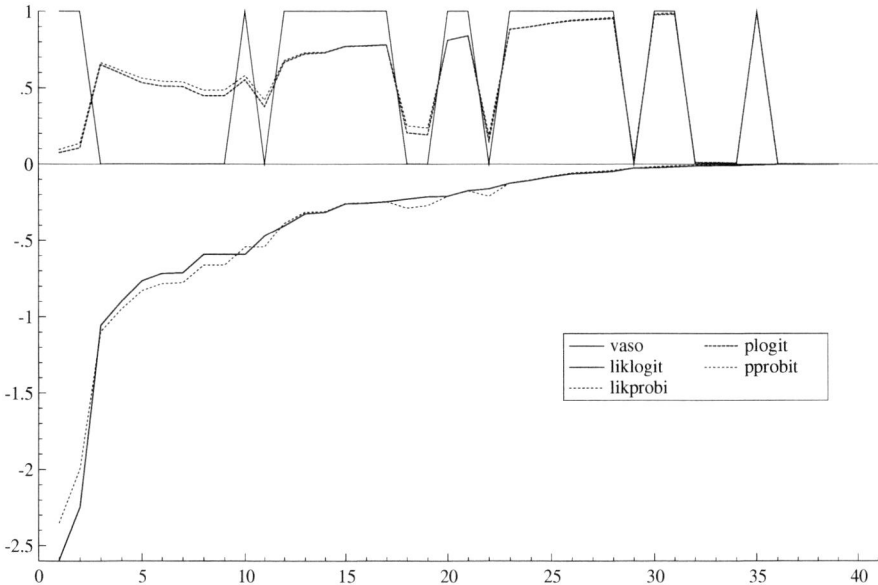

Figure 8.3 Comparison of the probit and logit models.

As an illustration of the possibilities and drawbacks of PcGive's ML option we did a multinomial logit with 4 states (numbered 0,1,2,3), 1700 observations and 24 parameters. The probabilities of observation i to be in state j are defined as:

$$\mathsf{p}_{ij} = \frac{e^{\mathbf{x}_i'\beta_j}}{\sum_{j=0}^3 e^{\mathbf{x}_i'\beta_j}}, \quad j = 0,\ldots,3, \quad \text{with } \beta_0 = 0.$$

The code rearranges this somewhat, to provide a numerically more stable calculation, see MNLOGIT.ALG. On a 90 Mhz Pentium this takes 10 minutes to converge (with strong convergence tolerance of 0.001), plus nearly 5 minutes to evaluate the variance numerically. When using the Limited dependent package within PcGive, which employs Newton's method with analytical first and second derivatives convergence takes 4 seconds. Most of the penalty comes out of having to evaluate the algebra code over and over again, rather than being able to use the hard-coded function.

8.5 Tobit estimation

In the standard tobit model (see, for example, Amemiya, 1985, Chapter 10, or Cramer, 1986, Chapter 11), the observations on the dependent variable are censored: the positive values are observed, but instead of negative values, we see only zeros. The analogue to (8.1) is:

$$y_i = \left\{ \begin{array}{ll} 0 & \text{if } y_i^* \leq 0, \\ y_i^* & \text{if } y_i^* > 0, \end{array} \right.$$

using

$$y_i^* = \mathbf{x}_i'\boldsymbol{\beta} + \epsilon_i, \text{ with } \epsilon_i \sim \text{IN}\left(0, \sigma^2\right).$$

Now $P\{y_i^* \leq 0\} = P(\mathbf{x}_i'\boldsymbol{\beta} + \epsilon_i \leq 0) = 1 - F_\epsilon(\mathbf{x}_i'\boldsymbol{\beta})$ (F_ϵ is symmetric). The log-likelihood can be seen to consist of a probit part and an OLS part:

$$\ell\left(\boldsymbol{\beta} \mid \mathbf{X}\right) = \sum_{\{y_i=0\}} \log\left(1 - F_\epsilon\left(\mathbf{x}_i'\boldsymbol{\beta}\right)\right) + \sum_{\{y_i>0\}} \log\left(f_\epsilon\left(y_i - \mathbf{x}_i'\boldsymbol{\beta}\right)\right).$$

Using (12.102):

$$\ell\left(\boldsymbol{\beta} \mid \mathbf{X}\right) = \sum_{\{y_i=0\}} \log\left(1 - F_\epsilon\left(\mathbf{x}_i'\boldsymbol{\beta}\right)\right) + c + \sum_{\{y_i>0\}} \left[\log\left(\sigma^{-1}\right) - \frac{1}{2}\frac{(y_i - \mathbf{x}_i'\boldsymbol{\beta})^2}{\sigma^2}\right]$$

Write Φ for the standard normal cdf:

$$1 - F_\epsilon(\mathbf{x}_i'\boldsymbol{\beta}) = 1 - \Phi\left(\mathbf{x}_i'\boldsymbol{\beta}/\sigma\right).$$

Using the indicator function $\mathcal{I}(\cdot)$ to indicate whether the outcome was observed, $\ell_i(\boldsymbol{\beta}|\mathbf{x}_i)$, the likelihood for individual i may be written as:

$$\mathcal{I}\left(y_i = 0\right)\log\left[1 - \Phi\left(\mathbf{x}_i'\boldsymbol{\beta}/\sigma\right)\right] + \mathcal{I}\left(y_i > 0\right)\left[\tfrac{1}{2}\log\left(\sigma^{-1}\right) - \tfrac{1}{2}\left(y_i/\sigma - \mathbf{x}_i'\boldsymbol{\beta}/\sigma\right)^2\right].$$

It is convenient to scale by σ, writing $\boldsymbol{\alpha} = \boldsymbol{\beta}/\sigma$, so that $\ell_i(\boldsymbol{\alpha}|\mathbf{x}_i)$ is:

$$\mathcal{I}\left(y_i = 0\right)\log\left[1 - \Phi\left(\mathbf{x}_i'\boldsymbol{\alpha}\right)\right] + \mathcal{I}\left(y_i > 0\right)\left[\tfrac{1}{2}\log\left(\sigma^{-1}\right) - \tfrac{1}{2}\left(y_i/\sigma - \mathbf{x}_i'\boldsymbol{\alpha}\right)^2\right].$$

The data set is TutTobit.in7, which holds data on expenditure on clothing for 150 individuals, with income and age. In algebra code, the likelihood is expressed as (the code is given in the file TutTobit.alg):

```
actual = expen;                          // y
fitted = &0 + &1 * inc/1000 + &2 * age/10;   // x'alpha
loglik = (actual <= 0)
  ? log( max(1.e-20, tailn(fitted)) )        // probit part
  : log(fabs(&3)) - 0.5 * (actual * fabs(&3) - fitted)^2;

&0=-3.3; &1=1.3; &2=2.3; &3=0.022;       // starting values
fitted = fitted/&3;// undo scaling, fitted is no longer needed
```

First of all, scaling of the parameters is important, preferably so that they fall between 0.1 and 1. Without that, the numerical derivatives are much more likely to fail. Also use good starting values (here based on OLS). Secondly, &3 is σ^{-1}, and the remaining parameters estimate $\alpha = \beta/\sigma$. More importantly, we take the absolute value of &3, reducing the singularity to a small region around 0. Consequently, it is possible to find a negative value for &3; in that case restart at the optimum, but with the absolute value of &3, which converges immediately. Finally, we don't allow $1 - F_\epsilon$ to get smaller than 10^{-20}. This helps with bad starting values, but should not make any difference close to the optimum.

The starting values were found from a full-sample OLS estimation:

	Coefficient	Std.Error	t-value	t-prob	Part.R^2
Constant	-151.482	48.56	-3.12	0.002	0.0621
inc	0.0608239	0.01710	3.56	0.001	0.0792
age	10.4385	3.113	3.35	0.001	0.0711
sigma	46.3493	RSS		315793.427	
R^2	0.23024	F(2,147) =	21.98	[0.000]**	
log-likelihood	-573.916	DW		2	

So: $\&0 = -151.48/46.3439$, $\&1 = (1000 \times 0.060824)/46.3439$, $\&2 = (100 \times 10.439)/46.3439$, $\&3 = 1/46.3439$.

The final results are:

```
EEQ( 3) Modelling actual by ML (using TutTobit.in7)
        The estimation sample is: 1 to 150
```

	Coefficient	Std.Error	t-value	t-prob
&0	-4.78177	1.207	-3.96	0.000
&1	1.27797	0.4053	3.15	0.002
&2	2.67282	0.7653	3.49	0.001
&3	0.0122297	0.001167	10.5	0.000

```
loglik = -374.9303539 for 4 parameters and 150 observations
```

Figure 8.4 gives a plot of the fitted values from the Tobit model and from OLS in the upper half, and expenditure in the lower half (both after sorting the database by expenditure).

8.6 ARMA estimation

Here we fit a model to generated ARMA$(2, 2)$ and in the next section to ARCH data. First run the batch file TutArma.fl in OxMetrics:

```
database("tutarma", 1, 1, 120, 1, 1);
algebra
{
    ranseed(-1);
```

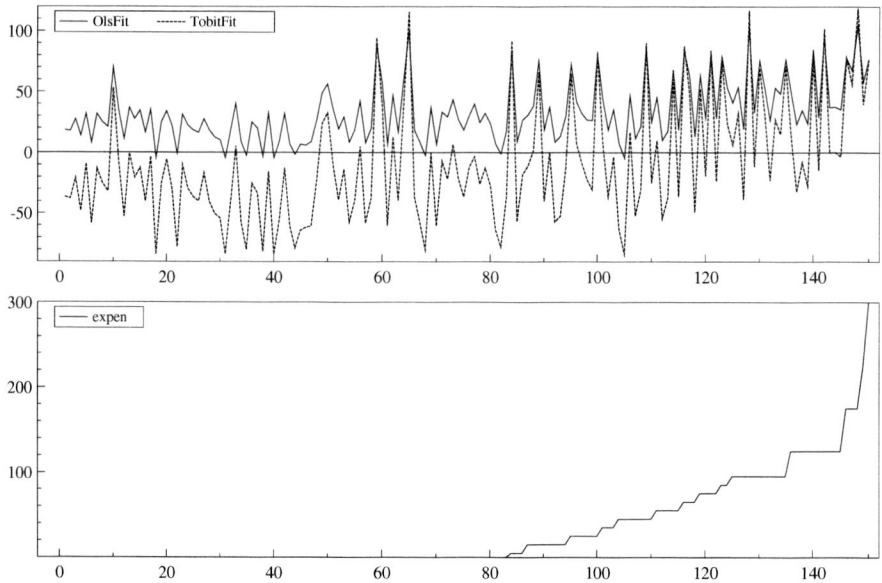

Figure 8.4   Comparison of fitted values from OLS and Tobit.

```
eps = rann();
arma22 = year() >= 3
    ? -1.4 * lag(arma22,1) - .5 * lag(arma22,2) + eps
    - .2 * lag(eps,1) - .1 * lag(eps,2)
    : 0;
arch = year() >= 3
    ? sqrt(1 + 0.6 * lag(arch,1)^2) * eps
    : 0;

arma22 = insample(1, 1, 17, 1) ? MISSING;
arch = insample(1, 1, 17, 1) ? MISSING;
}
```

This creates a database of 120 observations on an ARMA$(2, 2)$ and an ARCH process (the first 17 observations are thrown away).

For the ARMA$(2, 2)$ model

$$y_t = \theta_0 y_{t-1} + \theta_1 y_{t-2} + \epsilon_t + \theta_2 \epsilon_{t-1} + \theta_3 \epsilon_{t-2},$$

we can use NLS to mimimize the conditional sum of squares (CSS):

$$\sum_{t=3}^{T} (y_t - \theta_0 y_{t-1} - \theta_1 y_{t-2} - \theta_2 \epsilon_{t-1} - \theta_3 \epsilon_{t-2})^2$$

with $\epsilon_1 = \epsilon_2 = 0$. This treatment of the initial disturbances simplifies the estimation procedure. Exact maximum likelihood estimation requires specifying the distribution for the initial observations and disturbances. See Box and Jenkins (1976) or Harvey (1993) among others.

The code for estimating the ARMA$(2, 2)$ model is given in TutArma.alg:

```
actual = arma22;
fitted = (lag(actual,2) != MISSING)
        ? &1*lag(actual,1) + &2*lag(actual,2)
        +  &3*(lag(actual,1) - lag(fitted,1))
        +  &4*(lag(actual,2) - lag(fitted,2))
        : actual;
// starting values:
&1 = -1.4; &2 = -0.5; &3 = -0.2; &4 = -0.1;
```

Algebra is a vector language: each line can be interpreted as having an observation loop around it. This enables us to define 'fitted' recursively: when computing 'fitted' at time t, the value at $t - 1$ already exists. But we have to be careful, as this doesn't work for $t = 1$ and $t = 2$ where the second lag of 'fitted' cannot exist. The work-around is the conditional statement: in those two cases we assign the observed value, corresponding to a residual of zero. The final line gives the starting values. These lines can occur anywhere in the code, but are executed when the code is analyzed for errors, so before the proper algebra statements are executed. The syntax is restricted to '*parameter=value;*', as used in the code. In pseudo language the code can be interpreted as:

initialize $\hat{\theta}_0 = -1.4, \hat{\theta}_1 = -0.5, \hat{\theta}_2 = -0.2, \hat{\theta}_3 = -0.1$;

set actual, fitted to missing for the whole database period;

statement 1   for $t = T_1, \ldots, T_2$: actual $\leftarrow y_t$;

for $t = T_1, \ldots, T_1 + 2$: fitted $(\hat{y}_t) \leftarrow y_t$;

statement 2   for $t = T_1 + 3, \ldots, T_2$: fitted $(\hat{y}_t) \leftarrow \hat{\theta}_0 y_{t-1} - \hat{\theta}_1 y_{t-2} - \hat{\theta}_2 (y_{t-1} - \hat{y}_{t-1}) - \hat{\theta}_3 (y_{t-2} - \hat{y}_{t-2})$.

$T_1, \ldots, T_2$ is the sample used for estimation, and the result is that the first three ϵs in that sample are zero.

Estimation from observation 18 gives (remember that information criteria, etc. are switched off by default):

```
EQ( 5) Modelling actual by NLS (using tutarma)
       The estimation sample is: 18 to 120
```

	Coefficient	Std.Error	t-value	t-prob	Part.R^2
&1	-1.65563	0.2437	-6.79	0.000	0.3180
&2	-0.700066	0.2213	-3.16	0.002	0.0918
&3	0.0797921	0.2753	0.290	0.773	0.0008
&4	-0.301409	0.2016	-1.50	0.138	0.0221

```
sigma                   0.963591  RSS                    91.9221925
R^2                     0.942957  F(3,99) =       545.5 [0.000]**
log-likelihood          -140.291  DW                              2
no. of observations          103  no. of parameters              4
mean(actual)          -0.0110595  var(actual)                15.641

Standard errors based on information matrix
BFGS/warm-up using numerical derivatives (eps1=0.0001; eps2=0.005):
Strong convergence
```

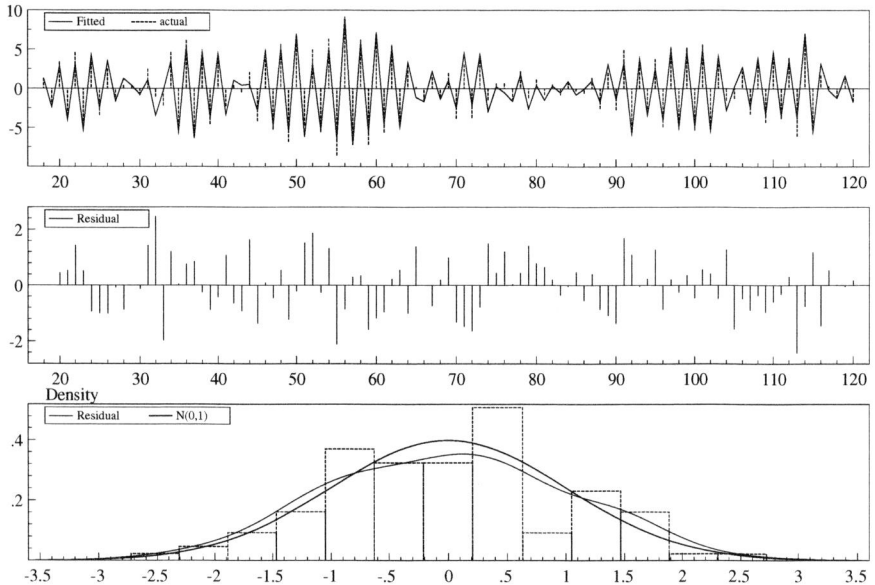

Figure 8.5   Graphical analysis of ARMA(2,2) model.

Graphic analysis is based on the 'actual' and 'fitted' values, with the residuals defined as the difference, see Figure 8.5. Tests are also available:

```
AR 1-2 test:     F(2,97)   =  0.11612 [0.8905]
ARCH 1-1 test:   F(1,97)   =   5.5023 [0.0210]*
Normality test:  Chi^2(2)  =  0.48103 [0.7862]
hetero test:     F(8,90)   =   0.9317 [0.4946]
hetero-X test:   F(14,84)  =  0.94068 [0.5199]
```

Tests that require an auxiliary regression use the derivatives of 'fitted' with respect to the parameters evaluated at the optimum, see §17.4.10.

8.7 ARCH estimation

Specify an ARCH(q) model as:

$$y_t = \mathbf{x}_t'\boldsymbol{\beta} + u_t, \quad \text{with } u_t = \sigma_t \epsilon_t, \quad \text{and } \sigma_t^2 = \alpha_0 + \sum_{j=1}^{q} \alpha_j u_{t-j}^2.$$

See, for example, Engle (1982) or Bollerslev, Chou and Kroner (1992). Assuming $\epsilon_t \sim$ IN$(0, 1)$ gives $u_t | u_{t-1} \cdots u_{t-q} \sim N(0, \sigma_t^2)$. So conditional on the past, the model is normal but heteroscedastic. The log-likelihood for observation t follows from (12.103)

$$\ell_t\left(\boldsymbol{\theta} | \mathcal{I}_{t-1}\right) = c - \tfrac{1}{2} \log\left(\sigma_t^2\right) - \tfrac{1}{2} \frac{(y_t - \mathbf{x}_t'\boldsymbol{\beta})^2}{\sigma_t^2}.$$

Fitting an ARCH(1) model to the generated data, with only a constant in the mean (that is, the only x is the intercept), is achieved by formulating (see TutArch.alg):

```
actual = arch;
fitted = &0;
res    = actual - fitted;
condv  = fabs(&1 + &2 * lag(res,1)^2);
loglik = -0.5 * (log(condv) + res^2/condv);
&0 = -0.05; &1 = 1.47; &2 = 0.56;    // starting values
```

with $\beta_0 = $ &0, $\alpha_0 = $ &1, $\alpha_1 = $ &2. The fabs() function takes the absolute value of its argument. This forces the variance to be positive, and improves the numerical behaviour of the optimization process considerably. The starting values are the coefficients from the ARCH test on the residuals from regressing the arch variable on a constant. The estimated model is, using 8 forecasts:

```
EQ( 3) Modelling actual by ML (using tutarma)
        The estimation sample is: 19 to 112

                  Coefficient  Std.Error  t-value  t-prob
&0                 -0.0150116    0.09534   -0.157   0.875
&1                  0.708277     0.1830     3.87    0.000
&2                  0.767728     0.2291     3.35    0.001
loglik = -69.92337936 for 3 parameters and 94 observations

Standard errors based on numerical second derivatives
BFGS/warm-up using numerical derivatives (eps1=0.0001; eps2=0.005):
Strong convergence
```

Graphic analysis and some tests are available, but this is not very helpful here because of the definition of 'actual' and 'fitted': the latter is only a constant. The result is that ARCH effects are not removed from 'actual'−'fitted', as seen from the test:

```
ARCH 1-1 test:    F(1,89)   =   36.930 [0.0000]**
Normality test:   Chi^2(2)  =   8.2419 [0.0162]*
```

More useful information is obtained from actual values $y_t/\hat{\sigma}_t$ and fitted values $x_t'\hat{\beta}/\hat{\sigma}_t$. Re-estimate adding the following to lines at the bottom of the algebra code:

```
actual = arch / sqrt(condv);
fitted = &0 / sqrt(condv);
```

The ARCH test has become insignificant:

```
ARCH 1-1 test:     F(1,89)   =    1.9815 [0.1627]
Normality test:    Chi^2(2)  =    3.4009 [0.1826]
```

Some graphical results are in Figure 8.6.

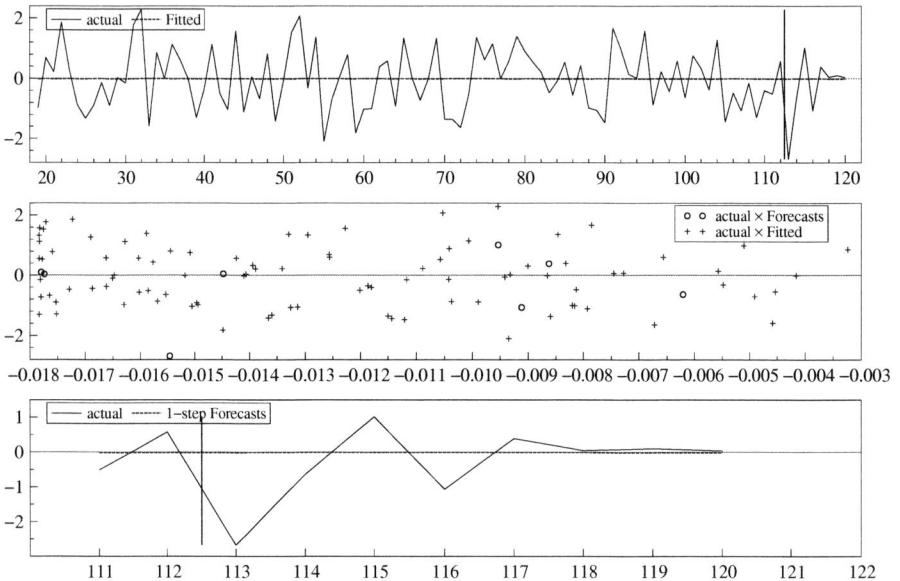

Figure 8.6 Graphical analysis for ARCH model using scaled actual and fitted.

As in the ARMA case, it makes a difference how the initial values are treated. In the ARCH algebra code, the first observations in the estimation use a value determined as actual–fitted when the algebra is run to determine the potential sample period, but left untouched during estimation (the value used in this case is 1.4714). It could be fixed by:

```
                              // loglik must already exist
condv  = lag(loglik,1) != MISSING && lag(res,1) != MISSING
  ? fabs(&1 + &2 * lag(res,1)^2) : 1;
```

This finishes our discussion of non-linear estimation using PcGive. We are confident that you can now experiment successfully with your own models.

Part III

The Econometrics of PcGive

Chapter 9

An Overview

The purpose of Part III is to explain the concepts, models, methods and methodology embodied in PcGive, and how to interpret its statistical and econometric output. For completeness, we occasionally refer to the module for system modelling which is fully described in Volume II, see Doornik and Hendry (2006a). The aim is to support the learning of econometrics by using the software at a computer, applying methods to data while learning about those methods. PcGive offers excellent facilities for learning econometrics at all levels from elementary courses, through intermediate stages to advanced graduate standard. Its ease of use, menu interface and virtual uncrashability make it a straightforward tool even for beginning economists and econometricians.

There are seven chapters on the econometrics of PcGive. First, we describe elementary-level material needed by both economists and econometricians, including notions of variation in data, the shape of distributions, measures of association, and time dependence, leading up to dummy variables, collinearity and nonsense regressions. The third 'learning' chapter is 11, which is at an intermediate level and considers the bulk of the features offered by PcGive. It provides an introductory explanation of econometrics, which also serves as a background to many of the features examined in the tutorials. The discussion is intuitive and discursive, and although mathematics is used, this is not at an advanced level. Topics addressed include linear dynamic models and their interpretation, multiple regression and instrumental variables, an introduction to modelling methodology and key econometric concepts, and diagnostic testing. Chapter 12 then describes the statistical theory of the normal distribution, of maximum likelihood estimation and of least squares, linking that to regression analysis (a distinction discussed shortly).

These chapters establish the main econometric tools, leading in Chapter 13 to an overview of the approach embodied in PcGive to sustain efficient econometric modelling. Chapter 14 considers nine important practical problems. The detailed discussion of the actual statistics reported in PcGive is in Chapters 15–16, relating respectively to data description and single-equation evaluation. As such, they are a reference to be used as needed, rather than read throughout at a single sitting. Conversely, it is advisable to read Chapters 11–13 prior to using PcGive for substantive research. The detailed table of contents is intended as a quick reference guide for locating explanations about any results obtained. References to sections are denoted by chapter.section, for example, §1.1, §2.4 etc. Equations are denoted by (chapter.number), for example, (12.17). Finally, figures are shown as chapter.number, for example, Figure 13.2.

The philosophy underlying PcGive is that economic time-series data are generated by a process of immense generality and complexity owing to the interacting behaviours and conflicting objectives of millions of individuals. The outcomes produced by the economic mechanism are measured with varying degrees of accuracy, but rarely perfectly, and sometimes not very well. The combination of the mechanism (the processes of production, transaction and consumption) and the measurement system is called the data generation process (DGP). The econometrician seeks to model the main features of the DGP in a simplified representation based on a small set of observable variables usually related to prior economic theory. Since many important data features are inevitably assumed absent in any economic theory, empirical models have to be developed interactively to characterize the data while being consistent with the theory. For example, a theory model might assume white-noise errors, whereas aggregation and the lack of a mapping of theory-decision periods to data-observation intervals may mean that the estimated model manifests substantial residual serial correlation (perhaps of a seasonal form). Equally, the 'deep' parameters of the theory may correspond to model coefficients which are not empirically constant over time. PcGive is designed to facilitate the process of model design, reveal problems with potential models, and test models to highlight their strengths and weaknesses.

Current research suggests that an important component of any modelling exercise is to estimate the most general model that it is reasonable to entertain *a priori*: see, for example, Hoover and Perez (1999), and Hendry (2000a, Ch 20). Thus, PcGive facilitates formulating general linear dynamic models, while still offering protection against the possibility that the initial generality is in fact too specific to adequately characterize the available data. This approach corresponds loosely to a constructive aspect of empirical modelling. Both aspects of model construction and testing to destruction are analyzed in Chapter 13.

Many econometrics packages focus on the estimation of economic models of varying degrees of complexity assuming that their qualitative characteristics are known beforehand, but the numerical values of their parameters need calibration from empirical evidence. While estimation represents a necessary ingredient in econometrics research, it is far from sufficient for practical empirical modelling. PcGive has been developed to aid the process of discovering 'good' models by offering a wide range of evaluation tools, some of which are sophisticated estimation methods reoriented to highlight potential model weaknesses. There is no royal road to developing good models, but some considerations which have proved helpful in related studies are discussed below, including an analysis of the criteria by which empirical models might be judged. A more extensive discussion is provided in Hendry (1993, 2000a) and Hendry (1995a).

Just as there is no 'best' way to drive a car, but many obviously bad ways (for example, with your eyes closed), so there are many necessary, but no sufficient, conditions for model validity. Delineating these necessary conditions, and analyzing the links between them, the available information and statistics for evaluating model adequacy is the focus for the discussion in Chapter 13. Here, we begin with data description as the first step towards mastering modern econometrics.

Chapter 10

Learning Elementary Econometrics Using PcGive

10.1 Introduction

This chapter explains how to use OxMetrics and PcGive to introduce students to econometrics, and as a complement to conventional elementary econometrics textbooks. Chapters 13–16 of this manual will be referenced frequently as they have been structured to complement and extend the ideas in the present chapter.

The chapter assumes that the reader has sufficient knowledge to operate PCs running under Windows, and is familiar with OxMetrics/PcGive in terms of its menus, mouse and keyboard. The Tutorials in Part II explain the mechanics of using the program. On-line, context-sensitive help about the program usage and the econometrics is always available. To load the data used in this chapter, access PCGTUT1.IN7 and PCGTUT1.BN7.

The chapter is also designed to help instructors in teaching econometrics. It is assumed that the instructor has prepared an appropriate data set in an .IN7 + .BN7 format: the PCGTUT data set used below is derived from `data.in7, data.bn7`. Also, it is obvious that the teacher must have explained enough of the usage of PcGive and the rudiments of Windows so that students can use the program. An overhead computer projection panel can be linked to a PC for classroom displays. The authors have found this to be an admirable and easy vehicle for illustrating econometrics concepts, models, and methods at all levels. As PcGive is essentially uncrashable and models can be formulated in batch files in advance of exercises as required, there is little risk of a serious problem developing — and should the worst happen, it can be turned into a salutory lesson on some of the real difficulties the students will face in undertaking empirical research!

As an initial small data set, we have selected 30 observations on the two variables *cons* and *inc*, which are artificial (computer-generated) data interpreted as aggregate consumers' expenditure and income in constant prices. First we view the data in the database, to see the numbers and determine their meaning, measurement, units and sample period. The data are quarterly (four times per year) over 1986(1)–1993(2), and the variables are in $100 \log$ units. This means that the change between any two points in time, say t to $t+1$, is approximately a percentage change: from 1993(1) to 1993(2), *cons* increased by 3 units from 407.23 to 410.23, which is therefore a 3% increase. Working back to the original units, divide by 100 and take antilogs (exponentials) to see that they are around 60, which is £billions (per quarter). Since consumers' expenditure must be positive, it is safe to take logs; the scaling by 100 converts changes to percentages. The reason for taking logs is to make economic time series more homogenous: back in 1900, consumers' expenditure was under £1billion, so a £1billion change then would have been 100% as against 1.5% in the 1980s.

10.2 Variation over time

Graphical inspection can highlight the salient features of the variables and reveal any peculiarities in the data, such as typing, or recording, errors. Those in Figure 10.1[1] also show the use of grid lines.

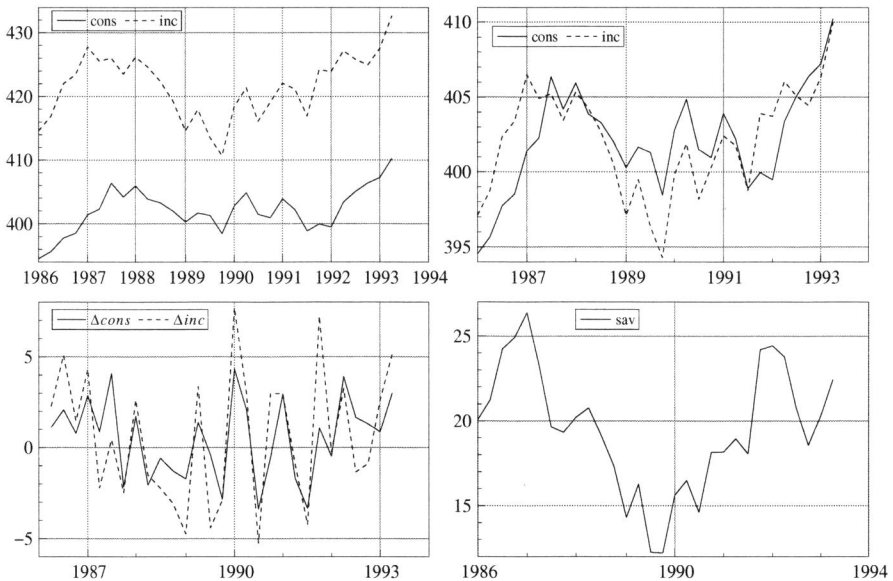

Figure 10.1 Time-series graphs of *cons* and *inc*.

The graph of *cons* and *inc* in Figure 10.1(a) reveals that they have gone through a boom-recession-boom cycle, and have ended higher than the initial observations (about

---

[1]Multiple graphs are numbered from left to right and top to bottom, so (b) is the top-right graph of four, and (c) the bottom left.

16% and 18% higher in fact). Further, they show no obvious signs of seasonality (regular variation across the quarters of the year). Figure 10.1(a) plots *cons* and *inc* in their original units, whereas Figure 10.1(b) matches them by means and ranges to maximize their apparent visual closeness: this helps reveal whether or not the two series move in the general way.

Now copy *cons* to a new variable, then revise the observation in 1987(1) from 401.41 to 301.41; it can be hard to notice this error in the database – and would be very hard amongst 500 data points – but a glance at its graph makes such an error clear. Remember to change the mistake back if you did not use a copy of *cons*.

Time-series graphs of the differences of, or changes in, each variable highlight the periods of positive and negative growth and show any synchrony between the series. Let Δ*cons* and Δ*inc* denote the changes from quarter to quarter (the Greek symbol Δ is often used in that sense in econometrics). Figure 10.1(c) shows that changes in these two series, unmatched, are clearly very close. Finally, Figure 10.1(d) plots the difference *inc–cons* which is called *sav* (actually, this is 100 times the savings ratio).

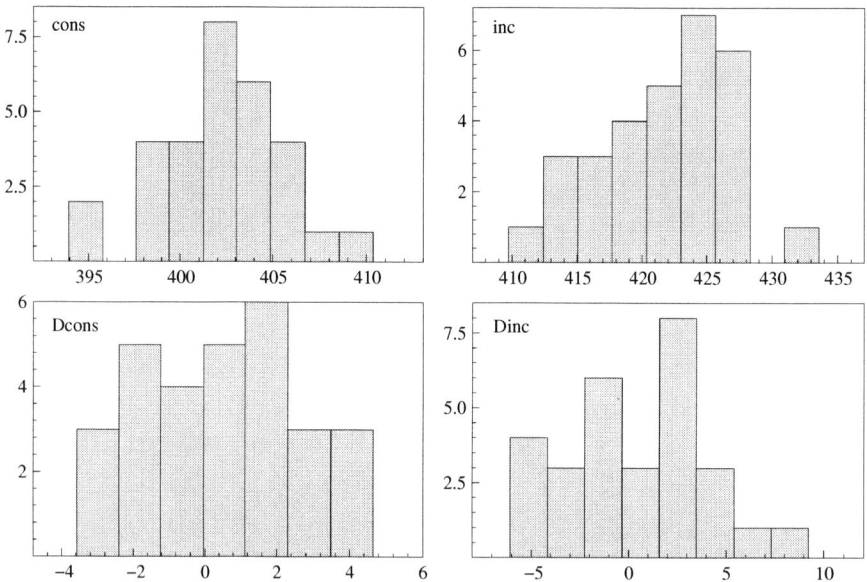

Figure 10.2   Histograms of *cons* and *inc*.

10.3 Variation across a variable

It is also useful to summarize data in terms of their distributional shape and low-order moments, and we illustrate this feature using the OxMetrics graphics. Click the graphics option and select *cons*, *inc* and their changes, then select Distribution/Frequencies as graph type. This leads to the outcomes in Figure 10.2(a)–(d). Here, there are too few data points to make the shape of the distributions very clear other than near symmetry, but we comment on several aspects in the next section.

Next, use descriptive statistics option in PcGive for the same four variables, and mark means, standard deviations, and correlations to produce the outcomes (we return to the correlations below). Since the data are in 100 logs, the standard deviations (s) of (3.2, 4.9, 2.2, 3.6) are in percentages of the original levels of the variables. Thus, the sample standard deviation is about 50% as large for the level as the change in *cons*, and 30% larger still for the level of *inc*. Roughly 95% of a symmetric distribution lies between $\bar{x}-2s$ and $\bar{x}+2s$ where $\bar{x}$ is the sample mean, so we might expect most changes in *cons* to fall in the range -4 to $+5$ (all of them actually do). Note that the sample on *cons* and *inc* is truncated by one observation when $\Delta cons$ and Δinc are included.

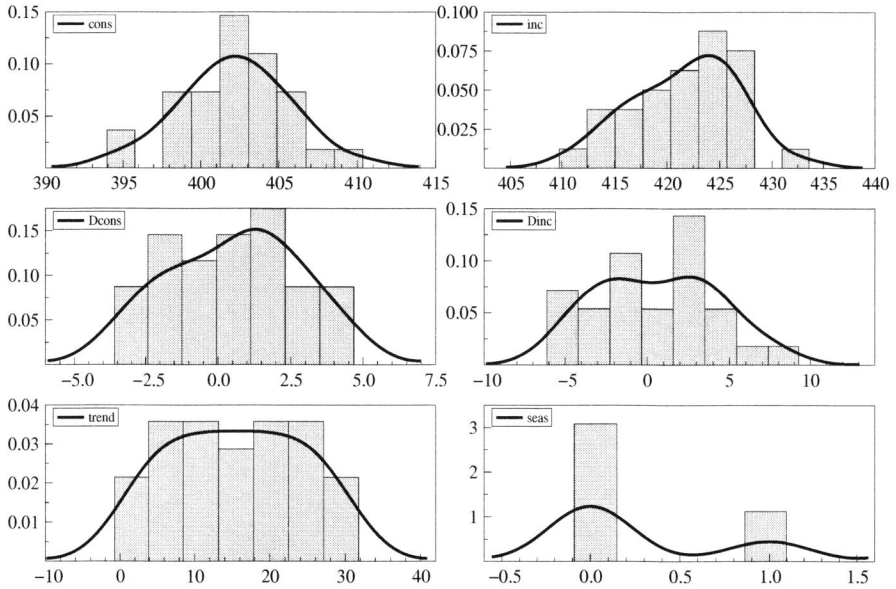

Figure 10.3   Histograms and densities for *cons* and *inc*.

The formulae for the mean and standard deviation of a sample $(x_1 \dots x_T)$ of T observations are:

$$\bar{x} = \frac{1}{T} \sum_{t=1}^{T} x_t \quad \text{and} \quad s = \sqrt{\frac{1}{T-1} \sum_{t=1}^{T} (x_t - \bar{x})^2}.$$

The sample standard deviation is sometimes denoted by $\hat{\sigma}$, where the ˆ shows that it is estimated from the data, when the population value is σ, and is often calculated by dividing by T rather than $T - 1$ (the degrees of freedom after removing the sample mean). The latter is used in OxMetrics for the Print database info option when viewing the database.

10.4 Populations, samples and shapes of distributions

Next, we relate the sample of data that was observed to the population of possible outcomes that might have occurred. We can use interpolated data densities to show the underlying shapes of the distributions (the estimated density and histogram graph type). As Figure 10.3 reveals, *cons* is unimodal and close to a normal distribution whereas $\Delta cons$ (the first difference) is nearer to a uniform distribution; *inc* and Δinc are more erratic – and the latter is nearly bimodal. The figure also shows other densities: the seasonal (called seas) is clearly bimodal, with one bump much larger than the other, and the trend is nearly uniform (can you explain these last two outcomes?).[2]

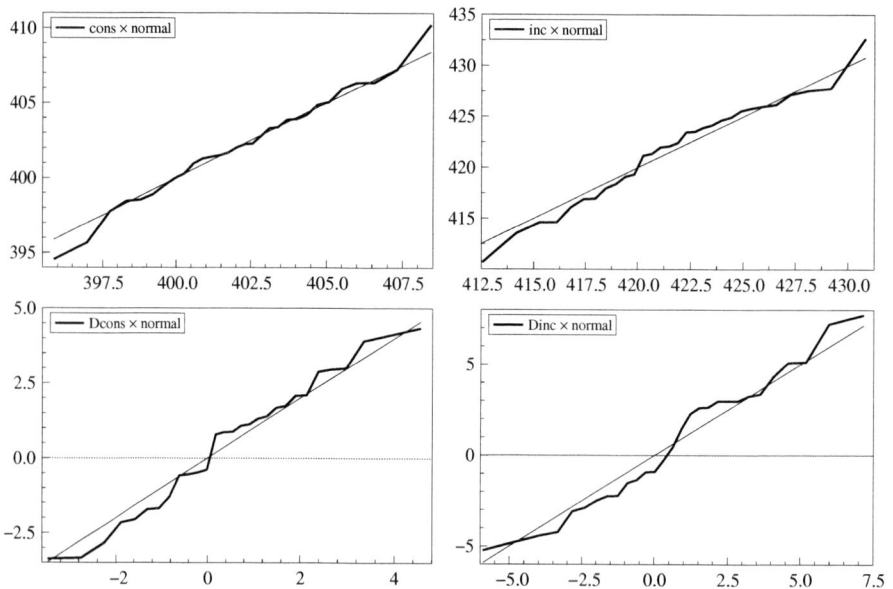

Figure 10.4   QQ plots for *cons* and *inc*.

The (cumulative) distribution function is one of the most basic concepts in probability, as it contains all the information about the probability behaviour of a random variable. Plot these for the same six variables (note that the normal is plotted automatically as well) and compare: the OxMetrics book discusses creating densities and

---

[2]To create these indicator variables in the database, use the algebra code: one = 1; trend = trend(); seas = season();. Note that they are automatically provided when estimating a model.

distributions for the standard statistical distributions. So-called QQ plots offer a picture of the closeness to normality of a variable: those in Figure 10.4 show the transformed cumulative distribution of the sample data with that for the normal (which is a straight line). There are departures in the tails, but otherwise little evidence against normality.

10.5 Correlation and scalar regression

Figure 10.1(b) highlighted the common movements in the two series first shown in Figure 10.1(a) by plotting them with a standard mean and range. There are many possible measures of co-movement, and correlation is a standardized measure of the closeness of a linear relationship, constructed to lie between -1 and $+1$. We have already computed a set of correlations above and these yielded the table shown below. All of them are positive (increases in any one series are associated with increases – rather than falls – in all of the others), and matching Figure 10.1, the correlation is higher between $\Delta cons$ and Δinc than between *cons* and *inc*. To understand the units (that is, when is a correlation high?), cross plot the pairs of variables (*cons,inc*) and ($\Delta cons, \Delta inc$), first with points, then with a line showing the correlation (four graphs in all) as in Figure 10.5.

	cons	inc	Dcons	Dinc
cons	1.0000			
inc	0.64553	1.0000		
Dcons	0.36771	0.54756	1.0000	
Dinc	0.12579	0.44095	0.76467	1.0000

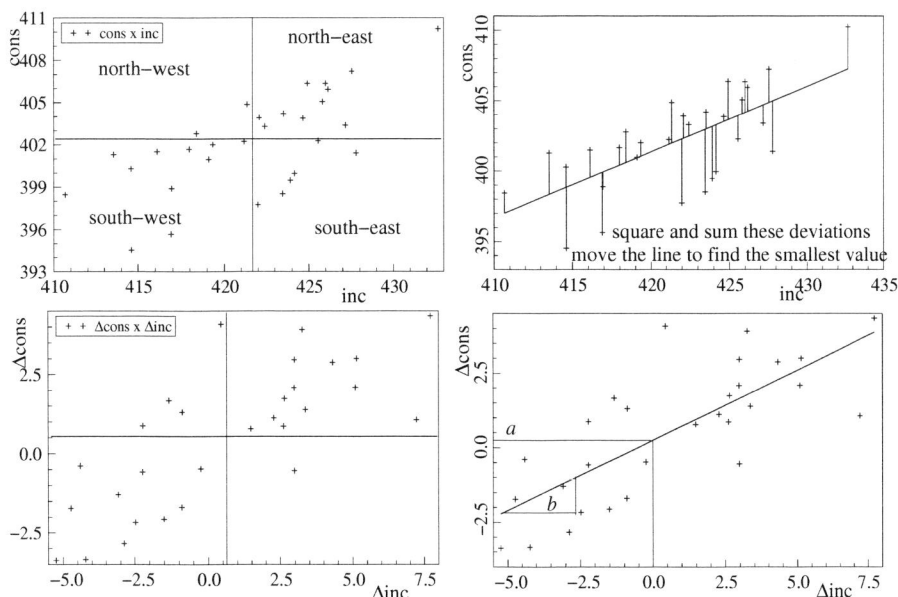

Figure 10.5   Scatter plots for *cons* and *inc*.

We have used the on-screen edit facilities to map out the region in Figure 10.5(a) into four quadrants using line drawing, placing the lines at the means of the variables (402, 422). The positive co-movement is clear from the excess of points in the north-east and south-west corners; a lack of correlation would be reflected by nearly equal numbers of points in each quadrant. Here we find the numbers of points to be:

Numbers of points for *cons, inc*

North-west	North-east
2	11
South-west	South-east
11	6

The preponderance of positively related points is clear. For ($\Delta cons, \Delta inc$) we have:

Numbers of points for $\Delta cons$, Δinc

North-west	North-east
4	13
South-west	South-east
12	1

matching the higher correlation.

The straight line shown in Figure 10.5(b) is defined by $y_t = a + bx_t$ where y_t denotes the variable on the vertical axis (*cons* here) and x_t is the variable on the horizontal axis (i.e., *inc*). The point a (called the intercept) is where the line cuts the y-axis when $x_t = 0$ (namely, 0.25), and b is the slope (measured relative to the positive direction of the x-axis). A unit change in x_t is associated with a change of b in y_t: Figure 10.5(d) illustrates. Now, the closer all the points are to the line, the higher the correlation.

A natural question concerns why the line is drawn as shown, rather than some other line. The answer is that we have picked 'the line of best fit' to the given data set. This is defined by minimizing the squared deviations of the points from the line: the vertical distances from the line are squared and summed and the values of a and b selected to minimize that sum as shown on Figure 10.5(b). We must find:

$$\min_{a,b} \sum_{t=1}^{T} (y_t - a - bx_t)^2 .$$

The values that do so are given by the famous formula:

$$\widehat{a} = \bar{y} - \widehat{b}\bar{x} \text{ and } \widehat{b} = \frac{\sum_{t=1}^{T} (y_t - \bar{y})(x_t - \bar{x})}{\sum_{t=1}^{T} (x_t - \bar{x})^2}, \tag{10.1}$$

where the ^ denotes that these are the best-fitting values, and $\bar{y}$ and $\bar{x}$ are the sample means. A value of $\widehat{b} = 0$ implies no slope, so the line is flat (that is, parallel to the horizontal axis); $\widehat{a} = 0$ forces the line through the origin.

Of course, we could have had the variables in the other order (*inc* first then *cons*) and that would have led to a different line: use the scatter plot facility to redraw the figure with both lines of best fit (the second, steeper line, defined by $x_t = c + dy_t$). The distance for the second line on the new figure is the horizontal distance, so it is no surprise that the line is somewhat different as we are minimizing a different sum of squared deviations. Indeed:

$$\widehat{c} = \bar{x} - \widehat{d}\bar{y} \text{ and } \widehat{d} = \frac{\sum_{t=1}^{T}(x_t - \bar{x})(y_t - \bar{y})}{\sum_{t=1}^{T}(y_t - \bar{y})^2}. \tag{10.2}$$

These two possible lines are closely related to the correlation coefficient, which we denote by r:

$$r = \frac{\sum_{t=1}^{T}(x_t - \bar{x})(y_t - \bar{y})}{\sqrt{\sum_{t=1}^{T}(x_t - \bar{x})^2 \sum_{t=1}^{T}(y_t - \bar{y})^2}}. \tag{10.3}$$

From (10.1) and (10.2), it can be seen that $\widehat{b}\widehat{d} = r^2$. When r = 1 (or −1) the two lines coincide; when r = 0, they are both parallel to their respective axes, so are at right angles to each other.

Using PcGive, it is easy to calculate the outcomes from fitting the line shown in the graph. The procedure is often called regression (somewhat loosely as we will see later). Access the Cross-section regression option and select *cons* as dependent (y_t) and *inc* as explanatory (x_t), leading to:

```
EQ( 1) Modelling cons by OLS (using PcgTut1.in7)
        The estimation sample is: 1986 (1) to 1993 (2)
```

	Coefficient	Std.Error	t-value	t-prob	Part.R^2
Constant	206.006	40.36	5.10	0.000	0.4820
inc	0.465140	0.09571	4.86	0.000	0.4576

sigma	2.58918	RSS	187.707974	
R^2	0.457558	F(1,28) =	23.62 [0.000]**	
log-likelihood	-27.5054	DW	0.317	
no. of observations	30	no. of parameters	2	
mean(cons)	402.148	var(cons)	11.5347	

The important information for the present is that the intercept (called Constant) is $\widehat{a} = 206$ and the slope $\widehat{b} = 0.465$. The numbers denoted Std.Error are the standard errors, or the standard deviations, of the estimated coefficients of the intercept and slope, so $\pm 2 \times 0.09571$ is an approximate 95% confidence interval around the central value $\widehat{b} = 0.4651$. The symbol R^2 is just the square of r = 0.676 and sigma (for $\widehat{\sigma}$) denotes the standard deviation of the residuals about the line, where the residuals are:

$$\widehat{u}_t = y_t - \widehat{a} - \widehat{b}x_t \text{ so } \widehat{\sigma} = \sqrt{\frac{1}{T-2}\sum_{t=1}^{T}\widehat{u}_t^2}. \tag{10.4}$$

Thus, the line is picked to yield the smallest value of $\widehat{\sigma}$. RSS denotes the residual sum of squares, namely:

$$RSS = \sum_{t=1}^{T} \widehat{u}_t^2.$$

The symbol F is a test of whether the correlation is zero, and ** denotes that it is definitely not (the probability is essentially zero of getting the value 23.62 for F when $r = 0$ – shown as [0.0000]).

The other statistics in the above results are the t-values and their probabilities, which test if the coefficients are zero by seeing if the estimated coefficient's 95% confidence interval includes zero; and the PartR^2s which are the (squared) partial correlations of each variable with the dependent variable, holding the remaining variables fixed, as explained above. When there is a lot of 'spreading' of the explanatory power between variables, the PartR^2s will be low even when the R^2 value is high: this reveals that the explanatory variables are substitutes rather than complements. Finally OLS is an acronym from ordinary least squares, which is a synonym for regression in the present context! We will return to explain the remaining information later.

The final issue is why $\widehat{a}$ and $\widehat{b}$ have standard errors or standard deviations. This happens because we view the data set as a sample from a much larger population that might have occurred. Had another sample been drawn, different values for $(\widehat{a}, \widehat{b})$ would result, and the standard errors measure how much variability might be expected on re-peated sampling from the same population. Since the data here are computer generated, it is easy to imagine drawing many other sets and plotting the distribution of the outcomes as a density like that in Figure 10.3: the standard deviation of that density is the coefficient standard error (Std.Error). Chapter 12 describes the theoretical analysis that delivers the formula for calculating the standard error: note the magic – we actually only have one sample, yet from that one sample, we can estimate how uncertain we are about the values $(\widehat{a}, \widehat{b})$ that themselves estimate the intercept and slope of the line in the population.

10.6 Interdependence

The concept of economic interdependence has already been illustrated by computing the matrix of correlations between all of the variables. In many economic data sets, all the correlations will be positive and many will exceed 0.9. This salient data feature is discussed below: it raises obvious dangers of confusing 'genuine' correlations between variables that really are connected with those that arise from the gradual evolution of the whole economy. The correlations are smaller for the changes in the variables, and this aspect will recur below as well. The formula in (10.3) explains part of the story, writing r as:

$$r = \frac{C(x_t, y_t)}{s(x_t)\, s(y_t)} \quad \text{where} \quad C(x_t, y_t) = \frac{1}{T-1} \sum_{t=1}^{T} (x_t - \bar{x})(y_t - \bar{y}). \tag{10.5}$$

$C(x_t, y_t)$ is called the covariance of x_t with y_t. Thus, the correlation coefficient is the ratio of the covariance to the product of the two variables' standard deviations. We know from above that the standard deviations are smaller after differencing; the covariances are as well, but fall by proportionately more owing to removing the 'common' trends and cycles from the data. However, correlations could also increase on differencing if (say) a trend masked opposite sign short-run correlations (see, for example, Hooker, 1901; this is a long-standing issue!).

10.7 Time dependence

Correlations (or dependencies) between successive values of the same variable often occur in economic time series. These are called serial (or auto) correlations. From Figure 10.1, when *cons* was high, the next value was also high, and when low, so was the next value. In general, we denote the current value of a variable by y_t and its previous (or lagged) value by y_{t-1}. The difference is then $\Delta y_t = y_t - y_{t-1}$.

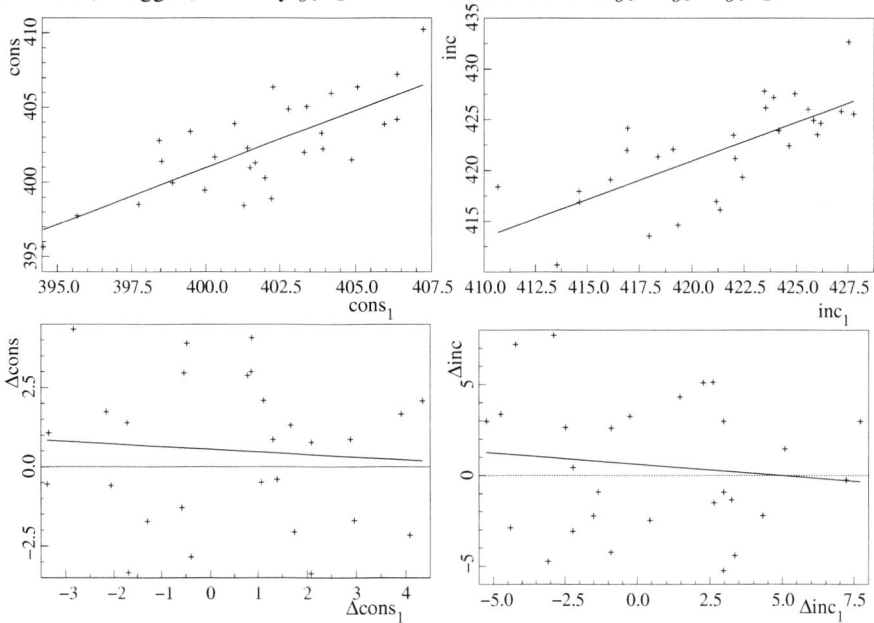

Figure 10.6   Lagged scatter plots for *cons* and *inc*.

Figure 10.1 also revealed that $\Delta cons$ jumped around considerably: high values were not followed by other high values very often. By simple algebra, when Δy_t is independent over time (so is not related to Δy_{t-1}), then $y_t \simeq y_{t-1}$ and hence y_t is serially correlated.

A useful way to see time dependence is to cross plot y_t against y_{t-1}, and Δy_t against Δy_{t-1} with a least-squares line (as in Figure 10.6). You may need to create the lagged values using the calculator (shown as $cons_1$ etc.). It is clear that *cons* and *inc* are both highly correlated with their own lagged values (Figure 10.6(a) and 10.6(b)), whereas $\Delta cons$ and Δinc are nearly unrelated (horizontal regression lines).

This idea can be generalized to two-period relations, namely the correlation of y_t with y_{t-2}. To summarize all such correlations at once, we plot a correlogram (or auto-correlation function, ACF) with the correlations $r_j = \text{corr}(y_t, y_{t-j})$ on the vertical axis and j on the horizontal, illustrated for four terms ($j = 1, \ldots, 4$) in Figure 10.7. This idea relates back to the salient feature of serial dependence of the time-series graphs of the variables in Figure 10.1, and provides a quantitative measurement of that aspect. Here, the correlograms for *cons* and *inc* have several large positive terms, whereas those for $\Delta cons$ and Δinc are nearly zero at all lags. The values of r_1 reflect the slopes of the plots in Figure 10.6. The horizontal dashed lines are $r_j \pm 2SE$ for the estimated autocorrelations, assuming the population value is zero: thus r_1 is unlikely to be zero for *cons* and *inc*.

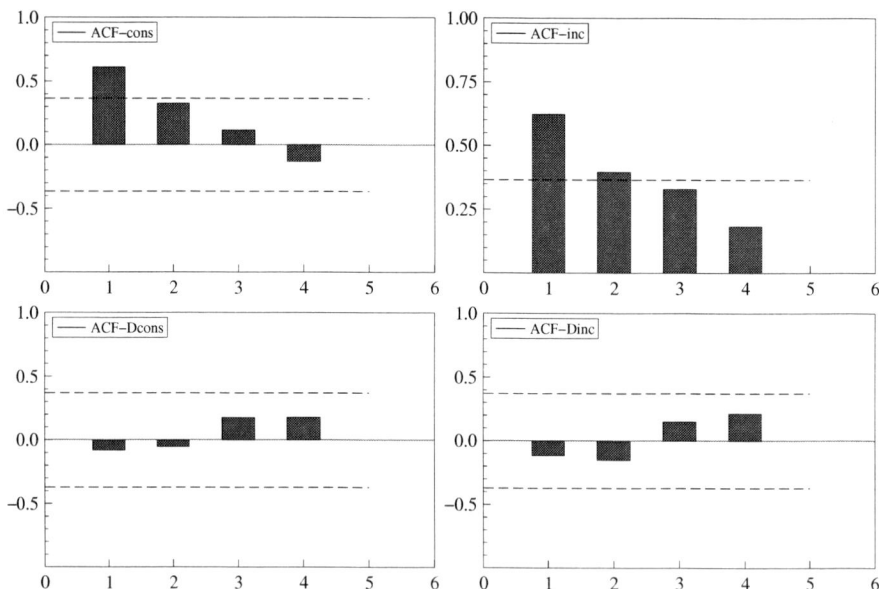

Figure 10.7   Correlograms for *cons* and *inc*.

We are in fact implicitly using regression, and can compute the slope coefficient for y_t on y_{t-1}, called a first-order autoregression ('regression on itself'), using that method. Select the Single-equation dynamic modelling option for *cons*, choose one lag, and accept to obtain (the last three lines are omitted):

```
EQ( 2) Modelling cons by OLS (using PcgTut1.in7)
        The estimation sample is: 1986 (2) to 1993 (2)

              Coefficient  Std.Error  t-value  t-prob Part.R^2
cons_1           0.764263     0.1282     5.96   0.000   0.5684
Constant         95.2765      51.51      1.85   0.075   0.1125

sigma             2.13872  RSS                123.501614
R^2               0.568417  F(1,27) =    35.56 [0.000]**
```

By now the statistics should be becoming more familiar: the intercept is 95.28 and the slope (i.e., the autoregressive coefficient) is 0.7643 which is approximately equal to the autocorrelation of $r_1 = 0.754$ (i.e., the square root of R^2). The value of r_1 is, therefore, just that of the correlation coefficient calculated as in (10.3) for *cons* and *cons*$_1$, and shows the slope of the regression line in the graph of that variable against its lagged value. Try to prove these connections for a first-order autoregression.

Returning to the correlogram $\{r_j\}$, a new idea occurs: we know corr (y_t, y_{t-1}) and corr (y_t, y_{t-2}) but part of each of these may be owing to the other – can we sort out the 'net' contributions of the one and two period lags? One notion might be to use the residuals from the first-order autoregression and correlate these with y_{t-2}; this approach gets close, but on reflection, you can probably see that it takes out too much of y_{t-1} at the first step (that is, it also takes out the bit of y_{t-2} in y_{t-1}). We believe the easiest way to understand the notion is to fit the regression of y_t on both y_{t-1} and y_{t-2} which is simple to perform in PcGive. Select the Single-equation dynamic modelling option for *cons* again but this time choose two lags and accept to obtain:

```
EQ( 3) Modelling cons by OLS (using PcgTut1.in7)
        The estimation sample is: 1986 (3) to 1993 (2)

              Coefficient  Std.Error  t-value  t-prob Part.R^2
cons_1           0.747621     0.2129     3.51   0.002   0.3304
cons_2          -0.0295917    0.2015    -0.147   0.884   0.0009
Constant         113.896      62.50      1.82   0.080   0.1173

sigma             2.20625  RSS                121.688116
R^2               0.490759  F(2,25) =    12.05 [0.000]**
```

The first slope coefficient is almost the same as that obtained when y_{t-1} alone was used, and consistent with that, the second is close to zero. We learn that most of corr (y_t, y_{t-2}) is due to the effect of y_{t-1}, and no 'net' 2-period lag operates. This is important in understanding the pattern we observed in the correlogram. The generalization we have developed is called the partial autocorrelation. The first slope coefficient shows the change in y_t from a change in y_{t-1} when y_{t-2} does not change: the second slope coefficient shows the change in y_t from a change in y_{t-2} when y_{t-1} does not change. Each shows the net effect of its variable – together they show the total effect. A great advantage of regression methods is this ease of generalization to any number of variables, where each coefficient measures the effects on the dependent variable of changing that explanatory variable when all other variables are held fixed. Chapter 12 describes the necessary algebra.

10.8 Dummy variables

Dummy variables are artificial creations with their non-zero values determined by us, rather than by nature. They are often called indicator variables as they indicate the presence of some state. We have already met three, namely the Constant, Trend and Seasonal (where the first does not vary, so indicates the constant state!). The Seasonal indicator variable (for non-annual data) is automatically created by PcGive to be unity in the first period of the year and zero elsewhere. PcGive only needs one seasonal from which the remaining seasonals for other periods are created by lagging: Seasonal_2 is Seasonal two periods lagged, and so has a unity in the third period of each year. Using the calculator or algebra, other dummies are easily created in a variety of forms for impulse effects (a 'blip' which is zero except for perhaps a couple of quarters where it is unity, often called a zero-one dummy); and step changes where the dummy is zero until a certain date and unity thereafter. Note that the scale of measurement of a dummy is ordinal ('on' differs from 'off') in that the 'on' effect can bear any relation to the 'off'. It is dangerous to create a dummy which takes three or more values (for example, some zeros, some unities and some twos) unless you are *certain* that the effect of the third is twice that of the second. However, we will do just that – for a specific purpose. Use the algebra to create the variable qrtr=period(); and using scatter plot, graph *cons*, *inc* and qrtr (after Next choose graph, select two series by a third). The figure will show the points as 1,2,3,4 depending on the quarter of the year, so the relation of *cons* to *inc* in each quarter can be viewed. For the present data, the picture in Figure 10.8a is not too informative, but see Davidson, Hendry, Srba and Yeo (1978) for a clearer example.

Next, graph *cons* and the trend over time, match for mean and range; then also cross plot them with the points joined; finally cross-plot them again, and insert a regression line as in Figure 10.8. The first cross plot (Figure 10.8c) shows precisely the time-series plot of *cons*; whereas the second cross plot shows the best-fitting trend line, which clearly differs from that obtained by just matching means and ranges (which is almost inevitably too steep).

Finally, note that a complete set of indicator variables is never needed (for example, a dummy for 'on' and a second dummy for 'off') and is said to be perfectly collinear. Try to compute a regression of *cons* on the quarterly seasonal with three lags: contrast the outcome with what happens when you use only two lags, where a constant is always included.

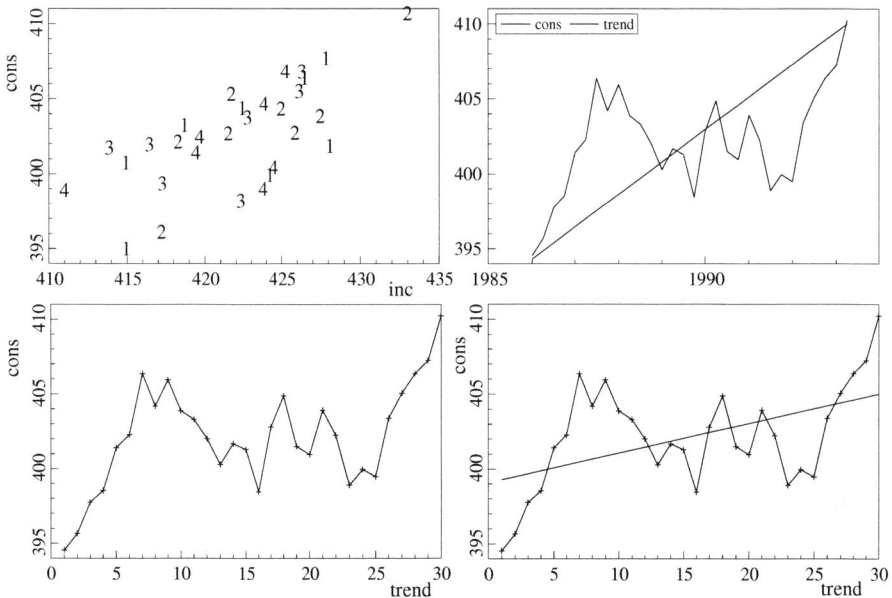

Figure 10.8 Relating time series and cross-plots using dummy variables.

10.9 Sample variability

Histograms and densities showed the data variability; this section focuses on the variability in the sample statistics. Use the zoom sample check box to cross plot *cons* against *inc* with a single regression line for the first half of the data only (to 1989(3)), then for the second half only. Now redo the cross plot for the whole sample period twice, but first fit two sequential lines then two recursive lines. The outcome is shown in Figure 10.9. The regression lines for the two subsamples clearly differ in slope and intercept, as Figure 10.9c makes clear (compute these numerically using the Single-equation dynamic modelling option to check). Nevertheless, as Figure 10.9d reveals, the first sample line is close to that obtained for the whole period.

Try fitting a number of sequential lines (four, for example) and consider the outcome, perhaps using several trend lines, to show growth-rate changes. This exercise should clarify the need to report coefficient standard errors.

10.10 Collinearity

Perfect linear dependence was shown in §10.8 above; this item relates to 'near linear dependence' between regressors – a more rigorous analysis is provided in §14.1. We introduced multiple regression above using the example of partial autocorrelation, and now use a finite distributed lag to show the effects of adding x_{t-1} to the regression of

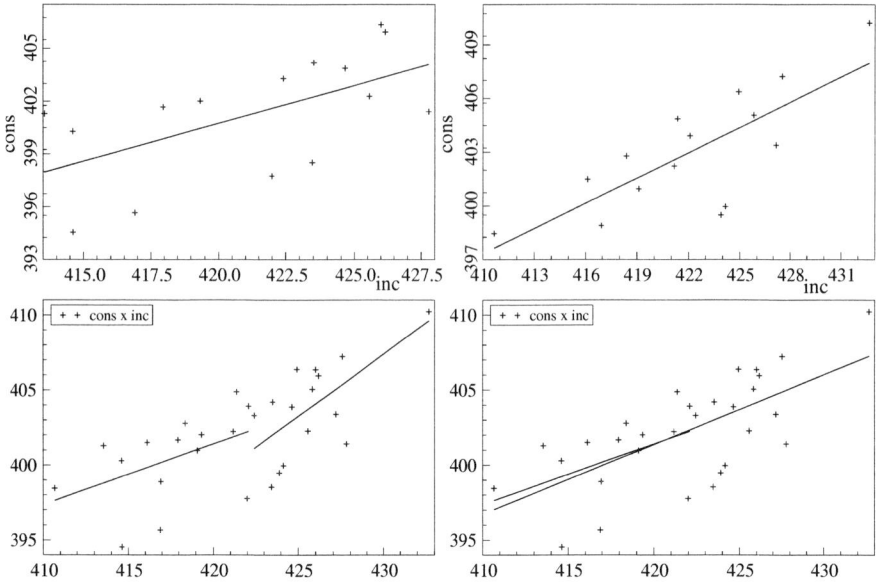

Figure 10.9   Changing regression lines.

y_t on x_t. This is called a distributed lag model because the lag coefficients on x show the distribution of the response of y over time (and when they are all positive, the coefficients can be normalized to add to unity, and hence are like a probability distribution). When x_t is highly autoregressive, a large increase in coefficient uncertainty usually results as the 'explanation' of y_t gets spread between x_t and x_{t-1} rather than concentrated on the former. Choose *cons* for y_t and *inc* for x_t and use the Single-equation dynamic modelling option with one lag on *inc* to produce:

```
EQ( 4) Modelling cons by OLS (using PcgTut1.in7)
        The estimation sample is: 1986 (2) to 1993 (2)

                 Coefficient  Std.Error  t-value  t-prob Part.R^2
Constant             202.060      44.39     4.55   0.000   0.4435
inc                 0.301206     0.1352     2.23   0.035   0.1602
inc_1               0.173896     0.1432     1.21   0.235   0.0537

sigma                2.46474  RSS                157.948781
R^2                 0.448039  F(2,26) =      10.55 [0.000]**
```

The standard error of the coefficient of x_t has increased by over 40% from the simple regression: this effect is often called collinearity, and is viewed as deriving from the high correlation between x_t and x_{t-1} when both are used to explain y_t.

At a somewhat more advanced level, instead of x_{t-1}, add Δx_t to the regression of y_t on x_t and consider the new output:

```
EQ( 5) Modelling cons by OLS (using PcgTut1.in7)
        The estimation sample is: 1986 (2) to 1993 (2)

                 Coefficient  Std.Error  t-value  t-prob Part.R^2
Constant             202.060      44.39     4.55   0.000   0.4435
inc                 0.475102     0.1053     4.51   0.000   0.4392
Dinc               -0.173896     0.1432    -1.21   0.235   0.0537

sigma                2.46474  RSS                 157.948781
R^2                 0.448039  F(2,26) =       10.55 [0.000]**
```

A glance establishes that all the regression statistics R^2, s, F etc. are identical to the earlier distributed lag estimates, and apart from the sign, so is the coefficient and standard error of Δinc. Only the coefficient and standard error of inc have altered (the former to the sum of the coefficients in the distributed lag), both close to those found in the simple regression of $cons$ on inc. In fact, these last two models are actually equivalent, as is easily seen algebraically:

$$d_1 x_t + d_2 x_{t-1} \equiv (d_1 + d_2) x_t - d_2 (x_t - x_{t-1}).$$

The differences in the standard errors between the two equivalent parametrizations are owing to the relatively low correlation between x_t and Δx_t, which must happen when x_t and x_{t-1} are highly correlated. This highlights the advantages of orthogonal parametrizations (ones where explanatory variables are not correlated) where these are feasible.

An alternative way to create collinearity is to add y_{t-1} to the regression of y_t on x_t; again use $cons$ and inc to obtain:

```
EQ( 6) Modelling cons by OLS (using PcgTut1.in7)
        The estimation sample is: 1986 (2) to 1993 (2)

                 Coefficient  Std.Error  t-value  t-prob Part.R^2
cons_1              0.634611    0.09665     6.57   0.000   0.6238
Constant             16.5568      40.59    0.408   0.687   0.0064
inc                 0.310060    0.06184     5.01   0.000   0.4916

sigma                1.55403  RSS                  62.7904156
R^2                 0.780575  F(2,26) =       46.25 [0.000]**
```

This time, despite the correlation between the explanatory variables, there is almost no increase in the standard error of the coefficient of inc (in fact $cons$ lagged and inc are only correlated 0.27). Notice the counterbalancing effects of the improvement in fit from the added variable against its interrelation with the previously-included variable. Contrast the outcomes in this section with those found from (say) regressing Δy_t on Δx_t (or that with Δy_{t-1} added).

10.11 Nonsense regressions

Even at an elementary level, a critical appreciation of econometric evidence is essential, especially for time-series econometrics. The issue of invalidly 'inferring causes from correlations' must be discussed: high (low) correlations do not by themselves confirm (refute) causal links. Rather, theory-models with well-defined causality links can be tested from data by checking on the presence and/or absence of certain correlations predicted by those models. Models which fail must be rejected, or at a minimum revised; models that are not rejected are consistent with the theory. This is a deductive exercise. Rigorously-tested, yet acceptable, models are then used in later analytical work, but causes are never inferred from correlations.

The most extreme cases of misleading correlations arise in what is known as the nonsense regressions problem. From an early date, economists discovered high correlations between what ought to be unrelated time-series variables and puzzled over these (for example, a high positive correlation between the murder rate and membership of the Church of England!: an early analysis is Yule, 1926, so again this is a long-standing issue). We have regularly challenged our econometrics classes to select any two variables from a large data set (being careful to exclude dummies other than constant and trend), and guarantee to produce a correlation of over 0.95 between the two chosen variables after at most one transformation on each variable selected. If the variables are trend free, we use the option to integrate (or cumulate) the two series chosen; otherwise we take the (trending) series as selected. Now a cross plot, or even a time-series graph with the ranges matched, shows the obviously high correlation, which can be confirmed using the Descriptive statistics calculations. A similar effect is achievable by adding trends to both series. In economics, one is unlikely to lose this challenge.

The underlying statistical problem was analyzed by Yule (1926) arising from either:

(1) integrated, but mutually-independent, time series (*nonsense regressions*); or
(2) variables depending on common third factors (*spurious regressions*).

In the former, the high level of serial correlation in each series individually is sufficient to ensure that it is highly correlated with other similarly integrated series; §11.2 presents the relevant concepts. Hendry and Morgan (1995) trace the history of the analysis.[3] The latter is more obvious, especially when both variables depend on a linear trend. Econometrics is a powerful body of knowledge precisely because one can (for example) predictably create nonsense regressions outcomes, as in Hendry (1980). Already we have moved towards an intermediate level where we can apply PcGive to a further range of topics. An exciting route lies ahead if you pursue the subject to a more advanced level where you will learn how to detect, and hence counter, such problems (see e.g. Hendry, 1995a). This requires an investment in some econometric theory to understand both the problems and their solutions, and Ch. 12 addresses that need.

---

[3] All the historical data sets used in their study, and that in Hendry (1995a) can be downloaded in PcGive format from the web: `www.nuff.ox.ac.uk/users/hendry`.

Chapter 11

Intermediate Econometrics

11.1 Introduction

The level envisaged in this chapter corresponds to a course involving *inter alia*, the properties of dynamic models, an introduction to unit roots and cointegration, model types (see §11.2–§11.4), interpreting linear equations (§11.5), multiple regression (§11.6, which builds on the algebra in Chapter 12), time-series concepts (§11.6.5), instrumental-variables estimation (§11.8), and inference and diagnostic testing (§11.9), leading on to model selection issues (§11.10).[1] Throughout, the econometric theory is to be illustrated by empirical applications which seek to highlight and explain how to resolve some of the central problems of econometrics. As might be anticipated in a book on a computer program, our emphasis is on practical procedures and solutions. Chapter 14 is devoted to an analysis of the last of these; this section concentrates on the other aspects. In fact, at an intermediate level where formal proofs are usually possible only for restrictive special cases (such as fixed regressors), Monte Carlo is almost certainly a better adjunct to theory derivations than empirical examples.[2] Nevertheless, an easy-to-use regression package also has an important role for illustrating concepts, methods and problems. To reiterate an earlier point, the discussion herein is intended to complement, and not substitute for, formal derivations of estimators, tests and their distributions. Chapter 12 provides the necessary background statistical material; an introduction to the basic notion of fitting by least squares was provided in the previous chapter.

---

[1] PcGive also provides multiple-equation software for empirically analyzing linear dynamic systems, but the estimation and identification of simultaneous equations systems and vector autoregressions, including cointegration, as well as forecasting, are all considered in Volume II: see Doornik and Hendry (2006a).

[2] PcNaive was released in 1991 as a Monte Carlo program specifically oriented to teaching econometrics: see Hendry and Neale (1987), and Hendry, Neale and Ericsson (1991). A Windows module is now available which writes the Ox code for a wide range of Monte Carlo programs, which additionally can be modified by users.

11.2 Linear dynamic equations

This section describes the forms of linear dynamic single equation models that occur frequently in time-series econometrics. A typology of possible equation forms is then analyzed in §11.4. Chapter 13 briefly generalizes the analysis to dynamic systems. First, however, we need to introduce the idea of stationarity.

11.2.1 Stationarity and non-stationarity

A variable y_t is said to be weakly stationary if its first two moments are finite and constant over time, and its correlogram $\{r_s\}$ is finite and independent of t for all s. We denote the expected value of y_t by $\mathsf{E}[y_t]$ and its second moment by $\mathsf{E}[y_t^2]$, so these must both be constant as a necessary condition to satisfy stationarity; otherwise the process is non-stationary.

There are many reasons why economics variables (like inflation, income etc.) may not be stationary (technical progress; policy regime changes etc.), which is bound to make it difficult to model their behaviour, since their means and variances may change from period to period. Thus, much econometric theory has assumed stationarity. If that is not a realistic characterization of economic data, then any resulting empirical analyses must be hazardous.

Consequently, recent effort has been devoted to developing models applicable to non-stationary data: a recent discussion is Hendry and Juselius (2000). The analysis below allows for some forms of non-stationarity, which we believe can be treated in an intermediate-level course. Notice that the final section of the previous chapter concerned one pernicious consequence of analyzing non-stationary processes as if they were stationary.

11.2.2 Lag polynomials

The class of models basic to PcGive is that of linear dynamic equations. The analysis of these follows from the use of a lag operator (denoted by L) such that $L^r x_t = x_{t-r}$ for any variable x_t. Notice that a difference, such as $\Delta y_t = y_t - y_{t-1}$, becomes $(1 - L) y_t$. More generally, scalar polynomials in L are denoted by:

$$d(L) = d_m L^m + d_{m+1} L^{m+1} + \cdots + d_r L^r = \sum_{r=m}^{n} d_r L^r,$$

where $d_m = 1$ is often imposed to normalize the polynomial. Usually, $m = 0$ and $n \geq 1$, and we assume that in the following, with $d_0 = 1$. The sum of the coefficients is important and is denoted by $d(1)$:

$$d(1) = \left(\sum_{r=0}^{n} d_r L^r \right)_{\rfloor L=1} = \sum_{r=0}^{n} d_r.$$

Using the sum, the polynomial can be rewritten as (using $n = 2$ to illustrate, and minimize the algebra):

$$
\begin{aligned}
d_0 + d_1 L + d_2 L^2 &= (d_0 + d_1 + d_2) - d_1 (1 - L) - d_2 (1 - L)(1 + L) \\
&= d(1) - d^*(L)(1 - L),
\end{aligned}
$$

where:

$$
d^*(L) = (d_1 + d_2) + d_2 L.
$$

In general, we can always write:

$$
d(L) = d(1) - d^*(L)\Delta \tag{11.1}
$$

which will prove important below.

Returning to dynamic models, the impact of $d(L)$ on x_t is given by:

$$
d(L) x_t = \sum_{r=0}^{n} d_r L^r x_t = \sum_{r=0}^{n} d_r x_{t-r}.
$$

Lag polynomials like $d(L)$ define autoregressions when the equation is of the form:

$$
a(L) y_t = \sum_{r=0}^{n} a_r y_{t-r} = \epsilon_t \tag{11.2}
$$

and ϵ_t is a serially-uncorrelated error (that is, white noise), often taken to be normal and independently distributed, with mean zero and constant variance:

$$
\epsilon_t \sim \text{IN}\left[0, \sigma_\epsilon^2\right].
$$

Alternatively, $d(L)$ defines a finite distributed lag when the model has the form:

$$
y_t = b(L) x_t + \epsilon_t = \sum_{r=0}^{p} b_r x_{t-r} + \epsilon_t. \tag{11.3}
$$

The autoregressive-distributed lag (ADL) class is given by:

$$
c(L) y_t = b(L) x_t + \epsilon_t \quad \text{or} \quad \sum_{j=0}^{n} c_j y_{t-j} = \sum_{r=0}^{p} b_r x_{t-r} + \epsilon_t. \tag{11.4}
$$

Many different xs may be used conjointly if required in models like (11.4), in which case the equation is written in a more convenient notation as:

$$
b_0(L) y_t = \sum_{i=1}^{k} b_i(L) x_{it} + \epsilon_t \tag{11.5}
$$

when there are k explanatory variables $(x_{1,t} \ldots x_{k,t})$. Of course, each $x_{i,t}$ will also exhibit some autoregressive behaviour in general.

11.2.2.1 Roots of lag polynomials

Many important properties of the dynamic model (11.4) are determined by the polynomials $a(L)$, $b(L)$ and $c(L)$. First, any polynomial of degree n has n (real or complex) roots λ_i, and can be expressed as the product of its roots:

$$d(L) = \sum_{r=0}^{n} d_r L^r = \prod_{i=1}^{n} (1 - \lambda_i L). \tag{11.6}$$

An important consequence of (11.6) is that:

$$d(1) = \prod_{i=1}^{n} (1 - \lambda_i). \tag{11.7}$$

The values of the roots determine the dynamic properties of the variables. For example, the model in (11.4) is a stable dynamic process if all the roots λ_i of the polynomial $c(L)$ satisfy $|\lambda_i| < 1$ (PcGive will calculate these roots).[3] Equally, the process in (11.2) is weakly stationary when all $|\lambda_i| < 1$ for $a(L)$. However, if in (11.2), a root of $a(L)$ is equal to unity, then from (11.7) $a(1) = 0$ so $a(L) = a^*(L)\Delta$, so that:

$$a(L)y_t = a^*(L)\Delta y_t = \epsilon_t,$$

and the first difference of y_t is weakly stationary. Thus, y_t itself is non-stationary, and is said to be integrated of order 1, denoted I (1), as it needs to be differenced to remove the unit root and become weakly stationary.[4] We now have one case where a process is non-stationary, but can be reduced to stationarity (here, by differencing).

11.2.2.2 Long-run solutions

Another important property, most relevant for $c(L)$ in (11.4), is when $c(1) \neq 0$, in which case it is possible to solve for the long-run outcome of the process. From (11.4):

$$c(L)y_t - b(L)x_t = \epsilon_t,$$

so that, using (11.1):

$$c(1)y_t - b(1)x_t = c^*(L)\Delta y_t - b^*(L)\Delta x_t + \epsilon_t. \tag{11.8}$$

When both Δy_t and Δx_t are stationarity, then $\mathsf{E}[\Delta y_t] = \mu_y$ and $\mathsf{E}[\Delta x_t] = \mu_x$ will be constant over time. Thus, if we take the expectation of both sides of (11.8):

$$\mathsf{E}[c(1)y_t - b(1)x_t] = \mathsf{E}[c^*(L)\Delta y_t - b^*(L)\Delta x_t + \epsilon_t] = c^*(1)\mu_y - b^*(1)\mu_x = K_0,$$

---

[3]The actual roots of $a(L) = 0$ are the inverse of the $\{\lambda_i\}$, and the term root here is a shorthand for eigenroot, where $a(L)$ is viewed as a scalar matrix polynomial, for consistency with eigenroots of dynamic systems below.

[4]If r roots of $a(L)$ are equal to unity in absolute value, then y_t is said to be integrated of order r, denoted I (r), as it needs to be differenced r times to remove the unit roots.

or:

$$E\left[y_t - \frac{b(1)}{c(1)}x_t - K_0\right] = E\left[y_t - K_1 x_t - K_0\right] = 0. \tag{11.9}$$

Then (11.9) is the long-run average solution to (11.4). Clearly, (11.9) requires that $c(1) \neq 0$ in order to be well defined, and $b(1) \neq 0$ to be non-trivial. In particular, when (y_t, x_t) are jointly weakly stationarity, then we can also write (11.9) as:

$$E[y_t] = K_0 + K_1 E[x_t]. \tag{11.10}$$

If $c(1) \neq 0$ and $b(1) \neq 0$ in (11.4) when y_t and x_t are both I(1), yet $\{y_t - K_1 x_t - K_0\}$ is I(0), then y_t and x_t are said to be cointegrated (the literature is vast: see *inter alia,* Engle and Granger, 1987, Granger, 1986, Hendry, 1986b, Banerjee and Hendry, 1992a, Banerjee, Dolado, Galbraith and Hendry, 1993, Hendry, 1995a, and Johansen, 1995): section 11.3 provides greater detail. Thus, cointegration is the property that linear combinations of variables also remove the unit roots. The solution in (11.9) remains valid in the cointegrated case. Section 11.4 assumes that x_t is I(1) and that y_t and x_t are cointegrated. Empirical evidence suggests that many economic time series are better regarded as integrated process than as stationary.

11.2.2.3 Common factors

Thirdly, (11.4) has common factors (denoted COMFAC) if some of the roots of $c(L)$ coincide with roots of $b(L)$. For example, when:

$$c(L) = (1 - \rho L)c^*(L) = \rho(L)c^*(L),$$

and at the same time:

$$b(L) = \rho(L)b^*(L),$$

then (11.5) can be written as:

$$\rho(L)c^*(L)y_t = \rho(L)b^*(L)x_t + \epsilon_t,$$

or dividing both sides by $\rho(L)$:

$$c^*(L)y_t = b^*(L)x_t + u_t \quad \text{where} \quad u_t = \rho u_{t-1} + \epsilon_t. \tag{11.11}$$

The error $\{u_t\}$ is, therefore, an autoregressive process, and is generated from the common factor in the original lag polynomials $c(L)$ and $b(L)$ (see Sargan, 1980b, and §11.4.7).

11.3 Cointegration

Once it is granted that economic time-series data are usually non-stationary, five issues arise:

(1) how important is the assumption of stationarity for modelling and inference?
(2) what are the effects of incorrectly assuming stationarity?
(3) what are the sources of non-stationarity?
(4) can the analysis be transformed back to one where stationarity is a valid assumption?
(5) if not, with what assumptions do we replace stationarity?

Essentially, the answers are 'very'; 'potentially hazardous'; 'many and varied'; 'sometimes, but it depends on the source of non-stationarity'; and 'several possibilities'. We expand on all of these below.

The issue in 1. was described under the heading of nonsense regressions in the previous chapter: the absence of stationarity can be crucially important in some settings, but matters less in others.

To answer 2., consider the following two simple random-walk processes:

$$\Delta y_t = \epsilon_t \text{ where } \epsilon_t \sim \text{IN}\left[0, \sigma_\epsilon^2\right] \tag{11.12}$$

$$\Delta x_t = \nu_t \text{ where } \nu_t \sim \text{IN}\left[0, \sigma_\nu^2\right] \tag{11.13}$$

setting $y_0 = 0$, $x_0 = 0$, with:

$$\mathsf{E}\left[\epsilon_t \nu_s\right] = 0 \,\forall t, s. \tag{11.14}$$

An economic equation of interest linking y_t and z_t is postulated to be:

$$y_t = \beta_0 + \beta_1 x_t + u_t \tag{11.15}$$

where β_1 is to represent the derivative of y_t with respect to z_t, namely:

$$\frac{\partial y_t}{\partial x_t} = \beta_1.$$

When estimated by OLS, equations like (11.15) implicitly assume $\{u_t\}$ is an IID process independent of x_t. A t-test of $\mathsf{H}_0: \beta_1 = 0$, namely dividing the estimated coefficient by the standard error:

$$t_{\beta_1=0} = \frac{\widehat{\beta}_1}{\text{SE}\left[\widehat{\beta}_1\right]} \tag{11.16}$$

where:

$$\widehat{\beta}_1 = \left(\sum_{t=1}^{T} x_t^2\right)^{-1} \sum_{t=1}^{T} x_t y_t, \tag{11.17}$$

is usually assumed to satisfy:

$$\mathsf{P}\left(\left|t_{\beta_1=0}\right| \geq 2.0 \mid \mathsf{H}_0\right) = 0.05. \tag{11.18}$$

In fact, serious over-rejection occurs using (11.18) with the conventional critical value of 2.

Why does such a large distortion occur? First, because β_1 is zero, then the model implies that $u_t = y_t$: but from (11.12), y_t has a unit root, so u_t exhibits dramatic serial correlation: this downwards biases the *estimated* standard error of $\widehat{\beta}_1$, $\mathrm{SE}[\widehat{\beta}_1]$, which is the denominator in (11.16). Secondly, and partly offsetting the first problem, $\widehat{\beta}_1$ is an unbiased estimator of β_1, so $\mathrm{E}[\widehat{\beta}_1] = 0$, since the z_t process is strongly exogenous, and can be taken as given, despite its non-stationary characteristics. Thus, 'on average' the numerator is zero. Thirdly, the non-stationarity induced by cumulating past errors causes the second moments of the data to grow much faster than in a stationary process (which grows at the sample size T). Instead, the processes in (11.28) and (11.29) grow at a rate proportional to T^2, since at each point:

$$y_t = \sum_{j=1}^{t} \epsilon_j$$

Consequently, one might expect $\mathrm{SE}[\widehat{\beta}_1]$ to decline very rapidly, because:

$$\mathrm{SE}\left[\widehat{\beta}_1\right] = \frac{\widehat{\sigma}_u}{\sqrt{\sum x_t^2}} = T^{-1} \frac{\widehat{\sigma}_u}{\sqrt{T^{-2} \sum x_t^2}},$$

where the denominator is now 'well behaved'. Unfortunately, the error variance is simultaneously rapidly increasing in T. If we ignore the effect of estimating β_1 and set $\widehat{u}_t = u_t$, then:

$$\widehat{\sigma}_u^2 = \frac{1}{T-2} \sum_{t=1}^{T} u_t^2 \simeq T \left(T^{-2} \sum_{t=1}^{T} u_t^2 \right).$$

Thus, $\mathrm{SE}[\widehat{\beta}_1]$ in fact decreases as $1/\sqrt{T}$ and so:

$$\mathrm{t}_{\beta_1=0} = \frac{\widehat{\beta}_1}{\mathrm{SE}\left[\widehat{\beta}_1\right]} \simeq \sqrt{T}\widehat{\beta}_1.$$

The dispersion of $\widehat{\beta}_1$ is huge: its actual variance $\mathrm{V}[\widehat{\beta}_1]$ is extremely large, so although the distribution is symmetric around zero, big positive and negative values both occur, inducing many big t-values.

The importance of this result is twofold:

(i) Although $\beta_1 = 0$, $\mathrm{t}_{\beta_1=0}$ diverges to infinity as T increases, and requires to be standardized by $1/\sqrt{T}$ to yield a well-behaved limiting distribution;

(ii) The resulting limiting distribution is non-standard, so that conventionally-calculated critical values are incorrect, even for the standardized distribution of $\mathrm{t}_{\beta_1=0}/\sqrt{T}$.

Consequently, processes with unit roots cannot be treated 'as if' they were stationary.

Concerning 3., there are many possible sources of non-stationarity, of which unit roots are just one. Non-stationarity seems endemic in economic life: legislative change is one obvious source of non-stationarity, often inducing structural breaks in time series, but it is far from the only one. We now consider a simple case where economic behaviour might induce a root (see Hendry and Juselius, 2000). If changes to long-run interest rates (R_l) were predictable, and $R_l > R_s$ (the short-term rate) – as usually holds, to compensate lenders for tying up their money – one could create a money machine. Just predict the forthcoming change in R_l, and borrow at R_s to buy bonds if you expect a fall in R_l (a rise in bond prices) or sell short if R_l is likely to rise. Such a scenario seems unlikely, so, we anticipate $E[\Delta R_{l,t}|\mathcal{I}_{t-1}] = 0$. As a model, this translates into:

$$R_{l,t} = R_{l,t-1} + \epsilon_t \tag{11.19}$$

where $E[\epsilon_t|\mathcal{I}_{t-1}] = 0$. The model in (11.19) has a unit coefficient on $R_{l,t-1}$, so as a dynamic relation, has a unit root. The whole of ϵ_t influences $R_{l,t}$, and next period, the whole of $R_{l,t}$ influences $R_{l,t+1}$ so the effect of ϵ_t persists indefinitely, and hence past errors accumulate with no 'depreciation'. This induces an ever increasing variance to the time series, violating stationarity.

The key development centers on 4.: transforming back to stationarity. One reason unit roots have attracted so much interest is that facilitate that step, but in two ways with very different implications. Most obviously, differencing removes a unit root and returns to a stationary process: indeed, that is precisely the reverse of how we generated the non-stationarity in (11.12). The second transformation is not so obvious, and requires a bit of explanation. Linear combinations of $I(1)$ processes are usually $I(1)$ as well. It may happen that the integration cancels between series to yield an $I(0)$ outcome: this is called cointegration as we noted above. As a possible example, consumption and income might be $I(1)$ but saving $(s_t = i_t - c_t)$ could be $I(0)$. Cointegrated processes define a 'long-run equilibrium trajectory' for the economy, departures from which induce equilibrium-correction mechanisms (EqCMs), which move the economy back towards its path.[5] Thus, linear combinations can also remove unit roots, and allow stationary inference (although the decision as to whether or not there is a unit root remains non-standard).

There are many possible tests for cointegration, and we first consider tests based on regression, when x_t can be treated as weakly exogenous for the parameters of the conditional model (see below, and e.g., Engle, Hendry and Richard, 1983).[6] Tests for genuine links between variables must take account of the outcome when there are no

---

[5]Davidson, Hendry, Srba and Yeo (1978), and much of the subsequent literature, referred to these as 'error corrections'.

[6]Regression methods can be applied to model $I(1)$ variables which are in fact linked (i.e., cointegrate). Most tests still have conventional distributions, apart from that corresponding to a test for a unit root.

links. To check that a 'nonsense regression' has not been estimated, one could test that the residuals of the levels regression are a stationary process using the Dickey–Fuller (*DF*) test for a unit root (perhaps augmented by lagged differences of residuals to whiten the error, denoted *ADF*). Let $\hat{u}_t = y_t - \hat{\kappa}x_t$ where $\hat{\kappa}$ is the OLS estimate of the long-run parameter κ, then the *DF*-statistic tests for H_0: $\rho = 0$ in:

$$\Delta\hat{u}_t = \rho\hat{u}_t + \omega_t. \tag{11.20}$$

A model like (11.20) based on $\hat{u}_t$, imposes a common factor on the dynamic structure (see Campos, Ericsson and Hendry, 1996, for a discussion of this drawback). Since such tests are not optimal, Kremers, Ericsson and Dolado (1992) contrast them with a direct test for H_0: $\phi_2 = 0$ in (say):

$$\Delta y_t = \phi_1\Delta x_t + \phi_2\left(y_{t-1} - \kappa x_{t-1}\right) + \omega_t, \tag{11.21}$$

where κ is not constrained to equal the short-run parameter ϕ_1 as in (11.20). Because the null rejection frequency of that test depends on the values of the 'nuisance' parameters ϕ_1 and σ_v^2, Kiviet and Phillips (1992) develop a test which is invariant to the values of ϕ_1 and σ_v^2 (this coincides with the test computed in PcGive, and discussed blow). Its distribution differs from the Dickey–Fuller distribution, so its critical values have been separately tabulated. Banerjee, Dolado, Galbraith and Hendry (1993) find the power of $t_{\phi_2=0}$ can be high relative to the *DF* test. However, when x_t is not weakly exogenous (and hence conditioning is invalid), the test is potentially a poor way of detecting cointegration, and so a multivariate method is needed. Thus, a partial answer to 5. is that we can allow for unit root non-stationarity.

Most dynamic equations have an intercept, and may have additional deterministic variables. In the general case of (11.5), simply interpret one of the regressors as the required variable. However, with integrated data, estimation and inference depend on which deterministic terms enter the model and the economic system, so care is required, but we leave a formal analysis to Volume II, where we can properly analyze multivariate cointegration.

PcGive is specifically designed to formulate, estimate, test, and analyze linear dynamic equations, and computes all of the statistics described above, and many more discussed in later sections. The empirical cloth on the present theory skeleton is presented in later sections once a few more concepts have been introduced.

11.4 A typology of simple dynamic models

Hendry, Pagan and Sargan (1984) provide a detailed analysis of single equation models like (11.5), and show that most of the widely-used empirical models are special cases of (11.5). There are nine distinct model types embedded in (11.5), a point most easily seen by considering the special case of $k = n = 1$ and $m = 0$, so that all of the polynomials are first order, and only one x variable is involved:

$$y_t = \alpha_1 y_{t-1} + \beta_0 x_t + \beta_1 x_{t-1} + \epsilon_t \text{ where } \epsilon_t \sim \text{IN}\left[0, \sigma_\epsilon^2\right] \qquad (11.22)$$

and $\text{IN}\left[\mu, \sigma^2\right]$ denotes an independent, normal random variable with mean μ and constant variance σ^2.

All nine of the following models are obtainable by further restrictions on this extremely simple case:

(1) static relationship;
(2) autoregressive process;
(3) leading indicator;
(4) growth-rate model;
(5) distributed lag;
(6) partial adjustment;
(7) autoregressive-error model (COMFAC);
(8) equilibrium-correction mechanism (EqCM);
(9) dead-start model.

Equation (11.22) is a specialization of the special case of a linear, single-equation dynamic model, with the apparently restrictive assumption that $\{\epsilon_t\}$ is a white-noise process. Yet most widely-used model types are schematically represented in (11.22), and the typology highlights their distinct characteristics, strengths and weaknesses.

To clarify the approach, we consider the nine cases in turn, deriving each via restrictions on the parameter vector:

$$\boldsymbol{\theta}' = (\alpha_1, \beta_0, \beta_1)$$

of (11.22), noting that an intercept and an error variance can be included without altering the implications in all models, and are omitted for simplicity of exposition. Four of the cases impose two restrictions on θ and five impose one, and these will be referred to respectively as one and two parameter models since σ^2 is common to all stochastic models. Table 11.1 lists the outcomes.

Three important issues must be clarified before proceeding: the status of $\{x_t\}$; the dependence of the model's properties on the data properties; and whether each model type is being treated as correctly specified or as an approximation to a more general DGP such as (11.5). These three problems arise in part because the analysis has not commenced from the most general system needed to characterize the observed data adequately, and in part because the DGP is unknown in practice, so we do not know which data properties to take as salient features in an analytical treatment (not to mention in empirical studies). A system formulation is offered in Chapter 13.

For the present, we treat $\{x_t\}$ as if it were (weakly) exogenous for the parameters of interest in θ (see Engle, Hendry and Richard, 1983, and §13.5.2). Heuristically,

Table 11.1   Model Typology.

Type of Model	θ'	Entailed Restrictions on (11.22)	
static regression	$(0, \beta_0, 0)$	$\alpha_1 = \beta_1 = 0$	no dynamics
autoregressive process	$(\alpha_1, 0, 0)$	$\beta_0 = \beta_1 = 0$	no covariates
leading indicator	$(0, 0, \beta_1)$	$\alpha_1 = \beta_0 = 0$	no contemporaneity
growth rate	$(1, \beta_0, -\beta_0)$	$\alpha_1 = 1,$ $\beta_1 = -\beta_0$	no levels
distributed lag	$(0, \beta_0, \beta_1)$	$\alpha_1 = 0$	finite lags
partial adjustment	$(\alpha_1, \beta_0, 0)$	$\beta_1 = 0$	no lagged x
autoregressive error	$(\alpha_1, \beta_0, -\alpha_1\beta_0)$	$\beta_1 = -\alpha_1\beta_0$	one common factor
error correction	(α_1, β_0, K)	$K = \dfrac{\beta_0 + \beta_1}{1 - \alpha_1}$	long-run response
dead-start	$(\alpha_1, 0, \beta_1)$	$\beta_0 = 0$	lagged variables

weak exogeneity ensures that we can take the conditioning variables as valid, and so analyze the conditional equation (11.22) without loss of any relevant information about θ, despite not also modelling the process determining x_t: this would be false if the model of x_t depended on θ. When x_t in (11.22) is weakly exogenous for θ, then if any member of the typology is valid, so must be every *less restricted*, but identifiable, member. That statement has profound implications not only for the general methodology of modelling, but also for such major issues of current contention as the practice of 'allowing for residual autocorrelation', the validity of analyzing over-identified simultaneous systems (the Sims critique: see Sims, 1980, and Hendry and Mizon, 1993), and the imposition of restrictions based on prior theory, including the Lucas critique (see Lucas, 1976, Favero and Hendry, 1992, and Ericsson and Irons, 1995).

As noted earlier, x_t is assumed to be I(1), and for convenience, we take $\{\Delta x_t\}$ to be a stationary process. This determines the answer to the second issue; but since some economic time series seem to be I(0) (e.g., unemployment), the case $x_t \sim I(0)$ remains relevant. If x_t and y_t are cointegrated, then $u_t = (y_t - K x_t) \sim I(0)$, but such a belief may be false, and the case $u_t \sim I(1) \ \forall K$ must be noted. The typology treats each case in turn, as if it were the correct specification, but notes both the historical success of such an assumption, and the likely consequences when it is incorrect.

11.4.1 Static regression

Equations of the form

$$y_t = b_0 x_t + u_t$$

(with b_0 and x_t vectors in general) have played a large role in many macro-econometric systems as erstwhile 'structural' equations (i.e., embodying the fundamental parameters of the behaviour of economic agents). In practice, $\{u_t\}$ has usually been highly autocorrelated (reminiscent of nonsense correlations – see Yule, 1926), so that conventional inference about b_0 is invalid (see, for example, Granger and Newbold, 1974, and Phillips, 1986). However, static equations reappeared as part of a two-stage strategy for investigating cointegration, with the focus on testing whether or not $\{u_t\}$ was I(1) against the alternative that it was I(0) (see Engle and Granger, 1987). Then, b_0 would be a direct estimator of K in (11.9). Even so, the success of such an estimator in finite samples has been questioned (see Banerjee, Dolado, Hendry and Smith, 1986), and is dependent on the mean lag between y and x, noting that a static equation imposes that mean lag at zero. Alternatively, the strategy of removing the autocorrelation in $\{u_t\}$ by fitting an autoregressive process is considered in §11.4.7. Finally, viewed as a structural equation, all of the restrictions on dynamics and covariates are testable against (11.5), as are the implicit restrictions highlighted in §13.5.

11.4.2 Univariate autoregressive processes

The equation

$$y_t = a_1 y_{t-1} + e_t$$

serves as our representative of univariate time-series models (see Box and Jenkins, 1976). If y_t is I(1), $a_1 = 1$, inducing a random walk when e_t is white noise. Autoregressive equations are widely used for *ex ante* forecasting, and have proved a powerful challenger to econometrics systems in that domain (see, for example, Nelson, 1972, and the vector analogues in Doan, Litterman and Sims, 1984; see Clements and Hendry, 1998, 1999, for an explanation based on other sources of non-stationarity than unit roots). In economics, the interdependence of economic decisions (for example, one person's income is another's expenditure) entails that univariate autoregressions must be derived, and hence are not autonomous processes – where an equation for y_t is autonomous if changes in the process generating x_t do not alter it. Here, the autoregression is obtained by eliminating, or marginalizing with respect to, x_t. For example, let $x_t = x_{t-1} + \nu_t$ where $\nu_t \sim \text{IN}\left[0, \sigma_t^2\right]$ when in fact $\alpha_1 = 1$ and $\beta_1 = -\beta_0$ in (11.22), then $y_t = y_{t-1} + \epsilon_t + \beta_0 \nu_t$ has a non-constant variance $\sigma_\epsilon^2 + \beta_0^2 \sigma_t^2$. Consequently, econometric models should both fit better than autoregressions (or else they are at least dynamically mis-specified), and should forecast better (or else the constancy of the econometric model must be suspect).

That both these requirements are sometimes not satisfied is owing in part to the inappropriateness of some current empirical methodological practices. A major objective of PcGive is to offer an alternative approach which circumvents such difficulties by commencing from a general dynamic specification that automatically embeds the relevant special cases.

11.4.3 Leading indicators

Models of the form

$$y_t = c_1 x_{t-1} + v_t$$

can be used in forecasting if x leads y with sufficient reliability (for example, orders arrive ahead of output). In the absence of a sound behavioural theory, however, c_1 need not be constant. If it is not, that will lead to poor forecasting, especially in periods of change when good forecasts are most needed. Moreover, there seems no good reason for excluding lagged ys, and if a general dynamic model is postulated, then the econometric considerations in §13.4, §13.5, §13.6 and §13.7 apply: see Emerson and Hendry (1996) and Clements and Hendry (1998).

11.4.4 Growth-rate models

The evolutionary and trend-like behaviour of many economic time series led earlier investigators to recommend differencing data prior to statistical analysis. One example is Granger and Newbold (1977) although, as argued in Hendry and Anderson (1977), there are other transformations (such as ratios) which potentially could also remove trends. That leads on to the concept of cointegration discussed in §11.4.8.

Growth-rate models have the form

$$\Delta y_t = d_0 \Delta x_t + \eta_t.$$

Such models successfully avoid nonsense regressions problems in I(1) data, and from the transformed dependent variable, a useful measure of goodness of fit can be calculated. Nevertheless, if the variance of Δx_t is large relative to that of Δy_t, d_0 must be small even if y_t and x_t are cointegrated with $K = 1$ (this is the permanent income issue in one guise: see Davidson, Hendry, Srba and Yeo, 1978). Further, although $y_t = K x_t$ implies $\Delta y_t = K \Delta x_t$, the converse is false in a stochastic world owing to integrating the error.

Alternatively, there are no *a priori* grounds for excluding levels from economic relationships since initial disequilibria cannot be assumed to be irrelevant: that is, the time path of Δy_t for a given sequence Δx_t may depend on the relationship between y_0 and x_0. Two further insights into the drawbacks of growth-rate models are discussed below in §11.4.7 and §11.4.8.

On the methodological level, a mistake sometimes committed in applied economics is to begin with a linear approximation to a steady-state theory of the form: $y_t = f(x_t)$, fit a static model thereto, discover severe residual autocorrelation and 'correct' that, either by differencing, or by using 'Cochrane–Orcutt' (but see their 1949 article, Cochrane and Orcutt, 1949, which does not recommend that procedure, as noted by Gilbert, 1989) but finding an autoregressive parameter near unity. While the goodness of fit may not be greatly worsened by imposing differencing, dynamic responses can be substantially distorted, and ignoring long-run feedbacks may distort policy strategies.

11.4.5 Distributed lags

Although using only one lag makes the resulting model highly schematic, but nevertheless the equation

$$y_t = f_0 x_t + f_1 x_{t-1} + \xi_t,$$

is representative of the class of finite distributed lags. Such models remain open to
the objections noted in §11.4.1 above, are highly dependent on whether x_t is weakly,
or strongly, exogenous unless ξ_t is white noise (which in practice it rarely is in this
class), and tend to suffer from collinearity owing to the inappropriate parametrization
of including many levels of the regressor (see Chapter 14). Imposing so-called *a priori*
restrictions on the lag coefficients to reduce the profligate parametrization has little to
recommend it, although such restrictions are at least potentially testable. It is hard to
see any theoretical grounds for excluding lagged ys, given that they are another way
of representing a distributed lag relationship; and as shown in §11.4.7, considerable
dangers exist in arbitrarily removing any residual autocorrelation from ξ_t.

11.4.6 Partial adjustment

The equation

$$y_t = g_0 x_t + g_1 y_{t-1} + \zeta_t$$

occurs regularly in empirical macro-economics, and can be derived from assuming a
long-run desired target of the form $y_t = K x_t$ subject to quadratic adjustment costs
(see, for example, Eisner and Strotz, 1963, and Nickell, 1985). While such a model
type seems reasonable in principle, it does not entail that the y and x variables which
agents use in their decision rules are precisely the levels analyzed by the economist.
For example, agents may use the (log of the) consumption-income ratio as their y_t, and
the growth rate of income as their x_t, rather than the levels of both.[7] The resulting
econometric specification, however, is wholly different despite the common element of
partial adjustment.

Even when y_t and x_t are cointegrated in levels, the partial adjustment model has
little to recommend it unless it happens to coincide with the DGP. The mean lag is
$g_1/(1 - g_1)$ whereas the median lag (the number of periods to reach the half-way stage
towards equilibrium) is zero for $g_0 \leq \frac{1}{2}$ and is $-\log(2g_1)/\log(g_1)$ for $g_0 > \frac{1}{2}$, so
that a skewed distribution is imposed irrespective of the data (see, for example, Hendry,
1995a, for the derivation of these formulae). When g_1 is near unity, both measures
entail extremely slow adjustment, exacerbated by any untreated positive residual autocorrelation. Further, x_t and y_{t-1} are usually highly correlated, so again an unfortunate

---

[7]The latter anyway seems suspect since few consumers appear to suffer great adjustment costs
in response to increases in their expenditure when income has risen.

parametrization is being selected. Since there are no good arguments for *a priori* excluding all the lagged *x*s, and plenty of empirical evidence to show that they do matter in many cases, this model type again seems suspect.[8]

11.4.7 Autoregressive errors or COMFAC models

As noted in §11.2, some of the roots of $a(L)$ and $b(L)$ in (11.4) may be equal, allowing cancellation. In the case of (11.22) with $\beta_0 \neq 0$, we can write the equation as:

$$(1 - \alpha_1 L)\, y_t = \beta_0 \left(1 + \frac{\beta_1}{\beta_0} L\right) x_t + \epsilon_t.$$

Thus, if and only if $\alpha_1 = -\beta_1/\beta_0$ or $\beta_1 + \alpha_1\beta_0 = 0$, then on dividing both sides by $(1 - \alpha_1 L)$, the equation can be rewritten as:

$$y_t = \beta_0 x_t + \frac{\epsilon_t}{(1 - \alpha_1 L)},$$

or letting $\rho = \alpha_1$:

$$y_t = \beta_0 x_t + u_t \quad \text{where} \quad u_t = \rho u_{t-1} + \epsilon_t, \tag{11.23}$$

yielding a static model with an autoregressive error. The term $(1 - \alpha_1 L)$ is a factor (in this simple case, the only factor) of $a(L)$ and similarly $(1 + (\beta_1/\beta_0) L)$ is a factor of $b(L)$, so that when these are equal there is a factor in common in $a(L)$ and $b(L)$ (leading to the name COMFAC). The converse that (11.23) induces a common factor is obvious, so there is an isomorphism between autoregressive errors and common factors in the lag polynomials: if you believe one, you must believe the other. Since (11.23) imposes restrictions on (11.22), these are testable, and rejection entails discarding the supposed reduction to (11.23) (see Hendry and Mizon, 1978). Thus, the ADL class includes all models with autoregressive errors.

Perhaps the greatest *non sequitur* in the history of econometrics is the assumption that autocorrelated residuals entail autoregressive errors, as is entailed in 'correcting serial correlation using Cochrane–Orcutt'. Dozens of mis-specifications in time-series data will induce residual autocorrelation without corresponding to common factors in the lag polynomials of the underlying general model (11.4). Indeed, the order of testing is incorrect: to estimate any models like (11.23) first necessitates establishing the validity of (11.4), then showing that $a(L)$ and $b(L)$ have common factors, and finally testing H_0: $\rho = 0$. Showing that $\rho \neq 0$ in equations like (11.23) does not prove that there are valid common-factor restrictions. PcGive offers algorithms for testing common-factor restrictions in equations like (11.5) using the Wald-test approach in Sargan (1980b). If

---

[8] Lags would arise naturally in the postulated model if the agents' y and x were not the levels the economist selects.

such restrictions are accepted, generalizations of (11.23) are estimable using the RALS estimator described in Chapter 16.

Two points of importance from (11.23) are that: (a) it imposes a zero mean lag irrespective of the actual lag responses, since the short-run and long-run responses are forced to be equal by the choice of model type; and (b) the growth-rate model of §11.4.4 can be reinterpreted as imposing a common factor then setting ρ to unity. We concur with the advice in the title of the paper by Mizon (1995).

11.4.8 Equilibrium-correction mechanisms

The issue of appropriate reparametrizations of $\boldsymbol{\theta}$ has arisen on several occasions above, and many alternatives are conceivable. One natural choice follows from rearranging (11.22) as:

$$
\begin{aligned}
\Delta y_t &= (\alpha_1 - 1)\, y_{t-1} + \beta_0 \Delta x_t + (\beta_1 + \beta_0)\, x_{t-1} + \epsilon_t \\
&= \beta_0 \Delta x_t + (\alpha_1 - 1)\, (y_{t-1} - Kx_{t-1}) + \epsilon_t,
\end{aligned}
\tag{11.24}
$$

where $K = (\beta_0 + \beta_1)/(1 - \alpha_1)$ is the long-run response in (11.9) above when $\alpha_1 \neq 1$. The new parameters in $f(\boldsymbol{\theta}) = \boldsymbol{\psi} = (\beta_0, (1 - \alpha_1), K)'$ correspond to the impact effect, the feedback effect and the long-run response: no restrictions are imposed in this transformation. The term $(y - Kx)_{t-1}$ was called an error-correction mechanism (EqCM) in Davidson, Hendry, Srba and Yeo (1978) since it reflected the deviation from the long-run equilibrium outcome, with agents correcting $(1 - \alpha_1)$ of the resulting disequilibrium each period. However, such a mechanism does not error correct between equilibria, so equilibrium-correction mechanism is more apposite – and has the same acronym (but is more often written EqCM). Sargan (1964) provides a real-wage example, and Hendry and Anderson (1977) considered some non-unit EqCMs. The special case $K = 1$ is of interest in econometrics as it corresponds to long-run proportionality (or homogeneity in log-linear models), but EqCMs are well defined for $K \neq 1$, although usually K will then need to be estimated. As Hendry, Pagan and Sargan (1984) note, logistic formulations or more general functions may be necessary to model agents' behaviour if they adjust more or less rapidly depending on the extent of disequilibrium (see Escribano, 1985).

Engle and Granger (1987) establish an isomorphism between EqCMs and cointegrated processes: if y_t and x_t are each I(1) and are cointegrated, then there exists an EqCM of the form $(y - Kx)$ and conversely. The former does not entail that the EqCM necessarily enters the y_t equation, rather than the x_t equation, and may enter both (which would violate weak exogeneity: see Hendry and Mizon (1993) for an example).

In our simple typology, the only EqCM case to impose any restrictions on (11.24) is $K = 1$ or $\alpha_1 + \beta_0 + \beta_1 = 1$, revealing that all long-run proportionality theories can be reproduced in static equilibrium by an appropriate EqCM. Here, this restriction yields:

$$\Delta y_t = \gamma_0 \Delta x_t - \gamma_1 (y - x)_{t-1} + \omega_t. \tag{11.25}$$

Thus, another interpretation of the growth-rate model §11.4.4 is revealed, namely, it corresponds to imposing long-run homogeneity ($\alpha_1 + \beta_0 + \beta_1 = 1$) and the absence of feedback from the level ($1 - \alpha_1 = 0$), which together entail a unit root. Consequently, small values of γ_0 are compatible with long-run proportionality. Since partial adjustment corresponds to the special case where $x = y^*$ (the desired target), it imposes $\gamma_0 = -\gamma_1$ to exclude the lagged x.

The parametrization in (11.25) has several advantages beyond being more interpretable: the regressors Δx_t and $(y - x)_{t-1}$ will not usually be highly correlated, being a current change and a lagged disequilibrium; and proportionality is easily tested by adding x_{t-1} as a (relatively non-collinear) regressor (however, such a test must allow for the possibility that $\{x_t\}$ may be I(1)). Further, a less strong lag shape is being imposed, since the mean lag is $(1 - \gamma_0)/\gamma_1$, which depends on both parameters, and can be small even if $(1 - \gamma_1)$ is around 0.9, whereas the median lag is zero for $\gamma_0 \geq \frac{1}{2}$ and is $-\log 2 (1 - \gamma_0)/\log(1 - \gamma_1)$ for $\gamma_0 < \frac{1}{2}$.

When the EqCM is the correct specification, the partial adjustment model may suffer from severe biases, and possibly residual autocorrelation, since it omits x_{t-1} which is highly correlated with x_t: because the coefficients of x_t and x_{t-1} are of similar magnitudes but opposite signs, this will drive the coefficient of x_t in the partial adjustment model close to zero (a common empirical problem), so that $g_0 \simeq 1 - g_1$ results. Note that $\beta_1 < 0$ in (11.22) need not entail any negative weights $\{w_i\}$ in the solved representation:

$$y_t = \sum_{i=0}^{\infty} w_i x_{t-i} + u_t.$$

Thus, do not delete lagged xs because their coefficients appear to have 'wrong signs', since on a reparametrization they may have the correct sign.

Finally, EqCMs can be confused with COMFAC models despite their very different implications for lag responses. This arises because COMFAC is an EqCM with the restriction that long-run and short-run responses are equal, as can be seen by rewriting (11.23) in the form:

$$y_t = \beta_0 x_t + \rho (y_{t-1} - \beta_0 x_{t-1}) + \epsilon_t,$$

or:

$$\Delta y_t = \beta_0 \Delta x_t + (\rho - 1)(y - \beta_0 x)_{t-1} + \epsilon_t. \tag{11.26}$$

Thus, the degree of mis-specification of (11.26) for (11.24) depends on the extent to which $(\alpha_1 - 1)(K - \beta_0) \neq 0$, which could be small even if $K = 1$ and, for example, $\beta_0 = 0.4$. Nevertheless, despite (11.24) and (11.26) having similar goodness of fit, the mean lag in (11.24) when $K = 1$ could be large at the same time as (11.26) imposes it at zero.

11.4.9 Dead-start models

The main consideration arising for this type of model is its exclusion of contemporaneous information. This could be because:

$$y_t = \alpha_1 y_{t-1} + \beta_1 x_{t-1} + \epsilon_t \qquad (11.27)$$

is structural, and hence is a partial adjustment type. Alternatively, (11.27) could be a derived form, from which x_t has been eliminated, in which case (11.27) is unlikely to be autonomous, and its parameters would be susceptible to alter with changes in the behaviour of the x_t process. In this second case, the coefficients are not interpretable since they are (unknown) functions of the correlations between x_t and (y_{t-1}, x_{t-1}).

Care is obviously required in selecting an appropriate type of model to characterize both a given theory and the associated data; some of the methodological considerations discussed below help clarify that choice.

11.5 Interpreting linear models

The notation for the linear model is the same as that in Chapter 12:

$$y_t = \sum_{i=1}^{k} \beta_i x_{i,t} + \epsilon_t = \boldsymbol{\beta}' \mathbf{x}_t + \epsilon_t \text{ with } \epsilon_t \sim \text{IN}\left[0, \sigma_\epsilon^2\right], \qquad (11.28)$$

where $\boldsymbol{\beta}$ is $k \times 1$ and $\mathsf{E}\left[\mathbf{x}_t \epsilon_t\right] = \mathbf{0}$. Grouping all the T observations:

$$\mathbf{y} = \mathbf{X}\boldsymbol{\beta} + \boldsymbol{\epsilon} \text{ with } \boldsymbol{\epsilon} \sim \mathsf{N}\left[\mathbf{0}, \sigma_\epsilon^2 \mathbf{I}_T\right] \qquad (11.29)$$

where $\mathbf{y}, \mathbf{X}, \boldsymbol{\epsilon}$ are respectively $T \times 1$, $T \times k$ and $T \times 1$.

First, we discuss the four distinct interpretations of (11.28), see Richard (1980) or Hendry, Pagan and Sargan (1984):

11.5.1 Interpretation 1: a regression equation

A regression is the conditional expectation of y_t given $\mathbf{x}_t$ (denoted by $\mathsf{E}\left[y_t | \mathbf{x}_t\right]$). Taking the conditional expectation in (11.28):

$$\mathsf{E}\left[y_t \mid \mathbf{x}_t\right] = \boldsymbol{\beta}' \mathbf{x}_t \qquad (11.30)$$

where $\boldsymbol{\beta}$ is a parameter of interest. Sufficient conditions to sustain that interpretation of (11.28) are a jointly stationary, multivariate-normal distribution for $(y_t, \mathbf{x}_t)$ with $\mathbf{x}_t$ weakly exogenous for $\boldsymbol{\beta}$. (A formal derivation of a conditional equation in a bivariate normal distribution is provided in Chapter 12. The properties of regression estimators are also discussed in that chapter: for example, that $\mathsf{V}\left[y_t - \boldsymbol{\beta}' \mathbf{x}_t\right]$ is minimized by the choice of $\widehat{\boldsymbol{\beta}}$). Notice that the minimal conditions which needed to justify (11.30) are not sufficient to sustain $\mathsf{E}\left[\mathbf{y}|\mathbf{X}\right] = \mathbf{X}\boldsymbol{\beta}$, which is used in Chapter 12, as that involves conditioning past ys on future xs.

11.5.2 Interpretation 2: a (linear) least-squares approximation

Here, the approximation is to a postulated general function:

$$y_t = \mathbf{f}(\mathbf{x}_t) + e_t,$$

chosen on the criteria that: (a) (11.28) is linear in $\mathbf{x}_t$; and (b) $\sum_{t=1}^{T} \epsilon_t^2$ is to be minimized. Graphically, β in (11.28) is not $\partial \mathbf{f}/\partial \mathbf{x}'$ (the tangent), owing to the second criterion, but must be a chord. If ϵ_t is non-normal, the regression would not be linear, whereas a linear approximation must be, so §11.5.1 and §11.5.2 are distinct. If, in practice, $\mathbf{f}$ is non-linear then (11.28) may be a poor approximation, $\{\epsilon_t\}$ could be autocorrelated, and forecasts could be poor (since $\partial \mathbf{f}/\partial \mathbf{x}_t'$ need not be constant). Of course, a quadratic or even a higher-order approximation to $\mathbf{f}(\mathbf{x})$ could be used. White (1980) provides a formal analysis of this case.

11.5.3 Interpretation 3: an autonomous contingent plan

In this interpretation:

$$y_t^p = \mathbf{x}_t' \boldsymbol{\beta},$$

is the planned value and:

$$y_t = y_t^p + u_t,$$

is the outcome, which deviates randomly from the plan (see Marschak, 1953, Bentzel and Hansen, 1955, and Hendry and Richard, 1983). Thus, (11.28) characterizes how agents form plans, and β is an invariant parameter (see Frisch, 1938). Since $\{u_t\}$ need not have a joint normal distribution, §11.5.3 and §11.5.1 are different; and $\mathbf{f}(\mathbf{x})$ might be approximated by a non-linear function of $\mathbf{x}_t$, so §11.5.2 and §11.5.3 also differ. For example, autoregressive-conditional heteroscedastic (ARCH) errors (so the variance at time t depends on the variance at time $t-1$) would be one instance where $\{u_t\}$ is not jointly normal, in which case, $\mathsf{E}[\mathbf{y}|\mathbf{X}] \neq \mathbf{X}\boldsymbol{\beta}$ need not hold although (11.28) could still be correct.

11.5.4 Interpretation 4: derived from a behavioural relationship

The final interpretation is:

$$\mathsf{E}[y_t \mid \mathcal{I}_{t-1}] = \boldsymbol{\beta}' \mathsf{E}[\mathbf{x}_t \mid \mathcal{I}_{t-1}],$$

or:

$$y_t^p = \boldsymbol{\beta}' \mathbf{x}_t^e,$$

where $\mathcal{I}_{t-1}$ denotes the universe of information available to agents at the time their plans are formulated. Here, the distinction is drawn between a plan (which is made about a variable that the relevant agent controls), and an expectation (which is formed about an uncontrolled variable). Let $\boldsymbol{\nu}_t = \mathbf{x}_t - \mathbf{x}_t^e$ and $\eta_t = y_t - y_t^p$ be the vector of expectational errors and the departure of the outcome from the plan respectively, with $\mathsf{E}\left[\boldsymbol{\nu}_t | \mathcal{I}_{t-1}\right] = \mathbf{0}$ and $\mathsf{E}\left[\eta_t | \mathcal{I}_{t-1}\right] = 0$, then:

$$y_t = \boldsymbol{\beta}' \mathbf{x}_t + \epsilon_t \text{ with } \epsilon_t = \eta_t - \boldsymbol{\beta}' \boldsymbol{\nu}_t,$$

so that $\mathsf{E}\left[\epsilon_t | \mathcal{I}_{t-1}\right] = 0$ but $\mathsf{E}\left[\epsilon_t | \mathbf{x}_t\right] \neq 0$ owing to their sharing the common component $\boldsymbol{\nu}_t$. In this setting, regression is inconsistent (and biased) for the parameter of interest $\boldsymbol{\beta}$, and may deliver non-constant estimates even when $\boldsymbol{\beta}$ is invariant when the process determining $\mathbf{x}_t$ alters. Clearly, §11.5.4 is distinct from §11.5.1–§11.5.3.

Merely asserting $y_t = \boldsymbol{\beta}' \mathbf{x}_t + \epsilon_t$ is not an adequate basis for econometric analysis, given the four distinct interpretations of equation (11.28) just described. Although the four interpretations happen to coincide in stationary, linear models with normal errors, the distinctions in §11.5.1–§11.5.4 are not formal: in practice, which one is valid entails quite different prognoses for the success (or failure) of any empirical study. When the $\mathbf{x}_t$ process varies enough, some discrimination is possible owing to the non-constancy of $\boldsymbol{\beta}$, and this is both the usual situation and that in which discrimination actually matters.

11.6 Multiple regression

The algebra of least-squares estimation is established in matrix notation in Chapter 12, and we merely record some of the most relevant formulae here. First, the OLS coefficient estimates and their estimated variances are:

$$\widehat{\boldsymbol{\beta}} = (\mathbf{X}'\mathbf{X})^{-1}\mathbf{X}'\mathbf{y} \text{ with } \widehat{\mathsf{V}\left[\widehat{\boldsymbol{\beta}}\right]} = \widehat{\sigma}_\epsilon^2 (\mathbf{X}'\mathbf{X})^{-1}.$$

Also the error variance estimate and the residual sum of squares are:

$$\widehat{\sigma}_\epsilon^2 = \frac{RSS}{(T-k)} \text{ when } RSS = \left(\mathbf{y} - \mathbf{X}\widehat{\boldsymbol{\beta}}\right)'\left(\mathbf{y} - \mathbf{X}\widehat{\boldsymbol{\beta}}\right).$$

Further, $\mathbf{M} = \mathbf{I}_T - \mathbf{X}(\mathbf{X}'\mathbf{X})^{-1}\mathbf{X}'$ is a symmetric, idempotent matrix which annihilates $\mathbf{X}$, so $\mathbf{M}\mathbf{X} = \mathbf{0}$ implying $\mathbf{M}\mathbf{y} = \mathbf{M}\boldsymbol{\epsilon} = \widehat{\mathbf{u}}$ (the vector of residuals $\mathbf{y} - \mathbf{X}\widehat{\boldsymbol{\beta}}$). Tests of H_0: $\boldsymbol{\beta} = \mathbf{0}$, or components thereof, are developed in Chapter 12. A simple empirical example with a constant and two other regressors is presented in §10.10.

It is a brave (foolhardy?) investigator who deems their model to coincide with the DGP, and most econometricians consider the possibility of various mis-specifications when appraising empirical research. A number of possibilities can be shown algebraically, such as omitting a relevant regressor. Denoting the OLS estimator of the mis-specified model by $\sim$, partition $\mathbf{X} = (\mathbf{X}_a : \mathbf{X}_b)$, and conformally let $\boldsymbol{\beta} = (\boldsymbol{\beta}_a' : \boldsymbol{\beta}_b')'$ which are $k_a \times 1$ and $k_b \times 1$ so that $k_a + k_b = k$. Then:

$$\widetilde{\boldsymbol{\beta}} = (\mathbf{X}_a'\mathbf{X}_a)^{-1}\mathbf{X}_a'\mathbf{y} \text{ and } \widetilde{\mathsf{V}\left[\widetilde{\boldsymbol{\beta}}_a\right]} = \widetilde{\sigma}_\epsilon^2 (\mathbf{X}_a'\mathbf{X}_a)^{-1} \text{ when } \widetilde{\sigma}_\epsilon^2 = \frac{\mathbf{y}'\mathbf{M}_a\mathbf{y}}{(T-k_a)},$$

and $\mathbf{M}_a$ has the same form as $\mathbf{M}$ but using only $\mathbf{X}_a$. Partitioned inversion of $(\mathbf{X'X})$ leads to the important numerical identity that:

$$\tilde{\beta}_a \equiv \widehat{\beta}_a + \mathbf{B}\widehat{\beta}_b \text{ where } \mathbf{B} = \left(\mathbf{X}_a'\mathbf{X}_a\right)^{-1}\mathbf{X}_a'\mathbf{X}_b.$$

If $\{\mathbf{x}_t\}$ is a stationary stochastic process, then:

$$\mathsf{E}\left[\tilde{\sigma}_\epsilon^2\right] \geq \mathsf{E}\left[\widehat{\sigma}_\epsilon^2\right],$$

since there is a component of $\mathbf{x}_{b,t}$ in the residual. Both the bias in $\tilde{\beta}_a$ and in the error variance were illustrated by the comparative regression results in §10.10. Tests for the significance of omitted variables can be undertaken from the Test menu; what would you conclude after getting significant test results for two different choices?

Despite a high correlation between $\mathbf{x}_{a,t}$ and $\mathbf{x}$, it is possible that:

$$\widehat{\mathsf{V}\left[\widehat{\beta}\right]} < \widehat{\mathsf{V}\left[\tilde{\beta}_a\right]},$$

owing to the reduction in $\widehat{\sigma}_\epsilon^2$ from $\tilde{\sigma}_\epsilon^2$ when $\mathbf{x}_{b,t}$ is added to the regression of y_t on $\mathbf{x}_{a,t}$. A more extensive treatment of collinearity is provided in Chapter 14. Finally, the Durbin–Watson test (DW: see Durbin and Watson, 1951) is often used to test for mis-specifications which result in residual autocorrelation: see §11.4.7.

11.6.1 Estimating partial adjustment

All these issues can be illustrated empirically, and we do so using the artificial data set called data.in7 and data.bn7, with the four variables CONS, INC, INFLAT and OUTPUT. The first regression is of CONS on INC and CONS lagged (that is, a partial adjustment form) which yields:[9]

```
EQ(1)  Modelling CONS by OLS (using data.in7)
       The estimation sample is: 1953 (2) to 1992 (3)
```

	Coefficient	Std.Error	t-value	t-prob	Part.R^2
CONS_1	0.823870	0.03300	25.0	0.000	0.8008
Constant	-45.6043	14.65	-3.11	0.002	0.0589
INC	0.223975	0.04158	5.39	0.000	0.1577

sigma	2.03715	RSS	643.24383	
R^2	0.977627	F(2,155) =	3387 [0.000]**	
log-likelihood	-110.91	DW	1.13	
no. of observations	158	no. of parameters	3	
mean(CONS)	875.848	var(CONS)	181.971	

---

[9]The exact form of the output depends on the options settings.

At first sight, the coefficients seem well determined, and the long-run effect of INC on CONS is close to unity. However, the DW statistic is low (especially as the model has a lagged dependent variable which biases DW towards 2). We will test the specification in the next section.

11.6.2 Heteroscedastic-consistent standard errors

Since residual autocorrelation and residual heteroscedasticity both bias estimated co-efficient standard errors, corrections have been developed. These can be computed in PcGive by selecting Test, Further output, which yields:

```
Heteroscedasticity consistent standard errors
           Coefficients        SE       HACSE        HCSE       JHCSE
CONS_1         0.82387   0.033004   0.048736    0.032659    0.033110
Constant       -45.604     14.647     19.361      13.642      13.778
INC            0.22398   0.041582   0.062002    0.040992    0.041563

           Coefficients      t-SE     t-HACSE     t-HCSE     t-JHCSE
CONS_1         0.82387    24.962      16.905      25.226     24.883
Constant       -45.604   -3.1135     -2.3554     -3.3428    -3.3100
INC            0.22398    5.3864      3.6124       5.4638     5.3889
```

The column above labelled HCSE denotes heteroscedastic-consistent standard errors (see Eicker, 1967, and White, 1980). Relative to the usual standard errors reported for regression estimation, HCSEs reflect any heteroscedasticity in the residuals which is related to the regressors. Consider OLS estimation in (11.28) when $\epsilon_t \sim \text{IN}\left[0, \sigma_t^2\right]$ with $\text{E}\left[\mathbf{x}_t \epsilon_s\right] = \mathbf{0} \ \forall t, s$, but we mistakenly believe that:

$$\epsilon_t \ \underset{h}{\widetilde{\ }} \ \text{IN}\left[0, \sigma_\epsilon^2\right],$$

where $\underset{h}{\widetilde{\ }}$ denotes 'is hypothesized to be distributed as'. To estimate β, we set to zero:

$$\sum_{t=1}^{T} \mathbf{x}_t \epsilon_t = \mathbf{0}. \tag{11.31}$$

Then, to derive the variance, we would analytically calculate:

$$\text{E}\left[\sum_{t=1}^{T} \mathbf{x}_t \epsilon_t \left(\sum_{t=1}^{T} \mathbf{x}_t \epsilon_t\right)'\right] = \text{E}\left[\sum_{t=1}^{T}\sum_{s=1}^{T} \mathbf{x}_t \epsilon_t \epsilon_s \mathbf{x}_s'\right] = \sum_{t=1}^{T} \sigma_t^2 \mathbf{x}_t \mathbf{x}_t',$$

from which the variance of $\widehat{\beta}$ is given by:

$$\mathbf{V} = \text{V}\left[\widehat{\beta}\right] = (\mathbf{X}'\mathbf{X})^{-1}\left(\sum_{t=1}^{T} \sigma_t^2 \mathbf{x}_t \mathbf{x}_t'\right)(\mathbf{X}'\mathbf{X})^{-1}. \tag{11.32}$$

This involves a weighted average of the xs with weights σ_t^2 proportional to the heteroscedastic error variances. The conventional variance estimator is:

$$\mathsf{V}\widehat{\left[\widehat{\boldsymbol{\beta}}\right]} = \widehat{\sigma}_\epsilon \left(\sum_{t=1}^{T} \mathbf{x}_t \mathbf{x}_t' \right)^{-1}.$$

When the weights σ_t^2 in (11.32) are not constant, the conventional variance estimator does not correctly reflect the estimation uncertainty.

Surprisingly, the correct variance formula in (11.32) can be estimated from the sample by replacing the unknown σ_t^2 by $\widehat{\epsilon}_t^2$ (see White, 1980):

$$\widehat{\mathbf{V}} = (\mathbf{X}'\mathbf{X})^{-1} \left(\sum_{t=1}^{T} \widehat{\epsilon}_t^2 \mathbf{x}_t \mathbf{x}_t' \right) (\mathbf{X}'\mathbf{X})^{-1}. \tag{11.33}$$

$\widehat{\mathbf{V}}$ is consistent for $\mathbf{V}$ (see White, 1980) and the conventional estimator of $\mathbf{V}$ arises when all $\{\sigma_t^2\}$ are constant. The square roots of the diagonal of $\widehat{\mathbf{V}}$ are the HCSEs above. When these are close to the OLS SEs, there is little evidence of distortion of inference from untreated heteroscedasticity. The JHCSEs denote Jackknife corrections (see MacKinnon and White, 1985).

Similarly, generalizations to allow for error autocorrelation have been obtained, and are reported above as HACSEs (see e.g., Andrews, 1991). However, in both cases in must be remembered that residual autocorrelation and residual heteroscedasticity may derive from dozens of causes, unrelated to the errors. In these common cases, the various forms of HCSE, HACSE etc. will not be useful – they merely serve to camouflage model mis-specification, not improve inference.

All reported statistics depend on assumptions about how well the model describes the data, and until these assumptions are established as valid, the interpretation of any empirical output is unclear. In the previous chapter, we considered the many assumptions made to derive the distribution of 't'-tests : the assumptions for HCSEs are weaker, but nonetheless strong – as just seen. As a first pass, we use Test, Graphical analysis to visually investigate the fit, the residuals, the residual correlogram, and the density of the residuals. The outcome is shown in Figure 11.1 and reveals a fair fit, but distinct residual autocorrelation, as well as a major group of 'outliers' in the residuals around 1973–4 (does this historical period ring any warning bells?).

More formal mis-specification tests will be considered shortly, but the graph shows substantial residual autocorrelation. How to proceed now?

11.6.3 Specific-to-general

To test a specification, investigators often add extra variables, so we first include lagged INC to obtain:

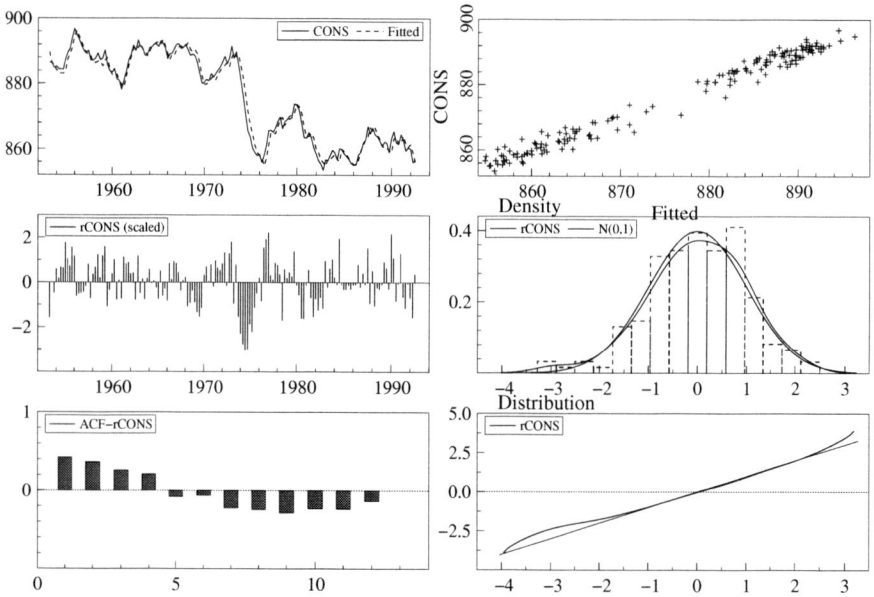

Figure 11.1   Goodness-of-fit measures for partial adjustment model.

EQ(2)   Modelling CONS by OLS (using data.in7)
         The estimation sample is: 1953 (2) to 1992 (3)

	Coefficient	Std.Error	t-value	t-prob	Part.R^2
CONS_1	0.985875	0.02762	35.7	0.000	0.8922
Constant	2.51140	11.39	0.220	0.826	0.0003
INC	0.495844	0.03797	13.1	0.000	0.5255
INC_1	-0.484913	0.04103	-11.8	0.000	0.4756

sigma	1.47998	RSS	337.313361
R^2	0.988268	F(3,154) =	4324 [0.000]**
log-likelihood	-59.915	DW	1.35
no. of observations	158	no. of parameters	4
mean(CONS)	875.848	var(CONS)	181.971

The added variable is highly significant, and so invalidates the first partial-adjustment model. The standard errors of both CONS and INC have fallen, despite adding the collinear variable INC_1, mainly because s has fallen markedly. Consistent with that feature, the partial r^2 values have increased.

Unfortunately, the model appears to have a common factor of unity suggesting that CONS and INC are not cointegrated (the lagged dependent variable coefficient is near unity, and the coefficients on INC and INC lagged are equal magnitude opposite sign). Three formal tests are possible, assuming the model is a good data description. First, we test for a common factor (Dynamic analysis, Test for common factors) to obtain:

```
COMFAC Wald test statistic table, COMFAC F(1,154) = 0.0306861 [0.8612]
Order   Cumulative tests                   Incremental tests
  1       Chi^2(1) = 0.030686 [0.8609]      Chi^2(1) = 0.030686 [0.8609]
```

The test easily accepts, so the model is now COMFAC rather than partial adjustment. The calculated values of the roots are also shown, and these are close to unity. Thus, we next test for a unit root by seeing if all the coefficients (other than the constant) add to unity: the linear restrictions test yields:

```
Test for linear restrictions (Rb=r):
R matrix
        CONS_1      Constant          INC         INC_1
        1.0000      0.00000        1.0000        1.0000
r vector
        1.0000
LinRes F(1,154) = 0.0648135 [0.7994]
```

This too accepts with ease. This suggests it is worth conducting the PcGive unit-root test (see Banerjee and Hendry, 1992b) (from the Test menu, Dynamic analysis, reported only in part here):

```
Tests on the significance of each variable
Variable    F-test            Value [ Prob]     Unit-root t-test
CONS        F(1,154) =     1274.1 [0.0000]**       -0.51143
Constant    F(1,154) = 0.048588 [0.8258]
INC         F(2,154) =     97.321 [0.0000]**        0.31073
```

Finally, the solved long run is badly determined and the unit-root test does not reject. All the evidence meshes: CONS and INC do not cointegrate.

```
Solved static long run equation for CONS
                 Coefficient  Std.Error  t-value  t-prob
Constant             177.794       1022.    0.174   0.862
INC                 0.773850       1.159    0.667   0.505
Long-run sigma = 104.775
```

```
ECM = CONS - 177.794 - 0.77385*INC;
WALD test: Chi^2(1) = 0.445497 [0.5045]
```

Again one must ask: how valid are these tests? A glance at the graphical diagnostics (corresponding to Figure 11.1) shows that the residual autocorrelation has not improved, so none of the SEs is reliable. More formal mis-specification tests are provided in the Test summary, and yield:

```
AR 1-5 test:       F(5,149) =    7.8187 [0.0000]**
ARCH 1-4 test:     F(4,146) =    6.1154 [0.0001]**
Normality test:    Chi^2(2) =    7.6549 [0.0218]*
hetero test:       F(6,147) =    1.0658 [0.3858]
hetero-X test:     F(9,144) =    1.0443 [0.4080]
RESET test:        F(1,153) =    2.6542 [0.1053]
```

There is indeed significant residual autocorrelation, and apparently autoregressive conditional heteroscedasticity (ARCH) as well (see Engle, 1982). However, the latter could be caused by the former (see Engle, Hendry and Trumbull, 1985), and merely shows the difficulty of interpreting outcomes when several tests reject. If we test for the omission from the equation of the remaining two variables in the database, we obtain:

```
Omitted variables test: F(2,152) = 67.5992 [0.0000] **
Added variables:
[0] = INFLAT
[1] = OUTPUT
```

Both seem to matter! All previous results are invalidated: how to proceed now? Does this explain the earlier problems? – or do they explain the latest results? or do further 'untreated problems' lurk unseen?

11.6.4 General-to-specific

It is precisely conundrums of the form just encountered that have led us to suggest an alternative approach to modelling. If at some stage you intend to investigate the relevance of a given phenomenon (for example, lagged INC, or INFLAT), include it in the model from the outset if sample size allows: this leads to general-to-specific modelling, discussed in greater detail in Chapter 14.

The initial general model should contain all the effects likely to be relevant, including sufficient lags to ensure no residual autocorrelation, then be tested for its validity. Once that has been established, further testing can proceed in confidence that conflicts will not arise. To illustrate, consider as an initial starting point a model involving CONS, INC, and INFLAT, adding their one-period lags:

```
EQ( 3) Modelling CONS by OLS (using data.in7)
        The estimation sample is: 1953 (2) to 1992 (3)
```

	Coefficient	Std.Error	t-value	t-prob	Part.R^2
CONS_1	0.798310	0.02716	29.4	0.000	0.8504
Constant	-20.2695	8.526	-2.38	0.019	0.0358
INC	0.498937	0.02833	17.6	0.000	0.6711
INC_1	-0.276105	0.03788	-7.29	0.000	0.2590
INFLAT	-0.793095	0.1840	-4.31	0.000	0.1090
INFLAT_1	-0.250612	0.2031	-1.23	0.219	0.0099

```
sigma                  1.07836   RSS                  176.753411
R^2                   0.993852   F(5,152) =      4915 [0.000]**
log-likelihood        -8.86069   DW                         1.95
no. of observations        158   no. of parameters             6
mean(CONS)             875.848   var(CONS)              181.971
```

The standard errors are much smaller than any previous results, and partial R^2 are higher, although the correlations between the regressors are quite large:

```
         Correlation matrix
              CONS      CONS_1      INC       INC_1     INFLAT
CONS         1.000
CONS_1       0.9866    1.000
INC          0.9422    0.9310    1.000
INC_1        0.9144    0.9414    0.9510    1.000
INFLAT      -0.3511   -0.2756   -0.1271   -0.07332   1.000
INFLAT_1    -0.4174   -0.3405   -0.1953   -0.1124    0.9266
```

Seven correlations exceed 0.9, yet every coefficient in the regression is well determined, although some are small. For example, the longest lag on INFLAT is irrelevant and could be eliminated. The goodness of fit as measured by s is 50% less than for the first equation, so the general model provides a usable baseline.

Next we test for a common factor:

```
COMFAC Wald test statistic table, COMFAC F(2,152) = 53.1042 [0.0000] **
Order   Cumulative tests                   Incremental tests
  1     Chi^2(2) =   106.21 [0.0000]**     Chi^2(2) =   106.21 [0.0000]**

Roots of lag polynomials:
            real        imag      modulus
CONS      0.79831     0.00000     0.79831
INC       0.55339     0.00000     0.55339
INFLAT   -0.31599     0.00000     0.31599
```

The COMFAC test strongly rejects, and the roots are now well below unity in absolute value.[10] Correspondingly, the long run is well determined, and the unit-root test rejects the null, so cointegration is obtained between CONS, INC and INFLAT:

```
Solved static long run equation for CONS
                Coefficient   Std.Error  t-value  t-prob
Constant          -100.498       37.53    -2.68   0.008
INC                1.10482     0.04185     26.4   0.000
INFLAT            -5.17480      0.5224    -9.91   0.000
Long-run sigma = 5.3466

ECM = CONS + 100.498 - 1.10482*INC + 5.1748*INFLAT;
WALD test: Chi^2(2) = 962.504 [0.0000] **

Tests on the significance of each variable
Variable     F-test          Value [ Prob]    Unit-root t-test
CONS         F(1,152) =     863.96 [0.0000]**       -7.4261**
Constant     F(1,152) =     5.6515 [0.0187]*
INC          F(2,152) =     159.04 [0.0000]**        6.8393
INFLAT       F(2,152) =     69.037 [0.0000]**       -11.1
```

---

[10]Neil Ericsson pointed out to us that, being a Wald test of non-linear restrictions, COMFAC is susceptible to how it is formulated (see e.g., Gregory and Veale, 1985): if the order of the variables was CONS, INFLAT, INC, the test statistic would have been $\chi^2(2) = 76.71 \, [0.000]^{**}$. The test still strongly rejects here, but has a much smaller value.

The model satisfies all the statistics in the diagnostic test summary, and Figure 11.2 shows the improved graphical performance: with a little experience, a glance at Figure 11.1 shows a failed model, whereas Figure 11.2 is fine. Hopefully, your experience is growing rapidly.

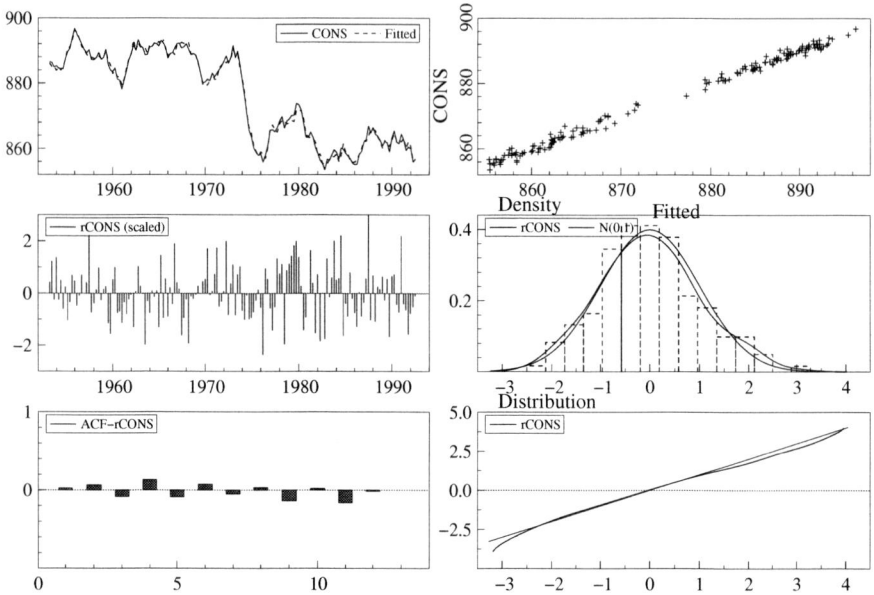

Figure 11.2   Goodness-of-fit measures for ADL.

11.6.5 Time series

PcGive allows all members of the typology to be estimated with ease, and as §11.4.1–§11.4.6 were considered in §11.6 above, we focus on §11.4.7 and §11.4.8 here, but in the opposite order.

11.6.6 Equilibrium correction

The concepts of I(1) behaviour and cointegration (or its absence) were explained above, and were illustrated using the general unrestricted model option by formulating a regression of y_t on x_t and setting the lag length of each variable at unity. After estimation, the long-run solution can be saved and graphed (called EqCM by default in the program). Above, we tested the model for a common factor by the COMFAC procedure and checked if the root was unity using the linear restrictions test: which of course assumed conventional critical values. The PcGive unit-root test was also applied. We now transform the preceding model to an EqCM.

First, CONS, INC and INFLAT are transformed to differences, and the right-hand side levels to EqCM form (denoted CI) using the rounded coefficients:

$$CI = CONS + 100 - INC + 5 \times INFLAT,$$

where income homogeneity is imposed. Add CI lagged one period to the model in differences (the current value of CI must be deleted) and estimate as:

```
EQ( 4)Modelling DCONS by OLS (using data.in7)
        The estimation sample is: 1953 (2) to 1992 (3)
```

	Coefficient	Std.Error	t-value	t-prob	Part.R^2
Constant	18.1489	1.726	10.5	0.000	0.4180
DINC	0.489427	0.02704	18.1	0.000	0.6802
DINFLAT	-0.709203	0.1826	-3.88	0.000	0.0892
CI_1	-0.195899	0.01848	-10.6	0.000	0.4218

```
sigma                   1.0962  RSS                   185.054987
R^2                   0.758689  F(3,154) =       161.4 [0.000]**
log-likelihood       -12.4866  DW                           1.88
no. of observations       158  no. of parameters               4
mean(DCONS)         -0.213409  var(DCONS)                4.85363
```

The outcome is a restricted, I(0), version of the ADL model, and all the coefficient estimates are well determined. The *s* value confirms that the restrictions are acceptable. Testing using the test summary yields:

```
AR 1-5 test:      F(5,149) =      1.4037 [0.2262]
ARCH 1-4 test:    F(4,146) =      1.2801 [0.2805]
Normality test:   Chi^2(2) =     0.17211 [0.9175]
hetero test:      F(6,147) =      0.5359 [0.7803]
hetero-X test:    F(9,144) =     0.76939 [0.6448]
RESET test:       F(1,153) =       1.057 [0.3055]
```

Thus, there is no evidence of mis-specification against the historical sample information. Figure 11.3 shows the goodness of fit and graphical statistics: we have added a regression line to the cross plot both to show its 45° angle, and to remind you that these graphs can be modified as flexibly as desired.

This concludes the EqCM analysis, except that the static regression in the next section both illustrates the Engle and Granger (1987) approach of OLS estimation of a cointegrating model (but see Banerjee, Dolado, Hendry and Smith, 1986), and shows the effects of 'correcting for residual autocorrelation'.

11.6.7 Non-linear least squares, COMFAC, and RALS

As an alternative to direct estimation of the EqCM, return to the general model in §11.6.4 (formulate a model, recall), but delete all the lagged variables, and estimate the resulting static regression (from 1953(2)). If the variables were I(1), this might be the first step of the Engle-Granger procedure.

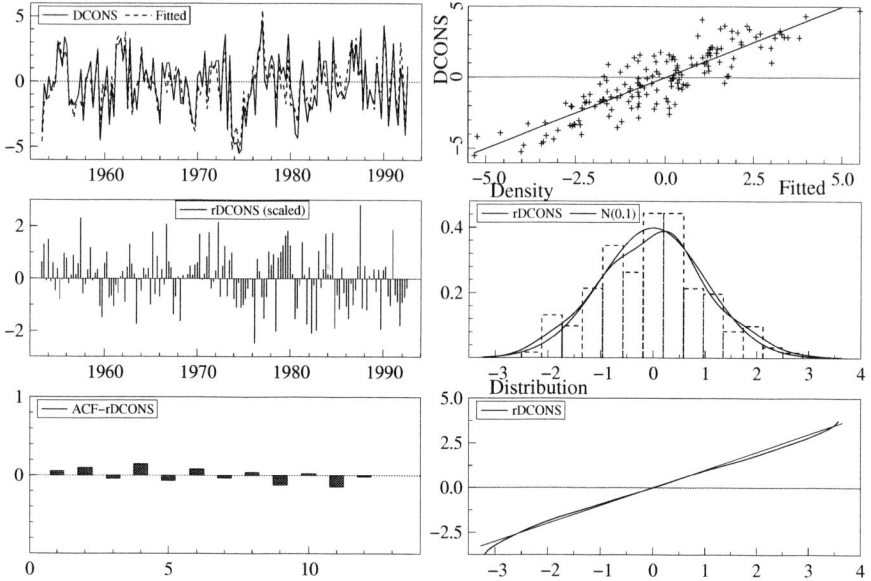

Figure 11.3 Goodness-of-fit measures for EqCM.

```
EQ( 5) Modelling CONS by OLS (using data.in7)
       The estimation sample is: 1953 (2) to 1992 (3)
```

	Coefficient	Std.Error	t-value	t-prob	Part.R^2
Constant	-147.330	22.00	-6.70	0.000	0.2244
INC	1.15256	0.02462	46.8	0.000	0.9340
INFLAT	-2.47521	0.2051	-12.1	0.000	0.4845

sigma	3.27725	RSS	1664.75407
R^2	0.942098	F(2,155) =	1261 [0.000]**
log-likelihood	-186.032	DW	0.601
no. of observations	158	no. of parameters	3
mean(CONS)	875.848	var(CONS)	181.971

RALS denotes rth-order autoregressive least squares, and is for estimating equations with valid common factors, so that their dynamics can be appropriately simplified to an autoregressive error. The residual sum of squares function for RALS is non-linear in the parameters, so an analytic formula for the optimum does not exist, although numerical methods can be used to locate it. In fact, one could always use numerical methods, even for OLS where an exact form does exist, although it might be a little slow. To illustrate this principle, we first re-fit the static OLS regression by numerical optimization, and compare the outcome with the result found by the analytical formula. Access the Nonlinear modelling choice on the Model menu, and formulate the instructions as follows:

```
actual = CONS;
fitted = &0 + &1*INC + &2*INFLAT;
&0 = -147.3301;
&1 = 1.152563;
&2 = -2.475206;
```

Estimate from 1953 (2); convergence is fast and the outcomes are almost identical (even though standard errors are calculated numerically, not from the variance formula): in particular, the RSS values match precisely.

```
EQ( 6) Modelling actual by NLS (using data.in7)
        The estimation sample is: 1953 (2) to 1992 (3)
```

	Coefficient	Std.Error	t-value	t-prob	Part.R^2
&0	-147.33	22.00	-6.70	0.000	0.2244
&1	1.1526	0.02462	46.8	0.000	0.9340
&2	-2.4752	0.2051	-12.1	0.000	0.4845

sigma	3.27725	RSS		1664.75407
R^2	0.942098	F(2,155) =	1261	[0.000]**
log-likelihood	-186.032	DW		0.601
no. of observations	158	no. of parameters		3
mean(actual)	875.848	var(actual)		181.971

```
Standard errors based on information matrix
BFGS/warm-up using numerical derivatives (eps1=0.0001; eps2=0.005):
Strong convergence
```

Following the route at the end of the previous section, for the static model of CONS on INC and INFLAT, the value of the DW statistic suggests a high degree of residual autocorrelation. This 'problem' might be 'corrected' by removing the autocorrelation, so we consider that possibility next. Recall the static model, and estimate from 1953(2) using Autoregressive Least Squares (RALS), with a first-order error process. At the RALS estimation dialog, use Grid to graph the log-likelihood as a function of the first-order autoregressive error parameter.[11] Multiple optima are quite common in RALS, and can be revealed by this procedure. Here, you will find that the optimum is on the boundary at unity – not an auspicious start. Use Estimate to start the numerical optimization, and OK to conclude.

```
EQ( 7) Modelling CONS by RALS (using data.in7)
        The estimation sample is: 1953 (2) to 1992 (3)
```

	Coefficient	Std.Error	t-value	t-prob	Part.R^2
Constant	403.491	34.87	11.6	0.000	0.4651
INC	0.519878	0.03548	14.7	0.000	0.5823
INFLAT	-0.724649	0.2449	-2.96	0.004	0.0538
Uhat_1	0.988354	0.01450	68.2	0.000	0.9679

---

[11]This is the concentrated (or profile) likelihood: for each autoregressive value the likelihood is maximized.

```
sigma                  1.43855  RSS                    318.693176
no. of observations        158  no. of parameters               4
mean(CONS)             875.848  var(CONS)                 181.971
```

```
NLS estimation using analytical derivatives (eps1=0.0001; eps2=0.005):
Strong convergence
Roots of error polynomial:
          real         imag      modulus
       0.98835      0.00000      0.98835
```

Consider these results in the light of §11.4.7, and use the RSS value to calculate a likelihood ratio test of COMFAC against the unrestricted dynamic model in §11.6 ($RSS_{\text{comfac}}(4) = 318.69$ and $RSS_{\text{unrest}}(6) = 176.75$):

$$\mathsf{F}_{T-K_1}^{K_1-K_2} = \frac{(318.69 - 176.75) \times 152}{176.75 \times 2} = 61.$$

The evidence fits like a glove: the DGP is not COMFAC, but EqCM. Figure 11.4 shows the RALS graphical output.

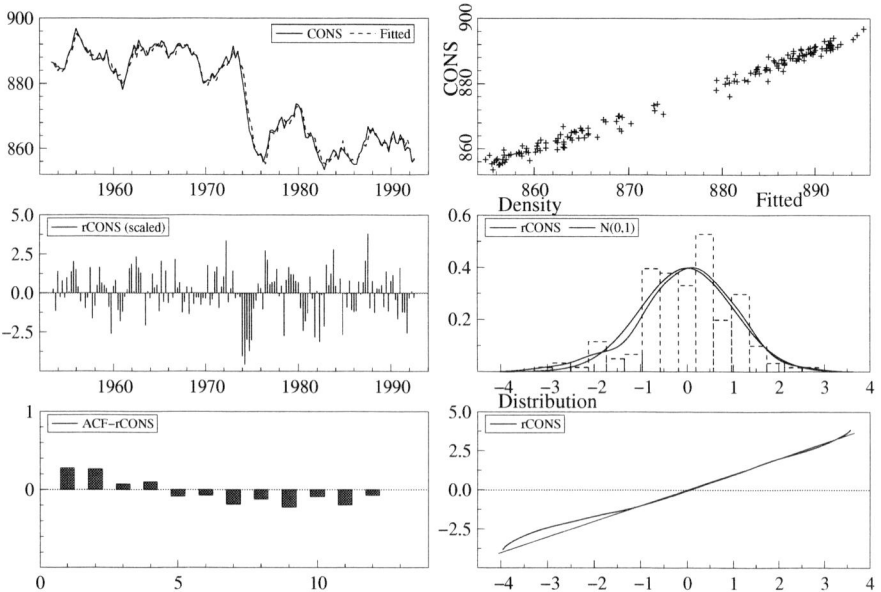

Figure 11.4   Goodness-of-fit measures for RALS.

11.7 Econometrics concepts

11.7.1 Innovations and white noise

It is possible to obtain a significant value on a COMFAC test, yet the residuals of the resulting RALS model be white noise according to the residual correlogram (Portmanteau) statistic; such an outcome illustrates a non-innovation white-noise process. The former outcome (i.e., COMFAC rejects) entails that a better model can be developed on the same information set (that is, a model which does not impose COMFAC) – so the error is not an innovation. The latter outcome shows that the same error is white noise (not serially correlated).

An alternative illustration of that distinction can be created by dropping the EqCM term from the model in §11.6. The correlogram statistic can be insignificant, but the omitted-variable test option shows that the EqCM term still matters, so that the residuals are not an innovation against lagged levels information (see Davidson, Hendry, Srba and Yeo, 1978, and Hendry and von Ungern-Sternberg, 1981, for empirical examples). Delete the equilibrium-correction term from the model in §11.6.6, and add in the 1-period lags of the three differences (so the resulting model has no long-run levels solution) to produce:

```
EQ( 8) Modelling DCONS by OLS (using data.in7)
        The estimation sample is: 1953 (3) to 1992 (3)
```

	Coefficient	Std.Error	t-value	t-prob	Part.R^2
DCONS_1	0.260429	0.07369	3.53	0.001	0.0764
Constant	-0.0644508	0.1042	-0.619	0.537	0.0025
DINC	0.527350	0.03262	16.2	0.000	0.6338
DINFLAT	-0.529530	0.2883	-1.84	0.068	0.0218
DINC_1	-0.00786886	0.04963	-0.159	0.874	0.0002
DINFLAT_1	-0.744058	0.2822	-2.64	0.009	0.0440

```
sigma               1.29654  RSS                 253.831609
R^2                 0.662972  F(5,151) =     59.41 [0.000]**
log-likelihood      -37.7134  DW                        2.27
no. of observations      157  no. of parameters            6
mean(DCONS)        -0.189886  var(DCONS)             4.79712
```

Figure 11.5 reports the corresponding graphical information: the correlogram is fairly flat and close to that of a white-noise process even though the errors contain the omitted EqCM, which would have a t-value of about **10** if entered directly in the model. An appropriate test for autocorrelated errors would reject, however. Also see the discussion in Hendry (1995a), and in §14.2 and §14.3.

11.7.2 Exogeneity

This analytic notion is described in §13.5.2, and recurs in §14.5: for a fuller treatment see Engle, Hendry and Richard (1983). To illustrate, it happens that, in the present

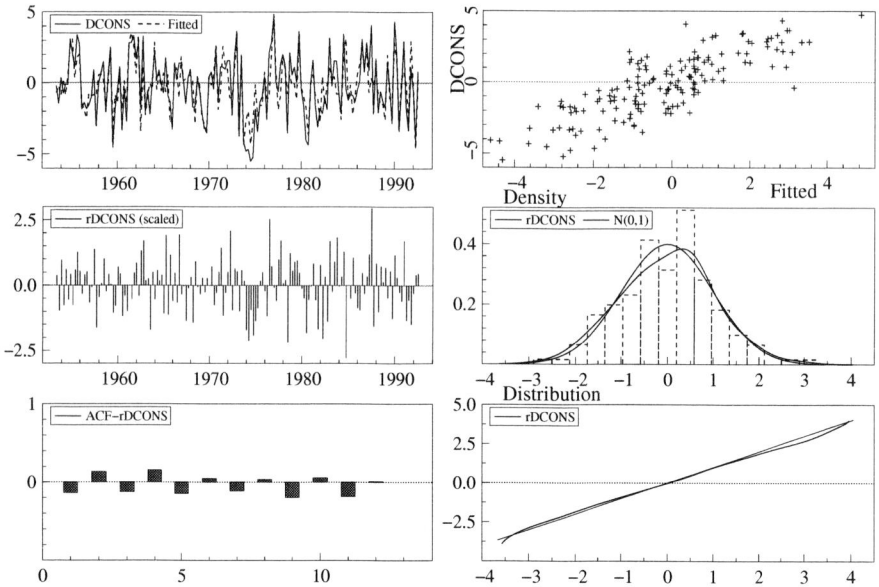

Figure 11.5   Mis-specified EqCM with near white-noise residuals.

data set, there is no valid consumption function with income weakly exogenous for invariant parameters of interest (CONS and INC are simultaneously determined); this is not easily tested at an intermediate level: however, instrumental variables methods (discussed below) could be used to investigate such a difficulty.

The comparison of §11.5.3 and §11.5.4 is illuminating since $\mathbf{x}_t$ is not weakly exogenous for β in the latter. The required exogeneity condition is that β can be learned from the conditional model alone, without loss of information. Thus, the $\mathbf{x}_t$ variables can be taken as given, or 'determined outside the model under consideration'. That this condition fails here is clear from the construction of the DGP in the Appendix. It also follows on the 'conventional' notion of exogeneity, since $\mathsf{E}[\mathbf{x}_t\epsilon_t] \neq \mathbf{0}$ in §11.5.4. Nevertheless, the 'conventional' notion of exogeneity is flawed, as we now explain. When the DGP is stationary, regressing y_t on $\mathbf{x}_t$ will deliver a coefficient vector α (say) with the property that $\mathsf{E}[y_t|\mathbf{x}_t] = \alpha'\mathbf{x}_t$, and so there exists a model $y_t = \alpha'\mathbf{x}_t + \xi_t$ where $\mathsf{E}[\mathbf{x}_t\xi_t] = \mathbf{0}$. Apparently, $\mathbf{x}_t$ is now 'exogenous'! Indeed, $\mathbf{x}_t$ is weakly exogenous for α in that model, but α is, of course, not the parameter of interest, β. However, the two parameters are related, which we illustrate by letting $\mathbf{x}_t = \mathbf{\Gamma}\mathbf{x}_{t-1} + \boldsymbol{\nu}_t$, so $\mathsf{E}[\mathbf{x}_t|\mathbf{x}_{t-1}] = \mathbf{\Gamma}\mathbf{x}_{t-1}$, and $\mathsf{E}[\boldsymbol{\nu}_t\boldsymbol{\nu}_t'] = \mathbf{\Omega}$. In §11.5.4, we saw that $\mathsf{E}[\boldsymbol{\nu}_t\eta_s] = \mathbf{0}\,\forall t, s$ was not sufficient for $\mathbf{x}_t$ to be weakly exogenous for β. Under stationarity, letting $\mathbf{\Phi} = \mathsf{E}[\mathbf{x}_t\mathbf{x}_t']$, then:

$$\alpha = \left(\mathsf{E}[\mathbf{x}_t\mathbf{x}_t']\right)^{-1}\left(\mathsf{E}[\mathbf{x}_ty_t]\right) = \left(\mathbf{I}_k - \mathbf{\Phi}^{-1}\mathbf{\Omega}\right)\beta,$$

and so depends on $\mathbf{\Gamma}$ and $\mathbf{\Omega}$. Thus, β cannot be obtained from α without knowledge of

$(\mathbf{\Gamma}, \mathbf{\Omega})$, which are the parameters of the $\{\mathbf{x}_t\}$ process, showing that the requirements for weak exogeneity are not satisfied: the parameter of interest can be obtained only by modelling $\{\mathbf{x}_t\}$. This case is most easily derived for a scalar x-process, where $\Phi = \Omega / \left(1 - \Gamma^2\right)$ and $\alpha = \Gamma^2 \beta$. This outcome is closely related to errors-in-variables models, such as permanent income.

Finally, the presence or absence of $\mathbf{x}_t$ in the equation is not germane to its weak exogeneity status. To show that, §11.5.4 entails that $y_t = \beta' \mathbf{\Gamma} \mathbf{x}_{t-1} + \epsilon_t + \beta' \nu_t$ and hence $\mathsf{E}[y_t | \mathbf{x}_{t-1}] = \beta' \mathbf{\Gamma} \mathbf{x}_{t-1}$ is a valid specification for regression. However, β can be obtained from $\beta' \mathbf{\Gamma}$ only if $\mathbf{\Gamma}$ is known, which necessitates estimating the marginal model for $\mathbf{x}_t$. That example reveals that $\mathbf{x}_t$ need not be weakly exogenous for the parameter of interest even when $\mathbf{x}_t$ is absent from the equation analyzed.

Importantly, non-stationarity is the more usual state for economic time series, in which case $\mathbf{\Gamma}$ and $\mathbf{\Omega}$ are likely to be non-constant, inducing non-constancy in α even when β is constant. Thus, we turn to investigating that issue.

11.7.3 Constancy and invariance

Recursive-estimation techniques are discussed formally in Chapter 12, but PcGive embodies graphical options which make parameter constancy, or its absence, easy to illustrate. The basic idea is straightforward. A tedious way to see if parameters are constant would be to fit the model to the first $M > k$ observations for k parameters, then to fit it to $M + 1$, $M + 2$ etc. up to T, yielding $T - M + 1$ estimates of each coefficient and its standard error over the sample. Plotting these would reveal any changes relative to the standard error measures. Fortunately, there are clever ways of doing so built into PcGive and we merely have to choose recursive estimation to obtain all the required statistics and associated tests. Use the same model as the final one for DCONS in §11.6.6, and estimate by RLS. Figure 11.6 illustrates the graphical output.

The first four plots are of the coefficient estimates at each point in the sample together with their approximate 95% confidence intervals ($\pm 2SE$ shown on either side); for most of the data set, the estimates are significantly different from zero, and are relatively constant over the sample once past the initial estimation. The fifth plot is of the 1-step ahead residuals (forecast errors) also with an approximate 95% confidence interval; the confidence bands are again reasonably constant, but increase somewhat around 1974. However, the final plot of the break-point Chow test (see Chow, 1960) shows that constancy is rejected at the 1% level over the oil-crisis period, and looking more carefully at the coefficient plots, the change in the coefficient of DINFLAT is noticeable.

Invariance is more complex to illustrate, so the artificial data set is helpful. (The Appendix shows the DGP for the tutorial data set.) Consider a sine wave – it is non-constant, but invariant to other changes. Above, we found that α was constant under stationarity, but not invariant to changes in the process generating $\mathbf{x}$. Thus, the two

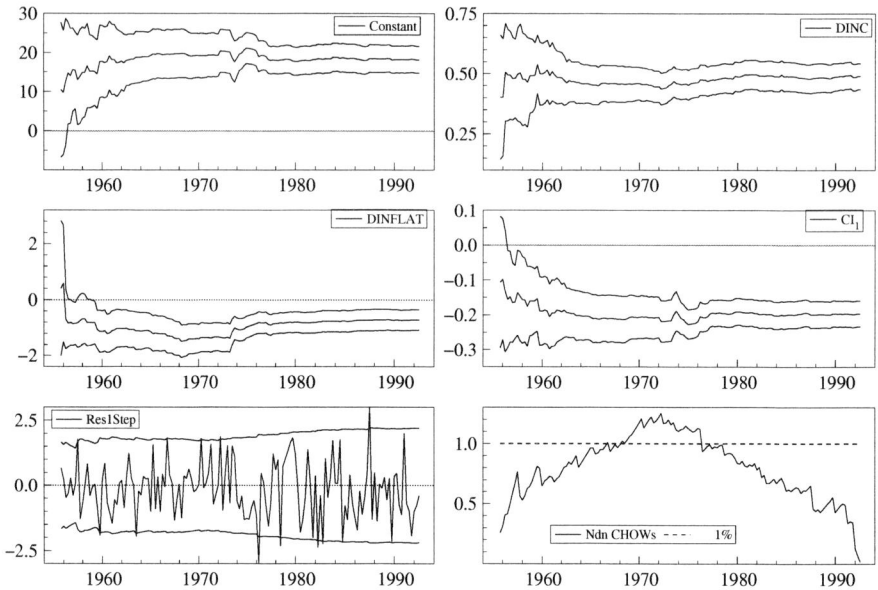

Figure 11.6   Recursive constancy statistics for EqCM.

concepts are distinct. To test for invariance in a regression model, one must first find changes in the processes generating the regressors, then check if any regression parameters shift at the same time: that would refute a claim of invariance. Here, a model of INFLAT on OUTPUT and INFLAT_1 is highly non-constant following 1973(3) (see Figure 11.7). This is precisely the point at which the coefficient of DINFLAT showed a shift in the conditional EqCM model, EQ(4), consistent with non-invariance of the inflation coefficient: see the last panel Figure 11.7. The common omitted factor in both models is the Oil-price jump. A more realistic case of invariance analysis is described in Hendry (1988).

11.7.4 Congruent models

We have now seen a variety of criteria that a model might reasonably be required to satisfy, such as white-noise, innovation errors, homoscedasticity, constant parameters that appear invariant to important historical and policy changes, and weakly exogenous conditioning variables for the parameters of interest. The first three relate to the ability of a model to characterize the past; the middle two, to its ability to describe the future; and the last to its validity in the present. A model which shows no departures from the data on any of the evaluation criteria is said to be congruent with the evidence. Non-congruent models can always be dominated by a model that explains the previous mis-match; and the DGP is clearly congruent with the data, so congruent models have much to recommend them. However, a sequence of congruent models of any given phe-

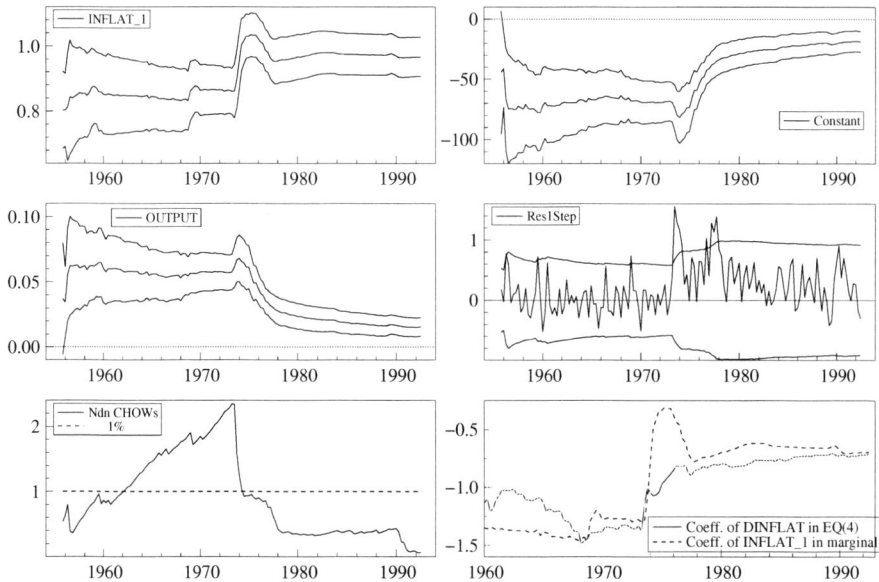

Figure 11.7 Recursive constancy statistics for marginal, and invariance comparison.

nomenon could be developed, each explaining more by augmenting the information set appropriately. Thus, we need a further criterion to choose between them, as discussed in the next section.

11.7.5 Encompassing rival models

Encompassing is easy to illustrate in PcGive, so we first explain the concept and its properties. Consider two rival explanations of a given variable denoted by M_1 and M_2. The question at issue is whether the M_2 model can explain features of the data which the M_1 model cannot. This is a test of M_1, with M_2 providing the alternative, to see whether M_2 captures any specific information not embodied in M_1. The converse is whether M_1 can account for all the results found by M_2, and that idea is formalized in the notion of encompassing (see Hendry and Richard, 1982, 1989, Mizon, 1984, and Mizon and Richard, 1986). A congruent undominated model should encompass (that is, account for) previous empirical findings claimed to explain the given dependent variable(s). Encompassing is denoted by $\mathcal{E}$ so if the relevant models are M_1 and M_2, then $M_1 \, \mathcal{E} \, M_2$ reads as 'M_1 encompasses M_2'. Notice that variance dominance (fitting better on the basis of error variance) is not sufficient for encompassing (the other model could still explain part of what the first did not), but is necessary (as the better-fitting model clearly explains some aspects better than the other).

The ease of handling general models allows embedding approaches to be almost automatic in PcGive. Encompassing and non-nested hypothesis tests are offered for

OLS and instrumental variables (IV), based on Cox (1961), Pesaran (1974) and Ericsson (1983), allowing pairs of single equation models to be tested directly. As argued in Hendry and Richard (1989), encompassing essentially requires a simple model to explain a more general one within which it is nested (often the union of the simple model with its rivals); this notion is called parsimonious encompassing and is denoted by $\mathcal{E}_p$. An important property of parsimonious encompassing is that it defines a partial ordering over models, since $\mathcal{E}_p$ is transitive, reflexive, and anti-symmetric. Since some aspects of inference must go wrong when a model is non-congruent, encompassing tests should only be conducted with respect to a 'baseline' congruent model; and is anyway unnecessary otherwise since non-congruence already demonstrates inadequacies (for a formal analysis, see Bontemps and Mizon, 2002).

To apply encompassing procedures, we need to have non-nested two models of interest. For the first, use the ADL (1 lag) of CONS on INC and INFLAT; and for the second CONS on OUTPUT with two lags of each, both from 1953(3). Formulate and estimate them in that order, then from the Test menu, select Encompassing to produce:

```
Encompassing test statistics: 1953 (3) to 1992 (3)

M1 is: CONS on
  Constant   CONS_1    INC     INC_1     INFLAT    INFLAT_1
M2 is: CONS on
  CONS_1    CONS_2    Constant      OUTPUT      OUTPUT_1    OUTPUT_2

Instruments used:
  Constant     CONS_1       INC          INC_1        INFLAT
  INFLAT_1     CONS_2       OUTPUT       OUTPUT_1     OUTPUT_2

sigma[M1] = 1.08126   sigma[M2] = 2.03616   sigma[Joint] = 1.09367

Test          Model 1 vs. Model 2            Model 2 vs. Model 1
Cox           N(0,1)  =   0.1961 [0.8445]    N(0,1)   =  -46.16 [0.0000]**
Ericsson IV   N(0,1)  =  -0.1929 [0.8471]    N(0,1)   =   24.69 [0.0000]**
Sargan        Chi^2(4) =  0.60786 [0.9622]   Chi^2(4) =  108.59 [0.0000]**
Joint Model   F(4,147) =  0.14861 [0.9634]   F(4,147) =  94.099 [0.0000]**
```

The tests produced are those due to Cox (1961), (distributed asymptotically as $N[0, 1]$ on the null of encompassing; Ericsson (1983) (an IV-based test with the same limiting distribution), another IV test developed by Sargan (1959), distributed as χ^2 with the degrees of freedom shown, and the F-test for each model being a valid simplification of the linear union of the two models under test. The second model clearly does not encompass the first on any of the tests, whereas the first is not rejected by the second. We conclude that the second is inferentially redundant and the first remains undominated. Since empirical models can be designed to satisfy a range of criteria (see §11.10), encompassing tests against models designed by other investigators offer a useful check against spurious findings.

11.8 Instrumental variables

The method of instrumental variables was developed to handle endogenous regressors in models, but using limited information. It may happen that in the linear equation (11.28), $E[y_t|\mathbf{x}_t] \neq \mathbf{x}_t'\boldsymbol{\beta}$ so that $E[\mathbf{x}_t\epsilon_t] \neq \mathbf{0}$. An example is a behavioural model. Then OLS estimation is not consistent for $\boldsymbol{\beta}$ (try proving this claim). Assume there is a $k \times 1$ vector $\mathbf{z}_t$ such that:

$$E[y_t \mid \mathbf{z}_t] = E[\mathbf{x}_t \mid \mathbf{z}_t]'\boldsymbol{\beta} \tag{11.34}$$

so $E[\mathbf{z}_t'\epsilon_t] = \mathbf{0}$. The role of $\mathbf{z}_t$ is purely instrumental in estimating $\boldsymbol{\beta}$, and its use leads to instrumental variables estimators (IVE) as follows (the case of more than k instruments is handled automatically by PcGive, but $\boldsymbol{\beta}$ is not estimable when there are fewer than k instruments).

We only consider the case where $E[\mathbf{Z}'\epsilon] = \mathbf{0}$ but in $\mathbf{y} = \mathbf{X}\boldsymbol{\beta} + \epsilon$, $E[\mathbf{X}'\epsilon] \neq \mathbf{0}$. Premultiply (11.29) by $\mathbf{Z}'$:

$$\mathbf{Z}'\mathbf{y} = \mathbf{Z}'\mathbf{X}\boldsymbol{\beta} + \mathbf{Z}'\epsilon \tag{11.35}$$

When $\text{rank}(T^{-1}\mathbf{Z}'\mathbf{X}) = k$, so that the matrix is invertible (which is also sufficient to identify $\boldsymbol{\beta}$: see White, 1984) then $\text{rank}(T^{-1}\mathbf{Z}'\mathbf{Z}) = k$. Thus, setting $\mathbf{Z}'\epsilon = \mathbf{0}$,,which it should be on average:

$$\widetilde{\boldsymbol{\beta}} = (\mathbf{Z}'\mathbf{X})^{-1}\mathbf{Z}'\mathbf{y} \tag{11.36}$$

which is the instrumental variables estimator. In large samples, its variance matrix is estimated by:

$$\widetilde{\sigma}_\epsilon^2 \left[\mathbf{X}'\mathbf{Z}(\mathbf{Z}'\mathbf{Z})^{-1}\mathbf{Z}'\mathbf{X}\right]^{-1} \tag{11.37}$$

where:

$$\widetilde{\epsilon} = \mathbf{y} - \mathbf{X}\widetilde{\boldsymbol{\beta}} \text{ and } \widetilde{\sigma}_\epsilon^2 = \frac{\widetilde{\epsilon}'\widetilde{\epsilon}}{T-k}. \tag{11.38}$$

Check that the formulae collapse to the OLS outcomes when $\mathbf{Z} = \mathbf{X}$. However, statistics like R^2 are not so easily defined.

The fourth case of §11.5 can be compared to the third when the IVs are variables in $\mathcal{I}_{t-1}$. When §11.5.3 holds with ϵ_t being an innovation against $\mathcal{I}_{t-1}$, then $E[y_t|\mathbf{x}_t] = \mathbf{x}_t'\boldsymbol{\beta}$ implies that $E[y_t|\mathcal{I}_{t-1}] = \boldsymbol{\beta}'E[\mathbf{x}_t|\mathcal{I}_{t-1}]$ also. The converse does *not* hold, however, otherwise types §11.5.3 and §11.5.4 would coincide. Check that you can prove this claim. Since the failure of OLS is owing to the $\{\mathbf{x}_t\}$ process being informative about the parameter of interest, the analysis of exogeneity above is directly relevant to clarifying when regression can be used.

The EqCM model of CONS in fact has INC endogenous owing to contemporaneous feedback, so we now estimate it by IV, using 1-lagged values of DCONS and DINC as instruments, as well as the other regressors (DINFLAT and the CI_1). The full sample estimates and test statistics are:

```
EQ( 9) Modelling DCONS by IVE (using data.in7)
        The estimation sample is: 1953 (3) to 1992 (3)

                       Coefficient  Std.Error  t-value  t-prob
DINC            Y        0.440453      0.1323     3.33   0.001
Constant                18.5348        1.884      9.84   0.000
DINFLAT                 -0.618109      0.2714    -2.28   0.024
CI_1                    -0.200159      0.02026   -9.88   0.000

sigma                    1.11086  RSS                 188.804732
Reduced form sigma       1.9202
no. of observations        157   no. of parameters          4
no. endogenous variables     2   no. of instruments         5
mean(DCONS)             -0.189886  var(DCONS)            4.79712

Additional instruments:
[0] = DCONS_1
[1] = DINC_1

Specification test: Chi^2(1) =   0.5315 [0.4660]
Testing beta = 0:   Chi^2(3) =   155.66 [0.0000]**
```

As can be seen by comparing with the earlier OLS results, the coefficients of INC and INFLAT are smaller, and their standard errors much larger. The EqCM coefficient is somewhat larger. The value of s is not much altered, but the much larger value of the 'reduced form' s (which measures the fit from regressing CONS on the instruments) shows the importance of contemporaneous information. The specification χ^2 tests for the independence of the instruments and the errors (see §16.3.3 and Sargan, 1958) does not reject, and the diagnostic tests yield similar outcomes to OLS. We conclude this section with the recursive statistics graphs (no equivalent of the Chow tests is provided for IV) shown in Figure 11.8. The parameters are reasonably constant, although that for INFLAT still shows signs of changing around the oil crisis.

11.9 Inference and diagnostic testing

Many aspects of inference and testing have occurred above, so a preliminary knowledge was implicitly assumed throughout. Formal derivations will not be presented (see Godfrey, 1988) but the intuition behind the Lagrange Multiplier (LM)-test for residual autocorrelation, ARCH etc. is useful. These statistics are essentially extrapolating from the likelihood function value when a parameter has been restricted (usually to zero) to what the likelihood value would be when the parameter was estimated. When the likelihood is quadratic, the score is linear and the extrapolation is completely successful (that is, the outcome is the same as a likelihood-ratio test). Asymptotically, as likelihoods are quadratic, LM-tests become fully powerful for the correct size (null rejection frequency).

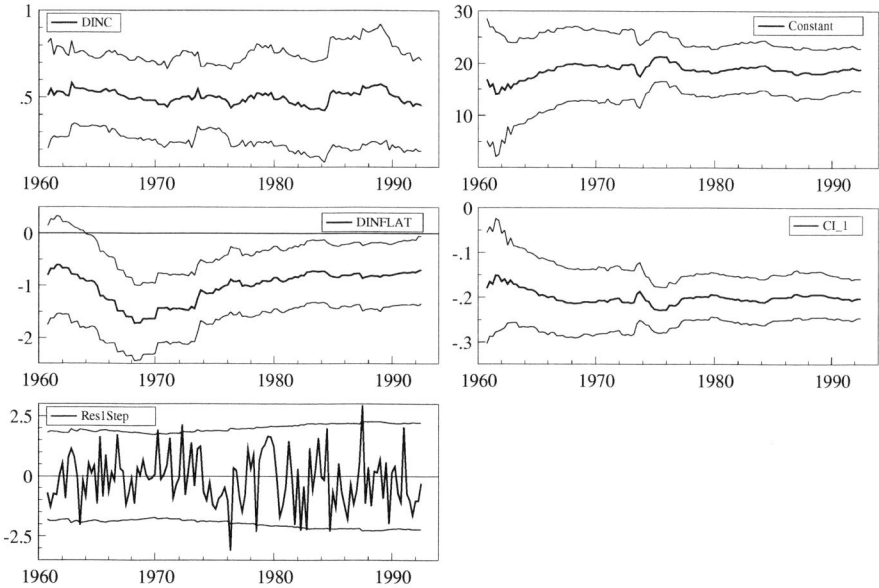

Figure 11.8 Recursive constancy statistics for IV estimation.

However, some statistics are LM-tests only under restrictive assumptions: for example, the Durbin–Watson test is an LM-test when the regressors are fixed, but ceases to be correct for lagged endogenous variables. A feature worth showing empirically is the flattening of the residual correlogram in models with lagged dependent variables. To do so, we contrast the residual autoregression coefficients and the associated F-test with those entailed in the equivalent length LM-test. When the model is mis-specified as a partial adjustment of CONS on INC and INFLAT, we find using the residuals:

```
Modelling Residual by OLS (using data.in7)
The estimation sample is: 1953 (4) to 1992 (3)
                 Coefficient  Std.Error  t-value  t-prob Part.R^2
Residual_1          0.169655    0.08000     2.12   0.036   0.0286
Residual_2          0.112725    0.08067     1.40   0.164   0.0126
Constant         -0.00413131     0.1027   -0.0402   0.968   0.0000

sigma               1.28233  RSS               251.586866
R^2               0.0486202  F(2,153) =      3.91 [0.022]*

Error autocorrelation coefficients in auxiliary regression:
  Lag Coefficient   Std.Error
   1     0.20089     0.08482
   2     0.14669     0.08458
RSS = 251.956  sigma = 1.65761

Testing for error autocorrelation from lags 1 to 2
  Chi^2(2) =      9.118 [0.0105]*  and F-form F(2,152) =    4.6545 [0.0109]*
```

Both tests happen to reject the null, but the LM F-test is about 20% larger, and its first-order autoregressive coefficient is about 25% larger.

A similar bias occurs even if there is no lagged dependent variable, but x_t is Granger-caused by y (see Granger, 1969, and Hendry and Mizon, 1999): again this is easy to demonstrate. Many other tests can be computed using PcGive, but in general, inference is better illustrated using Monte Carlo to simulate the actual distributions, sizes and powers. Nevertheless, the methodology of modelling is open to analysis at this stage, of which mis-specification tests are one aspect, so we turn to consider that.

11.10 Model selection

Some discussion, and empirical illustration, of the issue of model selection is imperative if econometrics is to find any practical use, even as a set of critical skills. Unfortunately, the topic is a vast one, often misunderstood (and subject to folklore, rather than fact), and so prone to disastrous outcomes in a teaching context. Nevertheless, we will first describe a general framework, then consider model design.

11.10.1 Three levels of knowledge

It is useful to distinguish between the three levels of knowledge potentially available in a theoretical analysis. Write the data set as $\mathbf{X}_T^1 = (\mathbf{x}_1 \ldots \mathbf{x}_T)$ and denote the DGP by the joint data density $\mathsf{D}_X \left(\mathbf{X}_T^1 | \boldsymbol{\theta} \right)$. Then:

(1) Both $\mathsf{D}_X (\cdot)$ and $\boldsymbol{\theta}$ being known corresponds to a probability theory course: that is, given $\mathsf{D}_X (\cdot | \boldsymbol{\theta})$, what xs will be observed, and with what probabilities of lying in various regions? The analyses in the first two sections above are examples of this level of knowledge.

(2) $\mathsf{D}_X (\cdot)$ known and $\boldsymbol{\theta}$ unknown corresponds to an estimation and inference course, that is, given $\mathbf{X}_T^1$ and knowledge of $\mathsf{D}_X (\cdot)$, how should one estimate $\boldsymbol{\theta}$? This route leads on to likelihood, maximum likelihood estimation etc., and characterizes the state of knowledge implicit in Chapter 12.

(3) Both $\mathsf{D}_X (\cdot)$ and $\boldsymbol{\theta}$ unknown corresponds to a modelling course: that is, given only $\mathbf{X}_T^1$ how do we discover, design or develop useful models of the observables, and what criteria characterize 'useful' etc.?

Since (3) is the realistic situation in empirical econometrics, §11.6 discussed a number of the background issues. The illustrations above fell in an intermediate state, as we knew the DGP, but did not use that knowledge except to explain the observed outcomes – and the reader did not necessarily know the DGP.

Two important issues arise once the limited knowledge of (3) is granted: first, the postulated likelihood function for an empirical model need not coincide with the actual density function of the observables; and secondly, models will inevitably be simplifications, not facsimiles of the economic mechanism. Both issues highlight that it is crucial to test empirical claims rigorously – and that feature is certainly built into Pc-Give. More fundamentally, we must first address the selection of the criteria by which to judge models, and the problems deriving from our ability to design empirical models to achieve such pre-specified criteria, even when the DGP does not satisfying those criteria. The former was briefly addressed above in the context of congruency, so we turn to the latter.

11.10.2 Modelling criteria

Sections 13.4 and 13.5 will consider more rigorously the range of relevant criteria for model selection in terms of necessary conditions for congruence. As noted earlier, a model is congruent when it matches the available evidence in all the dimensions examined (for example, has innovation, homoscedastic errors, constant parameters etc.). To check whether or not a model does match the evidence is a 'destructive' application of inference (testing in order to reject), and that destructive, or evaluation, aspect has been covered (in part) already in §11.6 above (see Baba, Hendry and Starr, 1992, for an example analyzing US M1 demand). We now seek more constructive criteria, always with the caveat that corroboration is not definitive (see e.g. Ericsson and Hendry, 1999).

Information criteria, which penalize for additional parameters more just than the degrees of freedom adjustment to $\widehat{\sigma}$, are often used – but assume that many of the necessary criteria for congruence are already satisfied. They are related to the use of R^2, $\bar{R}^2$ and $\widehat{\sigma}^2$ as model-selection criteria, and in finite samples seem preferable to those. PcGive provides three, namely the Schwarz, Hannan–Quinn, and final prediction error criteria (see Chapter 16), and uses the Schwarz criterion in general-to-specific modelling for selecting between congruent simplifications. However, within a class of models under comparison, nothing justifies the 'best' of these by any information criterion when they are all badly mis-specified – which emphasizes the prior need to have established the 'goodness' of the class as a data description. Thus, we come back to the need to develop congruent models, then select between these by encompassing.

That approach involves two stages: first formulate and test the general model; then simplify it to a parsimonious, undominated relation (model reduction). The first step is when we use mis-specification tests to evaluate the congruence of the general model; the use of diagnostic tests at later stages (during simplification) is merely as an aid to revealing invalid reductions. The statistical problems concern the probabilities of the mis-specification tests (which is relatively easy in technical terms, and could be resolved by a single 'portmanteau' test), and the consequences of 'revising the model in the light of test rejections'. The latter is only amenable to general discussion, since if the revision chanced to lead to specifying the DGP, the consequences would be brilliant – but that seems unlikely. Thus, we next consider the problem of 'covert', or implicit, design of models specifically to render insignificant any mis-specification tests.

11.10.3 Implicit model design

The reinterpretation of RALS estimation, following a significant residual autocorrelation test, as covert, or implicit, design should now be clear. Irrespective of the cause of the residual autocorrelation, a high enough order autoregressive error process fitted to the residuals can remove residual autocorrelation – and hence 'designs' the model according to a white-noise selection criterion. In the discussion of COMFAC, we noted that the order of hypothesis testing was incorrect. One must first establish the congruence of the general dynamic relation, then test for common factors in the dynamics, and finally test their significance when they the provide a valid reduction. More generally, we saw the problems with unstructured searches such as simple-to-general at the start of this chapter. A simple model of a complicated process can be made to 'work' by selecting a particular criterion (for example, white-noise residuals) and an associated test statistic, then successively correcting the problem until the test is insignificant. However, a second test (for example, COMFAC, or constancy) may still reject, forcing the entire exercise up to that point to be discarded, or lead to an unfounded strategy of patching the next mistake. Rejection means that all previous inferences were invalid, including even the existence of the initial problem. Thus, simple-to-general is an inefficient research strategy. Apparent residual autocorrelation (say) could derive from the wrong functional form (linear instead of log), or even parameter change: 'fixing' residual autocorrelation is then valueless. Also, alternative routes begin to multiply because simple-to-general is a divergent branching process – there are many possible solutions to each rejection, but the model evolves differently depending on which is selected, and in what order. Moreover, when should you stop testing or correcting previous rejections? There are obvious dangers in stopping at the first non-rejection (see the analysis of selecting the order of an autoregressive process in Anderson, 1971).

Conversely, with a pre-defined stopping point (that is, a general model in the background), a more coherent strategy is possible. The ordering of hypothesis tests is often clearer, rejections do not lead to a loss of previous work, and the tests are nested. Once the initial general model is rigorously tested for congruence, later tests are of reductions, not of model validity. Further, it is clear when to stop: when the selected model parsimoniously encompasses the initial general model, but fails to do so on further simplification. Of course, if the initial model is non-congruent, there is no alternative to a generalization, but that is not a telling argument against general-to-simple (denoted *Gets* below): a simpler starting point would fare even less well.

11.10.4 Explicit model design

Consequently, PcGive is easiest to use for sequential simplification following the testing for congruence of the initial general model (often called the statistical model: see

Spanos, 1986). Why simplify? We consider that parsimony is essential for test power and for interpretability, and is often found to sustain parameter constancy. Collinearity is not the driving force behind simplification: we saw above that models can be designed to have orthogonal parameters, however many regressors there are. On the other hand, orthogonality is useful for robustness and for testing for the marginal significance of each variable in isolation (that is, without strong *ceteris paribus* assumptions), as well as for interpretability. Thus, we aim to conclude with parsimonious models which have orthogonal regressors, as well as satisfying the necessary conditions for both congruence and encompassing.

Models can also be designed to be consistent with the available economic theory, which leads to the concept of an econometric model (which again must be congruent and should parsimoniously encompass the statistical model). Section 13.5.7 discusses sequential simplification in the theory of reduction (the Progress menu tracks explicit designs). Although it may seem to be useful to retain a subset of data throughout (for example, by initially loading only a time subset of the available data), since Neyman–Pearson testing for quality control can then be undertaken at the end of the analysis, what would you do next if this led to rejection after six months' work?

The process of model simplification can be surprisingly time consuming, so we have developed a companion program called PcGets: see Hendry and Krolzig (1999), and Krolzig and Hendry (2001), who build on Hoover and Perez (1999). There is now considerable Monte Carlo simulation evidence that *Gets* performs well, selecting a model from an initial general specification almost as often as the same criteria would when applied to the DGP (since test size leads to false rejections, and non-unit power to false acceptances of the null even when the analysis commences from the 'truth'). Watch this space – computer-based model selection is set to blossom in the near future.

A vast number of other aspects of model design could be illustrated, but we hope that the flavour of econometric modelling is now both well established and has proved interesting. Chapter 13 discusses the theory of reduction, model concepts, the information taxonomy, and modelling more formally, building on Hendry (1987). An overview is presented in Hendry and Richard (1983), and Hendry (1993, 2000a) provides a collection of papers on modelling methodology (see especially, Hendry, 2000b). Hendry and Doornik (1994) and Hendry, Neale and Srba (1988) extend the analysis to linear systems modelling, including recursive estimation of simultaneous systems and VARs. Hendry (1988) considers the refutability of the Lucas critique for models with current-dated expectations variables using such techniques. On the rapidly developing subject of cointegration, many of the currently proposed estimators and tests are easily calculated (see Engle and Granger, 1987, and Phillips, 1987 among others). The Johansen (1988) procedure is implemented in the system procedures discussed in Volume II. Monte Carlo is also useful as an illustrative tool, given the difficulty of analytical derivations of sampling distributions; but that is the subject of a separate program (see the companion book on Ox as well as Hendry, Neale and Ericsson, 1991).

Chapter 12

Statistical Theory

12.1 Introduction

We will review three main statistical tools: regression, maximum likelihood, and least squares. To explain these closely related methods of estimating unknown parameters, we first introduce the normal distribution for one variable, then the bivariate normal distribution, and finally a multivariate normal. A regression is a conditional relation and arises when looking at the conditional distribution of one random variable, denoted Y, given values of another, denoted Z (capital letters here denote random variables, and lower case their realizations). In a bivariate normal, the regression is linear, so has the form $E[Y|z] = \alpha + \beta z$ when $Z = z$, which provides an introductory case. In a multivariate normal, the regression remains linear, but involves several variables (k, say), denoted by a vector $\mathbf{z} = (z_1 \ldots z_k)'$.

Such regressions are defined in terms of unknown parameters, like α and β, and these require estimation from sample data. When samples are randomly drawn from a common population, and the linear regression holds for that population, then maximum likelihood or least squares will deliver 'good' estimates in general. These methods are described in §12.5 and §12.7.

12.2 Normal distribution

The normal, or Gaussian, density $f_{\times}\left(x|\mu_x, \sigma_x^2\right)$ of a random variable X is defined by:

$$f_{\times}\left(x \mid \mu_x, \sigma_x^2\right) = \left(2\pi\sigma_x^2\right)^{-\frac{1}{2}} \exp\left[-\frac{(x - \mu_x)^2}{2\sigma_x^2}\right] \tag{12.1}$$

where $|\mu_x| < \infty$ and $0 < \sigma_x^2 < \infty$ for $x \in \mathbb{R}$. The normal density function reaches a maximum at $x = \mu_x$ and is symmetric about μ_x which is the mean: $E[X] = \mu_x$. Its spread increases with σ_x^2 which is the variance: $E[(X - \mu_x)^2] = \sigma_x^2$; the square root $\sigma_x = \sqrt{\sigma_x^2}$ is the standard deviation. The normal distribution is denoted by $X \sim N\left[\mu_x, \sigma_x^2\right]$, and read as: X is distributed as a normal random variable with mean μ_x and variance σ_x^2.

170

Let $Y = (X - \mu_x)/\sigma_x$ so that $X = \sigma_x Y + \mu_x$. This linear transform from X to Y alters the density to:

$$f_y(y \mid \cdot) = \left(2\pi\sigma_x^2\right)^{-\frac{1}{2}} \exp\left[-\tfrac{1}{2} \; y^2\right] \sigma_x = (2\pi)^{-\frac{1}{2}} \exp\left[-\tfrac{1}{2} \; y^2\right]. \qquad (12.2)$$

This is the standardized form of the density, denoted by $Y \sim N[0,1]$. Note that $f_x(x) \geq 0$ since the exponential function is always positive, and that the density integrates to unity:

$$\int_{-\infty}^{\infty} (2\pi)^{-\frac{1}{2}} \exp\left[-\tfrac{1}{2} \; y^2\right] dy = 1.$$

12.3 The bivariate normal density

Consider two random variables denoted X and W. The correlation corr $[X,W] = \rho$ between X and W is defined by:

$$\rho = \frac{E\left[(X - \mu_x)(W - \mu_w)\right]}{\sqrt{E\left[(X - \mu_x)^2\right] E\left[(W - \mu_w)^2\right]}} = \frac{\sigma_{xw}}{\sigma_x \sigma_w}$$

where σ_{xw} is the covariance. It can be shown that $-1 \leq \rho \leq 1$. When X and W are distributed according to a standardized bivariate normal distribution, the formula for $f_{x,w}(x, w \mid \rho)$ is:

$$f_{x,w}(x, w \mid \rho) = \left(2\pi\sqrt{(1-\rho^2)}\right)^{-1} \exp\left[-\frac{\left(x^2 - 2\rho xw + w^2\right)}{2(1-\rho^2)}\right]. \qquad (12.3)$$

Since $\exp[\cdot]$ has a non-positive argument, its value is positive but less than unity, and hence:

$$\left(2\pi\sqrt{(1-\rho^2)}\right)^{-1} \geq f_{x,w}(x, w) \geq 0. \qquad (12.4)$$

For the standardized bivariate normal distribution, the covariance $E[XW] = \sigma_{xw} = \rho$, and $\rho = 0$ is necessary and sufficient to ensure independence between X and W.

Linear combinations of jointly normal variables are also normal. The proof is based on deriving the distribution of the random variables $(aX + bW : W)$ where $(X : W)$ is bivariate normal and $a \neq 0$.

12.3.1 Marginal and conditional normal distributions

The marginal distribution of W is normal, and from it we can obtain the conditional distribution of X given W denoted $f_{x|w}(x|w)$. By definition, the marginal density of W is:

$$f_w(w) = \int_{-\infty}^{\infty} f_{x,w}(x, w) \, dx. \qquad (12.5)$$

Calculating that expression for the standardized bivariate normal yields:

$$\int_{-\infty}^{\infty} \left(2\pi\sqrt{(1-\rho^2)}\right)^{-1} \exp\left[-\frac{\left(x^2 - 2\rho x w + w^2\right)}{2\left(1-\rho^2\right)}\right] dx. \qquad (12.6)$$

The term in $[\cdot]$ can be rewritten as $\left[(x - \rho w)^2 + \left(1 - \rho^2\right) w^2\right]$ (a result of use below). Since $\exp(a+b) = \exp(a)\exp(b)$, then $\int_{-\infty}^{\infty} f_{\text{x,w}}(x,w) dx$ is:

$$
\begin{aligned}
&\left(2\pi\sqrt{(1-\rho^2)}\right)^{-1} \int_{-\infty}^{\infty} \exp\left[-\frac{(x-\rho w)^2}{2\left(1-\rho^2\right)}\right] \cdot \exp\left[-\frac{\left(1-\rho^2\right) w^2}{2\left(1-\rho^2\right)}\right] dx \\
&= (2\pi)^{-\frac{1}{2}} \exp\left(-\tfrac{1}{2}w^2\right) \int_{-\infty}^{\infty} \left(2\pi\left(1-\rho^2\right)\right)^{-\frac{1}{2}} \cdot \exp\left[-\frac{(x-\rho w)^2}{2\left(1-\rho^2\right)}\right] dx.
\end{aligned}
\qquad (12.7)
$$

The term inside the integral is the density of a normal random variable with mean ρw and standard deviation $\sqrt{(1-\rho^2)}$ and hence the integral is unity. Thus, the marginal distribution of W is the term before the integral, and so is $\mathsf{N}[0,1]$. Note that $(X - \rho W)/\sqrt{(1-\rho^2)}$ and W are independent standardized normal random variables since they have zero means, unit variances, are jointly normal, and have a covariance of:

$$\mathsf{E}\left[\frac{W\left(X - \rho W\right)}{\sqrt{(1-\rho^2)}}\right] = 0 \qquad (12.8)$$

which checks the density factorization.

12.3.2 Regression

The term inside the integral in (12.7) is the conditional density since it is also true that:

$$f_{\text{x,w}}(x,w) = f_{\text{x|w}}(x \mid w) f_{\text{w}}(w). \qquad (12.9)$$

Thus:

$$(X \mid W = w) \sim \mathsf{N}\left[\rho w, \left(1 - \rho^2\right)\right].$$

The conditional expectation, $\mathsf{E}[X|W = w] = \rho w$, considered as a function of w, is the regression function, and ρ is the regression coefficient. The conditional mean is a linear function of w. Because the random variables are standardized, ρ is also the correlation coefficient (matching the requirement $|\rho| \leq 1$) but in general, the regression coefficient will not be ρ itself as shown below. The other conditional moments can be defined in a similar way, so that $\mathsf{V}[X|W = w]$ is the conditional variance function. For the normal distribution, $\mathsf{V}[X|W = w] = (1-\rho^2)$ does not depend on w, so the conditional variance is said to be homoscedastic (literally, constant variance).

Reverting to the unstandardized variables, $f_{\text{y,z}}(y, z)$ is:

$$\frac{1}{2\pi\sigma_y\sigma_z\sqrt{1-\rho^2}} \exp\left[-\frac{(y-\mu_y)^2}{2\left(1-\rho^2\right)\sigma_y^2} + \frac{\rho\left(y-\mu_y\right)\left(z-\mu_z\right)}{\left(1-\rho^2\right)\sigma_y\sigma_z} - \frac{(z-\mu_z)^2}{2\left(1-\rho^2\right)\sigma_z^2}\right] \qquad (12.10)$$

The marginal distribution of Z is $\mathsf{N}[\mu_z, \sigma_z^2]$, and by an equivalent factorization to (12.7) since $\rho = \sigma_{yz}/\sigma_y\sigma_z$ and $\sigma_y^2\left[1 - \rho^2\right] = \sigma_y^2 - (\sigma_{yz})^2/\sigma_z^2$:

$$(Y \mid Z = z) \sim \mathsf{N}\left[\alpha + \beta z, \omega^2\right] \tag{12.11}$$

where:

$$\alpha = \left(\mu_y - \beta\mu_z\right), \quad \beta = \left(\frac{\sigma_{zy}}{\sigma_z^2}\right) \text{ and } \omega^2 = \left(\sigma_y^2 - \frac{\sigma_{yz}^2}{\sigma_z^2}\right).$$

In general, therefore, $\beta = \rho\sigma_y/\sigma_z$. There are four important aspects of (12.11). First, for the normal distribution $\mathsf{E}[Y|Z = z]$ is a linear function of z. Unlike the normal distribution, many other distributions do not have linear regression functions, so $\mathsf{E}[Y|Z = z]$ may depend on higher powers of z. Secondly, the parameters of the conditional distribution, namely $(\alpha, \beta, \omega^2)$ depend on all the moments μ_y, μ_z, σ_y^2, σ_{zy} and σ_z^2 of $f_{\mathsf{y},\mathsf{z}}(y, z)$. However, the parameter sets $(\alpha, \beta, \omega^2)$ and (μ_z, σ_z^2) are variation free, in that for any given values of the second, the first set can freely take any values. Further, since σ_{yz}^2/σ_z^2 is non-negative, the variance of the conditional distribution is smaller than that of the unconditional distribution: that is, $\omega^2 \leq \sigma_y^2$. Finally, we have already commented on homoscedasticity which still holds.

12.4 Multivariate normal

12.4.1 Multivariate normal density

Going beyond the bivariate distribution necessitates matrix formulations, but in many respects these simplify the formulae. Denote the k-dimensional multivariate normal density of a random vector $\mathbf{V}$ of length k by $\mathbf{V} \sim \mathsf{N}_k[\boldsymbol{\mu}, \boldsymbol{\Sigma}]$ where $\mathsf{E}[\mathbf{V}] = \boldsymbol{\mu}$ is the vector of means (that is, for the ith element $\mathsf{E}[V_i] = \mu_i$), and $\boldsymbol{\Sigma}$ is the variance-covariance matrix of rank k:

$$\mathsf{E}\left[(\mathbf{V} - \boldsymbol{\mu})(\mathbf{V} - \boldsymbol{\mu})'\right] = \boldsymbol{\Sigma} \tag{12.12}$$

(that is, for the $(i, j)^{th}$ element $\mathsf{E}\left[(V_i - \mu_i)(V_j - \mu_j)\right] = \sigma_{ij}$). The multivariate normal density function is:

$$f_{\mathsf{v}}(\mathbf{v}) = \left[(2\pi)^k |\boldsymbol{\Sigma}|\right]^{-\frac{1}{2}} \exp\left[-\tfrac{1}{2}(\mathbf{v} - \boldsymbol{\mu})'\boldsymbol{\Sigma}^{-1}(\mathbf{v} - \boldsymbol{\mu})\right] \tag{12.13}$$

where $|\boldsymbol{\Sigma}|$ is the determinant of $\boldsymbol{\Sigma}$. When $k = 2$, (12.13) specializes to the bivariate case above. If all elements of $\mathbf{V}$ are independently and identically distributed (IID), having a normal distribution with mean μ and variance σ^2, we can write this as $\mathbf{V} \sim \mathsf{N}_k[\mu\boldsymbol{\iota}, \sigma^2\mathbf{I}]$, in which $\boldsymbol{\iota}$ is the $k \times 1$ vector of ones, and $\mathbf{I}$ is the $k \times k$ identity matrix. An alternative way of writing this is: $V_i \sim \mathsf{IN}[\mu, \sigma^2]$, $i = 1, \ldots, k$.

12.4.2 Multiple regression

To obtain multiple regression, partition $\mathbf{v}, \boldsymbol{\mu}$ and $\boldsymbol{\Sigma}$ conformably into:

$$\mathbf{v} = \begin{pmatrix} y \\ \mathbf{z} \end{pmatrix}, \ \boldsymbol{\mu} = \begin{pmatrix} \mu_y \\ \boldsymbol{\mu}_z \end{pmatrix} \text{ and } \boldsymbol{\Sigma} = \begin{pmatrix} \sigma_{yy} & \boldsymbol{\sigma}_{zy} \\ \boldsymbol{\sigma}_{yz} & \boldsymbol{\Sigma}_{zz} \end{pmatrix} \quad (12.14)$$

where the sub-vector $\mathbf{z}$ is $(k-1) \times 1$, and $\boldsymbol{\sigma}_{zy} = \boldsymbol{\sigma}'_{yz}$. The conditional distribution of Y given $\mathbf{Z} = \mathbf{z}$ is derived by factorizing the joint distribution. It is common in econometrics to adopt a shorthand where the lower-case letters denote both the outcome and the random variable (when no confusion is likely – but does sometimes ensue), and we will do so henceforth. The marginal distribution of $\mathbf{Z}$ is a special case of the general formula in (12.13):

$$f_{\mathbf{z}}(\mathbf{z}) = \left[(2\pi)^{(k-1)} \left| \boldsymbol{\Sigma}_{zz} \right| \right]^{-\frac{1}{2}} \exp\left[-\tfrac{1}{2} \ (\mathbf{z} - \boldsymbol{\mu}_z)' \boldsymbol{\Sigma}_{zz}^{-1} (\mathbf{z} - \boldsymbol{\mu}_z) \right]. \quad (12.15)$$

To derive the conditional distribution $f_{y|\mathbf{z}}(y|\mathbf{z})$ of Y given $\mathbf{z}$, express $f_{\mathbf{v}}(\cdot)$ in the transformed space of $(y|\mathbf{z})$ and $\mathbf{z}$. From §12.7.5, using partitioned inversion (see §12.7.5 below, or e.g., Hendry, 1995a, if this idea is unfamiliar):

$$\boldsymbol{\Sigma}^{-1} = \begin{pmatrix} \sigma_{yy\cdot z}^{-1} & -\sigma_{yy\cdot z}^{-1} \boldsymbol{\sigma}_{yz} \boldsymbol{\Sigma}_{zz}^{-1} \\ -\boldsymbol{\Sigma}_{zz}^{-1} \boldsymbol{\sigma}_{zy} \sigma_{yy\cdot z}^{-1} & \boldsymbol{\Sigma}_{zz}^{-1} \left(\mathbf{I}_{k-1} + \boldsymbol{\sigma}_{zy} \sigma_{yy\cdot z}^{-1} \boldsymbol{\sigma}_{yz} \boldsymbol{\Sigma}_{zz}^{-1} \right) \end{pmatrix}$$

where $\sigma_{yy\cdot z} = (\sigma_{yy} - \boldsymbol{\sigma}_{yz} \boldsymbol{\Sigma}_{zz}^{-1} \boldsymbol{\sigma}_{zy})$ and:

$$\left| \boldsymbol{\Sigma} \right| = \left| \boldsymbol{\Sigma}_{zz} \right| \left| \sigma_{yy} - \boldsymbol{\sigma}_{yz} \boldsymbol{\Sigma}_{zz}^{-1} \boldsymbol{\sigma}_{zy} \right| = \left| \boldsymbol{\Sigma}_{zz} \right| \left| \sigma_{yy\cdot z} \right|.$$

Letting $\boldsymbol{\beta}' = \boldsymbol{\sigma}_{yz} \boldsymbol{\Sigma}_{zz}^{-1}$, then $(\mathbf{v} - \boldsymbol{\mu})' \boldsymbol{\Sigma}^{-1} (\mathbf{v} - \boldsymbol{\mu})$ can be factorized as:

$$\left(y - \mu_y \right)^2 \sigma_{yy\cdot z}^{-1} - 2 \left(\mathbf{z} - \boldsymbol{\mu}_z \right)' \boldsymbol{\beta} \sigma_{yy\cdot z}^{-1} \left(y - \mu_y \right)$$
$$+ \left(\mathbf{z} - \boldsymbol{\mu}_z \right)' \boldsymbol{\beta} \sigma_{yy\cdot z}^{-1} \boldsymbol{\beta}' \left(\mathbf{z} - \boldsymbol{\mu}_z \right) + \left(\mathbf{z} - \boldsymbol{\mu}_z \right)' \boldsymbol{\Sigma}_{zz}^{-1} \left(\mathbf{z} - \boldsymbol{\mu}_z \right),$$

since $(y - \mu_y)\sigma_{yy\cdot z}^{-1}\boldsymbol{\beta}'(\mathbf{z} - \boldsymbol{\mu}_z)$ is a scalar and so equals its transpose; or on rearranging:

$$\left(y - \mu_y - \boldsymbol{\beta}' \left(\mathbf{z} - \boldsymbol{\mu}_z \right) \right)^2 \sigma_{yy\cdot z}^{-1} + \left(\mathbf{z} - \boldsymbol{\mu}_z \right)' \boldsymbol{\Sigma}_{zz}^{-1} \left(\mathbf{z} - \boldsymbol{\mu}_z \right)$$

Substituting these results in $f_{\mathbf{v}}(\cdot)$, then $f_{y|\mathbf{z}}(y|\mathbf{z})$ is:

$$\left[2\pi\sigma_{yy\cdot z} \right]^{-\frac{1}{2}} \exp\left[-\frac{1}{2} \frac{\left(y - \alpha - \boldsymbol{\beta}'\mathbf{z} \right)^2}{\sigma_{yy\cdot z}} \right] \quad (12.16)$$

where $\alpha = \mu_y - \boldsymbol{\beta}'\boldsymbol{\mu}_z$, or:

$$(Y \mid \mathbf{Z} = \mathbf{z}) \sim \mathsf{N}\left[\alpha + \boldsymbol{\beta}'\mathbf{z}, \sigma_{yy\cdot z} \right]. \quad (12.17)$$

The same four important points noted above hold for (12.17). Now, however, $\mathsf{E}\left[Y|\mathbf{Z} = \mathbf{z} \right]$ is a linear function of the vector $\mathbf{z}$, $(\alpha, \boldsymbol{\beta}, \sigma_{yy\cdot z})$ depend on all the moments of $f_{\mathbf{v}}(\cdot)$, and as $\boldsymbol{\sigma}_{yz} \boldsymbol{\Sigma}_{zz}^{-1} \boldsymbol{\sigma}_{zy}$ is non-negative, $\sigma_{yy\cdot z} \leq \sigma_{yy}$.

12.4.3 Functions of normal variables: χ^2, t and F distributions

Three important functions of normally distributed random variables are distributed as the χ^2, t, and F distributions. First, we define these three distributions, then consider generalizations. Let $Z \sim N[0, 1]$ then:

$$Z^2 \sim \chi^2(1),$$

where $\chi^2(1)$ is the chi-squared distribution with one degree of freedom. For a set of k independent random variables $Z_i \sim IN[0, 1]$:

$$\sum_{i=1}^{k} Z_i^2 \sim \chi^2(k), \tag{12.18}$$

where $\chi^2(k)$ is the χ^2-distribution with k degrees of freedom.

Next, let $X \sim N\left[\mu_x, \sigma_x^2\right]$ and let $\eta(k)$ be a $\chi^2(k)$ independently distributed from X then:

$$\tau = \frac{(X - \mu_x)\sqrt{k}}{\sigma_x\sqrt{\eta(k)}} \sim t(k)$$

where $t(k)$ is Student's t-distribution with k degrees of freedom.

Thirdly, let $\eta_1(k_1)$ and $\eta_2(k_2)$ be two independent chi-squareds of k_1 and k_2 degrees of freedom, then:

$$\phi = \frac{[\eta_1(k_1)/k_1]}{[\eta_2(k_2)/k_2]} \sim F(k_1, k_2)$$

where $F(k_1, k_2)$ is the F-distribution with k_1 and k_2 degrees of freedom. Note that $t(k)^2 \sim F(1, k)$ by using these three results. All of these distributions have been tabulated (in more modern terms, programmed into computer packages), and occur frequently in empirical research, in the sense that an underlying normal distribution is often assumed.

In the context of the multivariate normal, let $\mathbf{V} \sim N_k[\boldsymbol{\mu}, \boldsymbol{\Sigma}]$, then:

$$\eta(k) = (\mathbf{V} - \boldsymbol{\mu})' \boldsymbol{\Sigma}^{-1} (\mathbf{V} - \boldsymbol{\mu}) \sim \chi^2(k). \tag{12.19}$$

This result follows from the definition of a χ^2 by noting that any positive definite matrix $\boldsymbol{\Sigma}$ can be written as $\boldsymbol{\Sigma} = \mathbf{HH}'$ where $\mathbf{H}$ is a non-singular lower triangular matrix, so that:

$$\mathbf{H}^{-1}(\mathbf{V} - \boldsymbol{\mu}) = \boldsymbol{\zeta} \sim N_k[\mathbf{0}, \mathbf{I}], \tag{12.20}$$

and hence from (12.19):

$$\eta(k) = \boldsymbol{\zeta}'\boldsymbol{\zeta} = \sum_{i=1}^{k} \zeta_i^2 \sim \chi^2(k). \tag{12.21}$$

Partition ζ' into the k_1 and k_2 independent components $(\zeta'_1 : \zeta'_2)$, each of which is normal, then for $k_1 + k_2 = k$:

$$\eta_1(k_1) = \zeta'_1\zeta_1 \sim \chi^2(k_1) \quad \text{and} \quad \eta_2(k_2) = \zeta'_2\zeta_2 \sim \chi^2(k_2) \tag{12.22}$$

are also independent.

12.5 Likelihood

Assume we have a sample $x_1 \ldots x_T$, generated by a sequence of scalar random variables $X_1 \ldots X_T$ distributed with multivariate density $f_X(x_1 \ldots x_T | \theta)$ which is indexed by one unknown parameter $\theta \in \Theta \subseteq \mathbb{R}$. In empirical research, the underlying parameter(s) are unknown, and need to be estimated from the observed outcomes of the random processes. A major tool for accomplishing this is the likelihood function $L(\cdot)$ defined in terms of the density function of the sample, but exchanging the roles of variables and parameters:

$$f_X(x_1 \ldots x_T \mid \theta) \propto L(\theta \mid x_1 \ldots x_T) \quad \text{for } \theta \in \Theta. \tag{12.23}$$

$f_X(\cdot|\theta)$ maps from $\mathbb{R}^T$ to $\mathbb{R}_+$, whereas $L(\theta|x_1 \ldots x_T)$ maps from $\mathbb{R}$ to $\mathbb{R}_+$, so they are linked by a function $\varphi(x)$ which does not depend on θ. Any monotonic transformation of $L(\cdot)$ is also admissible, and this feature is useful when working with the log-likelihood function, and its first derivative. We set $\varphi(x)$ to unity so that the integral of the likelihood function is unity for a single random variable x:

$$\int_{-\infty}^{\infty} L(\theta \mid x) \, dx = 1. \tag{12.24}$$

The density function $f_X(\cdot|\theta)$ describes the mechanism generating observations on the random variables. (In other chapters, this mechanism is called the data generation process (DGP), and the joint density is then written as $D_X(\cdot)$.) For an independent sample $x_1 \ldots x_T$ of T observations on the random variable X, since the joint probability is then the product of the individual probabilities:

$$f_X(x_1 \ldots x_T \mid \theta) = \prod_{t=1}^{T} f_x(x_t \mid \theta). \tag{12.25}$$

For a given value of θ, the outcomes differ owing to random variation which is characterized by the form of $f_x(\cdot)$: for example, the location, spread, and shape of the distribution of a random sample $(x_1 \ldots x_T)$ are determined by $f_x(\cdot)$. At different points in the parameter space, the distribution also differs, so when the impact of distinct values of θ on $f_x(\cdot)$ is sufficiently marked, we might hope to infer what the value of θ is, taking into account the randomness arising from $f_x(\cdot)$.

For example, when $X \sim \text{IN}\,[\mu_x, 1]$ and $\mu_x = 0$, then $|x_t| < 2$ will occur roughly 95% of the time, whereas when $\mu_x = 5$, almost every observed x-value will exceed 2. Thus, the data on X yield information on μ_x, and from a sufficiently large sample, we may be able to determine the unknown parameter value precisely.

Since $f_X(\mathbf{x}) \geq 0$ for all $\mathbf{x} = (x_1 \ldots x_T)$, we can take the logarithm of $f_X(\mathbf{x}|\theta)$ and hence of $\text{L}(\theta|\cdot)$, which is denoted by $\ell(\theta|\cdot)$:

$$\ell(\theta \mid x_1 \ldots x_T) = \log \text{L}(\theta \mid x_1 \ldots x_T). \tag{12.26}$$

For an independent sample of T observations on X, using (12.25):

$$\ell(\theta \mid x_1 \ldots x_T) = \log \prod_{t=1}^{T} f_X(x_t \mid \theta) = \sum_{t=1}^{T} \ell(\theta \mid x_t). \tag{12.27}$$

Thus, the log-likelihood of an independent sample is the sum of the individual log-likelihoods.

12.6 Estimation

Maximum likelihood estimation (MLE) locates the value $\widehat{\theta}$ of θ which produces the highest value of the log-likelihood:

$$\widehat{\theta} = \underset{\theta \in \Theta}{\operatorname{argmax}}\, \ell(\theta \mid \mathbf{x}) = \underset{\theta \in \Theta}{\operatorname{argmax}} \sum_{t=1}^{T} \ell(\theta \mid x_t) \tag{12.28}$$

where the second equality holds for independent Xs. Since we are considering the sample realization $\mathbf{X} = \mathbf{x}$, $\ell(\theta|\mathbf{x})$ is written with the realization as an argument, but is thought of as a function of the random variable X as in (12.29) below. Thus, it makes sense to take the expectation of $\ell(\theta|\mathbf{x})$, to consider the large sample distribution of functions of $\ell(\theta|\mathbf{x})$ etc.

The form of any MLE depends on $f_X(\cdot)$. If the X_t are IID with a univariate normal distribution, θ is a two dimensional vector denoted by $\theta' = (\mu_x, \sigma_x^2)$ and so:

$$\ell(\theta \mid x_t) = -\tfrac{1}{2}\,\log(2\pi) - \log(\sigma_x) - \frac{(x_t - \mu_x)^2}{2\sigma_x^2} = \ell_t. \tag{12.29}$$

Hence, for an independent sample $(x_1 \ldots x_T)$:

$$
\begin{aligned}
\ell(\theta \mid \mathbf{x}) &= -\tfrac{T}{2}\log(2\pi) - T\log(\sigma_x) - 2\sigma_x^{-2}\textstyle\sum_{t=1}^{T}(x_t - \mu_x)^2 \\
&= -\tfrac{T}{2}\left(\log(2\pi) + \log(\sigma_x^2) + \sigma_x^{-2}\left[\widehat{\sigma}_x^2 + (\mu_x - \widehat{\mu}_x)^2\right]\right)
\end{aligned}
\tag{12.30}
$$

where $\widehat{\mu}_x = T^{-1}\sum_{t=1}^{T} x_t$ and $\widehat{\sigma}_x^2 = T^{-1}\sum_{t=1}^{T}(x_t - \widehat{\mu}_x)^2$. All the sample information is 'concentrated' in $(\widehat{\mu}_x, \widehat{\sigma}_x^2)$, so these statistics are sufficient for (μ_x, σ_x^2), in that the second line of (12.30) no longer depends explicitly on the $\{x_t\}$. From (12.30), $\ell\left(\boldsymbol{\theta}|\mathbf{x}\right)$ is maximized by minimizing $[\hat{\sigma}_x^2 + (\mu_x - \hat{\mu}_x)^2]/\sigma_x^2$. Setting $\mu_x = \hat{\mu}_x$ achieves the smallest value of the second component, and as $\hat{\sigma}_x^2$ corresponds to the smallest value of the sum of squares, $\hat{\sigma}_x^2 = \sigma_x^2$ lowers the remaining term to unity. The next section derives the MLE more formally.

12.6.1 The score and the Hessian

When the log-likelihood is differentiable, $\ell\left(\boldsymbol{\theta}|x\right)$ can be maximized by differentiating with respect to $\boldsymbol{\theta}$ and equating to zero (a necessary condition for a maximum). The first derivative of $\ell\left(\cdot\right)$ with respect to $\boldsymbol{\theta}$ is the score, denoted by:

$$\mathbf{q}\left(\theta\mid\mathbf{x}\right) = \frac{\partial\ell\left(\boldsymbol{\theta}|\mathbf{x}\right)}{\partial\boldsymbol{\theta}} = \sum_{t=1}^{T}\frac{\partial\ell_t\left(\boldsymbol{\theta}|\mathbf{x}\right)}{\partial\boldsymbol{\theta}} = \sum_{t=1}^{T}\mathbf{q}_t\left(\theta\mid\mathbf{x}\right) \tag{12.31}$$

where the second and third equalities hold for independent Xs. Solving for $\hat{\boldsymbol{\theta}}$ such that $\mathbf{q}(\hat{\boldsymbol{\theta}}) = \mathbf{0}$ yields the MLE (when the second derivative is negative). In the case of the normal distribution illustration (remember that we differentiate with respect to σ^2, not σ):

$$\mathbf{q}\left(\theta\mid\mathbf{x}\right) = \begin{pmatrix} q\left(\mu_x|\mathbf{x}\right) \\ q\left(\sigma_x^2|\mathbf{x}\right) \end{pmatrix} = \begin{pmatrix} T\left(\hat{\mu}_x - \mu_x\right)/\sigma_x^2 \\ -\frac{1}{2}T\sigma_x^{-2}\left[1 - \left\{\hat{\sigma}_x^2 + (\hat{\mu}_x - \mu_x)^2\right\}/\sigma_x^2\right] \end{pmatrix}. \tag{12.32}$$

Then $\mathbf{q}(\hat{\boldsymbol{\theta}}|\mathbf{x}) = \mathbf{0}$ occurs at $\hat{\boldsymbol{\theta}}' = \left(\hat{\mu}_x, \hat{\sigma}_x^2\right)$, where, as before:

$$\hat{\mu}_x = T^{-1}\sum_{t=1}^{T}X_t \text{ and } \hat{\sigma}_x^2 = T^{-1}\sum_{t=1}^{T}(X_t - \hat{\mu}_x)^2 \tag{12.33}$$

which are the sample mean and (unadjusted) variance. At the maximum $\hat{\boldsymbol{\theta}}$:

$$\ell\left(\hat{\boldsymbol{\theta}}\mid x\right) = -\frac{1}{2}T\left(\log\left(2\pi\right) + \log\left(\hat{\sigma}_x^2\right) + 1\right). \tag{12.34}$$

The second derivative of $\ell\left(\boldsymbol{\theta}|\mathbf{x}\right)$ with respect to $\boldsymbol{\theta}$ is the Hessian of the likelihood, and evaluated at $\hat{\boldsymbol{\theta}}$ can be shown to be negative. Differentiate $\mathbf{q}\left(\boldsymbol{\theta}|\mathbf{x}\right)$ with respect to $\boldsymbol{\theta}$ once more:

$$\mathbf{H}\left(\theta\mid\mathbf{x}\right) = \frac{\partial^2\ell\left(\boldsymbol{\theta}|\mathbf{x}\right)}{\partial\boldsymbol{\theta}\partial\boldsymbol{\theta}'} = \sum_{t=1}^{T}\frac{\partial^2\ell_t\left(\boldsymbol{\theta}|\mathbf{x}\right)}{\partial\boldsymbol{\theta}\partial\boldsymbol{\theta}'} = \sum_{t=1}^{T}\mathbf{H}_t\left(\theta\mid\mathbf{x}\right) \tag{12.35}$$

where the last two equalities hold for independent Xs. Thus, for the example from (12.32):

$$\mathbf{H}\left(\theta\mid\mathbf{x}\right) = \begin{pmatrix} -T/\sigma_x^2 & -T\left(\hat{\mu}_x - \mu_x\right)/\sigma_x^4 \\ -T\left(\hat{\mu}_x - \mu_x\right)/\sigma_x^4 & -T\sigma_x^{-6}\{\hat{\sigma}_x^2 + (\hat{\mu}_x - \mu_x)^2\} + \frac{1}{2}T\sigma_x^{-4} \end{pmatrix} \tag{12.36}$$

and when evaluated at $\widehat{\theta}$:

$$\mathbf{H}\left(\widehat{\theta} \mid \mathbf{x}\right) = \begin{pmatrix} -T\widehat{\sigma}_x^{-2} & 0 \\ 0 & -\frac{1}{2}T\widehat{\sigma}_x^{-4} \end{pmatrix},$$

which is negative definite, shows that the parameter estimates are uncorrelated, and that their precisions both depend inversely on σ_x and directly on T.

12.6.2 Maximum likelihood estimation

The justification for maximum likelihood is that the principle is general, and when the form of the data density is known and the sample size is sufficiently large, MLE usually yields estimators of θ that are as good as can be obtained. We now demonstrate that claim in a simple setting.

12.6.3 Efficiency and Fisher's information

Subject to reasonable regularity conditions, which ensure that the required derivatives exist etc., maximum likelihood estimators are consistent, and also tend to be efficient in large samples, such that no other method dominates MLE. This last claim can be proved to hold in finite samples for the special class of unbiased estimators defined by $\mathsf{E}[\widehat{\theta}] = \theta \; \forall \theta \in \Theta$, and this section outlines the proof in a scalar case. To simplify notation, we drop the reference to x in the arguments. The population value of the parameter is denoted by θ_p.

Five steps are required in the proof when $\ell(\theta)$ is a quadratic function of θ so that $q(\theta)$ is linear in θ. Hence $\mathsf{E}[q(\theta_p)^2] = H(\theta_p) = H$ is constant, and higher-order derivatives vanish: such a condition provides a good approximation in large samples.

(1) Expand $q(\theta_p)$ around $q(\widehat{\theta})$ in a Taylor series:

$$q\left(\theta_p\right) = q\left(\widehat{\theta}\right) + \frac{dq\left(\theta\right)}{d\theta}\bigg|_{\widehat{\theta}}\left(\theta_p - \widehat{\theta}\right) + \frac{1}{2}\frac{d^2q\left(\theta\right)}{d\theta^2}\bigg|_{\widehat{\theta}}\left(\theta_p - \widehat{\theta}\right)^2. \quad (12.37)$$

Since $q(\widehat{\theta}) = 0$ and $d^2q(\theta)/d\theta^2 = 0$ because H is constant:

$$q\left(\theta_p\right) = H \cdot \left(\theta_p - \widehat{\theta}\right) \quad (12.38)$$

so that:

$$\left(\widehat{\theta} - \theta_p\right) = -H^{-1}q\left(\theta_p\right). \quad (12.39)$$

Consequently, the MLE $\widehat{\theta}$ differs from θ_p by a linear function of $q(\theta_p)$. That last expression holds generally, but only as an approximation when $H(\theta)$ is not constant, needing iterative solution.

(2) Next, $E[q(\theta_p)] = 0$. Since we solve $q(\widehat{\theta}) = 0$ to obtain $\widehat{\theta}$, it is important that on average $E[q(\theta_p)]$ is indeed zero. Taking expectations in (12.38), for linear score functions $q(\theta_p)$, $E[\widehat{\theta}] = \theta_p$, so the MLE is unbiased under our assumptions.

(3) Since $E[q(\theta_p)] = 0$, the variance of $q(\theta_p)$ is $E[q(\theta_p)^2] = \mathcal{I}(\theta_p)$ which is Fisher's information. The key result is that:

$$E\left[q\left(\theta_p\right)^2\right] = \mathcal{I}\left(\theta_p\right) = -E\left[H\left(\theta_p\right)\right],$$

and hence Fisher's information is the negative of the Hessian ($\ell(\theta|x)$ must be equated with $D_x(x|\theta)$ in such derivations, although $\ell(\theta|x)$ is specified by the investigator and $D_x(x|\theta)$ by nature, so take care in practice).

(4) The variance of $\widehat{\theta}$ can be obtained from its definition as $E[(\widehat{\theta} - \theta_p)^2]$ and the Taylor-series expansion of $q(\theta_p)$ around $q(\widehat{\theta})$. With constant H, from (12.39):

$$E\left[\left(\widehat{\theta} - \theta_p\right)^2\right] = E\left[H\left(\theta_p\right)^{-1} q\left(\theta_p\right)^2 H\left(\theta_p\right)^{-1}\right] = H^{-1}\mathcal{I}H^{-1} = \mathcal{I}^{-1}$$

(12.40)

using (1) and (3). Thus, $V[\widehat{\theta}]$ is the inverse of Fisher's information. This result is of sufficient importance to merit a separate section, which then solves the fifth step.

12.6.4 Cramér–Rao bound

(5) Let $\widehat{\alpha}$ be any other unbiased estimator of θ so that $E[\widehat{\alpha}] = \theta_p$ with variance $E[(\widehat{\alpha} - \theta_p)^2] = V$. We now show that $V \geq \mathcal{I}^{-1}$ which proves that the MLE is the minimum-variance unbiased estimator here. First, a surprising intermediate result: $E[q(\theta_p)\widehat{\alpha}] = 1 \ \forall \widehat{\alpha}$ such that $E[\widehat{\alpha}] = \theta_p$. All unbiased estimators have a covariance of unity with the score. This is most easily seen with $\widehat{\theta}$ as the unbiased estimator, using the results in (1), (2) and (4). Now the squared correlation between $q(\theta_p)$ and $\widehat{\alpha}$ is:

$$r^2 = \frac{\left(E\left[q\left(\theta_p\right)\widehat{\alpha}\right]\right)^2}{V \cdot \mathcal{I}} = \frac{1}{V\mathcal{I}}.$$

(12.41)

Since a squared correlation must be between 0 and 1, $V \cdot \mathcal{I} \geq 1$ so that $V \geq \mathcal{I}^{-1}$. This result is the Cramér–Rao bound, and shows that no unbiased estimator $\widehat{\alpha}$ can have a smaller variance than $\mathcal{I}(\theta_p)^{-1}$; since the unbiased MLE had that variance, it is not dominated by any other $\widehat{\alpha}$. More generally, the Cramér–Rao bound holds for most MLEs as $T \to \infty$.

12.6.5 Properties of Fisher's information

Several other properties of Fisher's information merit note. First, since under independence $q(\theta_p) = \sum_{t=1}^{T} q_t(\theta_p)$:

$$
\begin{aligned}
\mathsf{E}\left[q(\theta_p)^2\right] &= \mathsf{E}\left[\left(\sum_{t=1}^{T} q_t(\theta_p)\right)^2\right] = \mathsf{E}\left[\sum_{s=1}^{T} \sum_{t=1}^{T} q_t(\theta_p) q_s(\theta_p)\right] \\
&= \sum_{s=1}^{T} \sum_{t=1}^{T} \mathsf{E}\left[q_t(\theta_p) q_s(\theta_p)\right].
\end{aligned}
\tag{12.42}
$$

Under independence, $\mathsf{E}[q_t(\theta_p)q_s(\theta_p)] = 0$, but otherwise is non-zero – which will pose
problems for estimation and inference.

Secondly, when $\mathsf{E}[q_t(\theta_p)q_s(\theta_p)] = 0$, (12.42) becomes:

$$
\mathsf{E}\left[q(\theta_p)^2\right] = \sum_{t=1}^{T} \mathsf{E}\left[q_t(\theta_p)^2\right] = \sum_{t=1}^{T} \mathcal{I}_t(\theta_p) = \mathcal{I}_{(T)}(\theta_p).
\tag{12.43}
$$

Thus, Fisher's information is additive for independent random variables. When
$\mathsf{E}[q_t(\theta_p)^2]$ is constant over t, then $\mathcal{I}_{(T)}(\theta_p) = T\mathcal{I}_0(\theta_p)$ where $\mathcal{I}_0(\theta_p)$ is Fisher's information for a single sample point. From the fact that $\mathcal{I}_{(T)}(\theta_p)$ is $T\mathcal{I}_0(\theta_p)$, we see that
information increases linearly with sample size in this setting. Conversely, when $\mathcal{I}_t(\theta_p)$
is not constant, inference difficulties may again ensue: see the discussion of HCSEs in
Chapter 11.

When $\mathcal{I}_t(\theta_p)$ is constant over t, $\mathsf{V}[q(\theta_p)] = T\mathcal{I}_0(\theta_p)$, so when $q(\theta_p)$ is a linear
function of θ_p for a normally distributed random variable (as in (12.30) when σ_x^2 is
known):

$$
q(\theta_p) \sim \mathsf{N}\left[0, T\mathcal{I}_0(\theta_p)\right] \quad \text{so that} \quad \sqrt{T} q(\theta_p) \sim \mathsf{N}\left[0, \mathcal{I}_0(\theta_p)\right].
\tag{12.44}
$$

From (12.39), $(\widehat{\theta} - \theta_p)$ is a linear function of $q(\theta_p)$, so:

$$
\sqrt{T}\left(\widehat{\theta} - \theta_p\right) \sim \mathsf{N}\left[0, \mathcal{I}_0(\theta_p)^{-1}\right].
\tag{12.45}
$$

This result is dependent on many strong assumptions which can be weakened.

Finally, when there is a set of sufficient statistics $g(\mathbf{X})$, since $h(\mathbf{x})$ does not depend
on θ, $q(\theta; \mathbf{x})$ is a function of $g(\mathbf{x})$, and hence so is $\mathcal{I}(\cdot)$. Thus, the MLE retains all of
the available information.

12.6.6 Estimating Fisher's information

Having established the MLE $\widehat{\theta}$ of θ and how to solve for it from $q(\widehat{\theta}) = 0$, we
now consider how to estimate $\mathsf{V}[\widehat{\theta}] = T\mathcal{I}_0(\theta_p)^{-1}$. The first way uses the result that
$T\mathcal{I}_0(\theta_p) = -\mathsf{E}[H(\theta_p)]$, which holds more generally than the quadratic log-likelihood
considered above. On replacing θ_p by $\widehat{\theta}$:

$$
\mathsf{V}\left[\widehat{\theta}\right] = -H\left(\widehat{\theta}\right)^{-1}.
\tag{12.46}
$$

Since $\widehat{\theta}$ converges on θ_p as $T \to \infty$ owing to consistency, whereas from (12.45), $\sqrt{T}(\widehat{\theta} - \theta_p)$ has a well-defined distribution, then $-T[H(\widehat{\theta})^{-1}]$ tends to $\mathcal{I}_0(\theta_p)^{-1}$.

However, $q(\widehat{\theta})^2$ cannot be used as an estimator of $\mathsf{V}[\widehat{\theta}]$ since $q(\widehat{\theta}) = 0$. Nevertheless, since $q(\widehat{\theta}) = \sum_{t=1}^{T} q_t(\widehat{\theta})$, and $q_t(\widehat{\theta}) \neq 0 \; \forall t$, the estimator:

$$\mathsf{V}\left[\widehat{\theta}\right] = \sum_{t=1}^{T} q_t\left(\widehat{\theta}\right)^2 \tag{12.47}$$

is feasible. Later, we confront the issues which arise when modelling data, since in any realistic application, the form of $f_\mathsf{X}(\mathbf{x}|\theta)$ is unknown, and one cannot be sure that the postulated likelihood function is proportional to the actual data density. Many of the above results depend on that identity, and important practical issues arise when it is invalid.

12.7 Multiple regression

Since linear models play a major role in econometrics, we consider the empirical counterpart of regression. This section formulates the conditional multiple regression model in §12.7.1, and the least squares estimator of its parameters in §12.7.2, followed by distributional results in §12.7.3. Parameter subset estimation is developed in §12.7.4, and partitioned inversion in §12.7.5. Finally, multiple and partial correlation are discussed in §12.7.6 and §12.7.7.

12.7.1 The multiple regression model

The notation adopted for the linear regression model, viewed as the mechanism which generated the observed data, is:

$$y_t = \beta'\mathbf{x}_t + u_t \text{ with } u_t \sim \mathsf{IN}\left[0, \sigma_u^2\right] \tag{12.48}$$

where $\beta = (\beta_1 \ldots \beta_k)' \in \mathbb{R}^k$ is the $k \times 1$ parameter vector of interest and $\mathbf{x}_t = (x_{1t} \ldots x_{kt})'$. Then $\beta'\mathbf{x}_t = \sum_{i=1}^{k} \beta_i x_{it}$. One of the elements in $\mathbf{x}_t$ is unity with the corresponding parameter being the intercept in (12.48). We interpret (12.48) as a regression equation, based on a joint normal distribution for $(y_t : \mathbf{x}_t')$ conditional on $\mathbf{x}_t$ so that from above:

$$\mathsf{E}\left[y_t \mid \mathbf{x}_t\right] = \beta'\mathbf{x}_t \text{ with } \mathsf{E}\left[\mathbf{x}_t u_t\right] = \mathbf{0}.$$

Hence $\mathsf{E}[(y_t - \gamma'\mathbf{x}_t)^2]$ is minimized at σ_u^2 by the choice of $\gamma = \beta$. Chapter 13 considers the conditions necessary to sustain a factorization of a joint density into a conditional model of y_t given $\mathbf{x}_t$, and a marginal model for $\mathbf{x}_t$ which is then ignored, and Chapter 11 considers other interpretations of linear equations like (12.48) and their implications.

Grouping the observations, so that $\mathbf{y}' = (y_1 \ldots y_T)$ and $\mathbf{X}' = (\mathbf{x}_1 \ldots \mathbf{x}_T)$, which is a $T \times k$ matrix with $\text{rank}(\mathbf{X}) = k$ and $\mathbf{u}' = (u_1 \ldots u_T)$:

$$\mathbf{y} = \mathbf{X}\boldsymbol{\beta} + \mathbf{u} \quad \text{with} \quad \mathbf{u} \sim \mathsf{N}_T \left[\mathbf{0}, \sigma_u^2 \mathbf{I}\right]. \tag{12.49}$$

To simplify the derivations, we assume that $\mathsf{E}\left[\mathbf{y} | \mathbf{X}\right] = \mathbf{X}\boldsymbol{\beta}$, and hence $\mathsf{E}\left[\mathbf{X}'\mathbf{u}\right] = \mathbf{0}$. Although conditioning on $\mathbf{X}$ is too strong to be justifiable in economics, and essentially entails an experimental setting, most of the results hold in large samples under weaker assumptions. The assumptions about $\mathbf{u}$ are almost equally strong, but less objectionable in practice given the discussion in Chapter 13.

12.7.2 Ordinary least squares

The algebra of what is conventionally called ordinary least squares (OLS) estimation can now be established: the OLS estimator is also the MLE under our present assumptions (see §12.6.2). However, the following algebraic results do not depend on the actual statistical status of $\mathbf{X}$, and hold even when conditioning is invalid. Naturally, any statistical results do depend on the status of $\mathbf{X}$, and the assumptions about $\mathbf{u}$.

OLS estimation seeks to find the value $\widehat{\boldsymbol{\beta}}$ of $\boldsymbol{\beta}$ which minimizes the quadratic function:

$$h\left(\boldsymbol{\beta}\right) = \left(\mathbf{y} - \mathbf{X}\boldsymbol{\beta}\right)' \left(\mathbf{y} - \mathbf{X}\boldsymbol{\beta}\right). \tag{12.50}$$

Either by differentiating $h\left(\boldsymbol{\beta}\right)$ with respect to $\boldsymbol{\beta}$ and solving the resulting expression equated to zero, or using the sample analogue of $\mathsf{E}\left[\mathbf{X}'\mathbf{u}\right] = \mathbf{0}$, namely $\mathbf{X}'(\mathbf{y} - \mathbf{X}\widehat{\boldsymbol{\beta}}) = \mathbf{0}$, the best value is given by:

$$\widehat{\boldsymbol{\beta}} = \left(\mathbf{X}'\mathbf{X}\right)^{-1} \mathbf{X}'\mathbf{y}. \tag{12.51}$$

It can be verified that the value $\widehat{\boldsymbol{\beta}}$ of $\boldsymbol{\beta}$ in (12.51) minimizes $h\left(\boldsymbol{\beta}\right)$ in (12.50).

To determine the properties of $\widehat{\boldsymbol{\beta}}$ as an estimator of $\boldsymbol{\beta}$ substitute for $\mathbf{y}$ from (12.49):

$$\widehat{\boldsymbol{\beta}} = \boldsymbol{\beta} + \left(\mathbf{X}'\mathbf{X}\right)^{-1} \mathbf{X}'\mathbf{u} \tag{12.52}$$

then taking expectations conditional on $\mathbf{X}$:

$$\mathsf{E}\left[\left(\widehat{\boldsymbol{\beta}} - \boldsymbol{\beta}\right) | \mathbf{X}\right] = \mathsf{E}\left[\left(\mathbf{X}'\mathbf{X}\right)^{-1} \mathbf{X}'\mathbf{u} | \mathbf{X}\right] = \left(\mathbf{X}'\mathbf{X}\right)^{-1} \mathbf{X}'\mathsf{E}\left[\mathbf{u}\right] = \mathbf{0}. \tag{12.53}$$

Next, $\mathsf{V}[\widehat{\boldsymbol{\beta}}]$ is given by:

$$\begin{aligned}
\mathsf{E}\left[\left(\widehat{\boldsymbol{\beta}} - \boldsymbol{\beta}\right)\left(\widehat{\boldsymbol{\beta}} - \boldsymbol{\beta}\right)' | \mathbf{X}\right] &= \mathsf{E}\left[\left(\mathbf{X}'\mathbf{X}\right)^{-1} \mathbf{X}'\mathbf{u}\mathbf{u}'\mathbf{X} \left(\mathbf{X}'\mathbf{X}\right)^{-1} | \mathbf{X}\right] \\
&= \left(\mathbf{X}'\mathbf{X}\right)^{-1} \mathbf{X}'\mathsf{E}\left[\mathbf{u}\mathbf{u}'\right] \mathbf{X} \left(\mathbf{X}'\mathbf{X}\right)^{-1} \\
&= \sigma_u^2 \left(\mathbf{X}'\mathbf{X}\right)^{-1}.
\end{aligned} \tag{12.54}$$

Further, letting $\widehat{\mathbf{u}} = (\mathbf{y} - \mathbf{X}\widehat{\boldsymbol{\beta}})$, σ_u^2 can be estimated by (note that the least-squares estimate of the variance is scaled by $T - k$, whereas the maximum-likelihood estimate of (12.33) is scaled by T):

$$\widehat{\sigma}_u^2 = \frac{\widehat{\mathbf{u}}'\widehat{\mathbf{u}}}{(T - k)} \tag{12.55}$$

when $\widehat{\mathbf{u}}'\widehat{\mathbf{u}} = RSS$ (an acronym for residual sum of squares). In turn, $\mathsf{V}[\widehat{\boldsymbol{\beta}}]$ can be estimated by:

$$\widehat{\mathsf{V}\left[\widehat{\boldsymbol{\beta}}\right]} = \widehat{\sigma}_u^2 \left(\mathbf{X}'\mathbf{X}\right)^{-1}. \tag{12.56}$$

From (12.49)–(12.54), since $\widehat{\boldsymbol{\beta}}$ is a linear function of the normally distributed vector u:

$$\widehat{\boldsymbol{\beta}} \sim \mathsf{N}_k \left[\boldsymbol{\beta}, \sigma_u^2 \left(\mathbf{X}'\mathbf{X}\right)^{-1}\right]. \tag{12.57}$$

Consequently, from (12.57):

$$\eta_1 = \frac{\left(\widehat{\boldsymbol{\beta}} - \boldsymbol{\beta}\right)' \left(\mathbf{X}'\mathbf{X}\right) \left(\widehat{\boldsymbol{\beta}} - \boldsymbol{\beta}\right)}{\sigma_u^2} \sim \chi^2\left(k\right). \tag{12.58}$$

Let $\mathbf{M} = \mathbf{I}_T - \mathbf{X}\left(\mathbf{X}'\mathbf{X}\right)^{-1}\mathbf{X}'$, which is a symmetric and idempotent $T \times T$ matrix, such that $\mathbf{M} = \mathbf{M}'$, $\mathbf{M} = \mathbf{M}^2$ and $\mathbf{M}\left(\mathbf{I}_T - \mathbf{M}\right) = \mathbf{0}$. From (12.58) and (12.51):

$$\begin{aligned} \sigma_u^2 \eta_1 &= \left[\mathbf{u}'\mathbf{X}\left(\mathbf{X}'\mathbf{X}\right)^{-1}\right]\left(\mathbf{X}'\mathbf{X}\right)\left[\left(\mathbf{X}'\mathbf{X}\right)^{-1}\mathbf{X}'\mathbf{u}\right] \\ &= \mathbf{u}'\mathbf{X}\left(\mathbf{X}'\mathbf{X}\right)^{-1}\mathbf{X}'\mathbf{u} \\ &= \mathbf{u}'\left(\mathbf{I} - \mathbf{M}\right)\mathbf{u}. \end{aligned} \tag{12.59}$$

Further, M annihilates X since $\mathbf{MX} = \mathbf{0}$, so that:

$$\mathbf{My} = \mathbf{y} - \mathbf{X}\left(\mathbf{X}'\mathbf{X}\right)^{-1}\mathbf{X}'\mathbf{y} = \mathbf{y} - \mathbf{X}\widehat{\boldsymbol{\beta}} = \widehat{\mathbf{u}} = \mathbf{Mu}, \tag{12.60}$$

where the last equality follows from premultiplying (12.49) by M. Consequently:

$$RSS = \mathbf{y}'\mathbf{My} = \mathbf{u}'\mathbf{Mu}. \tag{12.61}$$

Since M is real and symmetric, let $\mathbf{M} = \mathbf{H\Lambda H}'$ where $\boldsymbol{\Lambda}$ is the diagonal matrix of eigenvalues and H is the non-singular matrix of eigenvectors with $\mathbf{H}'\mathbf{H} = \mathbf{I}_T$. By idempotency:

$$\mathbf{M}^2 = \mathbf{H\Lambda H}'\mathbf{H\Lambda H}' = \mathbf{H\Lambda}^2\mathbf{H}' = \mathbf{M} = \mathbf{H\Lambda H}'$$

so $\boldsymbol{\Lambda}^2 = \boldsymbol{\Lambda}$ and all the eigenvalues of M are either zero or unity. Thus, rank(M) $= tr\left(\mathbf{M}\right) = tr\left(\boldsymbol{\Lambda}\right)$ so:

$$\text{rank}\left(\mathbf{M}\right) = tr\left(\mathbf{I}_T - \mathbf{X}\left(\mathbf{X}'\mathbf{X}\right)^{-1}\mathbf{X}'\right) = tr\left(\mathbf{I}_T\right) - tr\left(\left(\mathbf{X}'\mathbf{X}\right)^{-1}\mathbf{X}'\mathbf{X}\right) = \left(T - k\right) \tag{12.62}$$

There are $(T - k)$ unit and k zero eigenvalues, and M is singular of rank $(T - k)$.

12.7.3 Distributional results

Since $\mathbf{u} \sim N_T[\mathbf{0}, \sigma_u^2 \mathbf{I}]$, then $\mathbf{u}'\mathbf{u}/\sigma_u^2 \sim \chi^2(T)$. Because $\mathbf{M}$ is singular, we cannot apply the theorems of §12.4.3 on the distributions of functions of normal variables to $\mathbf{Mu}$ or $\mathbf{u}'\mathbf{Mu}$. An alternative route is nevertheless feasible. Collect all of the unit eigenvalues of $\mathbf{M}$ in the first $(T-k)$ diagonal elements of $\mathbf{\Lambda}$, with the last k diagonal elements being zeros. Let:

$$\boldsymbol{\nu} = \mathbf{H}'\mathbf{u} \sim N_T\left[\mathbf{0}, \sigma_u^2 \mathbf{H}'\mathbf{H}\right] = N_T\left[\mathbf{0}, \sigma_u^2 \mathbf{I}\right]$$

and consider the quadratic form:

$$\mathbf{u}'\mathbf{Mu} = \mathbf{u}'\mathbf{H}\mathbf{\Lambda}\mathbf{H}'\mathbf{u} = \boldsymbol{\nu}'\mathbf{\Lambda}\boldsymbol{\nu} = \boldsymbol{\nu}_1'\boldsymbol{\nu}_1, \qquad (12.63)$$

where $\boldsymbol{\nu}' = (\boldsymbol{\nu}_1' : \boldsymbol{\nu}_2')$ and $\boldsymbol{\nu}_1$ and $\boldsymbol{\nu}_2$ correspond to the unit and zero roots respectively in $\mathbf{\Lambda}$, so that $\boldsymbol{\nu}_1$ denotes the first $(T-k)$ elements of $\boldsymbol{\nu}$ corresponding to the unit eigenvalues of $\mathbf{M}$. Then $\boldsymbol{\nu}_1 \sim N_{T-k}[\mathbf{0}, \sigma_u^2 \mathbf{I}]$, and since $\boldsymbol{\nu} \sim N_T[\mathbf{0}, \sigma_u^2 \mathbf{I}]$, $\boldsymbol{\nu}_1$ and $\boldsymbol{\nu}_2$ are distributed independently. Hence:

$$\eta_2 = \frac{\mathbf{u}'\mathbf{Mu}}{\sigma_u^2} = \frac{\boldsymbol{\nu}_1'\boldsymbol{\nu}_1}{\sigma_u^2} \sim \chi^2(T-k). \qquad (12.64)$$

This result shows that an idempotent quadratic form in standardized normal variables is distributed as a χ^2 with degrees of freedom equal to the rank of the idempotent matrix. Also:

$$\eta_2 = \frac{(T-k)\widehat{\sigma}_u^2}{\sigma_u^2} \quad \text{so that} \quad \widehat{\sigma}_u^2 \sim \frac{\sigma_u^2}{(T-k)}\chi^2(T-k). \qquad (12.65)$$

The properties of $\widehat{\sigma}_u^2$ can be calculated from this last result using the χ^2-distribution. As $\eta_2 \sim \chi^2(T-k)$, then $\mathsf{E}[\eta_2] = T-k$ and $\mathsf{V}[\eta_2] = 2(T-k)$. Since $(\mathbf{I}_T - \mathbf{M}) = \mathbf{H}(\mathbf{I}_T - \mathbf{\Lambda})\mathbf{H}'$:

$$\mathbf{u}'(\mathbf{I}_T - \mathbf{M})\mathbf{u} = \boldsymbol{\nu}'(\mathbf{I}_T - \mathbf{\Lambda})\boldsymbol{\nu} = \boldsymbol{\nu}_2'\boldsymbol{\nu}_2,$$

so $\eta_1 = \boldsymbol{\nu}_2'\boldsymbol{\nu}_2/\sigma_u^2$. As $\boldsymbol{\nu}_1$ and $\boldsymbol{\nu}_2$ are distributed independently, η_1 and η_2 are also independent, matching their being $\chi^2(k)$ and $\chi^2(T-k)$ respectively. Tests of H_0: $\boldsymbol{\beta} = \mathbf{0}$ (or components thereof) follow from these results using the F-distribution, since $\mathbf{y} = \mathbf{u}$ when $\boldsymbol{\beta} = \mathbf{0}$, so that on H_0:

$$\mathbf{u}'(\mathbf{I}_T - \mathbf{M})\mathbf{u} = \mathbf{y}'(\mathbf{I}_T - \mathbf{M})\mathbf{y} = \widehat{\boldsymbol{\beta}}'(\mathbf{X}'\mathbf{X})\widehat{\boldsymbol{\beta}}, \qquad (12.66)$$

and hence:

$$\eta_\beta = \frac{(T-k)\eta_1}{k\eta_2} = \frac{(T-k)\mathbf{y}'(\mathbf{I}-\mathbf{M})\mathbf{y}}{k\mathbf{y}'\mathbf{My}} = \frac{(T-k)\widehat{\boldsymbol{\beta}}'(\mathbf{X}'\mathbf{X})\widehat{\boldsymbol{\beta}}}{k\,RSS} \underset{\mathsf{H}_0}{\sim} \mathsf{F}(k, T-k). \qquad (12.67)$$

The last expression for η_β is the statistic which is actually computed. If $\beta \neq \mathbf{0}$, then from (12.57) the numerator of η_β becomes a non-central χ^2 with non-centrality parameter $\beta'\mathbf{X}'\mathbf{X}\beta \geq 0$, whereas the denominator is unchanged. Thus, the statistic η_β will on average lead to values larger than the $F(k, T - k)$ anticipated under the null.

Finally, from (12.57) each element $\widehat{\beta}_i$ of $\widehat{\beta}$ is normally distributed with variance given by σ_u^2 times the ith diagonal element d_{ii} of $(\mathbf{X}'\mathbf{X})^{-1}$ and is independent of η_2. Thus:

$$\frac{\left(\widehat{\beta}_i - \beta_i\right)}{\widehat{\sigma}_u \sqrt{d_{ii}}} \sim t(T - k), \tag{12.68}$$

where $t(T - k)$ denotes Student's t-distribution with $(T - k)$ degrees of freedom and:

$$\widehat{\sigma}_u \sqrt{d_{ii}} = \mathsf{SE}\left(\widehat{\beta}_i\right) \tag{12.69}$$

is the standard error of $\widehat{\beta}_i$. On the hypothesis H_0: $\beta_i = 0$:

$$\tau_i = \frac{\widehat{\beta}_i}{\mathsf{SE}\left(\widehat{\beta}_i\right)} \underset{H_0}{\widetilde{}} t(T - k) \tag{12.70}$$

which is a computable statistic from sample evidence alone.

12.7.4 Subsets of parameters

Consider estimating a subset of k_b parameters β_b of β where $k_a + k_b = k$. Partition $\mathbf{X} = (\mathbf{X}_a : \mathbf{X}_b)$ and $\beta' = (\beta_a' : \beta_b')$ so that:

$$\mathbf{y} = \mathbf{X}_a\beta_a + \mathbf{X}_b\beta_b + \mathbf{u}. \tag{12.71}$$

Let $\mathbf{M}_a = \mathbf{I}_T - \mathbf{X}_a(\mathbf{X}_a'\mathbf{X}_a)^{-1}\mathbf{X}_a'$ which implies that $\mathbf{M}_a\mathbf{X}_a = \mathbf{0}$ then:

$$\mathbf{M}_a\mathbf{y} = \mathbf{M}_a\mathbf{X}_b\beta_b + \mathbf{M}_a\mathbf{u} \tag{12.72}$$

and hence:

$$\widehat{\beta}_b = (\mathbf{X}_b'\mathbf{M}_a\mathbf{X}_b)^{-1}\mathbf{X}_b'\mathbf{M}_a\mathbf{y}. \tag{12.73}$$

Consequently, $\widehat{\beta}_b$ can be calculated by first regressing $\mathbf{X}_b$ on $\mathbf{X}_a$ and saving the residuals $(\mathbf{M}_a\mathbf{X}_b)$, then regressing $\mathbf{y}$ on those residuals. Notice that the regressors need 'corrected', but the regressand does not. Thus, procedures for 'detrending' (for example), can be justified as equivalent to adding a trend to the model (see Frisch and Waugh, 1933, who first proved this famous result). From (12.72) and (12.73):

$$\widehat{\beta}_b = \beta_b + (\mathbf{X}_b'\mathbf{M}_a\mathbf{X}_b)^{-1}\mathbf{X}_b'\mathbf{M}_a\mathbf{u} \tag{12.74}$$

so that

$$\mathsf{V}\left[\widehat{\beta}_b\right] = \sigma_u^2(\mathbf{X}_b'\mathbf{M}_a\mathbf{X}_b)^{-1}. \tag{12.75}$$

Thus:

$$\widehat{\beta}_b \sim \mathsf{N}_{k_b} \left[\beta_b, \sigma_u^2 \left(\mathbf{X}_b' \mathbf{M}_a \mathbf{X}_b \right)^{-1} \right]. \tag{12.76}$$

Hypothesis tests about β_b follow analogously to the previous section. In particular, from §12.7.3 and (12.76):

$$\eta_b = \frac{\left(\widehat{\beta}_b - \beta_b \right)' \left(\mathbf{X}_b' \mathbf{M}_a \mathbf{X}_b \right) \left(\widehat{\beta}_b - \beta_b \right)}{k_b \widehat{\sigma}_u^2} \sim \mathsf{F}\left(k_b, T - k \right). \tag{12.77}$$

When $k_b = 1$, this matches (12.70) under H_0: $\beta_b = 0$, and when $k_b = k$, (12.77) reproduces (12.67) under H_0: $\beta = \mathbf{0}$. A useful case of (12.77) is $k_b = (k-1)$ and $\mathbf{X}_a = \iota$ (a $T \times 1$ vector of ones), so all coefficients other than the intercept are tested.

If, instead of estimating (12.71), $\mathbf{X}_a$ is omitted from the model in the incorrect belief that $\beta_a = \mathbf{0}$, the equation to be estimated becomes:

$$\mathbf{y} = \mathbf{X}_b \beta_b + \mathbf{e} \tag{12.78}$$

The resulting estimator of β_b, denoted by $\widetilde{\beta}_b = \left(\mathbf{X}_b' \mathbf{X}_b \right)^{-1} \mathbf{X}_b' \mathbf{y}$, confounds the effects of $\mathbf{X}_a$ and $\mathbf{X}_b$:

$$\begin{aligned} \widetilde{\beta}_b &= \left(\mathbf{X}_b' \mathbf{X}_b \right)^{-1} \mathbf{X}_b' \left(\mathbf{X}_a \beta_a + \mathbf{X}_b \beta_b + \mathbf{u} \right) \\ &= \mathbf{B}_{ba} \beta_a + \beta_b + \left(\mathbf{X}_b' \mathbf{X}_b \right)^{-1} \mathbf{X}_b' \mathbf{u} \end{aligned} \tag{12.79}$$

where $\mathbf{B}_{ba} = \left(\mathbf{X}_b' \mathbf{X}_b \right)^{-1} \mathbf{X}_b' \mathbf{X}_a$. Thus:

$$\mathsf{E}\left[\widetilde{\beta}_b \right] = \mathbf{B}_{ba} \beta_a + \beta_b, \tag{12.80}$$

which equals β_b if and only if $\mathbf{B}_{ba} \beta_a = \mathbf{0}$. Moreover, let $\mathbf{M}_b$ have the same form as $\mathbf{M}_a$ but using $\mathbf{X}_b$ then:

$$\mathsf{V}\left[\widetilde{\beta}_b \right] = \widetilde{\sigma}_u^2 \left(\mathbf{X}_b' \mathbf{X}_b \right)^{-1} \quad \text{where} \quad \widetilde{\sigma}_u^2 = \frac{\mathbf{y}' \mathbf{M}_b \mathbf{y}}{(T - k_b)} = \frac{\widetilde{\mathbf{u}}' \widetilde{\mathbf{u}}}{(T - k_b)} \tag{12.81}$$

when $\widetilde{\mathbf{u}} = \mathbf{y} - \mathbf{X}_b \widetilde{\beta}_b$ and:

$$\mathsf{E}\left[\widetilde{\sigma}_u^2 \right] = \sigma_u^2 + \frac{\beta_a' \mathbf{X}_a' \mathbf{M}_b \mathbf{X}_a \beta_a}{(T - k_b)} \geq \sigma_u^2. \tag{12.82}$$

Conventionally, $\widetilde{\beta}_b$ is interpreted as a biased estimator of β_b with bias given by $\mathbf{B}_{ba} \beta_a$. The estimated variance matrix in (12.81) may exceed, or be less than, that given by the relevant sub-matrix of (12.56), in the sense that the difference could be positive or negative semi-definite.

The sign of an estimated coefficient from (12.78) can be the same as, or the opposite to, that expected from prior theoretical reasoning, and the latter is sometimes called a 'wrong sign'. We interpret the outcome in (12.80) as delivering a different coefficient $\gamma_b = \mathbf{B}_{ba}\beta_a + \beta_b$ than β_b, consonant with the following argument. First:

$$\mathbf{X}_a \equiv \mathbf{M}_b\mathbf{X}_a + (\mathbf{I}_T - \mathbf{M}_b)\,\mathbf{X}_a = \mathbf{M}_b\mathbf{X}_a + \mathbf{X}_b\mathbf{B}_{ba}. \tag{12.83}$$

Consequently, from (12.71):

$$\begin{aligned} \mathbf{y} &= \left(\mathbf{M}_b\mathbf{X}_a + \mathbf{X}_b\mathbf{B}_{ba}\right)\beta_a + \mathbf{X}_b\beta_b + \mathbf{u} \\ &= \mathbf{X}_b\gamma_b + \left(\mathbf{u} + \mathbf{M}_b\mathbf{X}_a\beta_a\right) \\ &= \mathbf{X}_b\gamma_b + \mathbf{v} \end{aligned} \tag{12.84}$$

where $\mathsf{E}\,[\mathbf{v}] = \mathbf{M}_b\mathbf{X}_a\beta_a \neq \mathbf{0}$, but since $\mathbf{M}_b\mathbf{X}_b = \mathbf{0}$:

$$\mathsf{E}\,[\mathbf{X}_b'\mathbf{v}] = \mathsf{E}\,[\mathbf{X}_b'\mathbf{u}] + \mathbf{X}_b'\mathbf{M}_b\mathbf{X}_a\beta_a = \mathbf{0}. \tag{12.85}$$

Thus, the model is implicitly reparametrized by omitting $\mathbf{X}_a$, and OLS is an unbiased estimator of γ_b despite $\mathsf{E}\,[\mathbf{v}] \neq \mathbf{0}$. Under more general assumptions, a related large-sample result holds.

12.7.5 Partitioned inversion

The results on estimating subsets of parameters can be obtained by partitioned inversion of $(\mathbf{X}'\mathbf{X})$. Consider the matrix $(\mathbf{X}'\mathbf{X})^{-1}$. Let $\mathbf{H} = (\mathbf{X}_b'\mathbf{M}_a\mathbf{X}_b)$ and $\mathbf{G} = (\mathbf{X}_a'\mathbf{M}_b\mathbf{X}_a)$, then:

$$\begin{pmatrix} \mathbf{X}_a'\mathbf{X}_a & \mathbf{X}_a'\mathbf{X}_b \\ \mathbf{X}_b'\mathbf{X}_a & \mathbf{X}_b'\mathbf{X}_b \end{pmatrix}^{-1} = \begin{pmatrix} (\mathbf{X}_a'\mathbf{M}_b\mathbf{X}_a)^{-1} & -(\mathbf{X}_a'\mathbf{M}_b\mathbf{X}_a)^{-1}\mathbf{B}_{ba}' \\ -\mathbf{B}_{ab}(\mathbf{X}_b'\mathbf{M}_a\mathbf{X}_b)^{-1} & (\mathbf{X}_b'\mathbf{M}_a\mathbf{X}_b)^{-1} \end{pmatrix} \tag{12.86}$$

where $\mathbf{B}_{ab} = (\mathbf{X}_a'\mathbf{X}_a)^{-1}\mathbf{X}_a'\mathbf{X}_b$. Further, $\mathbf{X}'\mathbf{y}$ can be partitioned conformably as:

$$\begin{pmatrix} \mathbf{X}_a'\mathbf{y} \\ \mathbf{X}_b'\mathbf{y} \end{pmatrix} \tag{12.87}$$

and multiplication of (12.87) by (12.86) delivers (12.73) together with corresponding expressions for estimating β_a; the coefficient variance matrix follows from (12.86).

Alternatively, when $(\mathbf{X}'\mathbf{X})^{-1}$ is given by:

$$\begin{pmatrix} (\mathbf{X}_a'\mathbf{M}_b\mathbf{X}_a)^{-1} & -(\mathbf{X}_a'\mathbf{M}_b\mathbf{X}_a)^{-1}\mathbf{B}_{ba}' \\ -\mathbf{B}_{ba}(\mathbf{X}_a'\mathbf{M}_b\mathbf{X}_a)^{-1} & (\mathbf{X}_b'\mathbf{X}_b)^{-1} + \mathbf{B}_{ba}(\mathbf{X}_a'\mathbf{M}_b\mathbf{X}_a)^{-1}\mathbf{B}_{ba}' \end{pmatrix} \tag{12.88}$$

then multiplication of (12.87) by (12.88) delivers for the second row:

$$\begin{aligned} \widehat{\beta}_b &= -\mathbf{B}_{ba}(\mathbf{X}_a'\mathbf{M}_b\mathbf{X}_a)^{-1}\mathbf{X}_a'\mathbf{y} + (\mathbf{X}_b'\mathbf{X}_b)^{-1}\mathbf{X}_b'\mathbf{y} + \mathbf{B}_{ba}(\mathbf{X}_a'\mathbf{M}_b\mathbf{X}_a)^{-1}\mathbf{B}_{ba}'\mathbf{X}_b'\mathbf{y} \\ &= \widetilde{\beta}_b - \mathbf{B}_{ba}(\mathbf{X}_a'\mathbf{M}_b\mathbf{X}_a)^{-1}\mathbf{X}_a'\left(\mathbf{I}_T - \mathbf{X}_b(\mathbf{X}_b'\mathbf{X}_b)^{-1}\mathbf{X}_b'\right)\mathbf{y} \\ &= \widetilde{\beta}_b - \mathbf{B}_{ba}\widehat{\beta}_a \end{aligned} \tag{12.89}$$

from which it follows that:

$$\tilde{\beta}_b = \hat{\beta}_b + \mathbf{B}_{ba}\hat{\beta}_a. \tag{12.90}$$

Then (12.90) is the exact estimation analogue of (12.80): the simple regression estimate of β_b equals the corresponding multiple regression estimate of β_b plus the auxiliary regression matrix multiplied by the multiple regression estimate of the omitted effect. Consequently, a regression coefficient is interpretable as a partial derivative of y with respect to the relevant x only to the extent that all other effects have either been included in the regression, or are orthogonal to the variables under study.

12.7.6 Multiple correlation

Let $\hat{\mathbf{y}} = \mathbf{X}\hat{\beta}$, then $\mathbf{y} = \hat{\mathbf{y}} + \hat{\mathbf{u}}$ and $\mathbf{X}'\hat{\mathbf{u}} = \mathbf{0}$ since $\mathbf{MX} = \mathbf{0}$. Thus, $\hat{\mathbf{y}}'\hat{\mathbf{u}} = 0$ implying that:

$$\mathbf{y}'\hat{\mathbf{y}} = \hat{\mathbf{y}}'\hat{\mathbf{y}} \quad \text{and} \quad \mathbf{y}'\mathbf{y} = \hat{\mathbf{y}}'\hat{\mathbf{y}} + \hat{\mathbf{u}}'\hat{\mathbf{u}}. \tag{12.91}$$

A natural choice to measure the 'goodness of fit' between $\mathbf{y}$ and $\hat{\mathbf{y}} = \mathbf{X}\hat{\beta}$ is their correlation coefficient. When a constant is present in $\mathbf{X}$ as the vector of ones ι, since $\mathbf{MX} = \mathbf{0}$, then $\iota'\hat{\mathbf{u}} = \iota'\mathbf{M}\hat{\mathbf{u}} = 0$ and $T^{-1}\iota'\mathbf{y} = T^{-1}\iota'\hat{\mathbf{y}} = \bar{y}$ (the sample mean). Consequently, the squared correlation between $\mathbf{y}$ and $\hat{\mathbf{y}}$ is given by:

$$\mathsf{R}^2(\mathbf{y}, \hat{\mathbf{y}}) = \frac{\left[(\mathbf{y} - \iota\bar{y})'(\hat{\mathbf{y}} - \iota\bar{y})\right]^2}{\left[(\mathbf{y} - \iota\bar{y})'(\mathbf{y} - \iota\bar{y})\right]\left[(\hat{\mathbf{y}} - \iota\bar{y})'(\hat{\mathbf{y}} - \iota\bar{y})\right]}. \tag{12.92}$$

Substituting $(\mathbf{y} - \iota\bar{y}) = (\hat{\mathbf{y}} - \iota\bar{y}) + \hat{\mathbf{u}}$ takes deviations about means in $\mathbf{y} = \hat{\mathbf{y}} + \hat{\mathbf{u}}$, so using the results that $\hat{\mathbf{y}}'\hat{\mathbf{u}} = 0$ and $\iota'\hat{\mathbf{u}} = 0$:

$$\mathsf{R}^2 = \frac{(\hat{\mathbf{y}} - \iota\bar{y})'(\hat{\mathbf{y}} - \iota\bar{y})}{(\mathbf{y} - \iota\bar{y})'(\mathbf{y} - \iota\bar{y})}, \tag{12.93}$$

and hence:

$$\left(1 - \mathsf{R}^2\right) = \frac{\hat{\mathbf{u}}'\hat{\mathbf{u}}}{(\mathbf{y} - \iota\bar{y})'(\mathbf{y} - \iota\bar{y})}.$$

R^2 is the squared multiple correlation between y and $\mathbf{x}$. The statistic η_b in (12.77) for testing the hypothesis that all coefficients other than the intercept are zero can be written as a function of $\mathsf{R}^2/\left(1 - \mathsf{R}^2\right)$. On H_0: $\beta_b = \mathbf{0}$, since $\hat{\mathbf{y}} = \iota\hat{\beta}_a + \mathbf{X}_b\hat{\beta}_b$ and:

$$\hat{\beta}_a = \bar{y} - \bar{\mathbf{x}}_b'\hat{\beta}_b = \bar{y} - T^{-1}\iota'\mathbf{X}_b\hat{\beta}_b,$$

then:

$$\hat{\mathbf{y}} = \iota\bar{y} - T^{-1}\iota\iota'\mathbf{X}_b\hat{\beta}_b + \mathbf{X}_b\hat{\beta}_b = \iota\bar{y} + \mathbf{M}_a\mathbf{X}_b\hat{\beta}_b,$$

as $\mathbf{M}_a = \left(\mathbf{I}_T - \iota(\iota'\iota)^{-1}\iota'\right) = \left(\mathbf{I}_T - T^{-1}\iota\iota'\right)$, so that:

$$\eta_b = \frac{(T - k)\hat{\beta}_b'\mathbf{X}_b'\mathbf{M}_a\mathbf{X}_b\hat{\beta}_b}{(k - 1)\hat{\mathbf{u}}'\hat{\mathbf{u}}} = \frac{(T - k)(\hat{\mathbf{y}} - \iota\bar{y})'(\hat{\mathbf{y}} - \iota\bar{y})}{(k - 1)\hat{\mathbf{u}}'\hat{\mathbf{u}}} = \frac{(T - k)\mathsf{R}^2}{(k - 1)(1 - \mathsf{R}^2)}. \tag{12.94}$$

As $R^2 \to 1$, highly 'significant' results are bound to occur independently of their substance.

12.7.7 Partial correlation

The notion of a partial correlation, or a partial regression coefficient, is fundamental to interpreting econometric evidence. For empirical modelling, equations like (12.48) are usually formulated with the implicit assumption that:

$$\frac{\partial y_t}{\partial x_{it}} = \beta_i \text{ for } i = 1, \ldots, k. \tag{12.95}$$

OLS estimates $\widehat{\beta}_i$ are then interpreted as if they had the same properties. When $i = b$, β_b is a scalar so that X_b is a vector x_b, and the marginal distribution of $\widehat{\beta}_b$ is given in (12.76). Then the partial correlation $r_{by \cdot a}$ between y and x_b having removed the linear influence of X_a (assumed to contain ι) is the correlation between $M_a y$ and $M_a x_b$:

$$r_{by \cdot a} = \frac{y' M_a x_b}{\sqrt{(y' M_a y)(x'_b M_a x_b)}} = \frac{\widehat{\beta}_b \sqrt{(x'_b M_a x_b)}}{\sqrt{(y' M_a y)}}. \tag{12.96}$$

Note that $M_a y$ and $M_a x_b$ have zero means and that:

$$r^2_{by \cdot a} = \frac{\widehat{\beta}_b (x'_b M_a x_b) \widehat{\beta}_b}{y' M_a y}. \tag{12.97}$$

The numerator of $(1 - r^2_{by \cdot a})$ is $y' M_a y - \widehat{\beta}_b (x'_b M_a x_b) \widehat{\beta}_b = y' M^* y$ where:

$$\begin{aligned} M^* &= M_a - M_a x_b (x'_b M_a x_b)^{-1} x'_b M_a \\ &= M_a \left[I_T - M_a x_b (x'_b M_a x_b)^{-1} x'_b M_a \right] M_a \end{aligned} \tag{12.98}$$

so $M^* = M$. This last equality follows from applying (12.86) since $[\cdot]$ annihilates $M_a x_b$. As a check, by suitable rearrangement of the order of regressors, $M^* X = M^* (X_a : x_b) = 0 = MX$. From the earlier formula for τ_i when $i = b$:

$$\tau^2_b = \frac{(T - k) r^2_{by \cdot a}}{\left(1 - r^2_{by \cdot a}\right)}, \tag{12.99}$$

In the special case that $k = 2$ and $x_a = \iota$, (12.94) coincides with (12.99).

When X_a includes ι and $k_b > 1$, (12.98) holds in the form:

$$M = M_a - M_a X_b (X'_b M_a X_b)^{-1} X'_b M_a,$$

so that:

$$y' M y = y' M_a y - y' M_a X_b (X'_b M_a X_b)^{-1} X'_b M_a y = y' M_a y - \widehat{\beta}'_b X'_b M_a X_b \widehat{\beta}_b. \tag{12.100}$$

Substituting (12.100) in (12.77):

$$\eta_b = \frac{(T-k)\,(\mathbf{y}'\mathbf{M}_a\mathbf{y} - \mathbf{y}'\mathbf{M}\mathbf{y})}{k_b\widehat{\mathbf{u}}'\widehat{\mathbf{u}}} = \frac{(T-k)\,(\widetilde{\mathbf{u}}'\widetilde{\mathbf{u}} - \widehat{\mathbf{u}}'\widehat{\mathbf{u}})}{k_b\widehat{\mathbf{u}}'\widehat{\mathbf{u}}} = \frac{(T-k)}{k_b}\left(d\frac{\widetilde{\sigma}_u^2}{\widehat{\sigma}_u^2} - 1\right)$$

$$(12.101)$$

where $d = (T - k_a)/(T - k)$. Thus, when $\widehat{\sigma}_u^2 = \widetilde{\sigma}_u^2$, $\eta_b = 1$ and when $\widehat{\sigma}_u^2 > \widetilde{\sigma}_u^2$, $\eta_b < 1$. Deleting k_b regressors when the F-test for the significance of their coefficients is less than unity will lower the estimated residual standard error. For $k_b = 1$, deleting a single variable with $\tau_b^2 < 1$ will lower the estimated residual standard error.

12.7.8 Maximum likelihood estimation

As noted, OLS is also the MLE here. When $\mathbf{u} \sim \mathsf{N}_T[\mathbf{0}, \sigma_u^2\mathbf{I}]$, the conditional log-likelihood function is:

$$\ell\left(\boldsymbol{\beta}, \sigma_u^2 \mid \mathbf{X}; \mathbf{y}\right) = -\frac{T}{2}\log(2\pi) - \frac{T}{2}\log(\sigma_u^2) - \frac{(\mathbf{y} - \mathbf{X}\boldsymbol{\beta})'\,(\mathbf{y} - \mathbf{X}\boldsymbol{\beta})}{2\sigma_u^2} \qquad (12.102)$$

so the MLE minimizes the last term, which yields OLS. From above:

$$\ell\left(\boldsymbol{\beta}, \sigma_u^2 \mid \mathbf{X}; \mathbf{y}\right) = -\frac{T}{2}\log(2\pi) - \frac{T}{2}\log(\sigma_u^2) - \frac{\left(\widehat{\boldsymbol{\beta}} - \boldsymbol{\beta}\right)'\mathbf{X}'\mathbf{X}\left(\widehat{\boldsymbol{\beta}} - \boldsymbol{\beta}\right)}{2\sigma_u^2} - \frac{\widehat{\mathbf{u}}'\widehat{\mathbf{u}}}{2\sigma_u^2}$$

$$(12.103)$$

From (12.103), $(\widehat{\boldsymbol{\beta}}, \widehat{\sigma}_u^2)$ are jointly sufficient for $(\boldsymbol{\beta}, \sigma_u^2)$, and by independence, the joint distribution of $\widehat{\boldsymbol{\beta}}$ and $\widehat{\sigma}_u^2$ factorizes into the products of their marginals.

12.7.9 Recursive estimation

To understand the basis of recursive estimation, denote the specified equation by:

$$y_t = \boldsymbol{\beta}'\mathbf{x}_t + u_t \qquad (12.104)$$

where $\boldsymbol{\beta}$ is asserted to be constant, $\mathsf{E}\,[\mathbf{x}_t u_t] = \mathbf{0}\,\forall t$, $\mathsf{E}\,(u_t^2) = \sigma_u^2$, and $\mathsf{E}\,(u_t u_s) = 0$ if $t \neq s$. Let the complete sample period be $(1, \ldots, T)$, and consider the least-squares outcome on a subsample up to $t - 1$ (for $t > k$ when there are k regressors in $\mathbf{x}_{t-1}$):

$$\widehat{\boldsymbol{\beta}}_{t-1} = \left(\mathbf{X}'_{t-1}\mathbf{X}_{t-1}\right)^{-1}\mathbf{X}'_{t-1}\mathbf{y}_{t-1}, \qquad (12.105)$$

with $\mathbf{X}_{t-1} = (\mathbf{x}_1 \ldots \mathbf{x}_{t-1})'$ and $\mathbf{y}_{t-1} = (y_1 \ldots y_{t-1})'$. When the sample is increased by one observation, then:

$$\mathbf{X}'_t\mathbf{X}_t = \mathbf{X}'_{t-1}\mathbf{X}_{t-1} + \mathbf{x}_t\mathbf{x}'_t \qquad (12.106)$$

and:

$$\mathbf{X}'_t\mathbf{y}_t = \mathbf{X}'_{t-1}\mathbf{y}_{t-1} + \mathbf{x}_t y_t. \qquad (12.107)$$

However, given $\left(\mathbf{X}'_{t-1}\mathbf{X}_{t-1}\right)^{-1}$, one does not need to invert $(\mathbf{X}'_t\mathbf{X}_t)$ to calculate $\widehat{\boldsymbol{\beta}}_t$. Rather:

$$(\mathbf{X}'_t\mathbf{X}_t)^{-1} = \left(\mathbf{X}'_{t-1}\mathbf{X}_{t-1}\right)^{-1} - \frac{\boldsymbol{\lambda}_t\boldsymbol{\lambda}'_t}{1+\boldsymbol{\lambda}'_t\mathbf{x}_t}, \tag{12.108}$$

where

$$\boldsymbol{\lambda}_t = \left(\mathbf{X}'_{t-1}\mathbf{X}_{t-1}\right)^{-1}\mathbf{x}_t. \tag{12.109}$$

Thus, the inverse can be sequentially updated, and $\widehat{\boldsymbol{\beta}}_t$ follows directly. A similar updating formula is available for updating the residual sum of squares (RSS) from the innovations given by:

$$RSS_t = RSS_{t-1} + \frac{\nu_t^2}{1+\boldsymbol{\lambda}'_t\mathbf{x}_t} \tag{12.110}$$

where the innovations are the one-step ahead forecast errors:

$$\nu_t = y_t - \mathbf{x}'_t\widehat{\boldsymbol{\beta}}_{t-1}. \tag{12.111}$$

These are mean zero, independent random variables, with variance

$$\mathsf{E}\left[\nu_t^2\right] = \sigma_u^2\left(1+\boldsymbol{\lambda}'_t x_t\right) = \sigma_u^2\omega_t.$$

The standardized innovations are:

$$\frac{\nu_t}{\left(1+\boldsymbol{\lambda}'_t x_t\right)^{1/2}}.$$

From this, equation and parameter standard errors are readily calculated:

$$\widehat{\sigma}_t^2 = \frac{RSS_t}{t-k} \tag{12.112}$$

and:

$$\mathsf{V}\left[\widehat{\boldsymbol{\beta}}_t\right] = \widehat{\sigma}_t^2\left(\mathbf{X}'_t\mathbf{X}_t\right)^{-1} \tag{12.113}$$

where $\mathsf{V}\left[\cdot\right]$ denotes variance.

Finally, from the sequence of $\{RSS_{t-1}\}$, sequences of tests (for example, for parameter constancy) can be calculated, based on Chow (1960).

If instrumental variables estimators are used, the recursive formulae are similar but more cumbersome (see Hendry and Neale, 1987).

Chapter 13

Advanced Econometrics

13.1 Introduction

This chapter offers an overall description of the class of dynamic models handled by PcGive, the most frequently used concepts and modelling strategies, and the estimation and evaluation procedures available. The class of single-equation dynamic linear models analyzed by PcGive, including a model typology and distinctions between interpretations of linear models, were described in Chapter 11. Here we discuss dynamic systems in §13.2. The crucial concept of weak exogeneity is described in §13.3.2 as the basis for valid inference in single-equation conditional models which are nevertheless part of a dynamic economic system. That section also introduces several factorizations of data density functions, and relates these to such concepts as white noise and innovations. The discussion then turns to model evaluation in §13.4, an information taxonomy for model evaluation and design in §13.5, and the types of test used in §13.6. Section 13.7 considers modelling strategies, and the chapter concludes with a brief discussion of estimation techniques in §13.8.

13.2 Dynamic systems

The class of models basic to PcGive is that of linear dynamic single equations. Chapter 11 discussed the formulation and properties of such equations, their forms (in the typology), and their different interpretations. In economics, however, equations cannot be viewed in isolation: they are inherently part of a system. Here we note the structure of such systems, and lay the ground for determining when a single-equation analysis is likely to be valid despite the system context. Volume II (Doornik and Hendry, 2006a) analyzes linear dynamic systems *qua* systems, but PcGive provides single-equation methods that are applicable when one equation is the focus of interest from a system that otherwise is rather loosely specified. Dynamic systems are more extensively described in Volume II. For completeness, we give a brief overview here.

As in Chapter 11, dynamic linear equation analysis follows from the use of lag operators (denoted by L) such that $L^r x_t = x_{t-r}$ for a variable x_t. When $\mathbf{y}_t$ and $\mathbf{z}_t$ are $n \times 1$ and $k \times 1$ vectors of variables of modelled and non-modelled variables respectively, an expression like (11.4) constitutes a dynamic linear system. Since $L^r \mathbf{x}_t = \mathbf{x}_{t-r}$ for vectors as well, this enables us to describe the formulation of a dynamic system rather compactly.

The data sets of observations on $\{\mathbf{y}_t\}$ and $\{\mathbf{z}_t\}$ are denoted by $\mathbf{Y}_T^1 = (\mathbf{y}_1 \dots \mathbf{y}_T)$ and $\mathbf{Z}_T^1$ respectively where:

$$\mathbf{y}_t = \begin{pmatrix} y_{1,t} \\ y_{2,t} \\ \vdots \\ y_{n,t} \end{pmatrix} \text{ and } \mathbf{z}_t = \begin{pmatrix} z_{1,t} \\ z_{2,t} \\ \vdots \\ z_{k,t} \end{pmatrix}.$$

Formally, a dynamic system can be written as:

$$\mathbf{y}_t = \sum_{i=1}^{m} \boldsymbol{\pi}_{1i} \mathbf{y}_{t-i} + \sum_{j=0}^{r} \boldsymbol{\pi}_{2j} \mathbf{z}_{t-j} + \mathbf{v}_t \tag{13.1}$$

where $\mathbf{v}_t \sim \mathsf{N}_n[\mathbf{0}, \boldsymbol{\Omega}]$ for $t = 1, \dots, T$. Section 13.3.2 describes when $\mathbf{z}_t$ can be treated as weakly exogenous for the parameters of interest in the system, so that it is legitimate to treat $\{\mathbf{z}_t\}$ as determined outside the system in (13.1). Note that x_t in (11.4) may be endogenous in the system context (13.1) even though it is not jointly determined with y_t in (11.4). Also, m and r in (13.1) may differ between $\mathbf{y}_t$ and $\mathbf{z}_t$ as well as between variables within that partition.

Introducing matrix lag polynomials:

$$\boldsymbol{\pi}_1(L) = \sum_{i=0}^{m} \boldsymbol{\pi}_{1i} L^i \text{ and } \boldsymbol{\pi}_2(L) = \sum_{j=0}^{r} \boldsymbol{\pi}_{2j} L^j,$$

write (13.1) as:

$$\boldsymbol{\pi}_1(L) \mathbf{y}_t = \boldsymbol{\pi}_2(L) \mathbf{z}_t + \mathbf{v}_t,$$

where it is assumed that $\boldsymbol{\pi}_{10} = \mathbf{I}_n$ (the $n \times n$ identity matrix), and that $\boldsymbol{\pi}_1(1) \neq \mathbf{0}$ and $\boldsymbol{\pi}_2(1) \neq \mathbf{0}$, so that $\mathbf{y}$ and $\mathbf{z}$ are cointegrated. In conventional parlance, (13.1) is a reduced form, but since no structural model has been specified from which it can have been reduced, we refer to (13.1) as the system (see Hendry, Neale and Srba, 1988). When $\mathbf{z}_t$ is deterministic, (13.1) is closed and is a vector autoregression (VAR). However, at least conceptually, one could imagine extending the system to endogenize $\mathbf{z}_t$ and make a bigger VAR, so if $\boldsymbol{\pi}_{20} = \mathbf{0}$, (13.1) is part of a VAR (cut across equations), and if $\boldsymbol{\pi}_{20} \neq \mathbf{0}$ it is a VAR conditional on $\mathbf{z}_t$.

A model of the system is created by premultiplying (13.1) by a non-singular $n \times n$ matrix $\mathbf{B}$:

$$\mathbf{B}\mathbf{y}_t = \sum_{i=1}^{m} \mathbf{B}\pi_{1i}\mathbf{y}_{t-i} + \sum_{j=0}^{r} \mathbf{B}\pi_{2j}\mathbf{z}_{t-j} + \mathbf{B}\mathbf{v}_t, \tag{13.2}$$

or switching notation:

$$\mathbf{B}\left(L\right)\mathbf{y}_t = \mathbf{C}\left(L\right)\mathbf{z}_t + \mathbf{u}_t \quad \text{with} \quad \mathbf{u}_t \sim \mathsf{IN}_n\left[\mathbf{0}, \mathbf{\Sigma}\right]. \tag{13.3}$$

The system is said to be complete if $\mathbf{B}$ is non-singular. Let $\mathbf{A}$ be the matrix of all the coefficients:

$$\mathbf{A} = \left(\mathbf{B}_0 : \mathbf{B}_1 : \cdots : \mathbf{B}_m : -\mathbf{C}_0 : \cdots : -\mathbf{C}_r\right)$$

and $\mathbf{x}_t$ the column vector of all the variables $\left(\mathbf{y}_t \ldots \mathbf{y}_{t-m} : \mathbf{z}_t \ldots \mathbf{z}_{t-r}\right)$ then (13.3) can be written neatly as:

$$\mathbf{A}\mathbf{x}_t = \mathbf{u}_t \sim \mathsf{IN}_n\left[\mathbf{0}, \mathbf{\Sigma}\right].$$

The matrix $\mathbf{A}$ must be restricted if the $\{\mathbf{B}_i, \mathbf{C}_i\}$ are to be unique: otherwise, a further non-singular multiplication of (13.2) would produce a different model, yet one which looked exactly like (13.3), thereby destroying uniqueness. The rank and order conditions for identification apply: both are fully discussed in Volume II. The main issue of relevance to PcGive is that in any equation containing p right-hand side endogenous variables, the system of which it is part must contain at least p non-modelled variables not included in that equation: this is the order condition. When the sample of T observations on these p endogenous variables is just denoted by $\mathbf{Y}$ and the sample on the excluded but available non-modelled variables is $\mathbf{Z}$, then:

$$\text{rank}\left(\mathbf{Y}'\mathbf{Z}\right) = p,$$

is both necessary and sufficient for identification: this is the rank condition (see White, 1984).

All of the model types of §11.4 could occur within (13.3), and if $\mathbf{A}$ is over-identified, the imposed restrictions are testable. When developing a model of a system, it is sensible to commence from the unrestricted representation (13.1), test its validity, and then reduce the system to the model. All of the attributes needed for the model to match the evidence are called congruency (see §13.5) and these can be tested, but care is required in modelling integrated data. As a first step, cointegration tests can be conducted to establish the dimension of the cointegrating space, and the relevant set of cointegration restrictions and differences can be imposed to reduce the data to I(0). This order will facilitate later testing, since conventional limiting distributions can be used: see Phillips (1991) and Hendry and Mizon (1993) for discussions of modelling cointegrated processes, Johansen (1988) and Johansen and Juselius (1990) for analyses of the maximum likelihood estimator, and Hendry, Neale and Srba (1988) for an approach to structural system modelling in l(0) processes. Such a methodology implements the general-to-specific notion in the system context, and contrasts with the alternative of specifying a structural model at the outset and testing its restrictions against the (derived) reduced form. Since the latter may be invalid, it provides an unreliable benchmark for any tests. Techniques for estimating models, as well as general derivations of standard errors etc., are considered in §13.8 below; further detail on systems and models thereof is provided in Volume II, which includes the implementation of a complete modelling exercise on a dynamic cointegrated system.

Prior to proceeding, we note that since (13.1) is a model of itself, and there are likely to be valid parsimonious representations of the system (13.1), the critique in Sims (1980) lacks force. Specifying a model in structural form corresponds to imposing non-linear restrictions across functions of the πs in (13.1), and there are no *a priori* grounds for claiming that all possible restrictions are invalid. For example, if the response of $y_{1,t}$ to $y_{2,t}$ is very rapid compared to that of $y_{2,t}$ to $y_{1,t}$ in a second equation, a structural model of their joint representation can impose valid restrictions on the VAR. The application of encompassing discussed in §13.5 will clarify this issue further. At the heart of the issue of conditional estimation is the role of weak exogeneity in modelling single equations, so we now discuss that issue (see Engle, Hendry and Richard, 1983).

13.3 Data density factorizations

To undertake valid inference using a single-equation approach, some conditions must be fulfilled such that the system dependence of conditioning variables can be neglected without losing relevant information. These conditions are encapsulated in the concept of weak exogeneity. First, we introduce joint data density functions, and extend the notion of factorization introduced in Chapter 12.

13.3.1 Innovations and white noise

The data set of observations on $\{\mathbf{y}_t\}$ and $\{\mathbf{z}_t\}$ in (13.1) is denoted by $\mathbf{X}_T^1 = (\mathbf{x}_1 \dots \mathbf{x}_T)$ where $\mathbf{x}_t' = (\mathbf{y}_t' : \mathbf{z}_t')$. Thus:

$$\mathbf{X}_T^1 = \begin{pmatrix} \mathbf{y}_1 & \mathbf{y}_2 & \cdots & \mathbf{y}_T \\ \mathbf{z}_1 & \mathbf{z}_2 & \cdots & \mathbf{z}_T \end{pmatrix}.$$

Denote the process generating $\mathbf{X}_T^1$ by $\mathsf{D}_\mathsf{X}\left(\mathbf{X}_T^1 | \boldsymbol{\theta}_T^1, \mathbf{X}_0\right)$ where $\mathbf{X}_0$ are the initial conditions and $\boldsymbol{\theta}_T^1 \in \Theta$ are the 'parameters' of the process, which may depend on the historical time (hence the indexing by $1, \dots, T$). Since $\mathbf{X}_T^1 = (\mathbf{x}_1 \dots \mathbf{x}_T)$, the whole sample data density $\mathsf{D}_\mathsf{X}(\cdot)$ can be sequentially factorized as the product of terms like $\mathsf{D}_\mathsf{X}\left(\mathbf{x}_t | \mathbf{X}_{t-1}^1, \boldsymbol{\theta}_t, \mathbf{X}_0\right)$ which is each time period's density. This exploits the fact that if $\mathsf{P}(a)$ denotes the probability of an event a, then $\mathsf{P}(ab) = \mathsf{P}(a|b)\mathsf{P}(b)$, and this can be repeated starting at t, then $t - 1, \dots, 1$. Assume $\boldsymbol{\theta}_t = \boldsymbol{\theta} \,\forall t$ (constancy is the topic of §13.5.3), and let $\mathbf{X}_{t-1} = \left(\mathbf{X}_{t-1}^1, \mathbf{X}_0\right)$ so that $\mathsf{D_X}\left(\cdot\right)$ at every t is $\mathsf{D_X}\left(\mathbf{x}_t | \boldsymbol{\theta}, \mathbf{X}_{t-1}\right)$. Then:

$$\mathsf{D_X}\left(\mathbf{X}_T^1 \mid \boldsymbol{\theta}, \mathbf{X}_0\right) = \prod_{t=1}^{T} \mathsf{D_X}\left(\mathbf{x}_t \mid \boldsymbol{\theta}, \mathbf{X}_{t-1}\right). \tag{13.4}$$

Let:

$$\boldsymbol{\nu}_t = \mathbf{x}_t - \mathsf{E}\left[\mathbf{x}_t \mid \mathbf{X}_{t-1}\right],$$

then by construction, $\{\boldsymbol{\nu}_t\}$ is a mean innovation process since:

$$\mathsf{E}\left[\boldsymbol{\nu}_t \mid \mathbf{X}_{t-1}\right] = \mathsf{E}\left[\left(\mathbf{x}_t - \mathsf{E}\left[\mathbf{x}_t \mid \mathbf{X}_{t-1}\right]\right) \mid \mathbf{X}_{t-1}\right] = \mathbf{0}. \tag{13.5}$$

Moreover, since lagged $\boldsymbol{\nu}s$, denoted by $\mathbf{V}_{t-1}$, can be derived from $\mathbf{X}_{t-1}$ (by lagging their definition), they are also white noise:

$$\mathsf{E}\left[\boldsymbol{\nu}_t \mid \mathbf{V}_{t-1}\right] = \mathbf{0}. \tag{13.6}$$

Thus, the DGP can be expressed without loss in an innovation-error representation.

A well-known example is provided by the stationary first-order autoregressive process:

$$y_t = \mu y_{t-1} + e_t,$$

when $\{e_t\}$ is jointly normal and $\mathsf{E}\left[e_t e_s\right] = 0 \ \forall t \neq s$. Then, $\mathsf{D_Y}\left(y_1 \dots y_T | \mu, \sigma_e^2, y_0\right)$ is the multivariate normal density $\mathsf{N}_T\left[\mathbf{0}, \sigma_e^2 \boldsymbol{\Omega}\right]$ where $\boldsymbol{\Omega}$ is a $T \times T$ symmetric matrix with $\left(i, j\right)^{th}$ element:

$$\frac{\mu^{|i-j|}}{\left(1 - \mu^2\right)}.$$

The factorization of the joint density of $\left(y_1 \dots y_T\right)$ is:

$$\mathsf{D_Y}\left(y_1 \dots y_T \mid \mu, \sigma_e^2, y_0\right) = \prod_{t=1}^{T} \mathsf{D_Y}\left(y_t \mid \mathbf{Y}_{t-1}; \mu, \sigma_e^2\right)$$

which yields a product of individual density terms like $\mathsf{N}\left[\mu y_{t-1}, \sigma_e^2\right]$. Since $\nu_t = y_t - \mathsf{E}\left(y_t | \mathbf{Y}_{t-1}\right)$, then:

$$\nu_t = y_t - \mathsf{E}\left[y_t \mid y_{t-1}\right] = y_t - \mu y_{t-1} = e_t$$

is indeed the (mean) innovation (see e.g., Judge, Griffiths, Hill, Lütkepohl and Lee, 1985, Chapter 8).

13.3.2 Weak exogeneity

We can now formalize weak exogeneity. Its importance is that all current-dated regressors treated as conditioning variables must be weakly exogenous to sustain valid and efficient inferences (see Engle, Hendry and Richard, 1983). To relate the analysis more closely to that in Chapter 11, we only consider a bivariate system, where the two variables are $(y_t : z_t)$: the analysis generalizes by interpreting these as vectors.

First, note that the joint density $D_x(x_t | \theta, X_{t-1})$ is unaffected by 1-1 transformations of its parameters θ to ϕ (say) where:

$$\phi = f(\theta) \text{ and } \phi \in \Phi,$$

so that:

$$D_x(x_t \mid \theta, X_{t-1}) = D_x(x_t \mid \phi, X_{t-1}).$$

Secondly, we can partition into $\phi = (\phi_1 : \phi_2)$ to match the partition of x_t into $(y_t : z_t)$. Then, using the factorization in (13.4), if y_t is to be conditioned on z_t, we can factorize $D_x(\cdot)$ into a conditional and a marginal distribution:

$$D_x(x_t \mid \theta, X_{t-1}) = D_{y|z}(y_t \mid z_t, X_{t-1}, \phi_1) D_z(z_t \mid X_{t-1}, \phi_2). \tag{13.7}$$

This does not impose any restrictions, and hence loses no information.

Thirdly, some parameters, denoted μ, will be the focus of the econometric modelling exercise, and these are called parameters of interest. To avoid information loss from only modelling the conditional relation in (13.7), it must be possible to learn about μ from the factor:

$$D_{y|z}(y_t \mid z_t, X_{t-1}, \phi_1) \tag{13.8}$$

alone. Moreover, the resulting knowledge about μ must be equivalent to that which could have been gleaned from analyzing the joint density $D_x(\cdot)$. Two conditions ensure that equivalence. First:

(1) all the parameters of interest μ can be obtained from ϕ_1 alone; and

(2) ϕ_1 and ϕ_2 must be variation free (that is, impose no restrictions on each other):

$$(\phi_1 : \phi_2) \in \Phi_1 \times \Phi_2 \text{ where } \phi_1 \in \Phi_1 \text{ and } \phi_2 \in \Phi_2.$$

If so, z_t is said to be weakly exogenous for μ, and only the conditional model $D_{y|z}(y_t|z_t, X_{t-1}, \phi_1)$ needs to be estimated to determine μ, since the marginal model $D_z(z_t|X_{t-1}, \phi_2)$ contains no information about μ. For more extensive and expository discussions, see Ericsson (1992) and Hendry (1995a).

13.4 Model evaluation

In Chapter 11, the basic single-equation dynamic model was written as:

$$b_0(L) y_t = \sum_{i=1}^{k} b_i(L) z_{i,t} + \epsilon_t \tag{13.9}$$

where there are k explanatory variables $(z_{1,t} \ldots z_{k,t})$, $b_i(L)$ denotes a lag polynomial, and we have changed notation for the non-modelled variables from x to z to match the system notation above.

It is relatively easy to specify and analyze models such as those in (13.9), or any generalizations thereof, when they are regarded as mathematical formulations. Unfortunately, it is far more difficult to develop useful empirical relationships corresponding to these for a given time series on a set of variables. In particular, the orders of the lag lengths of every polynomial $b_0(L)$, $b_1(L)$ etc. must be established, as must the relevance of any given variable, the constancy of the entities called parameters, the validity of conditioning, the required functional form, and the properties of the unmodelled term. Indeed, this description begs the very issue of what defines the usefulness of an econometric relationship.

At a general level, the utility of anything depends on the purposes for which it is being developed. Hence if a completely specified loss function existed for judging a particular modelling exercise, it would seem natural to develop a model to optimize that criterion. Two problems arise, however, neither of which can be sidestepped. First, it is rare in econometrics to be able to fully specify the loss function. Models are wanted for prediction, for scenario or policy analyses, for testing economic hypotheses, and for understanding how the economy functions. Empirically, there often exist conflicts in criteria in selecting models to achieve such multiple objectives. For example, a model which predicts well historically may yield no insight into how a market will behave under some change in regulations, the implementation of which will cause that model to mispredict. Secondly, even assuming that a fully-specified loss function did exist and that the optimal model could be selected, there remains the difficulty of establishing how 'good' that best model is. For example, the best model that could be found may still suffer from non-constant parameters and hence yield a low level of utility; worse still, by not knowing this weakness, serious losses may accrue in the future. Thus, whatever the basis on which a model has been formulated or developed, there remains an issue of assessment or evaluation.

PcGive operates easily and efficiently to implement this aspect. Since we do not know how the economy works, we do not know the best way of studying it. Consequently, any model might correspond to reality, however unlikely its mode of creation; or unfortunately, it might transpire to be invalid, however clever and thorough its development. Nevertheless, taking a model as stated by its proprietor, a vast range of states of the world will be excluded by that model, and thus it is open to evaluation against the available information (see Hendry, 1987, for a more extensive analysis). For example, because its residual process is white noise, a particular model may claim to explain a given data set adequately; yet the residuals may not be an innovation process, so testing that latter hypothesis might reveal an important model weakness (as in the COMFAC procedure discussed in §11.4). This is the destructive testing aspect of PcGive, and accounts for its wide range of pre-programmed statistics for model evaluation.

Testing focuses on the empirical validity of assertions about a given model. Tests are statistics with a known distribution under a null hypothesis and some power against a specific alternative. The tests below are designed to have (central) t, F or χ^2 distributions under the null, and corresponding non-central distributions against some alternative. Usually, they are invariant to the direction of the departure from the null for a given class of alternatives, and only depend on the distance (that is, the overall extent of the departure: this holds for t^2, F and χ^2 statistics). However, most tests also have some power to detect other alternatives, so rejecting the null does not entail accepting the alternative, and in many instances, accepting the alternative would be a *non sequitur*. Rejection reveals model invalidity, albeit with some chance of a type-I error of incorrectly rejecting a valid null.

First, however, we need to delineate the relevant class of null hypotheses, and then derive associated test statistics for reasonable alternatives. The former task is considered in §13.5 in terms of a taxonomy of available information, and the latter in §13.6 where the main test principles are briefly described.

13.5 An information taxonomy

A further division of the data set $\mathbf{X}_t^1 = (\mathbf{x}_1 \ldots \mathbf{x}_t)$ into:

$$\mathbf{X}_T^1 = \left(\mathbf{X}_{t-1}^1 : \mathbf{x}_t : \mathbf{X}_T^{t+1}\right)$$

yields the trichotomy of the (past : present : future) relative to t. In addition, we allow for theory information, measurement information, and the information in rival models (see Hendry and Richard, 1982, 1983, and Gilbert, 1986, for expositions). Statistical tests can be constructed to evaluate a model against each element of this six-fold taxonomy. Such tests require formulating both the appropriate null hypothesis for the relevant information set, and devising a reasonable class of alternatives against which the test should have power. The taxonomy clarifies the relevant null hypotheses, and generally points up interesting alternatives against which to test model validity.

The six major aspects of model evaluation are discussed next, followed by a brief analysis of their relation to the theory of reduction.

13.5.1 The relative past

The residuals should be white noise and hence unpredictable from their own past as in (13.6). This entails that they should not be significantly autocorrelated. If they are autocorrelated, a better-fitting model can be developed by removing the autocorrelation, although this is not a recommended practice, since it may impose invalid common factors. PcGive provides valid tests and diagnostic information for residual autocorrelation, including Lagrange-multiplier tests for a wide range of orders of autoregressive errors, as well as residual correlograms and autoregressions.

Further, the errors should not be explainable from the information set being used. Alternatively expressed, the errors should be an innovation process which is unpredictable from lagged functions of the available data as in (13.5). Being white noise is a necessary, but not sufficient, condition for being an innovation, as shown above. A good example arises when removing autocorrelation by fitting, say, autoregressive error processes, since that automatically ensures the white noise, but may impose invalid common-factor restrictions and hence does not entail an innovation error (see Sargan, 1964, 1980a). This problem can be avoided by beginning with a general specification like (13.9) and testing for valid common factors prior to imposing them. In PcGive, the COMFAC tests to check such restrictions are based on Sargan's algorithms.

Neither white-noise errors nor innovations need be homoscedastic, so that the standard errors of OLS estimators in PcGive can allow for residual heteroscedasticity (the HCSEs in Chapter 11: see White, 1980, and MacKinnon and White, 1985). Tests of both autoregressive conditional heteroscedasticity (ARCH: see Engle, 1982) and unconditional heteroscedasticity are also provided. Similarly, tests for normality are included to check on the distributional assumptions underlying finite-sample inference.

To summarize these aspects relating to the (relative) past of the process, namely X_{t-1}^1, a reasonable null is that the unexplained component of a behavioural model should be a homoscedastic innovation.

13.5.2 The relative present

As noted above, all current-dated conditioning variables should be at least weakly exogenous (see Engle, Hendry and Richard, 1983) to sustain valid and efficient inferences. While weak exogeneity is not easy to test directly, tests of estimation consistency based on Engle (1984) can be calculated from stored regression predictions, using the fact that lagged variables are predetermined once the errors are innovations. These statistics test for the overall model specification and need not detect all forms of weak exogeneity failure: see Hendry (1995b). However, valid conditioning in conjunction with other hypotheses may entail many testable hypotheses: for example, parameter constancy in a structural equation, despite non-constancy in a reduced form or marginal processes, strongly supports weak exogeneity (see Favero and Hendry, 1992). Conversely, parameters of current endogenous variables (other than the dependent variable) should be estimated using instrumental variables (IV), or full-information maximum likelihood (FIML). Any instruments chosen must themselves be weakly exogenous for the parameters of interest (see §11.8 for the algebra of IV estimation).

Thus, for the (relative) present, namely x_t above, the crucial null hypothesis is that the conditioning variables (regressors or instruments) are valid.

13.5.3 The relative future

The parameters should be constant over time, where such 'parameters' are those entities which are anticipated on *a priori* grounds to be the basic invariants of the model. Here, an invariant is a parameter which remains constant over a range of interventions or regime shifts in policy (or marginal) variables. If z_t in (13.8) is weakly exogenous for the parameters of interest μ, and ϕ_1 is invariant to changes in the distribution of $\{z_t\}$, then z_t is super exogenous for μ. In this formulation, constancy is necessary for invariance.

PcGive calculates tests for parameter constancy based on Hansen (1992), and *ex post* 1-step forecast confidence bands, as well as offering recursive least squares (RLS) (see Hendry and Neale, 1987). Various types of constancy tests based on Chow (1960) are available.

Much of the power of PcGive resides in its recursive procedures. These are a useful tool for investigating issues of invariance and super exogeneity by showing that the behaviour of the z_t process did actually alter without changing the parameters of interest. This is one way of testing assertions that parameters are liable to suffer from the Lucas critique (see Hendry, 1988, and Favero and Hendry, 1992). The algebra of recursive estimation is described in Chapter 12. For recursive estimators, a large volume of output is generated, which can be analyzed graphically by plotting the recursive errors or coefficients etc. against t. The systems estimator is similar in structure, except that y_t becomes a vector of endogenous variables at time t.

Thus, in this group of tests about the (relative) future, denoted above by $\mathbf{X}_T^{t+1}$, the crucial null is parameter constancy.

13.5.4 Theory information

Econometrics is essentially concerned with the mutual interplay of economic theory and empirical evidence. Neither has precedence, and both are essential. It is difficult to characterize this information source in the abstract, partly because it is so pervasive, and partly because it is itself often under scrutiny. The role that theory information plays depends on the precise context, as is easily seen by contrasting exercises modelling the demand for cheese with modelling either the supply of money or the determination of an international exchange rate. Through national income accounts concepts, economics affects the measurement of the data variables, and theory models influence the choice of the data to examine, and the classes of models and functional forms to use, as well as suggesting the parametrizations of interest. Conversely, a major objective of a study in economics may be to test the validity of some theoretical propositions.

Not all theories are equal, and indeed theories differ greatly in their level, some being very low-level and well established (for example, those concerned with measuring the output of apples or the volume of visible imports); some being medium level and widely used but potentially open to revision as knowledge improves (for example, price indices, or concepts of the capital stock), and yet others being high level and under test (for example, a rational expectations, inter-temporal substitution theory of labour supply; or a surplus-rent theory of house price determination). Thus, that all observations are theory laden does not entail that data-based studies are impossible or even misguided; rather, the respective roles of evidence and theory will vary with the reliability of each in the given context (for a more extensive discussion, see Hendry, 1995a).

To test any theory requires a baseline, so first one must determine the extent to which that baseline satisfies the evaluation criteria. Thus, we are led to distinguish between the statistical model and the econometric model, where the former is the baseline and is judged on statistical criteria, and the latter is interpreted in the light of the economic theory, but tested against the former (see, for example, Spanos, 1986). This distinction is at its clearest for the system and the model thereof in the system module, where a test of over-identifying restrictions is automatically calculated to check the coherence between the two.

Overall, one can do little better than state the need for an econometric model to be at least low-level theory consistent.

13.5.5 Measurement information

This too is not open to a general discussion, but relates to the issues of data accuracy and admissibility. The latter concerns whether or not a given model could logically have generated the observed and future potential data. For example, the unemployment rate must lie between zero and unity; a logit transformation ensures that, but a linear model could generate negative unemployment (see White, 1990, for a critique). The relevance of such considerations depends on the problem under study, but since (for example) cointegration between the logarithms of any given set of I(1) variables need not entail cointegration between the levels, choosing the appropriate functional form can be vitally important.

The other key aspect is data measurement accuracy, and like apple pie, almost everyone favours more accurate data. Again we can only reiterate the obvious point that effort must be devoted to preparing the best available data, and to taking account of any known inaccuracies as well as the average level of their imprecision. Modelling the mismeasurement is sometimes possible (see Hendry, 1995a), and the use of instrumental variables rather than OLS is an example of doing so.

13.5.6 Rival models

The final necessary condition to ensure that an empirical model is in the set of useful contenders is that it is not dominated by any other model. More stringently, one might desire that no other model (M_2, say) explained features of the data which one's own model (M_1) could not. This idea was formalized in Chapter 11 by encompassing, and testing whether other models captured specific information not embodied in the model under test (see Hendry and Richard, 1982, 1989, Mizon, 1984, and Mizon and Richard, 1986). The contending model must encompass (denoted by $\mathcal{E}$) previous empirical models of the dependent variable (in symbols $M_1 \, \mathcal{E} \, M_2$).

Parsimonious encompassing (which is reflexive, antisymmetric and transitive) requires a congruent model to explain the results of a larger model within which it is nested. Let $\subset$ denote nesting when parsimonious encompassing is denoted by $\mathcal{E}_p$: if $M_1 \subset M_2$ then $M_1 \, \mathcal{E}_p \, M_2$ is that requirement. Consider a sequence of congruent models:

$$M_1 \subset M_2 \subset M_3.$$

When $M_1 \, \mathcal{E}_p \, M_2$ and $M_2 \, \mathcal{E}_p \, M_3$, then $M_1 \, \mathcal{E}_p \, M_3$. This follows because when $M_1 \, \mathcal{E}_p \, M_2$ and $M_2 \, \mathcal{E} \, M_1$ (by virtue of nesting it), then M_1 represents a limit to which M_2 can be validly reduced (although further reduction may be feasible as is entailed by the sequence $M_3 \rightarrow M_2 \rightarrow M_1$). Since M_2 is a valid reduction of M_3 by hypothesis, then M_1 must also be a valid reduction of M_3. Indeed, despite encompassing initially arising as a distinct concept in a different research area, it is an intimate component of the theory of reduction discussed in §13.5.7, and a further major reason for adopting a general-to-specific approach (see Bontemps and Mizon, 2002).

Let M^m be the minimal nesting model of two non-nested models M_1 and M_2 (so that neither M_1 nor M_2 is a special case of the other). M^m may be hard to synthesize, and may not be unique without arbitrary restrictions, but this difficulty reflects the inherent problems of any specific-to-general approach, and is not a difficulty for encompassing *per se*: the relevant issue of interest here is when M_1 does or does not encompass M_2, not the route by which the problem arose. If $M_1 \, \mathcal{E}_p \, M^m$, then M_2 can contain no specific information not already embodied in M_1 (since otherwise M^m would reflect that information, and M_1 could not be a valid reduction). Conversely, if $M_1 \, \mathcal{E} \, M_2$ then $M_1 \, \mathcal{E}_p \, M^m$. Thus, it should not matter whether M_1 is tested against M_2, $M_1 \cup M_2 = M^m$ or any combination thereof (including the orthogonal complement of M^m relative to M_1). Tests which are invariant to such common variables consequently seem essential, and the F-test for model simplification has that property for linear models. Chapter 11 provided an empirical illustration.

In the multi-equation context, the econometric model should encompass the statistical system (usually a VAR or unrestricted reduced form), and this is the test for over-identifying restrictions noted above (see Hendry and Mizon, 1993).

Consequently, the crucial null hypothesis in this information set is that the econometric model should parsimoniously encompass the statistical system.

13.5.7 The theory of reduction

The key concept underpinning the above analysis is that models are reductions of the DGP, obtained by transforming the initial variables to those which are to be investigated; marginalizing with respect to the many variables deemed irrelevant (but perhaps incorrectly treated as such); sequentially factorizing as in §13.5.1; and conditioning on other variables deemed to be weakly exogenous (as in §13.5.2): see Hendry and Richard (1982) and Hendry (1987). Every reduction induces a transformation of the original parameters λ of the DGP; consequently, invalid reductions may lead to the co-efficients of the resulting model not being constant or invariant – or even interpretable (as in so-called wrong signs). Thus, implicitly the analysis really begins with a far bigger set of variables $\mathbf{W}_T^1$ (say) than the set $\mathbf{X}_T^1$ considered by the current group of investigators, so, for example, $\mathbf{W}$ includes all the disaggregated variables which were eliminated when only aggregate time series were retained for analysis. The process of elimination or reduction then transforms λ into the θ_T^1 used above, although nothing guarantees that λ itself is constant.

The taxonomy of information sets §13.5.1–§13.5.6 arises naturally when considering each possible reduction step, so that reduction theory is invaluable in the context of model evaluation for delineating null hypotheses, and in the context of discovery for specifying the relevant design criteria. It also offers insights into many of the central concepts of econometrics in terms of whether a reduction does or does not involve a loss of information. Thus, we can consider the reverse of the taxonomy by relating extant concepts to associated reduction steps:

(1) the theory of sufficient statistics concerns when reduction by marginalizing with respect to a subset of observations retains all of the information relevant to the parameters of interest, as in aggregation;

(2) the concept of Granger non-causality concerns when there is no loss of information from marginalizing with respect to the entire history of a subset of variables (for example, the elements of $\mathbf{W}_{t-1}$ which are not included in $\mathbf{X}_{t-1}$): this concept is germane to marginalizing and not to conditioning (contrast Sims, 1980, with Engle, Hendry and Richard, 1983);

(3) the concept of an innovation concerns when there is no information remaining in lagged data: as shown above, all models can be expressed with innovation errors via sequential factorization; thus, all forms of autocorrelated-error representation are at best 'convenient simplifications';

(4) the concept of weak exogeneity concerns when there is no loss from ignoring information in the marginal distributions of the conditioning variables;

(5) the concept of invariance (or autonomy) concerns when the reduction sequence has successfully isolated constant parameters of the DGP;

(6) the concept of encompassing concerns when alternative models contain no additional information about the variables being modelled, so that an encompassing model represents a limit (though not necessarily the final limit) to the set of feasible reductions.

The theory of reduction also clarifies and extends the theory of encompassing by revealing that all models are comparable via the DGP. Indeed, the concept of reduction points up that model design is endemic, but because all models must arise as reductions of the DGP, the pertinent issue is their validity, not how they were designed. Some designs are inadvertent (as when residual autocorrelation is removed), whereas others are deliberate (as in general-to-specific). Thus, reduction theory even explains why the 'problems approach' to econometric modelling arises: overly reduced empirical representations of the DGP will usually manifest all sorts of symptoms of mis-specification. However, badly-designed models will often result from sequentially correcting such symptoms by adopting the alternative hypothesis corresponding to every null hypothesis that is rejected (see Hendry, 1979).

Models that are satisfactory against all six of the above information sets are called congruent and undominated (given the available information). Succinctly, PcGive is designed for efficiently developing congruent encompassing models and for evaluating existing models for potential departures from congruency.

13.6 Test types

Various test principles are commonly used in econometrics and the three main ones are Wald (W), Lagrange-multiplier (LM) and Likelihood-ratio (LR) tests (see Breusch and Pagan, 1980, and Engle, 1984). For example, the Chow (1960) test for parameter constancy is derivable from all three principles, whereas the test of over-identifying restrictions is LR, the portmanteau tests for autocorrelation in OLS are based on LM, and the COMFAC tests are Wald tests. In each instance, the choice of test type tends to reflect computational ease. Under the relevant null hypothesis and for local alternatives, the three test types are asymptotically equivalent; however, if equations are mis-specified in other ways than that under test, or the sample size is small, different inferences can result.

Although LM tests conventionally come in the form TR^2 (being distributed as χ^2), research indicates that F-forms have more appropriate significance levels and that χ^2 versions reject acceptable models too often (see Kiviet, 1987). (Incidentally, Kiviet's results also show that the Chow test and LM tests for autocorrelated residuals are approximately independently distributed.) Thus, PcGive tends to report F-forms when possible. Pagan (1984) exposits testing in terms of residual diagnostic procedures. Further details on econometric testing can be found in Harvey (1981, 1990), Spanos (1986), Godfrey (1988), Hendry (1995a) or in relevant chapters of Griliches and Intriligator (1984).

While a basic feature of PcGive is that most of the test statistics are calculated by a simple choice from a menu, others are inbuilt. For example, parameter constancy tests based on Hansen (1992) can be automatically undertaken with OLS estimation; alternatively, if the user initially specifies some post-sample observations, forecast-based tests are computed. Similar considerations apply to tests for the validity of any given choice of instrumental variables (automatic), and to the significance of lagged variables (computed by selecting Dynamic analysis). Note that the options in the Options dialog can be set to ensure automatic computation of the test summary, *inter alia*.

13.7 Modelling strategies

Turning now to constructive aspects of empirical research, since the DGP is unknown, any method of discovery might produce a Nobel-prize winning model, as illustrated by the apocryphal tale of Archimedes' 'Eureka' or Poincaré's memoirs (Poincaré, 1905). Nevertheless, different research strategies are likely to have different efficiencies. If one needs to estimate 'literally hundreds of regressions' (as in Friedman and Schwartz, 1982) to develop a single linear relationship between four or five variables, that strategy would seem to have a low level of efficiency relative to an approach which could locate at least as good a model in a couple of steps. This is the second aspect of Pc-Give, whereby it facilitates general-to-specific model simplification approaches (see, for example, Mizon, 1977, and Hendry and Mizon, 1978). Unsurprisingly, these mimic the theory of reduction in §13.5.7. Thus, PcGive provides easy ways of formulating polynomials like $b_i(L)$; solves for $b_0(1)$, $b_1(1)$ etc. (where the lag length n might be 8 for quarterly data), and provides associated standard errors; as well as tests for whether $(z_{t-m} \cdots z_{t-n})$ as a group contribute to the model's explanatory power. For single equations, common factor (COMFAC) simplifications can be checked, and long-run coefficients such as K_1 in (11.9) are derived, together with standard errors. Finally, all of the necessary conditions for model validity which were discussed in §13.5 above can be checked.

Naturally, a premium rests on a sensible specification of the initial general model, and that is where both economic theory and previous studies (to be encompassed in due course) play a major guiding role. Economic theories are powerful at specifying long-run equilibria (such as (11.9) above) which delineate the menu of variables, and earlier work often indicates at least minimal lag-length requirements. Once formulated, the general model should be transformed to an interpretable (probably orthogonal) parametrization and then simplified before rigorous testing. More detailed discussions are provided in Hendry (1986c, 1987, 1995a).

13.8 Model estimation

Like many of the other aspects considered above, appropriate estimation is a necessary, rather than a sufficient, condition for developing useful models. Given a particular model form and a distributional assumption about the data, the log-likelihood function can be formulated, and is denoted $\ell(\theta)$ where θ is the vector of unknown parameters of interest. Maximum likelihood (MLE) and least squares estimators are described in Chapter 12. In some cases, the set of first-order conditions defining the MLE may be non-linear and require iterative solution methods: this holds for any non-linear regression model. In large samples, for correctly specified problems, MLEs have many excellent statistical properties. Moreover, for models linear in both variables and parameters, almost all other estimation methods can be obtained as approximate solutions of the score equation based on choosing different initial values and selecting different numbers of iterative steps in alternative numerical methods. For example, simultaneous equations estimation is encapsulated in a simple formula called the estimator generating equation (EGE: see Hendry, 1976, and Hendry, Neale and Srba, 1988). Here we note that OLS and IVE are special cases of the EGE when an individual equation is being studied (even if that equation is implicitly part of a system).

The standard errors of $\hat{\theta}$ are usually calculated from the inverse of the information matrix or the negative inverse of the Hessian, although such a formula assumes a correctly-specified error (that is, a homoscedastic innovation). In PcGive, autocorrelation and heteroscedastic-consistent standard errors can be computed for OLS, but any differences from the conventional SEs reveals non-congruence.

The distributional assumptions for $\hat{\theta}$ implicit in inferences within PcGive (other than unit-root tests) are that, conditional, on having a congruent representation:

$$\sqrt{T}\mathbf{R}\left(\hat{\theta} - \theta_p\right) \xrightarrow{D} \mathsf{N}_n\left[\mathbf{0}, \mathbf{I}\right],$$

where T is the sample size, the probability limit of $\hat{\theta}$ is θ_p (the invariant parameter of interest), and $\mathbf{V} = \operatorname{plim} \mathbf{H}^{-1}$ such that $\mathbf{V}^{-1} = \mathbf{R}'\mathbf{R}$. This assumes that variables are transformed to I(0) and that all the components of congruency are valid. Naturally, these assumptions should be rigorously evaluated in order to sustain such a conditioning claim since 'the three golden rules of econometrics are test, test and test' (see Hendry, 1980). If a function of θ is of interest, say $\mathbf{g}(\theta) = \phi$ ($r \times 1$) the standard errors of $\hat{\phi} = \mathbf{g}(\hat{\theta})$ are derived from the Taylor-series approximation:

$$\hat{\phi} - \phi = \mathbf{J}\left(\hat{\theta} - \theta\right) \tag{13.10}$$

where

$$\mathbf{J} = \frac{\partial \mathbf{g}(\theta)'}{\partial \theta},$$

is the Jacobian matrix of the transformation, and hence:

$$\sqrt{T}\left(\hat{\phi} - \phi\right) \xrightarrow{D} \mathsf{N}_r\left[\mathbf{0}, \mathbf{J}\mathbf{V}\mathbf{J}'\right] \tag{13.11}$$

$\mathbf{J}$ can usually be derived analytically for cases of interest, but otherwise is calculated by numerical differentiation.

The preceding analysis of estimation (and implicitly also of testing) sidesteps an important issue which textbook notation also tends to camouflage, namely that estimation methods and associated tests are applied to the whole sample directly rather than recursively (adding observations one at a time). As stressed above, PcGive incorporates the recursive estimator RLS; multiple equation dynamic modelling contains the generalization to a system of equations with common regressors, and even recursive FIML. Such recursive estimators can yield evaluation information in a powerful way, yet for least squares are not computationally burdensome relative to direct methods (see Hendry and Neale, 1987).

13.9 Conclusion

PcGive explicitly embodies a methodical approach to econometric modelling which seeks to reflect the practical realities confronting the investigation of economic time-series data. This chapter has sketched the principles on which it is based. The next chapter, 14, confronts how PcGive might be used to handle a number of important practical problems.

Part IV completes the econometric discussion by explaining in detail the statistics reported by PcGive. Chapter 15 notes descriptive statistics, and Chapters 16 and 17 discuss statistics associated with single-equation modelling. These chapters could be read in a different order if desired, or left for later reference.

Chapter 14

Nine Important Practical Econometric Problems

Looking back over the sketch of the methodological approach underlying PcGive in Chapters 10–13, it seems worth spelling out how to tackle some of the detailed problems that confront practitioners in many time-series applications, and how the approach differs from that exposited in many econometrics textbooks. The nine issues selected below comprise: §14.1 multicollinearity, §14.2 residual autocorrelation, §14.3 dynamic specification, §14.4 non-nested hypotheses, §14.5 simultaneous equations bias, §14.6 identifying restrictions, §14.7 predictive failure, §14.8 non-stationarity, and §14.9 data mining.

This is not an exhaustive list, but does cover some of the areas of current contention as well as emphasizing the different approach built into PcGive.

14.1 Multicollinearity

The name multicollinearity was coined by Frisch (1934) (in his book on *Confluence Analysis*) to denote the existence of several exact linear relationships connecting a set of theoretical variables: collinearity was the name for when there was only one dependency. As such, the concept was initially unconnected with the present notion of very high correlations between observed variables (see Hendry and Morgan, 1989, for a history of how the present connotations evolved). Perfect collinearity is when an exact linear dependence exists between a set of variables (see §10.10), though more recently, 'collinearity' is generally used to refer to a state of 'near linear dependence'. For linear models, however, collinearity is not a property of the model itself, but of the way the model is parametrized. Consider the equation:

$$\mathsf{E}\left[y_t \mid \mathbf{z}_t\right] = \beta' \mathbf{z}_t \tag{14.1}$$

for k elements in β, expressed in model form as:

$$y_t = \beta' \mathbf{z}_t + \epsilon_t \ \ \text{where} \ \ \epsilon_t \sim \mathsf{IN}\left[0, \sigma_\epsilon^2\right]. \tag{14.2}$$

Since the model is linear, it is invariant under non-singular linear transformations in that all of its essential properties are unaffected. Let γ denote an arbitrary vector of constants, and $\mathbf{A}$ an arbitrary non-singular $k \times k$ matrix; both γ and $\mathbf{A}$ are chosen by the investigator. Then (14.2) can be transformed linearly to:

$$y_t - \gamma' \mathbf{z}_t = \left((\beta - \gamma)' \mathbf{A}^{-1} \right) \mathbf{A} \mathbf{z}_t + \epsilon_t, \tag{14.3}$$

or:

$$y_t^* = \beta^{*\prime} \mathbf{z}_t^* + \epsilon_t, \tag{14.4}$$

where $y_t^* = y_t - \gamma' \mathbf{z}_t$, $\mathbf{z}_t^* = \mathbf{A} \mathbf{z}_t$ and $\beta^* = \mathbf{A}^{-1'} (\beta - \gamma)$, so that:

$$\beta = \mathbf{A}' \beta^* + \gamma. \tag{14.5}$$

Transformations like (14.3) are used regularly in practice, as when moving from levels to either differences or differentials between variables. Since $\mathbf{A}$ is non-singular, either β^* can be estimated and β derived, or vice versa: the $\hat{\beta}$ from least squares estimates of (14.2) is always identical to that derived from $\hat{\beta}^*$, subject to possible numerical inaccuracies if the problem is extremely ill-conditioned in one parametrization. Direct standard errors of $\hat{\beta}$ (from (14.2)) or indirect from (14.5) will also be identical.

However, the supposed collinearity in the problem is not at all invariant. For example, let:

$$\mathbf{Q} = T^{-1} \sum_{t=1}^{T} \mathbf{z}_t \mathbf{z}_t',$$

(the sample second moment of the regressors), and select as the $\mathbf{A}$ matrix the inverse of the matrix of eigenvectors of $\mathbf{Q}$ denoted $\mathbf{H}^{-1}$ so $\mathbf{Q} = \mathbf{H} \mathbf{\Lambda} \mathbf{H}'$ where $\mathbf{\Lambda}$ is diagonal, then:[1]

$$\mathbf{Q}^* = T^{-1} \sum_{t=1}^{T} \mathbf{z}_t^* \mathbf{z}_t^{*\prime} = \mathbf{A} \mathbf{Q} \mathbf{A}' = \mathbf{H}^{-1} \mathbf{H} \mathbf{\Lambda} \mathbf{H}' \mathbf{H}^{-1'} = \mathbf{\Lambda}, \tag{14.6}$$

which is, of course, diagonal (see the related analysis in Leamer, 1983). The eigenvalues in $\mathbf{\Lambda}$ are not invariants of the model either, since other choices of $\mathbf{A}$ are admissible (compare Kuh, Belsley and Welsh, 1980).

Thus, the important issue in a model is not the degree of correlation between the variables, which is only loosely associated with the information content of the data, but the precision with which the parameters of interest (for example, β or β^*) can be determined.

Interpretable parameters often correspond to relatively orthogonal variables (see, for example, Davidson, Hendry, Srba and Yeo, 1978), and linear combinations of the original variables which lack variability can be deleted for parsimony. Consequently, PcGive

---

[1]This corresponds to Principal Components analysis but is not recommended as a practical procedure: it is merely one of a class of possible illustrations of the fact that collinearity is not a property of a model, but of a parametrization of that model.

advises transforming from β to β^* using information gained from previous studies and from theoretical analyses, rather than data-based transformations like Principal Components where the parameters will change if the sample is altered. Then $\beta^* s$ which are near zero (both in terms of statistical significance and economic importance) can be eliminated without much altering the estimates of those retained. The sequence of reductions and associated transformations is monitored by PcGive so that the validity of any given simplifications can be checked. The final parsimonious, interpretable model should generally not manifest much collinearity (in the sense of high intercorrelations of the $z^* s$), and can be tested against all the information sets described in §13.5.

14.2 Residual autocorrelation

It should be obvious by this stage how PcGive treats this issue! As discussed in §11.4 (especially §11.4.7), the analysis should commence from a sufficiently general lag specification such that the residuals should be close to white noise. If residual autocorrelation is discovered at any stage, it is taken as a symptom of poor model design, and the whole specification process should be reviewed. It is never arbitrarily assumed to be error autocorrelation, which was shown to correspond to residual autocorrelation only when there are common factors in the dynamics. However, if COMFAC tests suggest that valid common factors can be extracted, then a more parsimonious model with autoregressive errors can be designed and estimated (see Hendry and Mizon, 1978). Both the Wald tests based on Sargan (1980b), and the likelihood-ratio tests of RALS estimates against the general dynamic model, should be used prior to imposing common factors owing to the dependence of Wald tests on the formulation and potential multiple optima in the RALS likelihood function.

14.3 Dynamic specification

This is the obverse of §14.2, given the intimate links between dynamic and stochastic specification. PcGive assumes that general lag polynomials will be specified for every variable, so allows easy creation of any number of lags per variable. The theoretical analysis of the main single-equation dynamic models used in econometrics in §11.4 revealed the many weaknesses of arbitrarily assuming that one particular type happened to apply to the specific measure of the variables used in the problem under study. Consequently, a large section of PcGive is devoted to analyzing the empirical results arising from general dynamic models, in terms of long-run responses, roots of lag polynomials, etc. Simple procedures are offered for testing for unit roots, and for transforming to EqCMs.

14.4 Non-nested hypotheses

Many economic phenomena have competing theoretical explanations, especially in macro-economics. The traditional empirical approach in econometrics has been to formulate a model within the given theory framework and test its restrictions against data, corroborating or rejecting as the evidence is favourable or unfavourable. Unfortunately, the same data can corroborate conflicting models (as in Ahumada, 1985, for example). Moreover, if models are redesigned in the light of adverse test results (as happens in practice), then rejection of theory-models rarely occurs. The outcome of such methodologies is a proliferation of non-nested empirical models all claiming to be acceptable, despite being mutually inconsistent.

PcGive confronts this problem from two perspectives, both of which are implications of the theory of reduction discussed in Chapter 13 (for greater detail, see Hendry and Richard, 1983). First, remember that all models are derived from the process that actually generated the data, which is certainly a congruent representation, and hence are nested within that process. The model-based analogue is general-to-specific, which would eliminate many of the contending hypotheses if the initial general statistical model was formulated so as to embed the contending explanations as special cases: this was discussed in §14.3. Secondly, the traditional 'corroborate or reject' strategy is augmented by the requirement that an acceptable model should be able to account for the results obtained by rival explanations of the same phenomena: this is the theory of encompassing discussed in Chapter 13.5.6. Whether or not other hypotheses are non-nested with respect to the model under study ceases to matter in principle, although there are always practical problems in finite samples. The models must share a common probability framework, as well as seek to explain the same phenomena: the former may not occur, but will do so for any investigators who either claim their models are complete, or who accept the need for models to be congruent.

Encompassing is closely related to the well-established class of procedures called mis-specification analyses, where a data generation process (DGP) is assumed known and the consequences of various specification mistakes are studied (such as omitted variables). Since the DGP is indeed correct in such analyses, any specification errors postulated will occur precisely as the analysis predicts. In encompassing, the DGP is not known, but a model (say M_1) is implicitly claiming to represent it adequately. Other models (for example, M_2) are, by implication, mis-specified hypotheses. The encompassing question is whether or not M_1 mimics the DGP by correctly predicting the results of the mis-specified M_2: that provides a basis for testing if M_1 adequately represents the DGP. Failure to do so is a rejection of the adequacy of M_1; success suggests that M_2 is inferentially redundant.

Several encompassing statistics are preprogrammed in PcGive to test such hypotheses, both to evaluate any given model stringently, and to help reduce the proliferation of competing explanations. For an exposition, see Hendry and Richard (1989).

14.5 Simultaneous equations bias

The simultaneous equations paradigm is so dominant in both econometrics textbooks and Walrasian equilibrium economics that the prevalence of models with contemporaneous conditioning variables in the earlier analyses needs some comment. First, the theory of weak exogeneity described in §13.5 delineates those cases where contemporaneous conditioning is valid from those where it is not. If weak exogeneity is not sustainable, but the parameters of interest are identifiable (see §14.6 following), then the joint density must be analyzed to ensure efficient inference. If y_t depends on x_t and x_t on y_t then conditioning will not yield the parameters of interest. However, in other situations, contemporaneous conditioning can be valid. One sufficient condition is that agents form contingent plans, acting when the necessary information materializes: since the actual joint density $D_{y,x}(y_t, x_t | \theta)$ thereby factorizes into $D_y(y_t | x_t, \phi_1)$ and $D_x(x_t | \phi_2)$, and the former captures the parameters of interest, then weak exogeneity holds if the respective parameter spaces also satisfy the requirements for a cut, so that ϕ_1 and ϕ_2 are variation free.

Consider a situation in which both y_t and x_t are interest rates to be modelled, yet y_t is regressed on x_t. At first sight, simultaneity bias seems likely. However, $y_t - x_t$ (a spread) and x_t (a level) equally (and perhaps even more sensibly) could be analyzed as functions of past information alone, without any possibility of simultaneity bias. Thus, unless the first regression actually delivers a coefficient larger than unity, it seems odd to categorize it as being biased from y_t and x_t being simultaneous (even though in this example, y_t and x_t are indeed jointly determined). Thus, 'simultaneity' is another characteristic that is not invariant under linear transformations.

A more potent analysis ensues if some of the data density parameters vary over the sample, perhaps because of regime shifts. When any coefficients are biased, their bias is dependent on the particular data correlations, and hence will alter as those data correlations change (see, for example, Hendry and Neale, 1988). Thus, no constant conditional model can be obtained, and that is reasonably realistic of many macro-economic time series. Consequently, if a conditional model is constant, yet the marginal model for the conditioning variables is known to vary, this is a strong counter-argument to any claim of simultaneity bias (see Favero and Hendry, 1992). The recursive procedures in PcGive provide a powerful tool for such analyses. Hendry (1988) extends this analysis to models with expectational variables.

14.6 Identifying restrictions

Sims (1980) characterized as 'incredible' many of the over-identifying restrictions imposed in large macro-econometric models, proposing as an alternative a vector autoregression (VAR)-based methodology. The concepts and methods described above offer several insights into Sims' assertions. Identification' has three attributes, discussed in

Hendry (1997), namely 'uniqueness', 'satisfying the required interpretation', and 'correspondence to the desired entity'. Clearly, a non-unique result is not identified, so the first attribute is necessary: the discussion in Koopmans, Rubin and Leipnik (1950) of conditions for the uniqueness of coefficients in simultaneous systems makes that clear. However, it is insufficient to sustain useful models, since uniqueness can be achieved simply by imposing enough arbitrary restrictions (and that was indeed criticized by Sims, 1980, *inter alia*). Secondly, there may exist a unique combination of several relationships which is incorrectly interpreted as just one of those equations: for example, a mix of supply and demand forces in a reduced form that has a positive price effect, but is wrongly interpreted as a supply relation. Finally, a unique, interpretable model of a money-demand relation may in fact correspond to a Central Bank's supply schedule, and this too is sometimes called 'a failure to identify the demand relation'. Thus, Sims seems to be addressing the third aspect, and apparently claiming that the imposed restrictions do not correspond to 'reality'.

Taking that interpretation of Sims' critique, the restrictions embodied in some macro models have been both arbitrarily imposed and not tested. This could happen in practice from following a simple-to-general modelling strategy in which the restrictions arose merely because they were not considered. We concur with that criticism under this interpretation in those cases where it arises. Nevertheless, we propose an alternative solution, which focuses on two issues:

(1) which model isolates the actual invariants of the economic process (super exogeneity)?

(2) which if any model form (structural system or VAR) encompasses or accounts for the others' results?

Since VARs are derived, rather than autonomous, representations (relative to decision-making structures of economic agents), their constancy necessitates the constancy of every related parameter in the economic system, so they are unlikely to achieve (1). Conversely, their profligate parametrizations virtually ensure an excellent data fit, so that they are challenging rivals for any structural model to encompass, noting that variance dominance is necessary but not sufficient for encompassing here (see Hendry and Mizon, 1993).

As before, DGPs where parameters change in some of the marginal processes allow a more penetrating analysis of conditional models which claim to embody constant parameters of interest. Invalid restrictions on models in changing DGPs will generally lead to non-constant relationships, so that constant sub-systems against a background of a changing mechanism offer strong support to any claim about valid specification. Whether or not constant parameters need occur in models is considered in §14.7 below. Constant sub-systems cannot be confounded with any of the changing equations (except by chance cancelling), and are therefore identified relative to them. This last point derives from the analysis in Working's consolidation of identification conditions (Working, 1927). Finally, so-called identifying restrictions are no different in principle from any other form of restriction such as exclusion, linearity, homogeneity etc. Since maximum likelihood methods are equivariant to 1-1 transformations of the parameters (that is, when θ is mapped to $\psi = \mathbf{f}(\theta)$, then $\hat{\theta}$ is mapped to $\hat{\psi} = \mathbf{f}(\hat{\theta})$), estimating a structural model is equivalent to estimating the reduced form subject to certain within- and across-equation restrictions. It is well known that any just-identified model entails an unrestricted reduced form. Thus, unless Sims (1980) either denies the existence of any valid restrictions on reduced forms, which seems inconsistent with his ostensible views on VAR modelling in Doan, Litterman and Sims (1984), or denies that restrictions can ever correspond to a structural parametrization, which would exclude proportionalities between reduced form parameters *inter alia*, then his critique lacks force as an issue of principle, and becomes a practical concern as to whether specific structural models are indeed successful data reductions.

That introduces the topic of testing in simultaneous systems, and there are three related implications from Chapter 13. First, the conventional test of over-identifying restrictions is interpretable as a test of whether the structural model parsimoniously encompasses the unrestricted reduced form, or system as it was denoted above. Secondly, the system must itself be a valid baseline for testing against, which was the thrust of the general-to-specific notion as applied to modelling joint densities (see Hendry, Neale and Srba, 1988). Thirdly, identifying restrictions on structural parameters are meaningless if the claimed parameters are not constant. Consequently, a preferable modelling strategy seems to be: first construct a congruent statistical system (which may well be a VAR), then simplify it via interpretable restrictions (which may be structural), and finally test that the resulting econometric model both is congruent and parsimoniously encompasses the statistical system. This is precisely the strategy adopted in both Pc-Give for single equations and for systems.

14.7 Predictive failure

The prevalence of significant mispredictions and parameter changes in econometric models has been one of the greatest problems confronting applied econometricians (see, for example, Judd and Scadding, 1982, for a history of predictive failure in US money-demand modelling). However, views differ widely as to the explanation for the problem and Baba, Hendry and Starr (1992) propose one constant-parameter model over the period to 1989. To PcGive users, the sheer existence of the phenomenon of predictive failure is important: model discrimination is easier in worlds of parameter change than in constant processes. Next, it behoves modellers to check the historical constancy of any claimed relationship; all too often, public post-sample predictive failures merely highlight previously untested within-sample non-constancies (see Hendry, 1979, 1988): hence the easy-to-use recursive procedures and associated tests in PcGive. Third, the claim that certain predictive failures are owing to confounding expectations and behavioural dynamics (one aspect of the critique in Lucas, 1976) is testable (that is, potentially confirmable or refutable) by employing both encompassing and super exogeneity tests (see Hendry, 1988). Indeed, this point has been exploited in both preceding sections. Finally, it has proved possible in practice to develop models which have good track records over a decade or more (see, for example, Davidson, Hendry, Srba and Yeo, 1978, and Hendry and Ericsson, 1991). Even so, since nothing can guarantee the invariance of human behaviour, regular monitoring for innovation and change is wise. Models are a form of codified accumulated knowledge which progressively increase our understanding of economic behaviour, and consequently have to be adaptive to changing environments.

Some authors have argued for changing-parameter models as a better approximation than constant-parameter models to a reality characterized by predictive failure. It is important to realize that these two types of model only reflect different assumptions about which parameters are constant, as the former do not avoid constancy assumptions. For example, consider the model:

$$y_t = \mathbf{x}_t' \boldsymbol{\beta}_t + \epsilon_t \text{ where } \epsilon_t \sim \underline{\mathsf{IN}}\left[\underline{0}, \sigma^2\right]$$

and:

$$\boldsymbol{\beta}_t = \underline{\mathbf{K}} \boldsymbol{\beta}_{t-1} + \boldsymbol{\nu}_t \text{ with } \boldsymbol{\nu}_t \sim \underline{\mathsf{IN}}\left[\underline{\mathbf{0}}, \underline{\boldsymbol{\Omega}}\right]$$

where $\underline{\boldsymbol{\beta}}_0$ is given. Although the $\{\boldsymbol{\beta}_t\}$ evolve, the new constancies are shown underlined and include assumptions about constant error variances, constant (zero) serial correlation, constant distributional shape etc. Which set of constancies to adopt depends on the specification of the $\mathbf{x}_t$ as determinants of y_t, the functional form linking y_t to $\mathbf{x}_t$, and the constancies in the DGP. There are no principles favouring any particular type of constancy claim. What is important is that evidence should be presented on the actual constancy (or otherwise) of whatever meta-parameters are taken to be the basic constancies of the process being modelled. Similarly, the 'structural time-series models' in Harvey and Shephard (1992) can be re-represented as a restricted ARMA model, with constant parameters.

Predictive failure does not entail non-constant parameters in the initial model. This may seem paradoxical, but can be explained as follows: the definitions here are from Hendry (1995a), and the following analysis builds on Hendry (1996) and Hendry and Doornik (1997). A parameter $\boldsymbol{\theta} \in \Theta \subseteq \mathbb{R}^k$ must be constant across realizations of the stochastic process it indexes, but need not be constant over time. It is constant over a time interval $\mathcal{T} = \{\ldots, -1, 0, 1, 2, \ldots\}$ if $\boldsymbol{\theta}$ takes the same value for all $t \in \mathcal{T}$. A model is constant if all its parameters are. Even so, we have just seen that constant models can have time-varying coefficients, which are, in effect, latent variables that depend on more basic parameters that are constant.

All $1 - 1$ transforms of parameters are valid, so zero can be a population value of a parameter $\boldsymbol{\psi}$ in $\boldsymbol{\psi} = \mathbf{h}(\boldsymbol{\theta}) \in \Phi \subseteq \mathbb{R}^k$. Let the original parameters for the density $\mathsf{D}_{\mathsf{y}|\mathsf{z}}(\mathbf{y}_t|\mathbf{z}_t; \boldsymbol{\theta})$ of $\mathbf{y}_t$ over T_1 be $\boldsymbol{\theta}$ given a conditioning vector $\mathbf{z}_t$, where sequential factorization of the T_1-sample joint density yields:

$$\prod_{t=1}^{T_1} \mathsf{D}_{y|z} \left(\mathbf{y}_t \mid \mathbf{z}_t; \boldsymbol{\theta} \right). \tag{14.7}$$

Consider a setting where to adequately characterize the whole T-sample requires an extended model with parameters $\boldsymbol{\rho} \subseteq \mathbb{R}^K$ (for $K > k$) given K variables $\mathbf{x}_t$:

$$\prod_{t=1}^{T} \mathsf{D}_{y|z} \left(\mathbf{y}_t \mid \mathbf{x}_t; \boldsymbol{\rho} \right). \tag{14.8}$$

In (14.8), we assume that $\boldsymbol{\rho}$ is constant.

Prima facie, the model in (14.7) seems non-constant, but if there exists a $1 - 1$ mapping from $\boldsymbol{\rho}$ to $\boldsymbol{\delta}$ (say), such that:

$$\boldsymbol{\delta} = \mathbf{g} \left(\boldsymbol{\rho} \right) = \left(\boldsymbol{\theta}, \mathbf{0} \right), \tag{14.9}$$

then the model is constant despite the apparent expansion. For example, when $\mathbf{x}_t$ coincides with $\mathbf{z}_t$ over the T_1-sample, but is an alternative measure for the same construct over the forecast period, then (14.7) is:

$$\prod_{t=1}^{T_1} \mathsf{D}_{y|z} \left(\mathbf{y}_t \mid \mathbf{z}_t; \boldsymbol{\theta} \right) = \prod_{t=1}^{T_1} \mathsf{D}_{y|z} \left(\mathbf{y}_t \mid \mathbf{x}_t; \boldsymbol{\theta} \right), \tag{14.10}$$

and appropriate transforms of (14.8) can re-express it as:

$$\prod_{t=1}^{T} \mathsf{D}_{y|z} \left(\mathbf{y}_t \mid \mathbf{x}_t; \boldsymbol{\delta} \right) = \prod_{t=1}^{T} \mathsf{D}_{y|z} \left(\mathbf{y}_t \mid \mathbf{x}_t; \boldsymbol{\theta} \right). \tag{14.11}$$

An empirical example of this situation is when an outside interest rate r_c is used as a measure of the opportunity cost of holding money over a period where the own rate r_o is zero; the introduction of a non-zero own rate can induce forecast failure, perhaps countered by adding r_o to the model, thereby demonstrating apparent non-constancy. However, successfully replacing the previous measure by the differential $r_c - r_o$ as the correct measure of opportunity cost, with the coefficient on the added variable becoming zero, then reduces the model back to the original dimension with unchanged parameters.

Constancy has not lost its operational content because of this possibility: (14.7) is not constant for all T in the space of $(\mathbf{y}_t : \mathbf{z}_t)$. Moreover, there need be no $\mathbf{g}(\cdot)$ which reproduces the original parameters augmented by zeroes. However, the result does imply that there are no possible in-sample tests (up to T_1) for later predictive failure, since the observation of failure depends on how the model is extended, not on its within-sample properties.

At a practical level, the idea of designing models to have nearly orthogonal parametrizations offers some robustness to unmodelled changes since such changes get reflected in increased error variance rather than changing regression parameters.

14.8 Non-stationarity

Three particular forms of non-stationarity have appeared in this book:

(1) I(1), or integrated behaviour, removable by suitable differencing or cointegration transformations;
(2) parameter changes or regime shifts, removable for a subset of parameters of interest by establishing the invariants; and
(3) inherent non-stationarity owing to innovative human behaviour or natural processes, which as yet we do not know how to remove or model.

Concerning (1), it must be stressed that differencing can only remove unit roots and cannot *per se* remove either of (2) or (3) (although it will also mitigate regime shifts in deterministic factors: see Clements and Hendry, 1998, 1999). As noted in Chapter 11, however, analyzing only differences also removes all long-run or cointegrating information, and hence is not a sensible generic strategy. Conversely, long-run economic theoretic information should be tested as satisfying cointegration (see Engle and Granger, 1987, Granger, 1986, Johansen, 1988, Phillips, 1991, and Banerjee, Dolado, Galbraith and Hendry, 1993 *inter alia*).

Concerning (2), the establishing of constant and invariant parameters to characterize economic behaviour has been the main thrust of much of the earlier analysis. Many implications of constancy claims are testable and should be tested. Even though every marginal relationship may be affected by structural breaks, linear combinations (perhaps corresponding to conditional relations) need not be, just as linear combinations removed unit roots when cointegration was found: this is called co-breaking in Hendry (1995c).

Finally, (3) raises a number of interesting issues, most as yet unexplored. Can one establish whether or not a process is inherently non-stationary (in the sense of having non-constant unconditional first and second moments)? It is easy to invent complicated mechanisms dependent on mixtures of unlikely but time-independent events, which would seem to be non-stationary, despite having constant unconditional moments. How well can learning and innovation themselves be modelled by constant parameter processes? Theoretical analyses of R&D, technical change, financial innovation etc. have progressed, so a constant meta-parametrization in a high dimensional non-linear mechanism cannot be excluded *a priori*. This is especially important now that a theory for analyzing integrated processes is available to deal with, for example the accumulation of knowledge and technique. Do the various forms of non-stationarity interact? Here we are on slightly firmer ground – yes they do. A simple I(0) process with a large sustained shift will be quite well described as I(1) since differencing reduces the shift to a one-off blip (see Perron, 1989, and Hendry and Neale, 1991). For example, the artificial data used above have no unit roots, but seem I(1) on conventional scalar unit-root tests. Note, again, that a recursive testing procedure for a unit root may help clarify the relevant state of nature. Alternatively, tests for technical progress changing must allow for the distributional theory to be based on integrated and not on stationary processes. It would seem that lots of interesting findings await discovery in this area.

14.9 Data mining

Data mining has been characterized in many ways, with a common theme being the reuse of the same data to both estimate and revise a model. If that is the intended meaning of data mining, then in economics, either you must be omniscient or you will data mine: unless a model emerges perfect on the first try, it must be revised in the light of data evidence. Leamer (1978) offers an excellent treatment, commenting that his:

> 'book is about "data mining". It describes how specification searches can be legitimately used to bring to the surface the nuggets of truth that may be buried in a data set. The essential ingredients are judgment and purpose'.

Although the standpoint of PcGive is not Bayesian, much of the analysis, logic, and common sense are similar.

The tools relevant to this issue from Chapter 13 are:

(a) a dichotomy between the contexts of discovery (where you will reuse data in the process of model construction) and of evaluation (where one-off testing on genuinely new information allows valid model destruction);

(b) a theory of reduction to explain how empirical models are derived from the data generating mechanism and hence do not in general have autonomous errors;

(c) a typology of information sets which delineates the necessary conditions for a model to be congruent;

(d) the concept of model design to achieve congruency in the context of discovery, allowing conditioning of later inferences on the congruent model specification as the best representative of the DGP;

(e) a general-to-specific simplification approach to model design, mimicking reduction, moving from a congruent statistical model to a parsimonious and interpretable econometric model thereof, which is theory consistent and encompasses both the general model and other competing models;

(f) the notion that the validity of the chosen model is a property that is intrinsic to the model and not to the process of its discovery; later evaluation will sort the gold from the pyrites.

As a consequence, data mining has to be viewed as an unstructured activity leading some investigators to run 'literally hundreds of regressions' on data sets with fewer than one hundred observations. In such an approach, masses of ore are mined and sifted to pick out the bits of gold which appeal to the particular investigator. As remarked in

Hendry (1980), 'econometric fool's gold' is often the result. Gilbert (1986) neatly characterizes the view PcGive takes of such mining: divide all of the output into two piles, one consistent with (and encompassed by) the selected model and one inconsistent with it. 'Weak data mining' is when the second pile has any members and 'strong data mining' is when the anomalous findings are not reported as *caveats* to the claimed model. A related weak form is deliberate non-testing for fear of unfavourable results, so the research assistant does the first pre-filter (or loses the initial sifting sets of runs) – for an interesting analysis of the general problem in science, see Kohn (1987).

Conversely, once a congruent model has been developed by a structured search and rigorously tested, it is sensible to condition further inferences on that congruent model since by definition no better model is currently available. As an aside, all of the numerical values of coefficients, standard errors etc. are the same irrespective of the number of steps in the simplification (or search) process: the only issue is whether the precision recorded should in some sense be discounted because of the search process. If in fact the variances are too small owing to simplifying, over-rejection of such models outside of sample would occur: to date, the evidence is rather the opposite since many of the results seem surprisingly robust over long time periods (see Hendry, 1989).

A major recent development that has thrown considerable light on 'data mining' as a critique of empirical modelling is the computer automation of *Gets*, noted above. Moving from the relatively poor performance of every model-selection method investigated by Lovell (1983), Hoover and Perez (1999) achieved significant progress towards a viable *Gets* algorithm, which exhibited excellent simulation characteristics. *PcGets* has already shown that further improvements in design can induce markedly better selection behavior. For example, when the null model is true but the general model includes more than 40 variables, simplistic search procedures such as step-wise regression will find it under 20% of the time: yet re-running the Lovell simulation experiments, Hoover and Perez (1999) found it on almost 80% of trials at a 1% significance level, as against 97% using the pre-release version of *PcGets* reported in Hendry and Krolzig (1999). Thus, the performance of the first mechanized general-to-specific algorithms is excellent: yet these represent very early attempts at computer automation. For more extensive analyses, see Hendry (2000a), Hoover and Perez (2000) and Krolzig and Hendry (2001).

Part IV

The Statistical Output of PcGive

Chapter 15

Descriptive Statistics in PcGive

The Descriptive Statistics entry on the Model menu involves the formal calculation of statistics on database variables. Model-related statistics are considered in Chapters 16 and 17. This chapter provides the formulae underlying the computations. A more informal introduction is given in the tutorial Chapter 3. PcGive will use the largest available sample by default, here denoted by $t = 1, \ldots, T$. It is always possible to graph or compute the statistics over a shorter sample period.

15.1 Means, standard deviations and correlations

This reports sample means and standard deviations of the selected variables:

$$\bar{x} = \frac{1}{T} \sum_{t=1}^{T} x_t, \quad s = \sqrt{\frac{1}{T-1} \sum_{t=1}^{T} (x_t - \bar{x})^2}.$$

The correlation coefficient r_{xy} between x and y is:

$$r_{xy} = \frac{\sum_{t=1}^{T} (x_t - \bar{x})(y_t - \bar{y})}{\sqrt{\sum_{t=1}^{T} (x_t - \bar{x})^2 \sum_{t=1}^{T} (y_t - \bar{y})^2}}. \tag{15.1}$$

The correlation matrix of the selected variables is reported as a symmetric matrix with the diagonal equal to one. Each cell records the simple correlation between the two relevant variables. The same sample is used for each variable; observations with missing values are dropped.

15.2 Normality test and descriptive statistics

This is the test statistic described in §17.4.4, which amounts to testing whether the skewness and kurtosis of the variable corresponds to that of a normal distribution. Missing value are dropped from each variable, so the sample size may be different for each variable.

15.3 Correlogram (ACF) and Portmanteau statistic

This prints the correlogram of the selected variables, as described in §17.4.2. The same sample is used for each variable; observations with missing values are dropped.

15.4 Unit-root tests

A crucial property of any economic variable influencing the behaviour of statistics in econometric models is the extent to which that variable is stationary. If the autoregressive description

$$y_t = \alpha + \sum_{i=1}^{n} \gamma_i y_{t-i} + u_t, \tag{15.2}$$

has a root on the unit circle, then conventional distributional results are not applicable to coefficient estimates. As the simplest example, consider:

$$x_t = \alpha + \beta x_{t-1} + \epsilon_t \text{ where } \beta = 1 \text{ and } \epsilon_t \sim \text{IN}\left(0, \sigma_\epsilon^2\right),$$

which generates a random walk (with drift if $\alpha \neq 0$). Here, the autoregressive coefficient is unity and stationarity is violated. A process with no unit or explosive roots is said to be I(0); a process is I (d) if it needs to be differenced d times to become I(0) and is not I(0) if only differenced $d - 1$ times. Many economic time series behave like I(1), though some appear to be I(0) and others I(2).

The Durbin–Watson statistic for the level of a variable offers one simple characterization of this integrated property:

$$DW\left(x\right) = \frac{\sum_{t=2}^{T}\left(x_t - x_{t-1}\right)^2}{\sum_{t=1}^{T}\left(x_t - \bar{x}\right)^2}. \tag{15.3}$$

If x_t is a random walk, DW will be very small. If x_t is white noise, DW will be around 2. Very low DW values thus indicate that a transformed model may be desirable, perhaps including a mixture of differenced and disequilibrium variables.

An augmented Dickey–Fuller (ADF) test for I(1) against I(0) (see Dickey and Fuller, 1981) is provided by the t-statistic on $\hat{\beta}$ in:

$$\Delta x_t = \alpha + \mu t + \beta x_{t-1} + \sum_{i=1}^{n} \gamma_i \Delta x_{t-i} + u_t. \tag{15.4}$$

The constant or trend can optionally be excluded from (15.4); the specification of the lag length n assumes that u_t is white noise. The null hypothesis is H$_0$: $\beta = 0$; rejection of this hypothesis implies that x_t is I(0). A failure to reject implies that Δx_t is stationary, so x_t is I(1). This is a second useful description of the degree of integratedness of x_t. The Dickey–Fuller (DF) test has no lagged first differences on the right-hand side

$(n = 0)$. On this topic, see the *Oxford Bulletin of Economics and Statistics* (Hendry, 1986a, Banerjee and Hendry, 1992a), and Banerjee, Dolado, Galbraith and Hendry (1993). To test whether x_t is I(1), commence with the next higher difference:

$$\Delta^2 x_t = \alpha + \mu t + \beta \Delta x_{t-1} + \lambda x_{t-1} + \sum_{i=1}^{n} \gamma_i \Delta x_{t-i} + u_t. \tag{15.5}$$

Output of the ADF(n) test of (15.4) consists of:

coefficients	$\hat{\alpha}$ and $\hat{\mu}$ (if included), $\hat{\beta}, \hat{\gamma}_1, \ldots, \hat{\gamma}_n$,
standard errors	$\mathsf{SE}(\hat{\alpha}), \mathsf{SE}(\hat{\mu}), \mathsf{SE}(\hat{\beta}), \mathsf{SE}(\hat{\gamma}_i)$,
t-values	$\mathsf{t}_\alpha, \mathsf{t}_\mu, \mathsf{t}_\beta, \mathsf{t}_{\gamma_i}$,
$\hat{\sigma}$	as (16.8),
DW	(15.3) applied to $\hat{u}_t$,
DW(x)	(15.3) applied to x_t,
ADF(x)	t_β,
Critical values	
RSS	as (16.10).

Most of the formulae for the computed statistics are more conveniently presented in the next section on simple dynamic regressions, but the t-statistic is defined (e.g., for $\hat{\alpha}$) as $\mathsf{t}_\alpha = \hat{\alpha}/\mathsf{SE}(\hat{\alpha})$, using the formula in (16.5). Critical values are derived from the reponse surfaces in MacKinnon (1991), and depend on whether a constant, or constant and trend, are included (seasonals are ignored). Under the null ($\beta = 0$), $\alpha \neq 0$ entails a trend in $\{x_t\}$ and $\mu \neq 0$ implies a quadratic trend. However, under the stationary alternative, $\alpha = 0$ would impose a zero trend. Thus the test ceases to be similar if the polynomial in time $(1, t, t^2$ etc.) in the model is not at least as large as that in the data generating process (see, for example, Kiviet and Phillips, 1992). This problem suggests allowing for a trend in the model unless the data is anticipated to have a zero mean in differences. The so-called Engle-Granger two-step method amounts to applying the ADF test to residuals from a prior static regression (the first step). The response surfaces need to be adjusted for the number of variables involved in the first step: see MacKinnon (1991).

The default of PcGive is to report a summary test output for the sequence of ADF(n)...ADF(0) tests. The summary table consists of:

D-lag	j (the number of lagged differences),
t-adf	the t-value on the lagged level: t_β,
beta Y_1	the coefficient on the lagged level: β,
$\hat{\sigma}$	as (16.8),
t-DY_lag	t-value of the longest lag: t_{γ_j},
t-prob	significance of the longest lag: $1 - \mathsf{P}\left(|\tau| \leq \left|\mathsf{t}_{\gamma_j}\right|\right)$,
AIC	Akaike criterion, see §16.2.12
F-prob	significance level of the F-test on the lags dropped up to that point,

for $j = n, \ldots, 0$. Critical values are listed, and significance of the ADF test is marked by asterisks: * indicates significance at 5%, ** at 1%.

15.5 Principal component analysis

Principal component analysis (PCA) amounts to an eigenvalue analysis of the correlation matrix. Because the correlation matrix has ones on the diagonal, its trace equals k when k variables are involved. Therefore, the sum of the eigenvalues also equals k. Moreover, all eigenvalues are non-negative.

The eigenvalue decomposition of the $k \times k$ correlation matrix $\mathbf{C}$ is:

$$\mathbf{C} = \mathbf{H \Lambda H'},$$

where λ is the diagonal matrix with the ordered eigenvalues $\lambda_1 \geq \ldots \geq \lambda_k \geq 0$ on the diagonal, and $\mathbf{H} = (\mathbf{h}_1, \ldots, \mathbf{h}_k)$ the matrix with the corresponding eigenvectors in the columns, $\mathbf{H'H} = \mathbf{I}_k$. The matrix of eigenvectors diagonalizes the correlation matrix:

$$\mathbf{H'CH} = \mathbf{\Lambda}.$$

Let $(\mathbf{x}_1, \ldots, \mathbf{x}_k)$ denote the variables selected for principal components analysis (a $T \times k$ matrix), and $\mathbf{Z} = (\mathbf{z}_1, \ldots, \mathbf{z}_k)$ the standardized data (i.e. in deviation from their mean, and scaled by the standard deviation). Then $\mathbf{Z'Z}/T = \mathbf{C}$. The jth principal component is defined as:

$$\mathbf{p}_j = \mathbf{Zh}_j = \mathbf{z}_1 h_{1j} + \ldots + \mathbf{z}_k h_{kj},$$

and accounts for $100\lambda_j/k\%$ of the variation. The largest m principal components together account for $100\sum j = 1^m \lambda_j/k\%$ of the variation.

Principal components analysis is used to capture the variability of the data in a small number of factors. Using the correlation matrix enforces a common scale on the data (analysis in terms of the variance matrix is not invariant to scaling). Some examples of the use of PCA in financial applications are given in Alexander (2001, Ch.6).

PCA is sometimes used to reconstruct missing data on $\mathbf{y}$ in combination with data condensation. Assume that T observations are available on $\mathbf{y}$, but $T + H$ on the remaining data, then two methods could be considered:

Step	Data	Sample	Method	Output
1	$\mathbf{y} : \mathbf{X}$	T	PCA	$m, \lambda_1, \ldots, \lambda_m$
2	$\mathbf{X}$	$T + H$	PCA	$\mathbf{p}_1, \ldots, \mathbf{p}_m$
3	$\mathbf{P}$	$T + H$	$-$	$\widehat{\mathbf{y}}_1 = \mu_0 + \sum_{i=1}^m \lambda_i \mathbf{p}_i$
1	$\mathbf{X}$	$T + H$	PCA	$m, \mathbf{p}_1, \ldots, \mathbf{p}_m$
2	$\mathbf{y} : 1 : \mathbf{P}$	T	OLS	$\beta_0, \beta_1, \ldots, \beta_m$
3	$1 : \mathbf{P}$	$T + H$	$-$	$\widehat{\mathbf{y}}_2 = \widehat{\beta}_0 + \sum_{i=1}^m \widehat{\beta}_i \mathbf{p}_i$

Chapter 16

Model Estimation Statistics

Single equation estimation is allowed by:

OLS-CS ordinary least squares (cross-section modelling)
IVE-CS instrumental variables estimation (cross-section modelling)
OLS ordinary least squares
IVE instrumental variables estimation
RALS r^{th} order autoregressive least squares
NLS non-linear least squares
ML maximum likelihood estimation

Once a model has been specified, a sample period selected, and an estimation method chosen, the equation can be estimated. OLS-CS/IVE-CS and OLS/IVE only differ in the way the sample period is selected. In the first, **cross section**, case, all observations with missing values are omitted. Therefore, 'holes' in the database are simply skipped. In cross-section mode it is also possible to specify a variable *Sel* to select the sample by. In that case observations where *Sel* has a 0 or missing values are omitted from the estimation sample (but, if data is available, included in the prediction set). In **dynamic regression**, the observations must be consecutive in time, and the maximum available sample is the leading contiguous sample. The following table illustrates the default sample when regressing y on a constant:

	y	*Sel*	cross section		dynamic
			default	using *Sel*	
1980	.	0			
1981	.	0			
1982	4	0	∗		∗
1983	7	1	∗	∗	∗
1984	9	1	∗	∗	∗
1985	10	1	∗	∗	∗
1986	.	0			
1987	12	0	∗		

For ease of notation, the sample period is denoted $t = 1, \ldots, T + H$, after allowing for any lagged variables created where H is the forecast horizon. The data used for estimation are $\mathbf{X} = (\mathbf{x}_1 \ldots \mathbf{x}_T)$. The H retained observations $\mathbf{X}_H = (\mathbf{x}_{T+1} \ldots \mathbf{x}_{T+H})$ are used for static (1-step) forecasting and evaluating parameter constancy.

This chapter discusses the statistics reported by PcGive following model estimation. The next chapter presents the wide range of evaluation tools available following successful estimation. Sections marked with * denote information that can be shown or omitted on request. In the remainder there is no distinction between OLS/IVE and OLS-CS/IVE-CS.

16.1 Recursive estimation: RLS/RIVE/RNLS/RML

In most cases, recursive estimation is available:

RLS	recursive OLS
RIVE	recursive IVE
RNLS	recursive NLS
RML	recursive ML

Recursive OLS and IV estimation methods are initialized by a direct estimation over $t = 1, \ldots, M - 1$, followed by recursive estimation over $t = M, \ldots, T$. RLS and RIVE update inverse moment matrices (RLS formulae were given in §12.7.9). This is inherently somewhat numerically unstable, but, because it is primarily a graphical tool, this is not so important.

Recursive estimation of non-linear models is achieved by the brute-force method: first estimate for the full sample, then shrink the sample by one observation at a time. At each step the estimated parameters of the previous step are used as starting values, resulting in a considerably faster algorithm.

The final estimation results are always based on direct full-sample estimation, so unaffected whether recursive or non-recursive estimation is used. The recursive output can be plotted from the recursive graphics dialog.

16.2 OLS estimation

The algebra of OLS estimation is well established from previous chapters, see, for example, §12.7 and §11.6. The model is:

$$y_t = \boldsymbol{\beta}'\mathbf{x}_t + u_t, \quad \text{with } u_t \sim \mathsf{IN}\left(0, \sigma^2\right) \quad t = 1, \ldots, T,$$

or more compactly:

$$\mathbf{y} = \mathbf{X}\boldsymbol{\beta} + \mathbf{u}, \quad \text{with } \mathbf{u} \sim \mathsf{N}_T\left(\mathbf{0}, \sigma^2\mathbf{I}\right). \tag{16.1}$$

The vectors β and $\mathbf{x}_t$ are $k \times 1$. The OLS estimates of β are:

$$\hat{\beta} = (\mathbf{X}'\mathbf{X})^{-1}\mathbf{X}'\mathbf{y}, \tag{16.2}$$

with residuals

$$\hat{u}_t = y_t - \hat{y}_t = y_t - \mathbf{x}_t'\hat{\beta}, \quad t = 1, \ldots, T, \tag{16.3}$$

and estimated residual variance

$$\hat{\sigma}_u^2 = \frac{1}{T-k} \sum_{t=1}^{T} \hat{u}_t^2. \tag{16.4}$$

Forecast statistics are provided for the H retained observations (only if $H \neq 0$). For OLS, these are comprehensive 1-step ahead forecasts and tests, described below.

The estimation output is presented in columnar format, where each row lists information pertaining to each variable (its coefficient, standard error, t-value, etc.). Optionally, the estimation results can be printed in equation format,, which is of the form coefficient $\times$ variable with standard errors in parentheses underneath.

16.2.1 The estimated regression equation

The first column of these results records the names of the variables and the second, the estimated regression coefficients $\hat{\beta} = (\mathbf{X}'\mathbf{X})^{-1}\mathbf{X}'\mathbf{y}$. PcGive does actually not use this expression to estimate $\hat{\beta}$. Instead it uses the QR decomposition with partial pivoting, which analytically gives the same result, but in practice is a bit more reliable (i.e. numerically more stable). The QR decomposition of $\mathbf{X}$ is $\mathbf{X} = \mathbf{QR}$, where $\mathbf{Q}$ is $T \times T$ and orthogonal (that is, $\mathbf{Q}'\mathbf{Q} = \mathbf{I}$), and $\mathbf{R}$ is $T \times k$ and upper triangular. Then $\mathbf{X}'\mathbf{X} = \mathbf{R}'\mathbf{R}$.

The following five columns give further information about each of the magnitudes described below in §16.2.2 to §16.2.11.

16.2.2 Standard errors of the regression coefficients

These are obtained from the variance-covariance matrix:

$$\mathsf{SE}\left[\hat{\beta}_i\right] = \sqrt{\widehat{\mathsf{V}\left[\hat{\beta}_i\right]}} = \hat{\sigma}_u \sqrt{d_{ii}} \tag{16.5}$$

where d_{ii} is the ith diagonal element of $(\mathbf{X}'\mathbf{X})^{-1}$ and $\hat{\sigma}_u$ is the standard error of the regression, defined in (16.4).

16.2.3 t-values and t-probability

These statistics are conventionally calculated to determine whether individual coefficients are significantly different from zero:

$$\text{t-value} = \frac{\hat{\beta}_i}{\text{SE}\left[\hat{\beta}_i\right]} \tag{16.6}$$

where the null hypothesis H_0 is $\beta_i = 0$. The null hypothesis is rejected if the probability of getting a t-value at least as large is less than 5% (or any other chosen significance level). This probability is given as:

$$\text{t-prob} = 1 - \text{Prob}\left(|\tau| \leq |\text{t-value}|\right) \tag{16.7}$$

in which τ has a Student t-distribution with $T - k$ degrees of freedom. The t-probabilities do not appear when all other options are switched on.

When H_0 is true (and the model is otherwise correctly specified in a stationary process), a Student t-distribution is used since the sample size is often small, and we only have an estimate of the parameter's standard error: however, as the sample size increases, τ tends to a standard normal distribution under H_0. Large t-values reject H_0; but, in many situations, H_0 may be of little interest to test. Also, selecting variables in a model according to their t-values implies that the usual (Neyman–Pearson) justification for testing is not valid (see, for example, Judge, Griffiths, Hill, Lütkepohl and Lee, 1985).

16.2.4 Squared partial correlations

The final column lists the squared partial correlations under the header Part.R^2. The jth entry in this column records the correlation of the jth explanatory variable with the dependent variable, given the other $k - 1$ variables, see §12.7.7. Adding further explanatory variables to the model may either increase or lower the squared partial correlation, and the former may occur even if the added variables are correlated with the already included variables. If the squared partial correlations fall on adding a variable, then that is suggestive of collinearity for the given equation parametrization: that is, the new variable is a substitute for, rather than a complement to, those already included.

Beneath the columnar presentation an array of summary statistics is also provided as follows:

16.2.5 Equation standard error ($\hat{\sigma}$)

The equation standard error is the square root of the residual variance, which is defined as:

$$\hat{\sigma}_u^2 = \frac{1}{T - k} \sum_{t=1}^{T} \hat{u}_t^2, \tag{16.8}$$

where the residuals are defined as:

$$\hat{u}_t = y_t - \hat{y}_t = y_t - \mathbf{x}_t'\hat{\boldsymbol{\beta}}, \quad t = 1, \ldots, T. \tag{16.9}$$

16.2.6 Residual sum of squares (RSS)

$$RSS = \sum_{t=1}^{T} \hat{u}_t^2. \tag{16.10}$$

16.2.7 R²: squared multiple correlation coefficient

The variation in the dependent variable, or the total sum of squares (TSS), can be broken up into two parts: the explained sum of squares (ESS) and the residual sum of squares (RSS). In symbols, $TSS = ESS + RSS$, or:

$$\sum_{t=1}^{T} (y_t - \bar{y})^2 = \sum_{t=1}^{T} (\hat{y}_t - \bar{y})^2 + \sum_{t=1}^{T} \hat{u}_t^2,$$

and hence:

$$R^2 = \frac{ESS}{TSS} = \frac{\sum_{t=1}^{T} (\hat{y}_t - \bar{y})^2}{\sum_{t=1}^{T} (y_t - \bar{y})^2} = 1 - \frac{\sum_{t=1}^{T} \hat{u}_t^2}{\sum_{t=1}^{T} (y_t - \bar{y})^2},$$

assuming a constant is included (also see §12.7.6). Thus, R^2 is the proportion of the variance of the dependent variable which is explained by the variables in the regression. By adding more variables to a regression, R^2 will never decrease, and it may increase even if nonsense variables are added. Hence, R^2 may be misleading. Also, R^2 is dependent on the choice of transformation of the dependent variable (for example, y versus Δy) – as is the F-statistic below. The equation standard error, $\hat{\sigma}_u$, however, provides a better comparative statistic because it is adjusted by the degrees of freedom. Generally, $\hat{\sigma}$ can be standardized as a percentage of the mean of the original level of the dependent variable (except if the initial mean is zero) for comparisons across specifications. Since many economic magnitudes are inherently positive, that standardization is often feasible. If y is in logs, $100\hat{\sigma}$ is the percentage standard error.

R^2 is not reported if the regression does not have an intercept.

16.2.8 F-statistic

The formula was already given in (12.94):

$$\eta_\beta = \frac{R^2/(k-1)}{(1-R^2)/(T-k)} \sim F(k-1, T-k) \tag{16.11}$$

Here, the null hypothesis is that the population R^2 is zero, or that all the regression coefficients are zero (excluding the intercept). The value for the F-statistic is followed by its probability value between square brackets.

16.2.9 Log-likelihood

The log-likelihood for model (16.1) is:

$$\ell(\boldsymbol{\beta}, \sigma^2 | \mathbf{y}, \mathbf{X}) = -\tfrac{T}{2} \log 2\pi - \tfrac{T}{2} \log \sigma^2 - \tfrac{1}{2} \frac{\mathbf{u}'\mathbf{u}}{\sigma^2}.$$

Next, we can concentrate σ^2 out of the log-likelihood to obtain:

$$\ell_c(\boldsymbol{\beta} | \mathbf{y}, \mathbf{X}) = K_c - \tfrac{T}{2} \log \frac{\hat{\mathbf{u}}'\hat{\mathbf{u}}}{T},$$

where

$$K_c = -\tfrac{T}{2}(1 + \log 2\pi).$$

The reported log-likelihood includes the constant, so corresponds to:

$$\ell_c(\boldsymbol{\beta} | \mathbf{y}, \mathbf{X}) = K_c - \tfrac{T}{2} \log \frac{RSS}{T}.$$

16.2.10 Durbin–Watson test (DW)

This is a test for autocorrelated residuals and is calculated as:

$$DW = \frac{\sum_{t=2}^{T} (\hat{u}_t - \hat{u}_{t-1})^2}{\sum_{t=1}^{T} \hat{u}_t^2}. \tag{16.12}$$

DW is most powerful as a test of $\{u_t\}$ being white noise against:

$$u_t = \rho u_{t-1} + \epsilon_t \quad \text{where} \quad \epsilon_t \sim \text{IID}\left(0, \sigma_\epsilon^2\right).$$

If $0 < DW < 2$, then the null hypothesis is H_0: $\rho = 0$, that is, zero autocorrelation (so $DW = 2$) and the alternative is H_1: $\rho > 0$, that is, positive first-order autocorrelation.

If $2 < DW < 4$, then H_0: $\rho = 0$ and H_1: $\rho < 0$, in which case $DW^* = 4 - DW$ should be computed.

The significance values of DW are widely recorded in econometrics' textbooks. However, DW is a valid statistic only if all the $\mathbf{x}_t$ variables are non-stochastic, or at least strongly exogenous. If the model includes a lagged dependent variable, then DW is biased towards 2, that is, towards not detecting autocorrelation, and Durbin's h-test (see Durbin, 1970) or the equivalent LM-test for autocorrelation in §17.4.3 should be used instead. Also see §15.4 and §11.6 .

16.2.11 Mean and variance of dependent variable

The final entries list the number of observations used in the regressor (so after allowing for lags), and the number of estimated parameters. This is followed by the mean and variance of the dependent variable:

$$\bar{y} = \frac{1}{T} \sum_{t=1}^{T} y_t, \quad \sigma_y^2 = \frac{1}{T} \sum_{t=1}^{T} (y_t - \bar{y})^2.$$

16.2.12 *Information criteria

The four statistics reported are the Schwarz criterion (SC), the Hannan–Quinn (HQ) criterion, the Final Prediction Error (FPE), and the Akaike criterion (AIC). Here:

$$
\begin{aligned}
\text{SC} &= \log \tilde{\sigma}^2 + k \left(\log T\right)/T, \\
\text{HQ} &= \log \tilde{\sigma}^2 + 2k \left(\log \left(\log T\right)\right)/T, \\
\text{FPE} &= \left(T + k\right) \tilde{\sigma}^2 / \left(T - k\right), \\
\text{AIC} &= \log \tilde{\sigma}^2 + 2k/T.
\end{aligned}
\tag{16.13}
$$

using the maximum likelihood estimate of σ^2:

$$\tilde{\sigma}^2 = \frac{T-k}{T} \hat{\sigma}^2 = \frac{1}{T} \sum_{t=1}^{T} \hat{u}_t^2.$$

For a discussion of the use of these and related scalar measures to choose between alternative models in a class, see Judge, Griffiths, Hill, Lütkepohl and Lee (1985), §11.10.2 and §17.8 below.

16.2.13 *Heteroscedastic-consistent standard errors (HCSEs)

These provide consistent estimates of the regression coefficients' standard errors even if the residuals are heteroscedastic in an unknown way, see (11.33). Large differences between the corresponding values in §16.2.2 and §16.2.13 are indicative of the presence of heteroscedasticity, in which case §16.2.13 provides the more useful measure of the standard errors (see White, 1980). PcGive contains two methods of computing heteroscedastic-consistent standard errors: as described in White (1980) (labelled HCSE), or the Jack-knife estimator from MacKinnon and White (1985) (labelled JHCSE; for which the code was initially provided by James MacKinnon).

The heteroscedasticity and autocorrelation consistent standard errors are reported in the column labelled HACSE. This follows Andrews (1991).

16.2.14 *R^2 relative to difference and seasonals

The R^2 is preceded by the seasonal means $\bar{s}$ of the first difference of the dependent variable ($\overline{\Delta y}$ for annual data, four quarterly means for quarterly data, twelve monthly means for monthly data etc.).

The R^2 relative to difference and seasonals is a measure of the goodness of fit relative to $\sum(\Delta y_t - \bar{s})^2$ instead of $\sum(y_t - \bar{y})^2$ in the denominator of R^2 (keeping $\sum \hat{u}_t^2$ in the numerator), where $\bar{s}$ denotes the relevant seasonal mean. Despite its label, such a measure can be negative: if it is, the fitted model does less well than a regression of Δy_t on seasonal dummies.

16.2.15 *Correlation matrix of regressors

This reports the sample means and sample standard deviations of the selected variables:

$$\bar{x} = \frac{1}{T} \sum_{t=1}^{T} x_t, \quad s = \sqrt{\frac{1}{T-1} \sum_{t=1}^{T} (x_t - \bar{x})^2}.$$

The correlation matrix of the selected variables is reported as a lower-triangular matrix with the diagonal equal to one. Each cell records the simple correlation between the two relevant variables. The calculation of the correlation coefficient r_{xy} between x and y is:

$$r_{xy} = \frac{\sum_{t=1}^{T} (x_t - \bar{x})(y_t - \bar{y})}{\sqrt{\sum_{t=1}^{T} (x_t - \bar{x})^2 \sum_{t=1}^{T} (y_t - \bar{y})^2}}. \tag{16.14}$$

16.2.16 *Covariance matrix of estimated parameters

The matrix of the estimated parameters' variances is reported as lower triangular. Along the diagonal, we have the variance of each estimated coefficient, and off the diagonal, the covariances. The $k \times k$ variance matrix of $\hat{\beta}$ is estimated by:

$$\widehat{V\left[\hat{\beta}\right]} = \hat{\sigma}^2 \left(\mathbf{X}'\mathbf{X}\right)^{-1}, \tag{16.15}$$

where $\hat{\sigma}^2$ is the full-sample equation error variance. The variance-covariance matrix is only shown when requested, in which case it is reported before the equation output.

The remaining statistics only appear if observations were withheld for forecasting purposes:

16.2.17 1-step (ex post) forecast analysis

Following estimation over $t = 1, \ldots, T$, 1-step forecasts are given by:[1]

$$\hat{y}_t = \mathbf{x}_t'\hat{\beta}, \quad t = T + 1, \ldots, T + H, \tag{16.16}$$

which requires the observations $\mathbf{X}_H' = (\mathbf{x}_{T+1}, \ldots, \mathbf{x}_{T+H})$. The 1-step forecast error is the mistake made each period:

$$e_t = y_t - \mathbf{x}_t'\hat{\beta}, \quad t = T + 1, \ldots, T + H, \tag{16.17}$$

which can be written as:

$$e_t = \mathbf{x}_t'\beta + u_t - \mathbf{x}_t'\hat{\beta} = \mathbf{x}_t'\left(\beta - \hat{\beta}\right) + u_t. \tag{16.18}$$

Assuming that $\mathsf{E}[\hat{\beta}] = \beta$, then $\mathsf{E}[e_t] = 0$ and:

$$\mathsf{V}[e_t] = \mathsf{E}\left[e_t^2\right] = \mathsf{E}\left[\left(\mathbf{x}_t'\left(\beta - \hat{\beta}\right)\right)^2 + u_t^2\right] = \sigma_u^2\mathbf{x}_t'\left(\mathbf{X}'\mathbf{X}\right)^{-1}\mathbf{x}_t + \sigma_u^2. \tag{16.19}$$

This corresponds to the results given for the innovations in recursive estimation, see §12.7.9. The whole vector of forecast errors is $\mathbf{e} = (e_{T+1}, \ldots, e_{T+H})'$. $\mathsf{V}[\mathbf{e}]$ is derived in a similar way:

$$\mathsf{V}[\mathbf{e}] = \sigma^2\mathbf{I}_H + \mathbf{X}_H\mathsf{V}\left[\hat{\beta}\right]\mathbf{X}_H' = \sigma_u^2\left(\mathbf{I}_H + \mathbf{X}_H\left(\mathbf{X}'\mathbf{X}\right)^{-1}\mathbf{X}_H'\right). \tag{16.20}$$

Estimated variances are obtained after replacing σ_u^2 by $\hat{\sigma}_u^2$.

The columns respectively report the date for which the forecast is made, the realized outcome (y_t), the forecast $(\hat{y}_t)$, the forecast error $(e_t = y_t - \hat{y}_t)$, the standard error of the 1-step forecast $(\mathsf{SE}\,(e_t) = \sqrt{\mathsf{V}[e_t]})$, and a t-value (that is, the standardized forecast error $e_t/\mathsf{SE}\,(e_t)$).

16.2.18 Forecast test

A χ^2 statistic follows the 1-step analysis, comparing within and post-sample residual variances. Neither this statistic nor η_3 below measure absolute forecast accuracy. The statistic is calculated as follows:

$$\xi_1 = \sum_{t=T+1}^{T+H} \frac{e_t^2}{\hat{\sigma}_u^2} \overset{app}{\sim} \chi^2\,(H) \text{ on } \mathsf{H}_0. \tag{16.21}$$

---

[1]Dynamic forecasts are needed when the xs are also predicted for the forecast period. Dynamic forecasts are also implemented but the econometrics is discussed in Volume II (Doornik and Hendry, 2006a).

The null hypothesis is 'no structural change in any parameter between the sample and the forecast periods' (denoted 1 and 2 respectively), H_0: $\beta_1 = \beta_2$; $\sigma_1^2 = \sigma_2^2$. A rejection of the null hypothesis of constancy by ξ_3 below implies a rejection of the model used over the sample period – so that is a model specification test – whereas the use of ξ_1 is more as a measure of numerical parameter constancy, and it should not be used as a model-selection device (see Kiviet, 1986). However, persistently large values for this statistic imply that the equation under study will not provide very accurate *ex ante* predictions, even one step ahead. An approximate F-equivalent is given by:

$$\eta_1 = \frac{1}{H}\xi_1 \underset{app}{\widetilde{}} F\left(H, T - k\right) \text{ on } H_0. \tag{16.22}$$

A second statistic takes parameter uncertainty into account, taking the denominator from (16.19):

$$\xi_2 = \sum_{t=T+1}^{T+H} \frac{e_t^2}{\hat{\sigma}_u^2(1 + \mathbf{x}_t'\left(\mathbf{X'X}\right)^{-1}\mathbf{x}_t)} \underset{app}{\widetilde{}} \chi^2\left(H\right) \text{ on } H_0. \tag{16.23}$$

This test is not reported in single-equation modelling, but individual terms of the summation can be plotted in the graphical analysis.

16.2.19 Chow test

This is the main test of parameter constancy and has the form:

$$\eta_3 = \frac{\left(RSS_{T+H} - RSS_T\right)/H}{RSS_T/(T - k)} \underset{app}{\widetilde{}} F\left(H, T - k\right) \text{ on } H_0 \tag{16.24}$$

where H_0 is as for ξ_1. For fixed regressors, the Chow (1960) test is exactly distributed as an F, but is only approximately (or asymptotically) so in dynamic models.

Alternatively expressed, the Chow test is:

$$\eta_3 = H^{-1}\xi_3 = H^{-1}\mathbf{e}'\left(\widehat{V\left[\mathbf{e}\right]}\right)^{-1}\mathbf{e}. \tag{16.25}$$

We can now see the relation between ξ_3 and ξ_1: the latter uses $\widehat{V\left[\mathbf{e}\right]} = \hat{\sigma}_u^2\mathbf{I}$, obtained by dropping the (asymptotically negligible) term $V[\hat{\beta}]$ in (16.20). In small samples, the dropped term is often not negligible, so ξ_1 should not be taken as a test. The numerical value of ξ_1 always exceeds that of ξ_3: the difference indicates the relative increase in prediction uncertainty arising from estimating, rather than knowing, the parameters.

PcGive computes the Chow test efficiently, by noting that:

$$\hat{\sigma}_u^2\mathbf{e}'\left(\widehat{V\left[\mathbf{e}\right]}\right)^{-1}\mathbf{e} = \mathbf{e}'\left(\mathbf{I}_H - \mathbf{X}_H\left(\mathbf{X'X} + \mathbf{X}_H'\mathbf{X}_H\right)^{-1}\mathbf{X}_H'\right)\mathbf{e}. \tag{16.26}$$

16.2.20 t-test for zero forecast innovation mean (RLS only)

The recursive formulae from §12.7.9 are applicable over the sample $T+1, \ldots, T+H$, and under the null of correct specification and H_0 of ξ_1 above, then the standardized innovations $\{\nu_t/(\omega_t)^{1/2}\}$ in (12.111) are distributed as $\mathsf{IN}(0, \sigma_u^2)$. Thus:

$$\sqrt{H} \frac{\frac{1}{H} \sum_{t=T+1}^{T+H} \nu_t/(\omega_t)^{1/2}}{\hat{\sigma}_u} \sim \mathsf{t}(H-1) \text{ on } \mathsf{H}_0. \tag{16.27}$$

This tests for a different facet of forecast inaccuracy in which the forecast errors have a small but systematic bias. This test is the same as an endpoint CUSUM test of recursive residuals, but using only the forecasts sample (see Harvey and Collier, 1977).

16.3 IV estimation

Instrumental variables estimation was considered in §11.8. Here we write the model as:

$$y_t = \beta_0' \mathbf{y}_t^* + \beta_1' \mathbf{w}_t + \epsilon_t, \tag{16.28}$$

in which we have $n-1$ endogenous variables $\mathbf{y}_t^*$ and q_1 non-modelled variables $\mathbf{w}_t$ on the right-hand side (the latter may include lagged endogenous variables). We assume that we have q_2 additional instruments, labelled $\mathbf{w}_t^*$. Write $\mathbf{y}_t = (y_t : \mathbf{y}_t^{*\prime})'$ for the $n \times 1$ vector of endogenous variables. Let $\mathbf{z}_t$ denote the set of all instrumental variables (non-endogenous included regressors, plus additional instruments): $\mathbf{z}_t = (\mathbf{w}_t' : \mathbf{w}_t^{*\prime})'$, which is a vector of length $q = q_1 + q_2$.

16.3.1 *Reduced form estimates

The reduced form (RF) estimates are only printed on request. If $\mathbf{Z}' = (\mathbf{z}_1 \ldots \mathbf{z}_T)$, and $\mathbf{y}_t$ denotes all the n endogenous variables including y_t at t with $\mathbf{Y}' = (\mathbf{y}_1, \ldots, \mathbf{y}_T)$, then the RF estimates are:

$$\hat{\mathbf{\Pi}}' = (\mathbf{Z}'\mathbf{Z})^{-1} \mathbf{Z}'\mathbf{Y}, \tag{16.29}$$

which is $q \times n$. The elements of $\hat{\mathbf{\Pi}}'$ relevant to each endogenous variable are written:

$$\boldsymbol{\pi}_i = (\mathbf{Z}'\mathbf{Z})^{-1} \mathbf{Z}'\mathbf{Y}_i, \ i = 1, \ldots, n, \tag{16.30}$$

with $\mathbf{Y}_i' = (y_{i1}, \ldots, y_{iT})$ the vector of observations on the ith endogenous variable. Standard errors etc. all follow as for OLS above (using $\mathbf{Z}, \mathbf{Y}_i$ for $\mathbf{X}, \mathbf{y}$ in the relevant equations there).

16.3.2 Structural estimates

Generalized instrumental variables estimates for the $k = n - 1 + q_1$ coefficients of interest $\beta = (\beta_0' : \beta_1')'$ are:

$$\tilde{\beta} = \left(X'Z (Z'Z)^{-1} Z'X \right)^{-1} X'Z (Z'Z)^{-1} Z'y, \qquad (16.31)$$

using $x_t = (y_t^{*'} : w_t')'$, $X' = (x_1 \ldots x_T)$, $y = (y_1 \ldots y_T)'$, which is the left-hand side of (16.28), and Z is as in (16.29). This allows for the case of more instruments than explanatory variables ($q > k$), and requires $\text{rank}(X'Z) = k$ and $\text{rank}(Z'Z) = q$. If $q = k$ the equation simplifies to that of (11.36):

$$\tilde{\beta} = (Z'X)^{-1} Z'y. \qquad (16.32)$$

As for OLS, PcGive does not use expression (16.31) directly, but instead uses the QR decomposition for numerically more stable computation. The error variance is given by

$$\tilde{\sigma}_\epsilon = \frac{\tilde{\epsilon}'\tilde{\epsilon}}{T - k}, \quad \text{where } \tilde{\epsilon} = y - X\tilde{\beta}. \qquad (16.33)$$

The variance of $\tilde{\beta}$ is estimated by:

$$\widehat{V\left[\tilde{\beta}\right]} = \tilde{\sigma}_\epsilon^2 \left(X'Z (Z'Z)^{-1} Z'X \right)^{-1}. \qquad (16.34)$$

Again the output is closely related to that reported for least squares except that the columns for HCSE, partial r^2 and instability statistics are omitted. However, RSS, $\tilde{\sigma}$ and DW are recorded, as is the reduced form $\hat{\sigma}$ (from regressing y_t on z_t, already reported with the RF equation for y_t). Additional statistics reported are :

16.3.3 Specification χ^2

This tests for the validity of the choice of the instrumental variables as discussed by Sargan (1964). It is asymptotically distributed as $\chi^2(q_2-n+1)$ when the q_2-n+1 over-identifying instruments are independent of the equation error. It is also interpretable as a test of whether the restricted reduced form of the structural model (y_t on x_t plus x_t on z_t) parsimoniously encompasses the unrestricted reduced form (y_t on z_t directly):

$$\frac{\hat{\pi}' (Z'Z) \hat{\pi} - \tilde{\beta}' \left(X'Z (Z'Z)^{-1} Z'X \right) \tilde{\beta}}{\tilde{\epsilon}'\tilde{\epsilon}/T} \underset{app}{\widetilde{}} \chi^2(q_2 - n + 1), \qquad (16.35)$$

with $\hat{\pi} = (Z'Z)^{-1} Z'y$ being the reduced form estimates.

16.3.4 Testing $\beta = 0$

Reported is the χ^2 test of $\beta = 0$ (other than the intercept) which has a crude correspondence to the earlier F-test. On H_0: $\beta = 0$, the reported statistic behaves asymptotically as a $\chi^2 (k-1)$. First define

$$\xi_\beta = \tilde{\beta}' \left(\mathbf{X'Z} \left(\mathbf{Z'Z} \right)^{-1} \mathbf{Z'X} \right) \tilde{\beta}. \tag{16.36}$$

Then $\xi_\beta / \tilde{\sigma}_\epsilon \underset{app}{\widetilde{}} \chi^2(k)$ would test whether all k coefficients are zero (*cf.* equation (12.58)). To keep the intercept separate, we compute:

$$\frac{\xi_\beta - T\bar{y}^2}{\tilde{\sigma}_\epsilon^2} \underset{app}{\widetilde{}} \chi^2(k-1). \tag{16.37}$$

This amounts to using the formula for $\tilde{\beta}$ (eq. (16.31)) in ξ_β with $\mathbf{y} - \bar{y}\iota$ instead of $\mathbf{y}$.

16.3.5 Forecast test

A forecast test is provided if H observations are retained for forecasting. For IVE there are endogenous regressor variables: the only interesting issue is that of parameter constancy and correspondingly the output is merely ξ_1 of (16.21) using $\tilde{\sigma}_\epsilon$ and:

$$e_t = y_t - \mathbf{x}'_t \tilde{\beta}, \quad t = T+1, \ldots, T+H. \tag{16.38}$$

Dynamic forecasts (which require forecasts of the successive $\mathbf{x}_{T+1}, \ldots, \mathbf{x}_{T+H}$) could be obtained from multiple equation dynamic modelling, where the system as a whole is analyzed.

16.4 RALS estimation

As discussed in the typology in §11.4, if a dynamic model has common factors in its lag polynomials, then it can be re-expressed as having lower-order systematic dynamics combined with an autoregressive error process (called COMFAC: see model type §11.4.7, and §11.6.7). If the autoregressive error is of rth order, the estimator is called r^{th}-order Autoregressive Least Squares or RALS, and it takes the form:

$$\beta_0 (L) y_t = \sum_{i=1}^{m} \beta_i (L) z_{it} + u_t \text{ with } \alpha (L) u_t = \epsilon_t, \tag{16.39}$$

when:

$$\alpha (L) = 1 - \sum_{i=s}^{r} \alpha_i L^i. \tag{16.40}$$

This can be written as:

$$y_t = \mathbf{x}_t'\boldsymbol{\beta} + u_t, \quad u_t = \sum_{i=s}^{r} \alpha_i u_{t-i} + \epsilon_t, \quad t = 1, \ldots, T, \tag{16.41}$$

with $\epsilon_t \sim \mathsf{IN}\left(0, \sigma_\epsilon^2\right)$.

Maximizing:

$$f\left(\boldsymbol{\beta}, \boldsymbol{\alpha}\right) = -\tfrac{1}{T} \sum_{t=1}^{T} \epsilon_t^2 \tag{16.42}$$

as a function of the $(\boldsymbol{\beta}, \boldsymbol{\alpha})$ parameters yields a non-linear least squares problem necessitating iterative solution. However, conditional on values of either set of parameters, $f\left(\cdot\right)$ is linear in the other set, so analytical first and second derivatives are easy to obtain. There is an estimator-generating equation for this whole class (see Hendry, 1976, Section 7), but as it has almost no efficient non-iterative solutions, little is gained by its exploitation. Letting $\boldsymbol{\theta}$ denote all of the unrestricted parameters in $\beta_0\left(\cdot\right)$, $\{\beta_i\left(\cdot\right)\}$ and $\alpha\left(\cdot\right)$, then the algorithm programmed in PcGive for maximizing $f\left(\cdot\right)$ as a function of $\boldsymbol{\theta}$ is a variant of the Gauss–Newton class. Let:

$$\mathbf{q}\left(\boldsymbol{\theta}\right) = \frac{\partial \mathbf{f}}{\partial \boldsymbol{\theta}} \quad \text{and} \quad \mathbf{Q} = \mathsf{E}\left[\mathbf{q}\mathbf{q}'\right], \tag{16.43}$$

so that negligible cross-products are eliminated, then at the ith iteration:

$$\boldsymbol{\theta}_{i+1} = \boldsymbol{\theta}_i - s_i \mathbf{Q}_i^{-1} \mathbf{q}_i, \quad i = 0, \ldots, I, \tag{16.44}$$

where s_i is a scalar chosen by a line search procedure to maximize $f(\boldsymbol{\theta}_{i+1}|\boldsymbol{\theta}_i)$. The convergence criterion depends on $\mathbf{q}_i'\mathbf{Q}_i^{-1}\mathbf{q}_i$ and on changes in $\boldsymbol{\theta}_i$ between iterations. The bi-linearity of $f\left(\cdot\right)$ is exploited in computing $\mathbf{Q}$.

16.4.1 Initial values for RALS

Before estimating by RALS, OLS estimates of $\{\beta_i\}$ are calculated, as are LM-test values of $\{\alpha_i\}$, where the prespecified autocorrelation order is 'data frequency+1' (for example, 5 for quarterly data). These estimates are then used to initialize $\boldsymbol{\theta}$. However, the $\{\alpha_i\}$ can be reset by users. Specifically, for single-order processes, $u_t = \alpha_r u_{t-r} + \epsilon_t$, then α_r can be selected by a prior grid search. The user can specify the maximum number of iterations, the convergence tolerance, both the starting and ending orders of the polynomial $\alpha\left(L\right)$ in the form:

$$u_t = \sum_{i=s}^{r} \alpha_i u_{t-i} + \epsilon_t,$$

and whether to minimize $f\left(\cdot\right)$ sequentially over s, $s + 1, \ldots, r$ or merely the highest order, r.

16.4.2 Final estimates

On convergence, the variances of the θs are calculated (from $\mathbf{Q}^{-1}$), as are the roots of $\alpha(L) = 0$. The usual statistics for $\hat{\sigma}$, RSS (this can be used in likelihood-ratio tests between alternative nested versions of a model), t-values etc. are reported, as is $T^{-1}\sum(y_t - \bar{y})^2$ in case a pseudo-R^2 statistic is desired.

16.4.3 Analysis of 1-step forecasts

Rewrite the RALS model as:

$$y_t = \mathbf{x}'_t\boldsymbol{\beta} + \sum_{i=s}^{r} \alpha_i u_{t-i} + \epsilon_t \qquad (16.45)$$

with:

$$\hat{y}_t = \mathbf{x}'_t\hat{\boldsymbol{\beta}} + \sum_{i=s}^{r} \hat{\alpha}_i \hat{u}_{t-i} \qquad (16.46)$$

where $\hat{\boldsymbol{\beta}}$ and $\{\hat{\alpha}_i\}$ are obtained over $1, \ldots, T$. The forecast error is:

$$e_t = y_t - \hat{y}_t = \epsilon_t + \mathbf{x}'_t\left(\boldsymbol{\beta} - \hat{\boldsymbol{\beta}}\right) + \sum_{i=s}^{r} (\alpha_i u_{t-i} - \hat{\alpha}_i \hat{u}_{t-i}) \qquad (16.47)$$

or:

$$e_t = \epsilon_t + \mathbf{x}'_t\left(\boldsymbol{\beta} - \hat{\boldsymbol{\beta}}\right) + \sum_{i=s}^{r} \left[(\alpha_i - \hat{\alpha}_i)\,\hat{u}_{t-i} + \alpha_i\,(u_{t-i} - \hat{u}_{t-i})\right]. \qquad (16.48)$$

Now:

$$u_{t-i} - \hat{u}_{t-i} = \left(y_{t-i} - \mathbf{x}'_{t-i}\boldsymbol{\beta}\right) - \left(y_{t-i} - \mathbf{x}'_{t-i}\hat{\boldsymbol{\beta}}\right) = -\mathbf{x}'_{t-i}\left(\boldsymbol{\beta} - \hat{\boldsymbol{\beta}}\right). \qquad (16.49)$$

Consequently:

$$e_t = \epsilon_t + \left(\mathbf{x}'_t - \sum_{i=s}^{r} \alpha_i \mathbf{x}'_{t-i}\right)\left(\boldsymbol{\beta} - \hat{\boldsymbol{\beta}}\right) + \sum_{i=s}^{r} (\alpha_i - \hat{\alpha}_i)\,\hat{u}_{t-i}. \qquad (16.50)$$

Thus:

$$e_t = \epsilon_t + \mathbf{x}^{+\prime}_t\left(\boldsymbol{\beta} - \hat{\boldsymbol{\beta}}\right) + \hat{\mathbf{u}}'_r\left(\boldsymbol{\alpha} - \hat{\boldsymbol{\alpha}}\right) = \epsilon_t + \mathbf{w}'_t\left(\boldsymbol{\theta} - \hat{\boldsymbol{\theta}}\right), \qquad (16.51)$$

where we define $\mathbf{x}^{+\prime}_t = \mathbf{x}_t - \sum_s^r \alpha_i \mathbf{x}_{t-i}$, $\hat{\mathbf{u}}'_r = (\hat{u}_{t-s} \ldots \hat{u}_{t-r})$, $\mathbf{w}'_t = \left(\mathbf{x}^{+\prime}_t : \hat{\mathbf{u}}'_r\right)$, and $\boldsymbol{\theta}' = \left(\boldsymbol{\beta}' : \boldsymbol{\alpha}'\right)$ when $\boldsymbol{\alpha}' = (\alpha_s \ldots \alpha_r)$. $\mathsf{E}\,[e_t] \simeq 0$ for a correctly-specified model. Finally, therefore (neglecting the second-order dependence of the variance of $\mathbf{w}'_t(\boldsymbol{\theta} - \hat{\boldsymbol{\theta}})$ on $\hat{\boldsymbol{\theta}}$ acting through $\mathbf{w}_t$):

$$\mathsf{V}\,[e_t] = \sigma^2 + \mathbf{w}'_t\mathsf{V}\left[\hat{\boldsymbol{\theta}}\right]\mathbf{w}_t. \qquad (16.52)$$

$V[\hat{\boldsymbol{\theta}}]$ is the RALS variance-covariance matrix, and from the forecast-error covariance matrix, the 1-step analysis is calculated, as are parameter-constancy tests.

The output is as for OLS: the columns respectively report the date for which the forecast is made, the realized outcome (y_t), the forecast $(\hat{y}_t)$, the forecast error $(e_t = y_t - \hat{y}_t)$, the standard error of the 1-step forecast $(\mathsf{SE}\,(e_t) = \sqrt{\widehat{\mathsf{V}\,[e_t]}})$, and a t-value (that is, the standardized forecast error $e_t/\mathsf{SE}\,(e_t)$).

16.4.4 Forecast tests

The RALS analogues of the forecast test ξ_1 of (16.21), and of the Chow test η_3 in (16.25), are reported. The formulae follow directly from (16.47) and (16.52).

16.5 Non-linear modelling

16.5.1 Non-linear least squares (NLS) estimation

The non-linear regression model is written as

$$y_t = f\,(\mathbf{x}_t, \boldsymbol{\theta}) + u_t, \quad t = 1, \ldots, T, \text{ with } u_t \sim \mathsf{IN}\,(0, \sigma_u^2). \tag{16.53}$$

We take $\boldsymbol{\theta}$ to be a $k \times 1$ vector. For example:

$$y_t = \theta_0 + \theta_1 x_t^{\theta_2} + \theta_3 z_t^{1-\theta_2} + u_t.$$

Note that for fixed θ_2 this last model becomes linear; for example, for $\theta_2 = \frac{1}{2}$:

$$y_t = \theta_0 + \theta_1 x_t^* + \theta_3 z_t^* + u_t, \quad x_t^* = \sqrt{x_t},\ z_t^* = \sqrt{z_t},$$

which is linear in the transformed variables x_t^*, z_t^*. As for OLS, estimation proceeds by minimizing the sum of squared residuals:

$$\hat{\boldsymbol{\theta}} = \operatorname*{argmin}_{\boldsymbol{\theta}} \sum_{t=1}^{T} u_t^2 = \operatorname*{argmin}_{\boldsymbol{\theta}} \sum_{t=1}^{T} (y_t - f\,(\mathbf{x}_t, \boldsymbol{\theta}))^2. \tag{16.54}$$

In linear models, this problem has an explicit solution; for non-linear models the minimum has to be found using iterative optimization methods.

Instead of minimizing the sum of squares, PcGive maximizes the sum of squares divided by $-T$:

$$\hat{\boldsymbol{\theta}} = \operatorname*{argmax}_{\boldsymbol{\theta}} g\,(\boldsymbol{\theta} \mid y_t, \mathbf{x}_t) = \operatorname*{argmax}_{\boldsymbol{\theta}} \left\{ -\frac{1}{T} \sum_{t=1}^{T} u_t^2 \right\}. \tag{16.55}$$

As for RALS, an iterative procedure is used to locate the maximum:

$$\boldsymbol{\theta}_{i+1} = \boldsymbol{\theta}_i + s_i \mathbf{Q}\,(\boldsymbol{\theta}_i)^{-1}\,\mathbf{q}\,(\boldsymbol{\theta}_i), \tag{16.56}$$

with $\mathbf{q}\left(\cdot\right)$ the derivatives of $g(\cdot)$ with respect to θ_j (this is determined numerically), and $\mathbf{Q}\left(\cdot\right)^{-1}$ a symmetric, positive definite matrix (determined by the BFGS method after some initial Gauss-Newton steps). Practical details of the algorithm are provided in §16.5.3; Volume II gives a more thorough discussion of the subject of numerical optimization. Before using NLS you are advised to study the examples given in tutorial Chapter 8, to learn about the potential problems.

Output is as for OLS, except for the instability tests and HCSEs which are not computed. The variance of the estimated coefficients is determined numerically, other statistics follow directly, for example:

$$\hat{\sigma}_u^2 = \frac{1}{T-k} \sum_{t=1}^{T} \hat{u}_t^2, \text{ with } \hat{u}_t = y_t - f\left(\mathbf{x}_t, \hat{\boldsymbol{\theta}}\right). \tag{16.57}$$

Forecasts are computed and graphed, but the only statistic reported is the ξ_1 test of (16.21), using 1-step forecast errors:

$$e_t = y_t - f\left(\mathbf{x}_t, \hat{\boldsymbol{\theta}}\right), \quad t = T+1, \dots, T+H. \tag{16.58}$$

16.5.2 Maximum likelihood (ML) estimation

Maximum likelihood estimation was established in Chapter 12. We saw in (12.28) that for an independent sample of T observations and k parameters $\boldsymbol{\theta}$:

$$\hat{\boldsymbol{\theta}} = \operatorname*{argmax}_{\boldsymbol{\theta}} \ell\left(\boldsymbol{\theta} \mid \mathbf{X}\right) = \operatorname*{argmax}_{\boldsymbol{\theta}} \sum_{t=1}^{T} \ell\left(\boldsymbol{\theta} \mid \mathbf{x}_t\right). \tag{16.59}$$

This type of model can be estimated with PcGive, which solves the problem:

$$\max_{\boldsymbol{\theta}} \sum_{t=1}^{T} \ell\left(\boldsymbol{\theta} \mid \mathbf{x}_t\right). \tag{16.60}$$

Models falling in this class are, for example, binary logit and probit, ARCH, GARCH, Tobit, Poisson regression. Extensive examples are given in tutorial Chapter 8. As an example, consider the linear regression model. PcGive gives three ways of solving this:

(1) direct estimation (OLS);
(2) numerical minimization of the residual sum of squares (NLS);
(3) numerical maximization of the likelihood function (ML).

Clearly, the first method is to be preferred when available.

Estimation of (16.60) uses the same technique as NLS. The output is more concise, consisting of coefficients, standard errors (based on the numerical second derivative), t-values, t-probabilities, and 'loglik' which is $\sum_{t=1}^{T} \ell(\hat{\boldsymbol{\theta}}|\mathbf{x}_t)$. Forecasts are computed and graphed, but no statistics are reported.

16.5.3 Practical details

Non-linear model are formulated in algebra code. NLS requires the definition of a variable called `actual`, and one called `fitted`. It uses these to maximize minus the residual sum of squares divided by T:

$$-\frac{1}{T} \sum_{t=1}^{T} (actual_t - fitted_t)^2.$$

An example for NLS is:

```
actual = CONS;
fitted = &0 + &1 * INC + &2 * lag(INC,1);
&0   = 400;
&1   = 0.8;
&2   = 0.2;
```

This is just a linear model, and much more efficiently done using the normal options.

Models can be estimated by maximum likelihood if they can be written as a sum over the observations (note that the previous concentrated log-likehood cannot be written that way!). An additional algebra line is required, to define a variable called `loglik`. PcGive maximizes:

$$\sum_{t=1}^{T} loglik_t.$$

Consider, for example, a binary logit model:

```
actual = vaso;
xbeta = &0 + &1 * Lrate + &2 * Lvolume;
fitted = 1 / (1 + exp(-xbeta));
loglik = actual * log(fitted) + (1-actual) * log(1-fitted);
&0   = 0.74;
&1   = 1.3;
&2   = 2.3;
```

Here `actual` and `fitted` are not really that, but these variables define what is being graphed in the graphic analysis.

Note that algebra is a vector language without temporary variables, restricting the class of models that can be estimated. Non-linear models are *not* stored for recall and progress reports.

After correct model specification, the method is automatically set to Non-linear model (using ML if `loglik` is defined, NLS/RNLS otherwise); in addition, the following information needs to be specified:

(1) Estimation sample.
(2) The number of forecasts; enter the number of observations you wish to withhold for forecasting.
(3) Whether to use recursive estimation, and if so, the number of observations you wish to use for initialization.

NLS and ML estimation (and their recursive variants RNLS and RML) require *numerical optimization* to maximize the likelihood $\log \mathsf{L}\left(\phi\left(\theta\right)\right) = \ell\left(\phi\left(\theta\right)\right)$ as a non-linear function of θ. PcGive maximization algorithms are based on a Newton scheme:

$$\theta_{i+1} = \theta_i + s_i \mathbf{Q}_i^{-1} \mathbf{q}_i \qquad (16.61)$$

with

- θ_i parameter value at iteration i;
- s_i step length, normally unity;
- $\mathbf{Q}_i$ symmetric positive-definite matrix (at iteration i);
- $\mathbf{q}_i$ first derivative of the log-likelihood (at iteration i) (the score vector);
- $\delta_i = \theta_i - \theta_{i-1}$ is the change in the parameters;

PcGive uses the quasi-Newton method developed by Broyden, Fletcher, Goldfarb, Shanno (BFGS) to update $\mathbf{K} = \mathbf{Q}^{-1}$ directly. It uses numerical derivatives to compute $\partial \ell \left(\phi\left(\theta\right)\right) / \partial \theta_i$. However, for NLS, PcGive will try Gauss-Newton before starting BFGS. In this hybrid method, Gauss-Newton is used while the relative progress in the function value is 20%, then the program switches to BFGS.

Starting values must be supplied. The starting value for $\mathbf{K}$ consistes of 0s off-diagonal. The diagonal is the minimum of one and the inverse of the corresponding diagonal element in the matrix consisting of the sums of the outer-products of the gradient at the parameter starting values (numerically evaluated).

RNLS works as follows: starting values for θ and $\mathbf{K}$ for the first estimation ($T - 1$ observations) are the full sample values (T observations); then the sample size is reduced by one observation; the previous values at convergence are used to start with.

Owing to numerical problems it is possible (especially close to the maximum) that the calculated δ_i does not yield a higher likelihood. Then an $s_i \in [0, 1]$ yielding a higher function value is determined by a line search. Theoretically, since the direction is upward, such an s_i should exist; however, numerically it might be impossible to find one. When using BFGS with numerical derivatives, it often pays to scale the data so that the initial gradients are of the same order of magnitude.

The *convergence* decision is based on two tests. The first uses likelihood elasticities ($\partial \ell / \partial \log \theta$):

$$\begin{aligned} |q_{i,j}\theta_{i,j}| &\leq \epsilon \quad \text{for all } j \text{ when } \theta_{i,j} \neq 0, \\ |q_{i,j}| &\leq \epsilon \quad \text{for all } j \text{ with } \theta_{i,j} = 0. \end{aligned} \qquad (16.62)$$

The second is based on the one-step-ahead relative change in the parameter values:

$$\begin{aligned} |\delta_{i+1,j}| &\leq 10\epsilon \, |\theta_{i,j}| \quad \text{for all } j \text{ with } \theta_{i,j} \neq 0, \\ |\delta_{i+1,j}| &\leq 10\epsilon \quad \text{for all } j \text{ when } \theta_{i,j} = 0. \end{aligned} \qquad (16.63)$$

The status of the iterative process is given by the following messages:

(1) No convergence!

(2) Aborted: no convergence!

(3) Function evaluation failed: no convergence!

(4) Maximum number of iterations reached: no convergence!

(5) Failed to improve in line search: no convergence!
The step length s_i has become too small. The convergence test (16.62) was not passed, using tolerance $\epsilon = \epsilon_2$.

(6) Failed to improve in line search: weak convergence
The step length s_i has become too small. The convergence test (16.62) was passed, using tolerance $\epsilon = \epsilon_2$.

(7) Strong convergence
Both convergence tests (16.62) and (16.63) were passed, using tolerance $\epsilon = \epsilon_1$.

The chosen default values for the tolerances are:

$$\epsilon_1 = 10^{-4}, \ \epsilon_2 = 5 \times 10^{-3}. \tag{16.64}$$

You can:

(1) set the initial values of the parameters to zero or the previous values;

(2) set the maximum number of iterations;

(3) write iteration output;

(4) change the convergence tolerances ϵ_1 and ϵ_2. Care must be exercised with this: the defaults are 'fine-tuned'; some selections merely show the vital role of sensible choices!

NOTE 1: non-linear estimation can only continue after convergence.

NOTE 2: Restarting the optimization process leads to a Hessian reset.

Chapter 17

Model Evaluation Statistics

17.1 Graphic analysis

Graphic analysis focuses on graphical inspection of individual equations. Let y_t, $\hat{y}_t$ denote respectively the actual (that is, observed) values and the fitted values of the selected equation, with residuals $\hat{u}_t = y_t - \hat{y}_t$, $t = 1, \ldots, T$. When H observations are retained for forecasting, then $\hat{y}_{T+1}, \ldots, \hat{y}_{T+H}$ are the 1-step forecasts. NLS/RNLS/ML use the variables labelled 'actual' and 'fitted' for y_t, $\hat{y}_t$.

Eight different types of graph are available:

(1) *Actual and fitted values*
$(y_t, \hat{y}_t)$ over t. This is a graph showing the fitted $(\hat{y}_t)$ and actual values (y_t) of the dependent variable over time, including the forecast period.

(2) *Cross-plot of actual and fitted*
$\hat{y}_t$ against y_t, also including the forecast period.

(3) *Residuals (scaled)*
$(\hat{u}_t/\hat{\sigma})$ over t, where $\hat{\sigma}^2 = (T - k)^{-1} RSS$ is the full-sample equation error variance. As indicated, this graph shows the scaled residuals given by $\hat{u}_t/\hat{\sigma}$ over time.

(4) *Forecasts and outcomes*
The 1-step forecasts can be plotted in a graph over time: y_t and $\hat{y}_t$ are shown with error bars of ± 2SE (e_t) centered on $\hat{y}_t$ (that is, an approximate 95% confidence interval for the 1-step forecast); e_t are the forecast errors.

(5) *Residual density and histogram*
Plots the histogram of the standardized residuals $\hat{u}_t/\sqrt{(T^{-1}RSS)}$, $t = 1, \ldots, T$, the estimated density $\widehat{f_u(\cdot)}$ and a normal distribution with the same mean and variance (more details are in the OxMetrics book).

(6) *Residual correlogram (ACF)*
This plots the residual correlogram using $\hat{u}_t$ as the x_t variable in (17.13).

(7) *Partial correlogram (PACF)*
This plots the Partial autocorrrelation function (see §10.7 and the OxMetrics

book).

(8) *Forecasts Chow tests*
If available, the individual Chow $\chi^2(1)$ tests (see §16.23) are be plotted.

(9) *Residuals (unscaled)*
$(\hat{u}_t)$ over t;

(10) *Residual spectrum*
This plots the estimated spectral density (see the OxMetrics book) using $\hat{u}_t$ as the x_t variable.

(11) *Residual QQ plot against N(0,1)*
Shows a QQ plot of the residuals.

(12) *Residual density optionally with Histogram*
The histogram of the standardized residuals $\hat{u}_t/\sqrt{(T^{-1}RSS)}, t = 1, \ldots, T$, and the non-parametrically estimated density $\widehat{f_u}(\cdot)$ are graphed using the settings described in the OxMetrics book.

(13) *Residual distribution (normal quantiles)*
Plots the distribution based on the non-parametrically estimated density.

The residuals can be saved to the database for further inspection.

17.2 Recursive graphics (RLS/RIVE/RNLS/RML)

Recursive methods estimate the model at each t for $t = M - 1, \ldots, T$. The output generated by the recursive procedures is most easily studied graphically, possibly using the facility to view multiple graphs together on screen. The dialog has a facility to write the output to the editor, instead of graphing it. The recursive estimation aims to throw light on the relative future information aspect (that is, parameter constancy).

Let $\hat{\beta}_t$ denote the k parameters estimated from a sample of size t, and $y_j - \mathbf{x}'_j\hat{\beta}_t$ the residuals at time j evaluated at the parameter estimates based on the sample $1, \ldots, t$ (for RNLS the residuals are $y_j - f(\mathbf{x}_j, \hat{\beta}_t)$).

We now consider the generated output:

(1) *Beta coefficient ±2 Standard Errors*
The graph shows $\hat{\beta}_{it} \pm 2\mathsf{SE}(\hat{\beta}_{it})$ for each selected coefficient i $(i = 1, \ldots, k)$ over $t = M, \ldots, T$.

(2) *Beta t-value*
$\hat{\beta}_{it}/\mathsf{SE}(\hat{\beta}_{it})$ for each selected coefficient i $(i = 1, \ldots, k)$ over $t = M, \ldots, T$.

(3) *Residual sum of squares*
The residual sum of squares at each t is $RSS_t = \sum_{j=1}^{t}(y_j - \mathbf{x}'_j\hat{\beta}_t)^2$ for $t = M, \ldots, T$.

(4) *1-Step residuals ±2$\hat{\sigma}_t$*

The 1-step residuals $y_t - \mathbf{x}_t'\hat{\beta}_t$ are shown bordered by $0 \pm 2\hat{\sigma}_t$ over $M, \ldots, T$. Points outside the 2 standard-error region are either outliers or are associated with coefficient changes.

(5) *Standardized innovations*

The standardized innovations (or standardized recursive residuals) for RLS are: $\nu_t = (y_t - \mathbf{x}_t'\hat{\beta}_{t-1})/(\omega_t)^{1/2}$ where $\omega_t = 1 + \mathbf{x}_t' \left(\mathbf{X}_{t-1}'\mathbf{X}_{t-1}\right)^{-1} \mathbf{x}_t$ for $t = M, \ldots, T$.

As pointed out in §12.7.9, $\sigma^2\omega_t$ is the 1-step forecast error variance of (16.19), and $\hat{\beta}_{M-1}$ are the coefficient estimates from the initializing OLS estimation.

(6) *1-Step Chow tests*

1-step forecast tests are $F(1, t - k - 1)$ under the null of constant parameters, for $t = M, \ldots, T$. A typical statistic is calculated as:

$$\frac{(RSS_t - RSS_{t-1})(t - k - 1)}{RSS_{t-1}} = \frac{\nu_t^2/\omega_t}{\hat{\sigma}_{t-1}^2}. \tag{17.1}$$

Normality of y_t is needed for this statistic to be distributed as an F.

(7) *Break-point Chow tests*

Break-point F-tests are $F(T - t + 1, t - k - 1)$ for $t = M, \ldots, T$. These are, therefore, sequences of Chow tests and are also called $N\downarrow$ because the number of forecasts goes from $N = T - M + 1$ to 1. When the forecast period exceeds the estimation period, this test is not necessarily optimal relative to the covariance test based on fitting the model separately to the split samples. A typical statistic is calculated as:

$$\frac{(RSS_T - RSS_{t-1})(t - k - 1)}{RSS_{t-1}(T - t + 1)} = \frac{\frac{1}{T-t+1}\sum_{m=t}^{T}\nu_m^2/\omega_m}{\hat{\sigma}_{t-1}^2}. \tag{17.2}$$

This test is closely related to the CUSUMSQ statistic in Brown, Durbin and Evans (1975).

(8) *Forecast Chow tests*

Forecast F-tests are $F(t - M + 1, M - k - 1)$ for $t = M, \ldots, T$, and are called $N\uparrow$ as the forecast horizon increases from M to T. This tests the model over 1 to $M - 1$ against an alternative which allows any form of change over M to T. A typical statistic is calculated as:

$$\frac{(RSS_t - RSS_{M-1})(M - k - 1)}{RSS_{M-1}(t - M + 1)}. \tag{17.3}$$

The statistics in (17.1)–(17.3) are variants of Chow (1960) tests: they are scaled by 1-off critical values from the F-distribution at any selected probability level as an adjustment for changing degrees of freedom, so that the significant critical values become a straight line at unity. Note that the first and last values of (17.1) respectively equal the first value of (17.3) and the last value of (17.2).

The Chow test statistics are not calculated for RIVE/RML; the recursive RSS is not available for RML.

17.3 Dynamic analysis

The general class of models estimable in PcGive was discussed in Chapter 11 in the form:

$$b_0(L)\, y_t = \sum_{i=1}^{q} b_i(L)\, z_{it} + \epsilon_t \tag{17.4}$$

where $b_0(L)$ and the $b_i(L)$ are polynomials in the lag operator L. Now $q+1$ is the number of distinct variables (one of which is y_t), whereas k remains the number of estimated coefficients. For simplicity we take all polynomials to be of length m:

$$b_i(L) = \sum_{j=0}^{m} b_{ij} L^j, \quad i = 0, \ldots, q.$$

With $b_{00} = 1$ and using $a(L) = -\sum_{j=1}^{m} b_{0j} L^{j-1}$ we can write (17.4) as:

$$y_t = a(L)\, y_{t-1} + \sum_{i=1}^{q} b_i(L)\, z_{it} + \epsilon_t. \tag{17.5}$$

Finally, we use $\mathbf{a} = (b_{01}, \ldots, b_{0m})'$ and $\mathbf{b}_i = (b_{i0}, \ldots, b_{im})$, $i = 1, \ldots, q$.

In its unrestricted mode of operation, PcGive can be visualized as analyzing the polynomials involved, and it computes such functions as their roots and sums. This option is available if a general model was initially formulated, and provided OLS or IVE was selected.

17.3.1 Static long-run solution

When working with dynamic models, concepts such as equilibrium solutions, steady-state growth paths, mean lags of response etc. are generally of interest. In the simple model:

$$y_t = \beta_0 z_t + \beta_1 z_{t-1} + \alpha_1 y_{t-1} + u_t, \tag{17.6}$$

where all the variables are stationary, a static equilibrium is defined by:

$$\mathsf{E}\,[z_t] = z^* \quad \text{for all } t$$

in which case, $\mathsf{E}\,[y_t] = y^*$ will also be constant if $|\alpha_1| < 1$, and y_t will converge to:

$$y^* = K z^* \quad \text{where} \;\; K = \frac{(\beta_0 + \beta_1)}{(1 - \alpha_1)} \tag{17.7}$$

(cf. §11.4.8). For non-stationary but cointegrated data, reinterpret expression (17.7) as $\mathsf{E}\left[y_t - K z_t\right] = 0$.

PcGive computes estimates of K and associated standard errors. These are called static long-run parameters. If $b_0\left(1\right) \neq 0$, the general long-run solution of (17.4) is given by:

$$y^* = \sum_{i=1}^{q} \frac{b_i\left(1\right)}{b_0\left(1\right)} z_i^* = \sum_{i=1}^{q} K_i z_i^*. \tag{17.8}$$

The expression $y_t - \Sigma K_i z_{it}$ is called the equilibrium-correction mechanism (ECM) and can be stored in the data set. If common-factor restrictions of the form $b_j\left(L\right) = \alpha\left(L\right)\gamma_j\left(L\right)$, $j = 0, \ldots, q$ are imposed, then $\alpha\left(1\right)$ will cancel, hence enforced autoregressive error representations have no impact on derived long-run solutions.

The standard errors of $\hat{\mathbf{K}} = \left(\hat{K}_1 \ldots \hat{K}_q\right)'$ are calculated from:

$$\widehat{\mathsf{V}\left[\hat{\mathbf{K}}\right]} = \hat{\mathbf{J}} \widehat{\mathsf{V}\left[\hat{\beta}\right]} \hat{\mathbf{J}}' \text{ when } \mathbf{J} = \frac{\partial \mathbf{K}}{\partial \boldsymbol{\beta}'}. \tag{17.9}$$

PcGive calculates $\mathbf{J}$ analytically using the algorithm proposed by Bårdsen (1989).

PcGive outputs the solved static long-run equation, with standard errors of the coefficients. This is followed by a Wald test of the null that all of the long-run coefficients are zero (except the constant term). The $\widehat{\mathsf{V}[\hat{\mathbf{K}}]}$ matrix is printed when 'covariance matrix of estimated coefficients' is checked under the model options.

17.3.2 Analysis of lag structure

The $\hat{b}_i\left(L\right)$, $i = 0, \ldots, q$ of (17.4) and their standard errors are reported in tabular form with the $\hat{b}_i\left(1\right)$ (their row sums) and associated standard errors.

17.3.2.1 Tests on the significance of each variable

The first column contains F-tests of each of the $q + 1$ hypotheses:

$$\mathsf{H}_{v0} : \mathbf{a} = \mathbf{0}; \; \mathsf{H}_{vi} : \mathbf{b}_i = \mathbf{0} \text{ for } i = 1, \ldots, q.$$

These test the significance of each basic variable in turn. The final column gives the PcGive unit-root tests:

$$\mathsf{H}_{ui} : b_i\left(1\right) = 0 \text{ for } i = 0, \ldots, q.$$

If H_{ui}: $b_i\left(1\right) = 0$ cannot be rejected, there is no significant long-run level effect from z_{it}; if H_{vi}: $\mathbf{b}_i = \mathbf{0}$ cannot be rejected, there is no significant effect from z_{it} at any (included) lag. Significance is marked by * for 5% and ** for 1%. Critical values for the PcGive unit-root test (H_{u0}: $b_0\left(1\right) = 0$) are based on Ericsson and MacKinnon

(1999). For the unit-root test, only significance of the dependent variable is reported (not the remaining variables!),

Conflicts between the tests' outcomes are possible in small samples.

Note that $b_i(1) = 0$ and $\mathbf{b}_i = \mathbf{0}$ are not equivalent; testing $K_i = 0$ is different again. Using (17.6) we can show the relevant hypotheses:

$$
\begin{array}{ll}
\text{significance of each variable} & \mathrm{H}_{v0} : \alpha_1 = 0; \; \mathrm{H}_{v1} : \beta_0 = \beta_1 = 0, \\
\text{PcGive unit-root test} & \mathrm{H}_{u0} : \alpha_1 - 1 = 0, \\
\text{Additional unit-root tests} & \mathrm{H}_{u1} : \beta_0 + \beta_1 = 0, \\
\text{t-values from static long run} & \mathrm{H}_l : (\beta_0 + \beta_1)/(1 - \alpha_1) = 0.
\end{array}
$$

17.3.2.2 Tests on the significance of each lag

F-tests of each lag length are shown, beginning at the longest (m) and continuing down to 1. The test of the longest lag is conditional on keeping lags $(1, \ldots, m-1)$, that of $(m-1)$ is conditional on $(1, \ldots, m-2, m)$ etc.

17.3.3 Tests on the significance of all lags

Finally, F-tests of all lags up to m are shown, beginning at the longest $(1, \ldots, m)$ and continuing further from $(2, \ldots, m)$ down to $(m, \ldots, m)$. These tests are conditional on keeping no lags, keeping lag 1, down to keeping $(1, \ldots, m-1)$. Thus, they show the marginal significance of all longer lags.

17.3.4 COMFAC tests

COMFAC tests for the legitimacy of common-factor restrictions of the form:[1]

$$
\alpha(L) b_0^*(L) y_t = \alpha(L) \sum_{i=1}^{k} b_i^*(L) x_{it} + u_t \tag{17.10}
$$

where $\alpha(L)$ is of order r and * denotes polynomials of the original order minus r. The degrees of freedom for the Wald tests for COMFAC are equal to the number of restrictions imposed by $\alpha(L)$ and the Wald statistics are asymptotically χ^2 with these degrees of freedom if the COMFAC restrictions are valid. It is preferable to use the incremental values obtained by subtracting successive values of the Wald tests. These are χ^2 also, with degrees of freedom given by the number of additional criteria. Failure to reject common-factor restrictions does not entail that such restrictions must be imposed. For a discussion of the theory of COMFAC, see Hendry and Mizon (1978) and §11.4.7,

---

[1]Using Sargan's Wald algorithm (see Hendry, Pagan and Sargan, 1984 and Sargan, 1980b). Note that this non-linear Wald test is susceptible to formulation, so depends on the order of the variables.

§11.6.7; for some finite-sample Monte Carlo evidence see Mizon and Hendry (1980). COMFAC is not available for RALS.

When the minimum order of lag length in the $b_i\left(L\right)$ is unity or larger (m say), the Wald test sequence for $1, 2, \ldots, m$ common factors is calculated. Variables that are redundant when lagged (Constant, Seasonals, Trend) are excluded in conducting the Wald test sequence since they always sustain a common-factor interpretation.

17.3.5 Lag weights

Consider the simple model:

$$(1 - \alpha_1 L)\, y_t = (\beta_0 + \beta_1 L)\, z_t + u_t. \tag{17.11}$$

With $|\alpha_1| < 1$ this can be written as:

$$y_t = w\left(L\right) z_t + v_t,$$

when:

$$w\left(L\right) = (\beta_0 + \beta_1 L)\, /\left(1 - \alpha_1 L\right) = (\beta_0 + \beta_1 L)\left(1 + \alpha_1 L + \alpha_1^2 L^2 + \cdots\right).$$

Starting from an equilibrium z^* at $t = 0$, a one-off increment of δ to z^* has an impact on y^* at $t = 0, 1, 2, \ldots$ of $w_0 \delta,\ w_1 \delta,\ w_2 \delta,\ w_3 \delta, \ldots$ with the ws defined by equating coefficients of powers of L as:

$$w_0 = \beta_0, \quad w_1 = \beta_1 + \beta_0 \alpha_1, \quad w_2 = \alpha_1 w_1, \quad w_3 = \alpha_1 w_2, \ldots$$

PcGive can graph the normalized lag weights $w_0/w\left(1\right),\ w_1/w\left(1\right), \ldots,\ w_s/w\left(1\right)$ and the cumulative normalized lag weights $w_0/w\left(1\right),\ (w_0 + w_1)/w\left(1\right), \ldots,$ $(w_0 + \cdots + w_s)/w\left(1\right)$.

Lag weights are available for models estimated by OLS or IVE.

17.4 Diagnostic tests

17.4.1 Introduction

Irrespective of the estimator selected, a wide range of diagnostic tests is offered, intimately related to the model evaluation criteria discussed in Chapter 13, also see §11.6 and §11.9. Tests are available for residual autocorrelation, conditional heteroscedasticity, normality, unconditional heteroscedasticity/functional form mis-specification and omitted variables. Recursive residuals can be used if these are available. Tests for common factors and linear restrictions are discussed in §17.3.4 and §17.5 below, encompassing tests in §17.9. Thus, relating this section to the earlier information taxonomy in §13.5, the diagnostic tests of this section concern the past (checking that the errors are a homoscedastic, normal, innovation process relative to the information available), whereas the forecast statistics discussed in Chapter 16 concern the future and encompassing tests concern information specific to rival models.

Many test statistics in PcGive have either a χ^2 distribution or an F distribution. F-tests are usually reported as:

```
F(num,denom)   =  Value   [Probability]  /*/**
```
for example:
```
F(1, 155)      =  5.0088 [0.0266] *
```
where the test statistic has an F-distribution with one degree of freedom in the numerator, and 155 in the denominator. The observed value is 5.0088, and the probability of getting a value of 5.0088 or larger under this distribution is 0.0266. This is less than 5% but more than 1%, hence the star. Significant outcomes at a 1% level are shown by two stars. χ^2 tests are also reported with probabilities, as for example:

```
Normality Chi^2(2) = 2.1867 [0.3351]
```

The 5% χ^2 critical values with two degrees of freedom is 5.99, so here normality is not rejected (alternatively, Prob($\chi^2 \geq 2.1867$) = 0.3351, which is more than 5%). Details on the computation of probability values and quantiles for the F and χ^2 tests are given under the `probf`, `probchi`, `quanf` and `quanchi` functions in the Ox reference manual (Doornik, 2006).

Some tests take the form of a likelihood ratio (LR) test. If ℓ is the unrestricted, and ℓ_0 the restricted log-likelihood, then $-2(\ell_0 - \ell)$ has a $\chi^2(s)$ distribution, with s the number of restrictions imposed (so model ℓ_0 is nested in ℓ).

Many diagnostic tests are calculated through an auxiliary regression. For single-equation tests, they take the form of TR^2 for the auxiliary regression so that they are asymptotically distributed as $\chi^2(s)$ under their nulls, and hence have the usual additive property for independent $\chi^2 s$. In addition, following Harvey (1990) and Kiviet (1986), F-approximations are calculated because they may be better behaved in small samples:

$$\frac{R^2}{1 - R^2} \cdot \frac{T - k - s}{s} \sim F(s, T - k - s) \qquad (17.12)$$

17.4.2 Residual correlogram and Portmanteau statistic

The correlogram or sample autocorrelation function (ACF) of a variable x_t is the series $\{r_j\}$ where r_j is the correlation coefficient between x_t and x_{t-j} for $j = 1, \ldots, s$:[2]

$$r_j = \frac{\sum_{t=j+1}^{T} (x_t - \bar{x}) (x_{t-j} - \bar{x})}{\sum_{t=1}^{T} (x_t - \bar{x})^2}. \qquad (17.13)$$

Here $\bar{x} = \frac{1}{T} \sum_{t=j}^{T} x_t$ is the sample mean of x_t.

---

[2]Old version of PcGive (version 9 and before) used the running mean in the denominator. The difference with the current definition tends to be small, and vanishes asymptotically.

The residual correlogram is defined as above, but using the residuals from the econometric regression, rather than the data. Thus, this reports the series $\{r_j\}$ of correlations between the residuals $\hat{u}_t$ and $\hat{u}_{t-j}$. Inaddition, PcGive prints the partial autocorrelation function (PACF) (see the OxMetrics book).

It is possible to calculate a statistic based on '$T *$ (sum of s squared autocorrelations)', with s the length of the correlogram, called the Portmanteau statistic:

$$\mathsf{LB}\,(s) = T^2 \sum_{j=1}^{s} \frac{r_j^2}{T-j}. \tag{17.14}$$

This is corresponds to Box and Pierce (1970), but with a degrees of freedom correction as suggested by Ljung and Box (1978). It is designed as a goodness-of-fit test in stationary, autoregressive moving-average models. Under the assumptions of the test, $\mathsf{LB}(s)$ is asymptotically distributed as $\chi^2(s-n)$ after fitting an AR(n) model. A value such that $\mathsf{LB}(s) \geq 2s$ is taken as indicative of mis-specification for large s. However, small values of such a statistic should be treated with caution since residual autocorrelations are biased towards zero (like DW) when lagged dependent variables are included in econometric equations. An appropriate test for residual autocorrelation is provided by the LM test in §17.4.3 below.

17.4.3 Error autocorrelation test (not for RALS, ML)

This is the Lagrange-multiplier test for r^{th} order residual autocorrelation, distributed as $\chi^2(r)$ in large samples, under the null hypothesis that there is no autocorrelation (that is, that the errors are white noise). In standard usage, $r \simeq \frac{1}{2}s$ for s in §17.4.2 above, so this provides a type of Portmanteau test (see Godfrey, 1978). However, any orders from 1 up to 12 can be selected to test against:

$$u_t = \sum_{i=p}^{r} \alpha_i u_{t-i} + \epsilon_t \text{ where } 0 \leq p \leq r.$$

As noted above, the F-form suggested by Harvey (1981, see Harvey, 1990) is the recommended diagnostic test. Following the outcome of the F-test (and its p-value), the error autocorrelation coefficients are recorded. For an autoregressive error of order r to be estimated by RALS, these LM coefficients provide good initial values, from which the iterative optimization can be commenced. The LM test is calculated by regressing the residuals on all the regressors of the original model and the lagged residuals for lags p to r (missing residuals are set to zero). The LM test $\chi^2(r-p+1)$ is TR^2 from this regression (or the F-equivalent), and the error autocorrelation coefficients are the coefficients of the lagged residuals. For an excellent exposition, see Pagan (1984).

17.4.4 Normality test

Let μ, σ_x^2 denote the mean and variance of $\{x_t\}$, and write $\mu_i = \mathsf{E}\left[x_t - \mu\right]^i$, so that $\sigma_x^2 = \mu_2$. The skewness and kurtosis are defined as:

$$\sqrt{\beta_1} = \frac{\mu_3}{\mu_2^{3/2}} \text{ and } \beta_2 = \frac{\mu_4}{\mu_2^2}. \tag{17.15}$$

Sample counterparts are defined by

$$\bar{x} = \frac{1}{T}\sum_{t=1}^{T} x_t, \quad m_i = \frac{1}{T}\sum_{t=1}^{T}(x_t - \bar{x})^i, \quad \sqrt{b_1} = \frac{m_3}{m_2^{3/2}} \text{ and } b_2 = \frac{m_4}{m_2^2}. \tag{17.16}$$

A normal variate will have $\sqrt{\beta_1} = 0$ and $\beta_2 = 3$. Bowman and Shenton (1975) consider the test:

$$e_1 = \frac{T\left(\sqrt{b_1}\right)^2}{6} + \frac{T\left(b_2 - 3\right)^2}{24} \overset{a}{\sim} \chi^2(2), \tag{17.17}$$

which subsequently was derived as an LM test by Jarque and Bera (1987). Unfortunately e_1 has rather poor small sample properties: $\sqrt{b_1}$ and b_2 are not independently distributed, and the sample kurtosis especially approaches normality very slowly. The test reported by PcGive is based on Doornik and Hansen (1994), who employ a small sample correction, and adapt the test for the multivariate case. It derives from Shenton and Bowman (1977), who give b_2 (conditional on $b_2 > 1 + b_1$) a gamma distribution, and D'Agostino (1970), who approximates the distribution of $\sqrt{b_1}$ by the Johnson S_u system. Let z_1 and z_2 denote the transformed skewness and kurtosis, where the transformation creates statistics which are much closer to standard normal. The test statistic is:

$$e_2 = z_1^2 + z_2^2 \overset{app}{\sim} \chi^2(2). \tag{17.18}$$

Table 17.1 compares (17.18) with its asymptotic form (17.17). It gives the rejection frequencies under the null of normality, using $\chi^2(2)$ critical values. The experiments are based on 10 000 replications and common random numbers.

Table 17.1   Empirical size of normality tests.

T	nominal probabilities of e_2				nominal probabilities of (17.17)			
	20%	10%	5%	1%	20%	10%	5%	1%
50	0.1734	0.0869	0.0450	0.0113	0.0939	0.0547	0.0346	0.0175
100	0.1771	0.0922	0.0484	0.0111	0.1258	0.0637	0.0391	0.0183
150	0.1845	0.0937	0.0495	0.0131	0.1456	0.0703	0.0449	0.0188
250	0.1889	0.0948	0.0498	0.0133	0.1583	0.0788	0.0460	0.0180

PcGive reports the following statistics under the normality test option, replacing x_t by the residuals u_t:

mean	$\bar{x}$
standard deviation	$\sigma_x = \sqrt{m_2}$
skewness	$\sqrt{b_1}$
excess kurtosis	$b_2 - 3$
minimum	
maximum	
asymptotic test	e_1
normality test $\chi^2(2)$	e_2 $\left[P\left(\chi^2(2) \geq e_2 \right) \right]$

17.4.5 Heteroscedasticity test using squares (not for ML)

This test is based on White (1980), and involves an auxiliary regression of $\{\hat{u}_t^2\}$ on the original regressors (x_{it}) and all their squares (x_{it}^2). The null is unconditional homoscedasticity, and the alternative is that the variance of the $\{u_t\}$ process depends on $\mathbf{x}_t$ and on the x_{it}^2. The output comprises TR^2, the F-test equivalent, the coefficients of the auxiliary regression, and their individual t-statistics, to help highlight problem variables. Variables that are redundant when squared are automatically removed.

17.4.6 Heteroscedasticity test using squares and cross-products (not for ML)

This test is that of White (1980), and only calculated if there is a large number of observations relative to the number of variables in the regression. It is based on an auxiliary regression of the squared residuals $(\hat{u}_t^2)$ on all squares and cross-products of the original regressors (that is, on $r = \frac{1}{2}k(k+1)$ variables). That is, if $T >> k(k+1)$, the test is calculated; redundant variables are automatically removed. The usual χ^2 and F-values are reported; coefficients of the auxiliary regression are also shown with their t-statistics to help with model respecification. This is a general test for heteroscedastic errors: H_0 is that the errors are homoscedastic or, if heteroscedasticity is present, it is unrelated to the xs.

In previous versions of PcGive this test used to be called a test for functional form mis-specification. That terminology was criticized by Godfrey and Orme (1994), who show that the test does not have power against omitted variables.

17.4.7 ARCH test

This is the ARCH (AutoRegressive Conditional Heteroscedasticity) test: see Engle, 1982) which in the present form tests the hypothesis $\gamma = \mathbf{0}$ in the model:

$$E\left[u_t^2 \mid u_{t-1}, \ldots, u_{t-r} \right] = c_0 + \sum_{i=1}^{r} \gamma_i u_{t-i}^2$$

where $\gamma = (\gamma_1, \ldots, \gamma_r)'$. Again, we have TR^2 as the χ^2 test from the regression of $\hat{u}_t^2$ on a constant and $\hat{u}_{t-1}^2$ to $\hat{u}_{t-r}^2$ (called the ARCH test) which is asymptotically distributed as $\chi^2(r)$ on H_0: $\boldsymbol{\gamma} = \mathbf{0}$. The F-form is also reported. Both first-order and higher-order lag forms are easily calculated (see Engle, 1982, and Engle, Hendry and Trumbull, 1985).

17.4.8 RESET (OLS only)

The RESET test (Regression Specification Test) due to Ramsey (1969) tests the null of correct specification of the original model against the alternative that powers of $\hat{y}_t$ such as $(\hat{y}_t^2, \hat{y}_t^3 \ldots)$ have been omitted (PcGive only allows squares). This tests to see if the original functional form is incorrect, by adding powers of linear combinations of xs since by construction, $\hat{y}_t = \mathbf{x}_t' \hat{\boldsymbol{\beta}}_t$.

17.4.9 Parameter instability tests (OLS only)

Parameter instability statistics are reported for σ^2, followed by the joint statistic for all the parameters in the model (also see §17.4.9), based on the approach in Hansen (1992). Next, the instability statistic is printed for each parameter $(\beta_1, \ldots, \beta_k, \sigma^2)$.

Large values reveal non-constancy (marked by * or **), and indicate a fragile model. Note that this measures within-sample parameter constancy, and is computed if numerically feasible (it may fail owing to dummy variables), so no observations need be reserved. The indicated significance is only valid in the absence of non-stationary regressors.

17.4.10 Diagnostic tests for NLS

The LM tests for autocorrelation, heteroscedasticity and functional form require an auxiliary regression involving the original regressors x_{it}. NLS uses $\partial f(\mathbf{x}_t, \boldsymbol{\theta})/\partial \theta_i$ (evaluated at $\hat{\boldsymbol{\theta}}$) instead. The auxiliary regression for the autocorrelation test is:

$$\hat{u}_t = \sum_{i=1}^{k} \beta_i \left(\frac{\partial f(\mathbf{x}_t, \boldsymbol{\theta})}{\partial \theta_i} \right)_{|\hat{\boldsymbol{\theta}}} + \sum_{i=p}^{r} \alpha_i \hat{u}_{t-i} + \epsilon_t. \tag{17.19}$$

These three tests are not computed for models estimated using ML.

17.5 Linear restrictions test

Writing the model in matrix form as $\mathbf{y} = \mathbf{X}\boldsymbol{\beta} + \mathbf{u}$, the null hypothesis of p linear restrictions can be expressed as H_0: $\mathbf{R}\boldsymbol{\beta} = \mathbf{r}$, with $\mathbf{R}$ a $(p \times k)$ matrix and $\mathbf{r}$ a $p \times 1$ vector. This test is well explained in most econometrics textbooks, and uses the unrestricted estimates (that is, it is a Wald test).

The subset form of the linear restrictions tests is: H_0: $\beta_i = \cdots = \beta_j = 0$: any choice of coefficients can be made, so a wide range of specification hypothesis can be tested.

17.6 General restrictions

Writing $\hat{\theta} = \hat{\beta}$, with corresponding variance-covariance matrix $V\left[\hat{\theta}\right]$, we can test for (non-) linear restrictions of the form (see §A1.1 for the syntax):

$$\mathbf{f}(\boldsymbol{\theta}) = \mathbf{0}.$$

The null hypothesis $H_0 : \mathbf{f}(\boldsymbol{\theta}) = \mathbf{0}$ will be tested against $H_1 : \mathbf{f}(\boldsymbol{\theta}) \neq \mathbf{0}$ through a Wald test:

$$w = \mathbf{f}\left(\hat{\boldsymbol{\theta}}\right)' \left(\hat{\mathbf{J}} V\widetilde{\left[\hat{\boldsymbol{\theta}}\right]} \hat{\mathbf{J}}'\right)^{-1} \mathbf{f}\left(\hat{\boldsymbol{\theta}}\right)$$

where $\mathbf{J}$ is the Jacobian matrix of the transformation: $\mathbf{J} = \partial\mathbf{f}(\boldsymbol{\theta})/\partial\boldsymbol{\theta}'$. PcGive computes $\hat{\mathbf{J}}$ by numerical differentiation. The statistic w has a $\chi^2(s)$ distribution, where s is the number of restrictions (that is, equations in $\mathbf{f}(\cdot)$). The null hypothesis is rejected if we observe a significant test statistic.

17.7 Test for omitted variables (OLS)

Lag polynomials of any variable in the database can be tested for omission. Variables that would change the sample or are already in the model are automatically deleted. The model itself remains unchanged. If the model is written in matrix form as $\mathbf{y} = \mathbf{X}\boldsymbol{\beta} + \mathbf{Z}\boldsymbol{\gamma} + \mathbf{u}$, then $H_0: \boldsymbol{\gamma} = \mathbf{0}$ is being tested. The test exploits the fact that on H_0:

$$\sqrt{T}\hat{\boldsymbol{\gamma}} \overset{D}{\sim} N_p\left(\mathbf{0}, \sigma^2\left(\mathbf{Z}'\mathbf{M}_X\mathbf{Z}/T\right)^{-1}\right) \quad \text{with } \mathbf{M}_X = \mathbf{I}_T - \mathbf{X}\left(\mathbf{X}'\mathbf{X}\right)^{-1}\mathbf{X}', \quad (17.20)$$

then:

$$\frac{\hat{\boldsymbol{\gamma}}'\left(\mathbf{Z}'\mathbf{M}_X\mathbf{Z}\right)\hat{\boldsymbol{\gamma}}}{\hat{\sigma}^2} \cdot \frac{T - k - p}{p} \sim F\left(p, T - k - p\right) \quad (17.21)$$

for p added variables.

Since $(\mathbf{X}'\mathbf{X})^{-1}$ is precalculated, the F-statistic is easily computed by partitioned inversion. Computations for IVE are more involved.

17.8 Progress: the sequential reduction sequence

Finally, because of the methodological arguments advanced in Chapter 13, PcGive has specific procedures programmed to operate when a general-to-specific mode is adopted.[3] In PcGive, when a model is specified and estimated by least squares or instrumental variables, then the general dynamic analysis is offered: see §17.3.

---

[3]Note that PcGive does not *force* you to use a general-to-specific strategy. However, we hope to have given compelling arguments in favour of adopting such a modelling strategy.

However, while the tests offered are a comprehensive set of Wald statistics on variables, lags and long-run outcomes, a reduction sequence can involve many linear transformations (differencing, creating differentials etc.) as well as eliminations. Consequently, as the reduction proceeds, PcGive monitors its progress, which can be reviewed at the progress menu. The main statistics reported comprise:

(1) The number of parameters, the log-likelihood and the SC, HQ and AIC information criteria for each model in the sequence.

(2) F-tests of each elimination conditional on the previous stage.

17.9 Encompassing and 'non-nested' hypotheses tests

Once appropriate data representations have been selected, it is of interest to see whether the chosen model can explain (that is, account for) results reported by other investigators. Often attention has focused on the ability of chosen models to explain each other's residual variances (variance encompassing), and PcGive provides the facility for doing so using test statistics based on Cox (1961) as suggested by Pesaran (1974). Full details of those computed by PcGive for OLS and IVE are provided in Ericsson (1983). Note that a badly-fitting model should be rejected against well-fitting models on such tests, and that care is required in interpreting any outcome in which a well-fitting model (which satisfies all of the other criteria discussed in Chapter 13) is rejected against a badly-fitting, or silly, model (see Mizon, 1984, Mizon and Richard, 1986, and Hendry and Richard, 1989). The Sargan test is for the restricted reduced form parsimoniously encompassing the unrestricted reduced form, which is implicitly defined by projecting y_t on all of the non-modelled variables. The F-test is for each model parsimoniously encompassing their union. This is the only one of these tests which is invariant to the choice of common regressors in the two models.[4] Thus, the F-test yields the same numerical outcome for the first model parsimoniously encompassing either the union of the two models under consideration, or the orthogonal complement to the first model relative to the union. In PcGive, tests of both models encompassing the other are reported.

---

[4]For example, if either the first or both models have the lagged dependent variable y_{t-1}, the same F-value is produced. However, a different value will result if only the second model has y_{t-1}.

Part V

Appendices

Appendix A1

Algebra and Batch for Single Equation Modelling

PcGive is mostly menu-driven for ease of use. To add flexibility, certain functions can be accessed through entering commands. The syntax of these commands, which can be seen as little computer languages, is described in this chapter.

Algebra is described in the OxMetrics manuals. Algebra commands are executed in OxMetrics, via the Calculator, the Algebra editor, or as part of a batch run.

A1.1 General restrictions

Restrictions have to be entered when testing for parameter restrictions and for imposing parameter constraints for estimation. The syntax is similar to that of algebra, albeit more simple.

Restrictions code may consist of the following components:

(1) *Comment*
(2) *Constants*
(3) *Arithmetic operators*

These are all identical to algebra. In addition there are:

(4) *Parameter references*

Parameters are referenced by an ampersand followed by the parameter number. Counting starts at 0, so, for example, &2 is the third parameter of the model. What this parameter is depends on your model. Make sure that when you enter restrictions through the batch language, you use the right order for the coefficients. In case of IV estimation PcGive will reorder your model so that the endogenous variables come first.

Consider, for example, the following unconstrained model:

$$\text{CONS}_t = \beta_0 \text{CONS\_1}_t + \beta_1 \text{INC}_t + \beta_2 \text{INC\_1}_t + \beta_3 \text{INFLAT}_t + \beta_4 + u_t.$$

Then &0 indicates the coefficient on CONS_1, etc.

Restrictions for *testing* are entered in the format: $f(\theta) = 0$;. The following restrictions test the significance of the long-run parameters in this unconstrained model:

```
(&1 + &2) / (1 - &0) = 0;
&3 / (1 - &0) = 0;
```

A1.2 Non-linear models

A1.2.1 Non-linear least squares

A non-linear model is formulated in Algebra code. The following extensions are used:

(1) *parameter references*

Parameters are referenced by an ampersand followed by the parameter number. The numbering does not have to be consecutive, so your model can use for example &1, &3 and &4.

Consider, for example, the following specification of the fitted part:

```
fitted = &0*lag(CONS,1) + &1*INC + &3*INFLAT + &4;
```

(2) *starting values*

Starting values are entered in the format: &*parameter=value*;. For example:

```
&0 = 0;   &1 = 1;   &3 = -1;   &4 = 1;
```

The following two variables must be defined for NLS to work:

(1) `actual`

Defines the actual values (the y variable).

(2) `fitted`

Defines the fitted values (the $\hat{y}$ variable).

Together, these formulate the whole non-linear model, as in the following example:

```
actual = CONS;
fitted = &0 + &1*lag(CONS,1) + &2*INC - &1*&2*lag(INC,1);
```

You are advised to work through the examples in Chapters 5 and 8 before trying to estimate models by NLS or RNLS. Also see §16.5.1.

A1.2.2 Maximum likelihood

Maximum likelihood models are defined using the three variables:

(1) `actual`

(2) `fitted`

(3) `loglik`

Both `actual` and `fitted` only define the variables being used in the graphic analysis and the residual based tests. The `loglik` variable defines the function to be maximized. Parameters and starting values are as for NLS. See Chapter 8 and §16.5.2.

A1.3 PcGive batch language

PcGive allows models to be formulated, estimated and evaluated through batch commands. Such commands are entered in OxMetrics. Certain commands are intercepted by OxMetrics, such as those for loading and saving data, as well as blocks of algebra code. The remaining commands are then passed on to the active module, which is PcGive in this case. This section gives an alphabetical list of the PcGive batch language statements. There are two types of batch commands: function calls (with or without arguments) terminated by a semicolon, and commands, which are followed by statements between curly brackets.

Anything between `/*` and `*/` is considered comment. Note that this comment cannot be nested. Everything following `//` up to the end of the line is also comment.

OxMetrics allows you to save the current model as a batch file, and to rerun saved batch files. If a model has been created interactively, it can be saved as a batch file for further editing or easy recall in a later session. This is also the most convenient way to create a batch file.

If an error occurs during processing, the batch run will be aborted and control returned to OxMetrics. A warning or out of memory message will have to be accepted by the user (press `Enter`), upon which the batch run will resume.

In the following list, function arguments are indicated by *words*, whereas the areas where statement blocks are expected are indicated by .... Examples follow the list of descriptions. For terms in double quotes, the desired term must be substituted and provided together with the quotes. A command summary is given in Table A1.1. For completeness, the Table A1.1 also contains the commands which are handled by OxMetrics. Consult the OxMetrics book for more information on those commands.

`adftest("`*var*`",` *lag, deterministic*`=1,` *summary*`=1);`
>The *var* argument specifies the variable for the ADF test, *lag* is the lag length to be used. The *det* argument indicates the choice of deterministic variables:
>
>0   no deterministic variables,
>1   constant,
>2   constant and trend,
>3   constant and seasonals,
>4   constant, trend and seasonals.
>
>Finally, the summary argument indicates whether a summary table is printed (1) or full output (0).

`arorder(`*ar1, ar2*`);`

Specifies the starting and ending order for RALS estimation. Note that the estimation sample must allow for the specified choice.

dynamics;

Does part of the dynamic analysis: the static long-run solution and the lag structure analysis.

estimate("*method*"=OLS, *year1*=-1, *period1*=0, *year2*=-1, *period2*=0, *forc*=0, *init*=0);

Estimate a system. The presence of default arguments implies that the shortest version is just: estimate(), which estimates by OLS using the maximum possible sample, and no forecasts. Similarly, a call to estimate("OLS", 1950, 1) corresponds to estimate("OLS", 1950, 1, -1, 0, 0, 0).
The *method* argument is one of:

OLS-CS	ordinary least squares (cross-section regression),
IVE-CS	instrumental variables estimation (cross-section regression),
OLS	ordinary least squares,
IVE	instrumental variables estimation,
RALS	autoregressive least squares (also see arorder),
NLS	non-linear least squares (non-linear modelling),
ML	maximum likelihood (non-linear modelling).

year1(period1) – year2(period2) is the estimation sample. Setting year1 to −1 will result in the earliest possible year1(period1), setting year2 to −1 will result in the latest possible year2(period2).

forc is the number of observations to withhold from the estimation sample for forecasting.

init is the number of observations to use for initialization of recursive estimation (not if *method* is RALS); no recursive estimation is performed if *init* = 0.

forecast(*nforc, hstep*=0, *setype*=1);

Prints *nforc* dynamic forecasts (when *hstep* is zero) or *hstep* forecasts. The last argument is the standard error type: 0 to not compute; 1 for error variance only (the default); 2 to include parameter uncertainty. For example, forecast(8) produces eight dynamic forecasts with error-variance based standard errors; forecast(8,4) produces the 4-step forecasts (note that the first three will coincide with 1,2,3-step respectively). Use the store command next to store the forecasts if necessary.

nonlinear { ... }

Formulates a non-linear model. The code between { } must conform to the syntax of §A1.2.

output("*option*");

Prints further output:

option	
correlation	print correlation matrix of variables,
covariance	print covariance matrix of coefficients,
equation	print the model equation format,
forecasts	print the static forecasts,
HCSE	Heteroscedasticity-consistent standard errors
infcrit	report information criteria,
instability	report instability tests,
latex	print the model in latex format,
r2seasonals	report R^2 about seasonals,
reducedform	print the reduced form,
sigpar	significant digits for parameters (second argument),
sigse	significant digits for standard errors (second argument).

option("*option*", *argument*);

    The first set relates to maximization:

option	argument	value
maxit	maximum number of iterations	default: 1000,
print	print every # iteration	0: do not print,
compact	compact or extended output	0 for off, 1 on,
strong	strong convergence tolerance	default: 0.005,
weak	set weak convergence tolerance	default: 0.0001,

    The second set of options adds further output automatically:

option	argument	value
equation	add equation format	0 for off, 1 on,
infcrit	report information criteria	0 for off, 1 on.
instability	report instability tests	0 for off, 1 on,
HCSE	Heteroscedasticity-consistent SEs	0 for off, 1 on,
r2seasonals	report R^2 about seasonals	0 for off, 1 on,

progress;

    Reports the modelling progress.

store("*name*", "*rename*"="");

    Use this command to store residuals, etc. into the database, the default name is used. Note that if the variable already exists, it is overwritten without warning. The *name* must be one of: residuals, fitted, res1step, stdinn, rss, eqse, innov, loglik.

    The optional second argument replaces the default name. For example store("residuals") stores the residuals under the name Residual; store("residuals", "xyz") stores them under the name xyz.

system { Y=...; Z=...; U=...; A=...; }

    Specify the system, consisting of the following components:

Y endogenous variables;
A additional instruments (optional);
Z non-modelled variables;
U unrestricted variables (optional, treated as Z).

The variables listed are separated by commas, their base names (that is, name excluding lag length) must be in the database. If the variable names are not a valid token, the name must be enclosed in double quotes.

The following special variables are recognized: Constant, Trend, Seasonal and CSeason.

Note that when IVE/RIVE are used PcGive reorders the model as follows: the endogenous variables first and the additional instruments last. This reordering is relevant when specifying restrictions.

test("*test*", *lag1*=0, *lag2*=0);
Performs a specific test using the specified lag lengths.

"ar"	test for autocorrelated errors from *lag1* to *lag2*;
"arch"	ARCH test up to order *lag1*;
"comfac"	test for common factor;
"encompassing"	tests the two most recent models for encompassing;
"hetero"	heteroscedasticity test (squares);
"heterox"	heteroscedasticity test (squares and cross products);
"instability"	instability tests;
"normal"	normality test;
"rescor"	residual correlogram up to lag *lag1*;
"reset"	Reset test using powers up to *lag1*.

testgenres { ... }
Used to test for general restrictions: specify the restrictions between { }, conforming to §A1.1.

testlinres { ... }
Test for linear restrictions. The content is the matrix dimensions followed by the $(R : r)$ matrix.

testres { ... }
Test for exclusion restrictions. The content lists the variables to be tested foe exclusion, separated by a comma (remember that variable names that are not proper tokens must be enclosed in double quotes).

testsummary;
Do the test summary.

We finish with an annotated example using most commands. To run this file, we assume that OxMetrics is loaded with data.in7, and that PcGive has been started.

```
package("PcGive", "Single-equation");
usedata("data.in7");
system
{
    Y = CONS, INC;          // endogenous variables
    Z = CONS_1, INC_1,      // non-modelled variables
        Constant;
    A = OUTPUT, OUTPUT_1;   // additional instruments, optional
}
estimate("IVE", 0, 0, 0, 0, 8);
                        // Estimate by IV over maximum sample:
                        // 1953(2)-1992(3), use 8 forecasts
testsummary;            // Do the test summary.
dynamics;               // Do dynamic analysis.
store("residuals");     // store the residuals
testgenres              // Test for general restrictions.
{
    &1 - &2 = 0;        // coeff of CONS_1 - coeff of INC_1.
}
testlinres              // Test for linear restrictions.
{                       // same restriction
    1 5
    0 1 -1 0 0
}
```

Table A1.1   Batch language syntax summary.

adftest("*var*", *lag*, *deterministic*=1, *summary*=1);
algebra {...}
appenddata("*filename*", "*group*");
appresults("*filename*");
arorder(*ar1*, *ar2*);
break;
chdir("*path*");
command("*command_line*");
database(*year1*, *period1*, *year2*, *period2*, *frequency*);
dynamics;
estimate("*method*"=OLS, *year1*=-1, *period1*=0, *year2*=-1, *period2*=0, *forc*=0, *init*=0);
exit;
forecast(*nforc*, *hstep*=0, *setype*=1);
loadalgebra("*filename*");
loadbatch("*filename*");
loadcommand("*filename*");
loaddata("*filename*");
module("*name*");
nonlinear {...}
print("*text*");
println("*text*");
option("*option*", *argument*);
progress;
savedata("*filename*");
saveresults("*filename*");
setdraw("*option*", *i1*=0, *i2*=0, *i3*=0, *i4*=0, *i5*=0);
store("*name*", "*rename*"="");
system {...}
test("*test*", *lag1*=0, *lag2*=0);
testlinres {...}
testgenres {...}
testsummary;
usedata("*databasename*");

Appendix A2

PcGive Artificial Data Set
(data.in7/data.bn7)

The following four-equation log-linear artificial data generation process was created using DAGER (see Hendry and Srba, 1980):

$$\Delta c_t = -0.9 + 0.4 \, \Delta y_t + 0.15 \, (y - c)_{t-1} - 0.9 \, \Delta p_t + \epsilon_{1t} \qquad (A2.1)$$

$$\Delta y_t = -75.0 + 0.3 \, \Delta c_t + 0.25 \, (q - y)_{t-1} + 0.25 \, \Delta q_t + \epsilon_{2t} \qquad (A2.2)$$

$$\Delta p_t = 0.3 + 0.7 \, \Delta p_{t-1} + 0.08 \, (q - 1200)_{t-1} + \epsilon_{3t} \qquad (A2.3)$$

$$\Delta q_t = 121.3 - 0.1 \, q_{t-1} - 1.30 \, \Delta p_{t-1} + \epsilon_{4t} \qquad (A2.4)$$

The $\{\epsilon_{it}\}$ were generated as IN $(0, \sigma_{ii}^2)$ where $(\sigma_{11}, \sigma_{22}, \sigma_{33}, \sigma_{44}) = (1, 3, 0.25, 4)$ with zero covariances. The variables are interpreted such that $x_t = 100 \log X_t \, (\forall x)$. The conditional latent roots of the dynamics for the 'domestic' economy (c_t, y_t) are $0.8 \pm 0.044i$, so the modulus is 0.80 and the period 115 'quarters', whereas for the world economy $(\Delta p_t, q_t)$ the roots are $0.8 \pm 0.31i$, with modulus 0.86 and period 17.2 'quarters'. Data were generated for a sample supposed to represent 1953(1) to 1992(3), with an 'oil crisis' in 1973(3). Thus, there were 159 observations on $(c_t, y_t, \Delta p_t, q_t)$ with an autonomous shock to the world economy intercepts (equations (A2.3) and (A2.4)) at observation 83. This shock left the system dynamics unaltered and only directly affected Δp_t and q_t. The long-run equilibrium of the system was shifted from:

$$
\begin{array}{lll}
 & c = y - 6\Delta p - 6 & [C = \exp(-6\Delta p - 0.06) \, Y] \\
 & y = q - 300 & [Y = 0.05 \, Q] \\
\text{with:} & \Delta p = 1 & [\dot{p} = 1\% \text{ per quarter}] \\
 & q = 1200 & [Q = 162, 755] \\
\text{to:} & \Delta p = 2 & [\dot{p} = 2\% \text{ per quarter}] \\
 & q = 1180 & [Q = 133, 252]
\end{array}
$$

Thus, 'equilibrium' inflation $(\dot{p})$ doubled and world output fell by about 18%. Correct modelling of the system necessitates different intercepts pre/post-1973(3) in equations (A2.3) and (A2.4). The structural break was included so that issues of predictive failure would be meaningful (see Hendry, 1979).

To ease recognition of the variables, they were respectively named CONS, INC, INFLAT and OUTPUT. Simultaneous equations estimation closely replicates these co-efficients of the DGP and the long-run solutions. Note that estimating (A2.2) by OLS yields a spectacular example of simultaneity bias and (A2.3) without the oil dummy shows massive predictive failure. Also, (A2.1) by RLS indicates evidence of parameter non-constancy owing to the change in the simultaneity bias at the oil crisis: most mis-specifications also lead to predictive failure.

Appendix A3

Numerical Changes From Previous Versions

A3.1 From version 9 to 10

There are a only few minor changes: the RESET test now uses direct regression instead of partioned inverse, resulting in small differences; the t-test for zero innovation mean is now implemented as in the documentation; NLS standard errors are now based on the information matrix; NLS AR test can be slightly different (as could the heteroscedasticity tests when degrees of freedom differ); RALS ARCH test degrees of freedom now use T after allowing for lagged residuals. The residual correlogram uses the more standard textbook definition now (i.e. in deviation from the full sample mean, instead of the running mean).

A3.2 From version 8 to 9

The major change is the adoption of the QR decomposition with partial pivoting to compute OLS and IV estimates. There are also some minor improvements in accuracy, the following tests are the most sensitive to such changes: encompassing, heteroscedasticity and RESET. The heteroscedasticity tests could also differ in the number of variables removed owing to singularity.

A3.3 From version 7 to 8

The numerical results generated by PcGive version 8 are unchanged from version 7, apart from a marginal increase in accuracy of several diagnostic tests. Also, a new version of the normality test is used now, which uses a small sample correction.

References

Ahumada, H. (1985). An encompassing test of two models of the balance of trade for Argentina, *Oxford Bulletin of Economics and Statistics*, **47**, 51–70.

Alexander, C. (2001). *Market Models: A Guide to Financial Data Analysis*. Chichester: John Wiley and Sons.

Amemiya, T. (1981). Qualitative response models: A survey, *Journal of Economic Literature*, **19**, 1483–1536.

Amemiya, T. (1985). *Advanced Econometrics*. Oxford: Basil Blackwell.

Anderson, T. W. (1971). *The Statistical Analysis of Time Series*. New York: John Wiley & Sons.

Andrews, D. W. K. (1991). Heteroskedasticity and autocorrelation consistent covariance matrix estimation, *Econometrica*, **59**, 817–858.

Baba, Y., Hendry, D. F. and Starr, R. M. (1992). The demand for M1 in the U.S.A., 1960–1988, *Review of Economic Studies*, **59**, 25–61.

Banerjee, A., Dolado, J. J., Galbraith, J. W. and Hendry, D. F. (1993). *Co-integration, Error Correction and the Econometric Analysis of Non-Stationary Data*. Oxford: Oxford University Press.

Banerjee, A., Dolado, J. J., Hendry, D. F. and Smith, G. W. (1986). Exploring equilibrium relationships in econometrics through static models: Some Monte Carlo evidence, *Oxford Bulletin of Economics and Statistics*, **48**, 253–277.

Banerjee, A., Dolado, J. J. and Mestre, R. (1998). Error-correction mechanism tests for cointegration in a single equation framework, *Journal of Time Series Analysis*, **19**, 267–283.

Banerjee, A. and Hendry, D. F. (1992a). Testing integration and cointegration, *Oxford Bulletin of Economics and Statistics*, **54**. Special issue.

Banerjee, A. and Hendry, D. F. (1992b). Testing integration and cointegration: An overview, *Oxford Bulletin of Economics and Statistics*, **54**, 225–255.

Bårdsen, G. (1989). The estimation of long run coefficients from error correction models, *Oxford Bulletin of Economics and Statistics*, **50**.

Bentzel, R. and Hansen, B. (1955). On recursiveness and interdependency in economic models, *Review of Economic Studies*, **22**, 153–168.

Bollerslev, T., Chou, R. S. and Kroner, K. F. (1992). ARCH modelling in finance – A review of the theory and empirical evidence, *Journal of Econometrics*, **52**, 5–59.

Bontemps, C. and Mizon, G. E. (2002). Congruence and encompassing, In Stigum, B. P. (ed.), *Econometrics and the Philosophy of Economics*. Princeton: Princeton University Press. forthcoming.

Bowman, K. O. and Shenton, L. R. (1975). Omnibus test contours for departures from normality based on $\sqrt{b_1}$ and b_2, *Biometrika*, **62**, 243–250.

Box, G. E. P. and Jenkins, G. M. (1976). *Time Series Analysis, Forecasting and Control.* San Francisco: Holden-Day. First published, 1970.

Box, G. E. P. and Pierce, D. A. (1970). Distribution of residual autocorrelations in autoregressive-integrated moving average time series models, *Journal of the American Statistical Association*, **65**, 1509–1526.

Breusch, T. S. and Pagan, A. R. (1980). The Lagrange multiplier test and its applications to model specification in econometrics, *Review of Economic Studies*, **47**, 239–253.

Brown, R. L., Durbin, J. and Evans, J. M. (1975). Techniques for testing the constancy of regression relationships over time (with discussion), *Journal of the Royal Statistical Society B*, **37**, 149–192.

Campos, J., Ericsson, N. R. and Hendry, D. F. (1996). Cointegration tests in the presence of structural breaks, *Journal of Econometrics*, **70**, 187–220.

Chambers, E. A. and Cox, D. R. (1967). Discrimination between alternative binary response models, *Biometrika*, **54**, 573–578.

Chow, G. C. (1960). Tests of equality between sets of coefficients in two linear regressions, *Econometrica*, **28**, 591–605.

Clements, M. P. and Hendry, D. F. (1998). *Forecasting Economic Time Series.* Cambridge: Cambridge University Press.

Clements, M. P. and Hendry, D. F. (1999). *Forecasting Non-stationary Economic Time Series.* Cambridge, Mass.: MIT Press.

Cochrane, D. and Orcutt, G. H. (1949). Application of least squares regression to relationships containing auto-correlated error terms, *Journal of the American Statistical Association*, **44**, 32–61.

Cox, D. R. (1961). Tests of separate families of hypotheses, In *Proceedings of the Fourth Berkeley Symposium on Mathematical Statistics and Probability*, Vol. 1, pp. 105–123 Berkeley: University of California Press.

Cramer, J. S. (1986). *Econometric Applications of Maximum Likelihood Methods.* Cambridge: Cambridge University Press.

Cramer, J. S. (2001). *The LOGIT Model: An Introduction for Economists* 3rd edition. London: Timberlake Consultants Press.

D'Agostino, R. B. (1970). Transformation to normality of the null distribution of g_1, *Biometrika*, **57**, 679–681.

Davidson, J. E. H., Hendry, D. F., Srba, F. and Yeo, J. S. (1978). Econometric modelling of the aggregate time-series relationship between consumers' expenditure and income in the United Kingdom, *Economic Journal*, **88**, 661–692. Reprinted in Hendry, D. F., *Econometrics: Alchemy or Science?* Oxford: Blackwell Publishers, 1993, and Oxford University Press, 2000.

Dickey, D. A. and Fuller, W. A. (1981). Likelihood ratio statistics for autoregressive time series with a unit root, *Econometrica*, **49**, 1057–1072.

Doan, T., Litterman, R. and Sims, C. A. (1984). Forecasting and conditional projection using realistic prior distributions, *Econometric Reviews*, **3**, 1–100.

Doornik, J. A. (2006). *Object-Oriented Matrix Programming using Ox* 5th edition. London: Timberlake Consultants Press.

Doornik, J. A. and Hansen, H. (1994). A practical test for univariate and multivariate normality,

Discussion paper, Nuffield College.

Doornik, J. A. and Hendry, D. F. (1992). *PCGIVE 7: An Interactive Econometric Modelling System*. Oxford: Institute of Economics and Statistics, University of Oxford.

Doornik, J. A. and Hendry, D. F. (1994). *PcGive 8: An Interactive Econometric Modelling System*. London: International Thomson Publishing, and Belmont, CA: Duxbury Press.

Doornik, J. A. and Hendry, D. F. (2006a). *Modelling Dynamic Systems using PcGive: Volume II* 3rd edition. London: Timberlake Consultants Press.

Doornik, J. A. and Hendry, D. F. (2006b). *OxMetrics: An Interface to Empirical Modelling* 4th edition. London: Timberlake Consultants Press.

Durbin, J. (1970). Testing for serial correlation in least squares regression when some of the regressors are lagged dependent variables, *Econometrica*, **38**, 410–421.

Durbin, J. and Watson, G. S. (1951). Testing for serial correlation in least squares regression II, *Biometrika*, **38**, 159–178.

Eicker, F. (1967). Limit theorems for regressions with unequal and dependent errors, In *Proceedings of the Fifth Berkeley Symposium on Mathematical Statistics and Probability*, Vol. 1, pp. 59–82 Berkeley: University of California.

Eisner, R. and Strotz, R. H. (1963). *Determinants of Business Investment*. Englewood Cliffs, NJ: Prentice-Hall.

Emerson, R. A. and Hendry, D. F. (1996). An evaluation of forecasting using leading indicators, *Journal of Forecasting*, **15**, 271–291.

Engle, R. F. (1982). Autoregressive conditional heteroscedasticity, with estimates of the variance of United Kingdom inflation, *Econometrica*, **50**, 987–1007.

Engle, R. F. (1984). Wald, likelihood ratio, and Lagrange multiplier tests in econometrics, in Griliches and Intriligator (1984), Ch. 13.

Engle, R. F. and Granger, C. W. J. (1987). Cointegration and error correction: Representation, estimation and testing, *Econometrica*, **55**, 251–276.

Engle, R. F., Hendry, D. F. and Richard, J.-F. (1983). Exogeneity, *Econometrica*, **51**, 277–304. Reprinted in Hendry, D. F., *Econometrics: Alchemy or Science?* Oxford: Blackwell Publishers, 1993, and Oxford University Press, 2000; and in Ericsson, N. R. and Irons, J. S. (eds.) *Testing Exogeneity*, Oxford: Oxford University Press, 1994.

Engle, R. F., Hendry, D. F. and Trumbull, D. (1985). Small sample properties of ARCH estimators and tests, *Canadian Journal of Economics*, **43**, 66–93.

Ericsson, N. R. (1983). Asymptotic properties of instrumental variables statistics for testing non-nested hypotheses, *Review of Economic Studies*, **50**, 287–303.

Ericsson, N. R. (1992). Cointegration, exogeneity and policy analysis: An overview, *Journal of Policy Modeling*, **14**, 251–280.

Ericsson, N. R. and Hendry, D. F. (1999). Encompassing and rational expectations: How sequential corroboration can imply refutation, *Empirical Economics*, **24**, 1–21.

Ericsson, N. R. and Irons, J. S. (1995). The Lucas critique in practice: Theory without measurement, In Hoover, K. D. (ed.), *Macroeconometrics: Developments, Tensions and Prospects*. Dordrecht: Kluwer Academic Press.

Ericsson, N. R. and MacKinnon, J. G. (1999). Distributions of error correction tests for cointegration, International finance discussion paper no. 655, Federal Reserve Board of Governors, Washington, D.C. www.bog.frb.fed.us/pubs/ifdp/1999/655/default.htm.

Escribano, A. (1985). Non-linear error correction: The case of money demand in the UK (1878–1970), Mimeo, University of California at San Diego.

Favero, C. and Hendry, D. F. (1992). Testing the Lucas critique: A review, *Econometric Reviews*, **11**, 265–306.

Finney, D. J. (1947). The estimation from individual records of the relationship between dose and quantal response, *Biometrika*, **34**, 320–334.

Fletcher, R. (1987). *Practical Methods of Optimization*, 2nd edition. New York: John Wiley & Sons.

Friedman, M. and Schwartz, A. J. (1982). *Monetary Trends in the United States and the United Kingdom: Their Relation to Income, Prices, and Interest Rates, 1867–1975*. Chicago: University of Chicago Press.

Frisch, R. (1934). *Statistical Confluence Analysis by means of Complete Regression Systems*. Oslo: University Institute of Economics.

Frisch, R. (1938). Statistical versus theoretical relations in economic macrodynamics, Mimeograph dated 17 July 1938, League of Nations Memorandum. Reproduced by University of Oslo in 1948 with Tinbergen's comments. Contained in Memorandum 'Autonomy of Economic Relations', 6 November 1948, Oslo, Universitets Økonomiske Institutt. Reprinted in Hendry D. F. and Morgan M. S. (1995), *The Foundations of Econometric Analysis*. Cambridge: Cambridge University Press.

Frisch, R. and Waugh, F. V. (1933). Partial time regression as compared with individual trends, *Econometrica*, **1**, 221–223.

Gilbert, C. L. (1986). Professor Hendry's econometric methodology, *Oxford Bulletin of Economics and Statistics*, **48**, 283–307. Reprinted in Granger, C. W. J. (ed.) (1990), *Modelling Economic Series*. Oxford: Clarendon Press.

Gilbert, C. L. (1989). LSE and the British approach to time-series econometrics, *Oxford Review of Economic Policy*, **41**, 108–128.

Godfrey, L. G. (1978). Testing for higher order serial correlation in regression equations when the regressors include lagged dependent variables, *Econometrica*, **46**, 1303–1313.

Godfrey, L. G. (1988). *Misspecification Tests in Econometrics*. Cambridge: Cambridge University Press.

Godfrey, L. G. and Orme, C. D. (1994). The sensitivity of some general checks to omitted variables in the linear model, *International Economic Review*, **35**, 489–506.

Granger, C. W. J. (1969). Investigating causal relations by econometric models and cross-spectral methods, *Econometrica*, **37**, 424–438.

Granger, C. W. J. (1986). Developments in the study of cointegrated economic variables, *Oxford Bulletin of Economics and Statistics*, **48**, 213–228.

Granger, C. W. J. and Newbold, P. (1974). Spurious regressions in econometrics, *Journal of Econometrics*, **2**, 111–120.

Granger, C. W. J. and Newbold, P. (1977). The time series approach to econometric model building, In Sims, C. A. (ed.), *New Methods in Business Cycle Research*, Ch. 1. Minneapolis: Federal Reserve Bank of Minneapolis.

Gregory, A. W. and Veale, M. R. (1985). Formulating Wald tests of non-linear restrictions, *Econometrica*, **53**, 1465–1468.

Griliches, Z. and Intriligator, M. D. (eds.)(1984). *Handbook of Econometrics*, Vol. 2–3. Amsterdam: North-Holland.

Hansen, B. E. (1992). Testing for parameter instability in linear models, *Journal of Policy Modeling*, **14**, 517–533.

Harvey, A. C. (1981). *The Econometric Analysis of Time Series*. Deddington: Philip Allan.

Harvey, A. C. (1990). *The Econometric Analysis of Time Series,* 2nd edition. Hemel Hempstead: Philip Allan.

Harvey, A. C. (1993). *Time Series Models,* 2nd edition. Hemel Hempstead: Harvester Wheatsheaf.

Harvey, A. C. and Collier, P. (1977). Testing for functional misspecification in regression analysis, *Journal of Econometrics*, **6**, 103–119.

Harvey, A. C. and Shephard, N. G. (1992). Structural time series models, In Maddala, G. S., Rao, C. R. and Vinod, H. D. (eds.), *Handbook of Statistics*, Vol. 11. Amsterdam: North-Holland.

Hendry, D. F. (1976). The structure of simultaneous equations estimators, *Journal of Econometrics*, **4**, 51–88. Reprinted in Hendry, D. F., *Econometrics: Alchemy or Science?* Oxford: Blackwell Publishers, 1993, and Oxford University Press, 2000.

Hendry, D. F. (1979). Predictive failure and econometric modelling in macro-economics: The transactions demand for money, In Ormerod, P. (ed.), *Economic Modelling*, pp. 217–242. London: Heinemann. Reprinted in Hendry, D. F., *Econometrics: Alchemy or Science?* Oxford: Blackwell Publishers, 1993, and Oxford University Press, 2000.

Hendry, D. F. (1980). Econometrics: Alchemy or science?, *Economica*, **47**, 387–406. Reprinted in Hendry, D. F., *Econometrics: Alchemy or Science?* Oxford: Blackwell Publishers, 1993, and Oxford University Press, 2000.

Hendry, D. F. (1986a). Econometric modelling with cointegrated variables, *Oxford Bulletin of Economics and Statistics*, 48(3). Special issue.

Hendry, D. F. (1986b). Econometric modelling with cointegrated variables: An overview, *Oxford Bulletin of Economics and Statistics*, **48**, 201–212. Reprinted in R.F. Engle and C.W.J. Granger (eds), Long-Run Economic Relationships, Oxford: Oxford University Press, 1991, 51–63.

Hendry, D. F. (1986c). Using PC-GIVE in econometrics teaching, *Oxford Bulletin of Economics and Statistics*, **48**, 87–98.

Hendry, D. F. (1987). Econometric methodology: A personal perspective, In Bewley, T. F. (ed.), *Advances in Econometrics*, Ch. 10. Cambridge: Cambridge University Press.

Hendry, D. F. (1988). The encompassing implications of feedback versus feedforward mechanisms in econometrics, *Oxford Economic Papers*, **40**, 132–149. Reprinted in Ericsson, N. R. and Irons, J. S. (eds.) *Testing Exogeneity*, Oxford: Oxford University Press, 1994.

Hendry, D. F. (1989). Comment on intertemporal consumer behaviour under structural changes in income, *Econometric Reviews*, **8**, 111–121.

Hendry, D. F. (1993). *Econometrics: Alchemy or Science?* Oxford: Blackwell Publishers.

Hendry, D. F. (1995a). *Dynamic Econometrics*. Oxford: Oxford University Press.

Hendry, D. F. (1995b). On the interactions of unit roots and exogeneity, *Econometric Reviews*, **14**, 383–419.

Hendry, D. F. (1995c). A theory of co-breaking, Mimeo, Nuffield College, University of Oxford.

Hendry, D. F. (1996). On the constancy of time-series econometric equations, *Economic and*

Social Review, **27**, 401–422.

Hendry, D. F. (1997). On congruent econometric relations: A comment, *Carnegie–Rochester Conference Series on Public Policy*, **47**, 163–190.

Hendry, D. F. (2000a). *Econometrics: Alchemy or Science?* Oxford: Oxford University Press. New Edition.

Hendry, D. F. (2000b). Epilogue: The success of general-to-specific model selection, in *Econometrics: Alchemy or Science?* (2000a), pp. 467–490. New Edition.

Hendry, D. F. and Anderson, G. J. (1977). Testing dynamic specification in small simultaneous systems: An application to a model of building society behaviour in the United Kingdom, In Intriligator, M. D. (ed.), *Frontiers in Quantitative Economics*, Vol. 3, pp. 361–383. Amsterdam: North Holland Publishing Company. Reprinted in Hendry, D. F., *Econometrics: Alchemy or Science?* Oxford: Blackwell Publishers, 1993, and Oxford University Press, 2000.

Hendry, D. F. and Doornik, J. A. (1994). Modelling linear dynamic econometric systems, *Scottish Journal of Political Economy*, **41**, 1–33.

Hendry, D. F. and Doornik, J. A. (1997). The implications for econometric modelling of forecast failure, *Scottish Journal of Political Economy*, **44**, 437–461. Special Issue.

Hendry, D. F. and Ericsson, N. R. (1991). Modeling the demand for narrow money in the United Kingdom and the United States, *European Economic Review*, **35**, 833–886.

Hendry, D. F. and Juselius, K. (2000). Explaining cointegration analysis: Part I, *Energy Journal*, **21**, 1–42.

Hendry, D. F. and Krolzig, H.-M. (1999). Improving on 'Data mining reconsidered' by K.D. Hoover and S.J. Perez, *Econometrics Journal*, **2**, 202–219.

Hendry, D. F. and Mizon, G. E. (1978). Serial correlation as a convenient simplification, not a nuisance: A comment on a study of the demand for money by the Bank of England, *Economic Journal*, **88**, 549–563. Reprinted in Hendry, D. F., *Econometrics: Alchemy or Science?* Oxford: Blackwell Publishers, 1993, and Oxford University Press, 2000.

Hendry, D. F. and Mizon, G. E. (1993). Evaluating dynamic econometric models by encompassing the VAR, In Phillips, P. C. B. (ed.), *Models, Methods and Applications of Econometrics*, pp. 272–300. Oxford: Basil Blackwell.

Hendry, D. F. and Mizon, G. E. (1999). The pervasiveness of Granger causality in econometrics, In Engle, R. F. and White, H. (eds.), *Cointegration, Causality and Forecasting*. Oxford: Oxford University Press.

Hendry, D. F. and Morgan, M. S. (1989). A re-analysis of confluence analysis, *Oxford Economic Papers*, **41**, 35–52.

Hendry, D. F. and Morgan, M. S. (1995). *The Foundations of Econometric Analysis*. Cambridge: Cambridge University Press.

Hendry, D. F. and Neale, A. J. (1987). Monte Carlo experimentation using PC-NAIVE, In Fomby, T. and Rhodes, G. F. (eds.), *Advances in Econometrics*, Vol. 6, pp. 91–125. Greenwich, Connecticut: Jai Press Inc.

Hendry, D. F. and Neale, A. J. (1988). Interpreting long-run equilibrium solutions in conventional macro models: A comment, *Economic Journal*, **98**, 808–817.

Hendry, D. F. and Neale, A. J. (1991). A Monte Carlo study of the effects of structural breaks on tests for unit roots, In Hackl, P. and Westlund, A. H. (eds.), *Economic Structural Change*,

Analysis and Forecasting, pp. 95–119. Berlin: Springer-Verlag.

Hendry, D. F., Neale, A. J. and Ericsson, N. R. (1991). *PC-NAIVE, An Interactive Program for Monte Carlo Experimentation in Econometrics. Version 6.0.* Oxford: Institute of Economics and Statistics, University of Oxford.

Hendry, D. F., Neale, A. J. and Srba, F. (1988). Econometric analysis of small linear systems using PC-FIML, *Journal of Econometrics*, **38**, 203–226.

Hendry, D. F., Pagan, A. R. and Sargan, J. D. (1984). Dynamic specification, in Griliches and Intriligator (1984), Ch. 18. Reprinted in Hendry, D. F., *Econometrics: Alchemy or Science?* Oxford: Blackwell Publishers, 1993, and Oxford University Press, 2000.

Hendry, D. F. and Richard, J.-F. (1982). On the formulation of empirical models in dynamic econometrics, *Journal of Econometrics*, **20**, 3–33. Reprinted in Granger, C. W. J. (ed.) (1990), *Modelling Economic Series*. Oxford: Clarendon Press and in Hendry D. F., *Econometrics: Alchemy or Science?* Oxford: Blackwell Publishers 1993, and Oxford University Press, 2000.

Hendry, D. F. and Richard, J.-F. (1983). The econometric analysis of economic time series (with discussion), *International Statistical Review*, **51**, 111–163. Reprinted in Hendry, D. F., *Econometrics: Alchemy or Science?* Oxford: Blackwell Publishers, 1993, and Oxford University Press, 2000.

Hendry, D. F. and Richard, J.-F. (1989). Recent developments in the theory of encompassing, In Cornet, B. and Tulkens, H. (eds.), *Contributions to Operations Research and Economics. The XXth Anniversary of CORE*, pp. 393–440. Cambridge, MA: MIT Press.

Hendry, D. F. and Srba, F. (1980). AUTOREG: A computer program library for dynamic econometric models with autoregressive errors, *Journal of Econometrics*, **12**, 85–102. Reprinted in Hendry, D. F., *Econometrics: Alchemy or Science?* Oxford: Blackwell Publishers, 1993, and Oxford University Press, 2000.

Hendry, D. F. and von Ungern-Sternberg, T. (1981). Liquidity and inflation effects on consumers' expenditure, In Deaton, A. S. (ed.), *Essays in the Theory and Measurement of Consumers' Behaviour*, pp. 237–261. Cambridge: Cambridge University Press. Reprinted in Hendry, D. F., *Econometrics: Alchemy or Science?* Oxford: Blackwell Publishers, 1993, and Oxford University Press, 2000.

Hendry, D. F. and Wallis, K. F. (eds.)(1984). *Econometrics and Quantitative Economics*. Oxford: Basil Blackwell.

Hooker, P. H. (1901). Correlation of the marriage rate with trade, *Journal of the Royal Statistical Society*, **64**, 485–492.

Hoover, K. D. and Perez, S. J. (1999). Data mining reconsidered: Encompassing and the general-to-specific approach to specification search, *Econometrics Journal*, **2**, 167–191.

Hoover, K. D. and Perez, S. J. (2000). Truth and robustness in cross-country growth regressions, unpublished paper, Economics Department, University of California, Davis.

Jarque, C. M. and Bera, A. K. (1987). A test for normality of observations and regression residuals, *International Statistical Review*, **55**, 163–172.

Johansen, S. (1988). Statistical analysis of cointegration vectors, *Journal of Economic Dynamics and Control*, **12**, 231–254. Reprinted in R.F. Engle and C.W.J. Granger (eds), Long-Run Economic Relationships, Oxford: Oxford University Press, 1991, 131–52.

Johansen, S. (1995). *Likelihood-based Inference in Cointegrated Vector Autoregressive Models*. Oxford: Oxford University Press.

Johansen, S. and Juselius, K. (1990). Maximum likelihood estimation and inference on cointegration – With application to the demand for money, *Oxford Bulletin of Economics and Statistics*, **52**, 169–210.

Judd, J. and Scadding, J. (1982). The search for a stable money demand function: A survey of the post-1973 literature, *Journal of Economic Literature*, **20**, 993–1023.

Judge, G. G., Griffiths, W. E., Hill, R. C., Lütkepohl, H. and Lee, T.-C. (1985). *The Theory and Practice of Econometrics,* 2nd edition. New York: John Wiley.

Kiviet, J. F. (1986). On the rigor of some mis-specification tests for modelling dynamic relationships, *Review of Economic Studies*, **53**, 241–261.

Kiviet, J. F. (1987). *Testing Linear Econometric Models*. Amsterdam: University of Amsterdam.

Kiviet, J. F. and Phillips, G. D. A. (1992). Exact similar tests for unit roots and cointegration, *Oxford Bulletin of Economics and Statistics*, **54**, 349–367.

Kohn, A. (1987). *False Prophets*. Oxford: Basil Blackwell.

Koopmans, T. C. (ed.)(1950). *Statistical Inference in Dynamic Economic Models*. No. 10 in Cowles Commission Monograph. New York: John Wiley & Sons.

Koopmans, T. C., Rubin, H. and Leipnik, R. B. (1950). Measuring the equation systems of dynamic economics, in Koopmans (1950), Ch. 2.

Kremers, J. J. M., Ericsson, N. R. and Dolado, J. J. (1992). The power of cointegration tests, *Oxford Bulletin of Economics and Statistics*, **54**, 325–348.

Krolzig, H.-M. and Hendry, D. F. (2001). Computer automation of general-to-specific model selection procedures, *Journal of Economic Dynamics and Control*, **25**, 831–866.

Kuh, E., Belsley, D. A. and Welsh, R. E. (1980). *Regression Diagnostics. Identifying Influential Data and Sources of Collinearity*. Wiley Series in Probability and Mathematical Statistics. New York: John Wiley.

Leamer, E. E. (1978). *Specification Searches. Ad-Hoc Inference with Non-Experimental Data*. New York: John Wiley.

Leamer, E. E. (1983). Let's take the con out of econometrics, *American Economic Review*, **73**, 31–43. Reprinted in Granger, C. W. J. (ed.) (1990), *Modelling Economic Series*. Oxford: Clarendon Press.

Ljung, G. M. and Box, G. E. P. (1978). On a measure of lack of fit in time series models, *Biometrika*, **65**, 297–303.

Lovell, M. C. (1983). Data mining, *Review of Economics and Statistics*, **65**, 1–12.

Lucas, R. E. (1976). Econometric policy evaluation: A critique, In Brunner, K. and Meltzer, A. (eds.), *The Phillips Curve and Labor Markets*, Vol. 1 of *Carnegie-Rochester Conferences on Public Policy*, pp. 19–46. Amsterdam: North-Holland Publishing Company.

MacKinnon, J. G. (1991). Critical values for cointegration tests, In Engle, R. F. and Granger, C. W. J. (eds.), *Long-Run Economic Relationships*, pp. 267–276. Oxford: Oxford University Press.

MacKinnon, J. G. and White, H. (1985). Some heteroskedasticity-consistent covariance matrix estimators with improved finite sample properties, *Journal of Econometrics*, **29**, 305–325.

Makridakis, S., Wheelwright, S. C. and Hyndman, R. C. (1998). *Forecasting: Methods and Applications* 3rd edition. New York: John Wiley and Sons.

Marschak, J. (1953). Economic measurements for policy and prediction, In Hood, W. C. and Koopmans, T. C. (eds.), *Studies in Econometric Method*, No. 14 in Cowles Commission

Monograph. New York: John Wiley & Sons.

McFadden, D. L. (1984). Econometric analysis of qualitative response models, in Griliches and Intriligator (1984), Ch. 24.

Mizon, G. E. (1977). Model selection procedures, In Artis, M. J. and Nobay, A. R. (eds.), *Studies in Modern Economic Analysis*, pp. P97–120. Oxford: Basil Blackwell.

Mizon, G. E. (1984). The encompassing approach in econometrics, in Hendry and Wallis (1984), pp. 135–172.

Mizon, G. E. (1995). A simple message for autocorrelation correctors: Don't, *Journal of Econometrics*, **69**, 267–288.

Mizon, G. E. and Hendry, D. F. (1980). An empirical application and Monte Carlo analysis of tests of dynamic specification, *Review of Economic Studies*, **49**, 21–45. Reprinted in Hendry, D. F., *Econometrics: Alchemy or Science?* Oxford: Blackwell Publishers, 1993, and Oxford University Press, 2000.

Mizon, G. E. and Richard, J.-F. (1986). The encompassing principle and its application to nonnested hypothesis tests, *Econometrica*, **54**, 657–678.

Nelson, C. R. (1972). The prediction performance of the FRB-MIT-PENN model of the US economy, *American Economic Review*, **62**, 902–917.

Nickell, S. J. (1985). Error correction, partial adjustment and all that: An expository note, *Oxford Bulletin of Economics and Statistics*, **47**, 119–130.

Pagan, A. R. (1984). Model evaluation by variable addition, in Hendry and Wallis (1984), pp. 103–135.

Perron, P. (1989). The Great Crash, the oil price shock and the unit root hypothesis, *Econometrica*, **57**, 1361–1401.

Pesaran, M. H. (1974). On the general problem of model selection, *Review of Economic Studies*, **41**, 153–171.

Phillips, P. C. B. (1986). Understanding spurious regressions in econometrics, *Journal of Econometrics*, **33**, 311–340.

Phillips, P. C. B. (1987). Time series regression with a unit root, *Econometrica*, **55**, 277–301.

Phillips, P. C. B. (1991). Optimal inference in cointegrated systems, *Econometrica*, **59**, 283–306.

Poincaré, H. (1905). *Science and Hypothesis.* New York: Science Press.

Ramsey, J. B. (1969). Tests for specification errors in classical linear least squares regression analysis, *Journal of the Royal Statistical Society B*, **31**, 350–371.

Richard, J.-F. (1980). Models with several regimes and changes in exogeneity, *Review of Economic Studies*, **47**, 1–20.

Sargan, J. D. (1958). The estimation of economic relationships using instrumental variables, *Econometrica*, **26**, 393–415.

Sargan, J. D. (1959). The estimation of relationships with autocorrelated residuals by the use of instrumental variables, *Journal of the Royal Statistical Society B*, **21**, 91–105. Reprinted as pp. 87–104 in Sargan J. D. (1988), *Contributions to Econometrics*, Vol. 1, Cambridge: Cambridge University Press.

Sargan, J. D. (1964). Wages and prices in the United Kingdom: A study in econometric methodology (with discussion), In Hart, P. E., Mills, G. and Whitaker, J. K. (eds.), *Econometric Analysis for National Economic Planning*, Vol. 16 of *Colston Papers*, pp. 25–63. London: Butterworth Co. Reprinted as pp. 275–314 in Hendry D. F. and Wallis K. F. (eds.) (1984).

Econometrics and Quantitative Economics. Oxford: Basil Blackwell, and as pp. 124–169 in Sargan J. D. (1988), *Contributions to Econometrics*, Vol. 1, Cambridge: Cambridge University Press.

Sargan, J. D. (1980a). The consumer price equation in the post-war British economy. An exercise in equation specification testing, *Review of Economic Studies*, **47**, 113–135.

Sargan, J. D. (1980b). Some tests of dynamic specification for a single equation, *Econometrica*, **48**, 879–897. Reprinted as pp. 191–212 in Sargan J. D. (1988), *Contributions to Econometrics*, Vol. 1, Cambridge: Cambridge University Press.

Shenton, L. R. and Bowman, K. O. (1977). A bivariate model for the distribution of $\sqrt{b_1}$ and b_2, *Journal of the American Statistical Association*, **72**, 206–211.

Sims, C. A. (1980). Macroeconomics and reality, *Econometrica*, **48**, 1–48. Reprinted in Granger, C. W. J. (ed.) (1990), *Modelling Economic Series*. Oxford: Clarendon Press.

Spanos, A. (1986). *Statistical Foundations of Econometric Modelling*. Cambridge: Cambridge University Press.

White, H. (1980). A heteroskedastic-consistent covariance matrix estimator and a direct test for heteroskedasticity, *Econometrica*, **48**, 817–838.

White, H. (1984). *Asymptotic Theory for Econometricians*. London: Academic Press.

White, H. (1990). A consistent model selection, In Granger, C. W. J. (ed.), *Modelling Economic Series*, pp. 369–383. Oxford: Clarendon Press.

Working, E. J. (1927). What do statistical demand curves show?, *Quarterly Journal of Economics*, **41**, 212–235.

Yule, G. U. (1926). Why do we sometimes get nonsense-correlations between time-series? A study in sampling and the nature of time series (with discussion), *Journal of the Royal Statistical Society*, **89**, 1–64.

Author Index

Subject Index